Other Titles for the Creative Professional

Looking Good on the Web
By Daniel Gray

Flash™ 4 Web Animation f/x and Design
By Ken Milburn and John Croteau

Flash™ ActionScript f/x and Design
By Bill Sanders

Adobe LiveMotion™ f/x and Design
By Daniel Gray

Paint Shop Pro™ 6 Visual Insight
By Ramona Pruitt and Joshua Pruitt

QuarkXpress™ 4 In Depth
By William Harrel and Elaine Betts

Adobe PageMill® 3 f/x and Design
By Daniel Gray

Illustrator® 9 f/x and Design
By Sherry London

Painter® 6 f/x and Design
By Sherry London and Rhoda Grossman

Photoshop® 5 In Depth
By David Xenakis and Sherry London

Adobe InDesign™ f/x and Design
By Elaine Betts

To Gus Bailey who, over the course of 30 years, has been there, through all my ups and downs.
—Richard Shrand

About the Author

Richard Schrand is a former award-winning broadcaster who recently turned his interest in computers and digital art into a new career. He created the Nashville, TN, based company, GRFX ByDesign in 1998, focusing on corporate image reconstruction and 3D design and animation.

During his broadcasting career, Richard worked for both local and national broadcast facilities as a reporter, anchor, upper-level manager, and promotion and marketing consultant. He handled program publicity while at NBC Television Network in Los Angeles, handling shows such as *Days Of Our Lives*, *Family Ties*, *Wheel Of Fortune*, and many others. He also helped create the daytime drama, *Generations*.

His computer-program writing career began a little over a year ago when he began writing tutorials for various Web-based 3D sites. He writes tutorials covering Adobe Illustrator and Pixels:3D for the Graphics Resource Club's Web site. Richard is also the author of *Canoma Visual Insight*, published by The Coriolis Group.

Acknowledgments

The transition from an idea to a solid entity like the book you hold in your hands is accomplished through the vast talents of dozens of people, some of whom I am literally in contact with daily and some of whom I have never met (which, in many cases I can say to them: "Thank your lucky stars for that!"). And this book is no exception.

I'd like to acknowledge and thank Beth Kohler and Don Eamon, the guiding forces at The Coriolis Group. I owe you two my profound gratitude. To Meg Turecek, Production Coordinator and layout artist; April Nielsen, Designer; Michelle McConnell, CD-ROM Developer; and Patti Davenport, Marketing Specialist, who did a superb job of making both the book and the CD-ROM look great... thank you!

To Lynn Grillo, fellow author and all-around saint who shared her knowledge and experience with me without ever calling me something untoward (although I know she probably thought it!).

To everyone on the GoLive team, especially John Kranz and his crew of sleep-deprived gurus. Great job guys. And the constant emails kept me sane while everything was happening.

To my agent, David Fugate, and Maureen at Waterside Productions. These two are the tops when it comes to taking care of my incessant needs.

To my parents, Ed and Jane, for their love and support.

And last but not least, to my wife, Sharon, my daughters Cyndi and Courtney, and my twin sons Richard and Brandon (who often made my concentration fly right out the window). I love you all.

—Richard Shrand

Contents at a Glance

Table of Contents

Introduction

Welcome to the World of Web Design

You have surfed the Web and marveled at some of the magnificent designs and fascinating effects. You've studied them, wondered how to they were achieved, and then returned to your design work, shaking your head and thinking you could never duplicate the quality of what you've seen. Well, get that thought out of your head right now. With GoLive 5, you have the tools at your disposal to not only create the site of your dreams, but to literally create new and exciting looks by combining different elements in new and exciting ways.

What is GoLive 5?

Adobe GoLive 5 is the latest upgrade to the high-end Web design software package that has literally taken the Web-design world by storm. With GoLive 5, you have all the creative tools to build and publish world class Web sites with unprecedented ease. Create your image files, link to them in GoLive 5, and then place them wherever you want on your Web page, with pixel-by-pixel precision. Additionally, with the fantastic new features built into GoLive 5, the Web-design process has become even simpler.

A number of years back, GoLive 5 started life as CyberStudio. A company called GoLive Systems, Inc. created it (hence, the name, which Adobe kept after they purchased it). Many people, although that is incorrect to do so, still call it GoLive CyberStudio. Between the time when CyberStudio 3 was on the market and when Adobe purchased and released GoLive 4, Adobe was also marketing their PageMill Web-creation program. In many ways, this was the little brother to CyberStudio in that it had all the drag-and-drop features that were becoming the Adobe standard, but it just wasn't as powerful as CyberStudio. However, for fledgling Web designers who weren't willing to spend the time to learn HTML (HyperText Markup Language), it was the end-all Web production tool. Along came GoLive 4, and Adobe's Web-design presence went through an astounding metamorphosis. I was a user of PageMill, but I quickly upgraded to GoLive. My favorite way to describe the differences between PageMill and the new product: GoLive 4 was PageMill on steroids. In a rather strange way, it was.

So what's so special about GoLive—and GoLive 5 in particular? To me, it's the way in which this program quietly goes about its business. Beneath that unassuming exterior lies a power that continues to become apparent as you delve further into the program. Layer upon layer of possibilities lurk among a plethora of Actions, tools, and layout options that literally pounce on you when you finally discover them. It's not, however, as ominous as it sounds. If you are like me and enjoy the trip as mush as you do reaching the destination, GoLive 5 will not disappoint.

The GoLive 5 Trip Planner

I wanted to give you, the reader, the power to explore without feeling the oft-experienced tremor of concern of "Oh my! Am I going to mess something up if I do this?" I also wanted to whet your creative appetite with some fun ideas and then show you ways to accomplish them. This isn't a book designed to replace the user manual. Many times throughout this work, I'll suggest you go back to the program's documentation to either refresh your memory on a certain element or to get a feel for it before working out the projects contained here. This book is also designed to help you decipher some of the more complicated aspects of GoLive, such as implementing Cascading Style Sheets or creating forms and tables. I also occasionally fill the pages with my own view of design techniques, especially as they relate to the Web. Sometimes, you'll agree with me, sometimes not. Often, I go against the so-called accepted view of the day.

My design techniques have been honed over an almost three-decade stint in the broadcast industry where, for two decades, I oversaw the visual aspects of everything from television station logos to animations to program production. Throughout that time, I always tried to find a happy medium between the old and the new. As new toys became available, it was easy to produce a commercial or promotional announcement and use 100 new effects in a 30-second spot because. . . well, because it could be done. But were the effects pertinent to the message? Were they there because they added to that message or there because they looked nifty? Most of the time, unfortunately, it was because of the latter. This isn't to say that I've not had some horrendous ideas myself or that I didn't fall into that same "nifty" trap. It means that I tried my best to find what worked best (in my humble estimation) for the project at hand.

I also started my broadcasting career before videotape took over. Our news footage was shot on film. Real film. We had massive developers that processed the film; then we spliced it together and put it onto a gigantic reel to play back in the telecine area. All programs produced on the local level were done live. It was a time of experimentation; of not worrying about the bottom line so much as finding new and creative ways to tell stories. That's how I see the Web today; in this same creative light. In this Internet medium, creativity rules and experimentation is not only necessary, it's expected. That's what GoLive 5 allows you to do—to experiment to your heart's content, to try new and exciting things to make your site stand out, and to stand ready for that next big advance in Internet technology.

A little later in this Introduction, I'll give you a quick overview of what each chapter contains so that you can go directly to the one that interests you the most or that has a high-priority for your immediate tasks.

Who This Book Is For

This book is designed to give you the ideas and techniques you need to create visually stimulating Web sites that keep surfers coming back for more. If you have experience with Adobe GoLive 4, this book will help refresh you on the returning features—because, if you're like me, you reach the point of using the same ones over and over again and tend to forget about some of the other intriguing options of the program. If you are a seasoned professional, this book will help you discover the amazing new features in GoLive 5 that provide numerous ways to streamline your workflow, many of which are not found in GoLive 4. If you are a Webmaster, version 5's new features enable you to design a Web site before putting even the first page together and help expedite the workflow in production groups.

The changes are so great, they might even make you want to put in a few extra hours of work each day just to explore them. Ok, maybe that's going a bit too far. The following sections will break it down a bit more.

Intermediate-Level Designer

If you have a personal Web site or if you have created sites for clients but are now looking for new creative and intriguing ways to expand them, this book will help you. You'll learn about the rich, full-featured content creation tools that will immediately assist you in setting your sites apart from the competition. This book will also present you with the ammunition to expand your knowledge of Web-site creation by following the examples and experimenting with the various demos that I've included on the companion CD-ROM.

Professional Web Designer

GoLive 5 has added dozens of powerful new tools to use to help you quickly and easily create rich, interactive sites. Additionally, GoLive 5 now provides tools that allow you to modify artwork that you've created without ever leaving the program. GoLive has implementation new animation, video, and audio editing tools that make it easy to import MIDI, AVI, QuickTime, Flash, Fireworks, and LiveMotion files. There's even working support for manipulating vector graphics that gives the professional Web designer even more power to create memorable Web sites.

Teams and Team Captains

If you are part of a development team or if you are the producer overseeing a number of design professionals, GoLive 5 will make your task even easier. If you're a producer, you can literally design a site within GoLive without creating full layouts. If you're part of a team, dynamic elements allow you to share information, designs, artwork, and more quickly and efficiently. So if you're a team leader or part of a team working at different workstations in one location or multiple locations, GoLive's tools give you the power to efficiently manage your workflow.

A New Chapter in Web Creation

Now, let's look at what is contained in each chapter. You'll then be able to focus on a particular need more easily, and more easily figure out where you want to go—or what you want to do—next.

Chapter 1—Getting to Know GoLive 5

Some significant changes have been made to GoLive. In this chapter, you will learn what they are so that you can zoom through the standard learning curve inherent to all program upgrades.

Chapter 2—Smart Tools

Here, you will learn about the new Smart Tools that come with the GoLive 5. You can now import an image or animation file in its native format and tell GoLive to retain that link. If you need to modify an image, simply double-click on it, and GoLive will open the program that created the file so that you can make your changes. Then, all changes that you made within GoLive are automatically reflected on the Web page.

Chapter 3—Frames and Tables

Significant improvements have been made to these two areas. In this chapter, you will discover new ways to employ these oft-misunderstood tools so that you have more control over the way in which your sites are displayed—no matter which Web browser a visitor might use.

Chapter 4—Forms

Forms are a great way of controlling your presentations. In this chapter, discover their power and ways to use them to full advantage.

Chapter 5—Cascading Style Sheets

Many people (including myself at first) were confused when it came to creating Cascading Style Sheets. Chapter 5 demystifies this area, giving you ideas on how to create and work with both Internal and External style sheets.

Chapter 6—Bring a Site to Life

Adding animations to your site has never been easier. Here, you'll explore the various tools that you can use to create Shockwave and streaming video presentations for inclusion on your Web site.

Chapter 7—Using the QuickTime Editor

Adobe has updated the way in which GoLive creates QuickTime movies. This chapter goes over the advances that have been made with the QuickTime Editor to help you build full-motion videos without leaving GoLive.

Chapter 8—Fun With Sonics

In this chapter, you learn about the programs that let you create high-quality streaming audio for inclusion in your Web site designs. Here, you'll also find information on how to save your sound-related files for optimal streaming.

Chapter 9—DHTML Techniques

If you're familiar with GoLive 4, then you probably know about the Floating Box. There have been a lot of changes to this feature, and in this chapter you'll discover how to manipulate multiple Floating Box layers to create exciting animations that don't involve streaming media.

Chapter 10—Site Design

Improved visualization tools give Web-site designers the ability to monitor the interactivity between the pages. Additionally, the customizable design interface makes it a pleasant task to check for missing links. In this chapter, you will discover the power of this extremely useful tool.

Chapter 11—The Creative Group Environment

The evolving face of Web production has seen changes in the way a Web site is created. Teams of designers, artists, and technical personnel often work together to create the sites that you see on the Web. In this chapter, you will discover how GoLive 5 has is positioned to meet the work group environment.

Chapter 12—Adobe Products

Learn about the latest products in the Adobe library and how GoLive 5 interacts with them. This chapter is definitely worth the read if you are a current Photoshop, Illustrator, or other Adobe product user.

Chapter 13—Other Applications

As is the case with virtually every application, to wring the most out of your site development, you will want to turn to other programs to help you build the best Web sites possible. This chapter goes beyond the standard applications and looks at other, more esoteric, programs that can make your site stand out.

Chapter 14—WebObjects

What are they? Are WebObjects right for your needs? This chapter looks at Apple's current crop of applications, which are completely supported by GoLive.

Chapter 15—Constructing a Site

Follow along as I use the various design functions of GoLive 5, as well as many of the plug-ins discussed throughout this book, to rebuild my company's Web site. After you complete this chapter, you'll be amply armed to take on the Web by using your new knowledge and GoLive 5's powerful features.

The World (Wide Web) Is Your Oyster

With GoLive 5, the Web is truly your oyster. It's the last bastion of incredibly open-ended creativity. There is no place else left where you have such creative freedom without the bottom-line looming over every decision you make. Of course, if you're working for a large corporation, you still have to deliver the message cleanly and succinctly so that the company continues to grow. Additionally, if you are building your own business, you want to feature it in the best possible way. However, when it boils down to downright creative freedom and expression, your ability to bring your vision to life is the only thing that can hold you back.

GoLive 5 has the power to turn your vision into reality and throughout this book, you'll find many hints, tips, and tricks that will help you do just that. Also, as I stated previously, you'll get to know me (and my thoughts on design and the direction the Web is going), all at no extra charge. What a deal!

If you've read this introduction, I'm sure that you're now more than ready to begin discovering what makes Adobe GoLive 5 such a hot program. Thanks for putting up with me so far, and now let's move on to Chapter 1.

Part I

What's New

Chapter 1

Getting to Know GoLive 5

This chapter introduces the new features in GoLive 5. It's written in a way to help you more easily become familiar with the locations of the application's features and to guide you to the areas you want to explore further.

How to Read this Chapter

If I were a smart aleck, I'd say the best way to look at this chapter is with the book right side up and the pages facing toward you. However, I'm not a smart aleck, so you don't have to worry about bad jokes like this. The best way to look at this chapter is as a glorified tease, designed to whet your appetite. You'll quickly learn what Adobe GoLive 5 offers and how it has been expanded from its predecessor. If you are an experienced GoLive 5 user, you can choose to either skip this chapter or to scan it for features you haven't yet used.

Take the time to look over this chapter and determine the first area you want to investigate. You'll find so much to explore in so little time, especially if you—like me—are under deadlines from numerous clients, family members wanting the latest pictures scanned (and placed on disc) of their child stuffing birthday cake up their sibling's nose, the boss wanting that report yesterday, or the dog, frantic to be let out. This, then, is your detailed catalogue designed to bridge that gap between flipping through the pages, hoping to glimpse the topic you want to explore more in depth, and taking a day off to read this book from cover to cover.

Expanding Creativity

In the beginning, the act of creating any type of Web site—whether static or graphically intensive and interactive—was limited to those learned few who had the time and interest in learning HTML code. These people spent countless hours exploring and expanding the abilities of the Web, creating new and exciting codes that allowed faster and more interesting visitor interactions. To keep up with current trends, these developers expanded their knowledge base by developing and learning JavaScript, Cooperative Distributed Meta-Librarian Protocol (CDML), Extensible Markup Language (XML), Active Server Page (ASP), ColdFusion, and other scripting languages to, once again, make the surfing experience an exciting adventure. Soon, the masses began to learn the basics of scripting, creating their personal and business sites using text editors, and learning basic skills, such as writing rollover scripts.

During this time, a symbiotic relationship was formed between graphic artists and scripters. In many cases, graphic designers wanted to focus on their artistic vision without having to get into this other field of endeavor, and many of the people creating the HTML and Java scripts didn't want to worry about the artistic side. In general, both sides of the Web creation teams thought: "Why should I, after working my tush off to study the skills and techniques of my chosen field, have to go back to school to learn an entirely new set of skills that don't fall into my area of interest?" Therefore, the two fields—the technical and artistic—came together to help each other create bigger and better sites without having to venture into new lands.

Yet, change was inevitable. More and more people were connecting to the Web, creating a need for sites that allowed the general masses the ability to stake a claim to their own little plot of the cyberuniverse. Program developers began to see the need for programs that simplified the process of creating exciting Web sites, whereas the downtrodden masses began to cry out for easier ways to create those amazing effects they saw as they surfed.

Adobe GoLive 5 is the answer to those needs. Not only can Mary Jones from Tuscaloosa create a fully interactive Web site that includes rollovers, animation, and visitor interactions, but professional designers can also build professional sites in a third the time it used to take. Finally, if you are one of the purists who believe the only way to truly create a Web site is by writing thousands of lines of code, you can use GoLive 5 to do this as well.

Starting Up

When working with any program, you want to set it up in the most efficient way possible for your workflow. This set-up process is especially true for GoLive, which can quickly devour the viewing area of your monitor. To work with all the tool palettes and screens, you'll need at least a 15-inch screen (preferably, larger) set to a resolution of at least 1024x768 with True Color (if you're on a PC) or Millions Of Colors (if you are working on a Macintosh).

If possible—and you're equipped for it—multiple monitors can truly be a lifesaver when working in GoLive. You can assign the workspace to one monitor and the various palettes to the other. As you can see in Figure 1.1, this kind of setup gives you all the screen real estate you need.

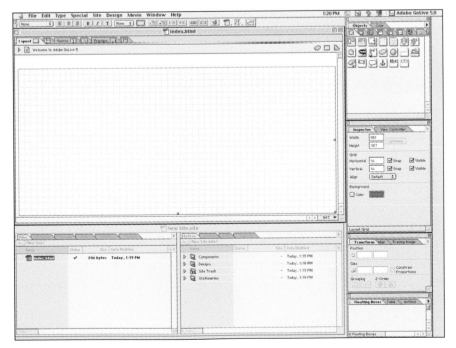

Figure 1.1

The initial screen setup, in 1024x768 resolution. As you see, at this resolution, all windows can be opened and positioned for easy access. This example shows a Macintosh screen.

If you have worked with GoLive 4, you'll see that the interface has changed a great deal. If, however, you are new to GoLive with this version, the available tools are so numerous that you might feel a bit (how shall I put this?) overwhelmed. Therefore, before you go on, you should look at how GoLive 5 has expanded your ability to build intriguingly interactive sites.

A Change in Management

No, I do not mean management in the sense of those in high-ranking positions in your company. Rather, by management here, I mean a change in the way you work with the various windows. In GoLive version 4, the Options, Inspector, and Color management windows could be moved off to the side where they collapsed into little squares and locked themselves to the edge of your monitor. Rather than dragging the windows to the side of the screen as was true of version 4, the docking procedure is now handled by using the Control key and clicking on the title bar of the window. As Figure 1.2 shows, the new docking method allows you to see exactly which palettes are docked where. This change expedites finding the palette you want to use. To undock, you merely click on the tab to reopen the window.

As you can see in Figure 1.3, each of the windows contains tabbed sections that allow you to easily move between the different design elements you'll need. As with other Adobe applications, the tabs can be "torn away," as shown in Figure 1.4, to form a separate, self-contained screen. Alternatively, Figure 1.5 shows how tabs can be merged into different groups that follow your way of thinking and working.

Figure 1.2

The new look when docking the palette windows.

For those of you who have become used to the old way of moving the different windows out of the way, this management revision in GoLive 5 will be one of your biggest challenges. However, if you use Photoshop, Illustrator, or any other Adobe product on a regular basis, you'll quickly feel right at home with these changes.

Figure 1.3

New tabbed sections make it easy to have access to many features without looking for them in the pull-down menus at the top of the screen.

Figure 1.4

You can now separate the tabs into self-contained screens.

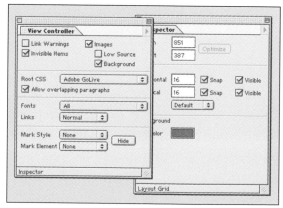

The Options Palette

This palette gives you all the tools you need to build your site. The Options palette is broken down into nine basic sections, many of which have expanded elements. Now, it's time to see what's new in this area.

The Basic Options

Basic Options consists of a mix of the old and the new. Figure 1.6 shows the five new tools in this section, as well as the returning ones from GoLive 4.

The five new tools are as follows:

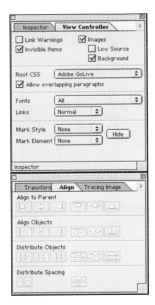

- *SWF tool*—This tool is designed for use specifically for Shockwave movies created with Adobe LiveMotion, Flash, Fireworks, Director, and whatever other programs you might use that generates this type of file.

- *QuickTime tool*—This specific plug-in tool imports QuickTime movies you've created. Prior to version 5, one plug-in tool imported any file, be it a QT, Real, Shockwave, AVI, MOV, or other format.

Figure 1.5
You can merge the different screens, as you can with other Adobe applications.

- *Real tool*—Again, a plug-in that specifically lets you import RealMedia files. If you used RealProducer to generate video files, use this tool to import them onto your Web site.

- *SVG tool*—Scalable vector graphics are the hot new item for designers. This tool allows you to import vector graphics created in Illustrator, Freehand, or Pagemaker. SVG is a new World Wide Web Consortium (W3C) standard that has been recently implemented.

- *Object tool*—This tool replaces GoLive 4's ActiveX tool. It lets you place and work with ActiveX elements.

The Smart Objects

This area contains entirely new and exciting elements, as well as housing some of the options that were available with GoLive 4 that have the potential to increase your workflow dramatically. Smart Objects will be discussed in greater detail in Chapter 2. As a quick rundown, the Smart Objects give you added design power by actually allowing you to link to the file in the original file format (psd, ai, liv, and so on). To modify these files during the design process, simply double-click on the specific Smart Objects placeholder. The program that created the file launches and the file opens in its original saved form. If, for example, you saved a layered Photoshop file, this file opens with all layers still intact. You can make changes, resave the file, and see it instantly updated in GoLive.

Figure 1.6
The Basic Options, with five new features.

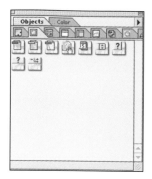

Figure 1.7
The new Smart tools will become an invaluable asset to your creative workflow.

Note: GoLive 5 actually shows you your Shockwave files, rather than just displaying a placeholder icon.

Figure 1.8
Three new Site Options give you the power to work online with other designers.

The following list shows these new options (see Figure 1.7):

- *Smart Photoshop*
- *Smart Illustrator*
- *LiveMotion*
- *Smart Rollover*
- *Smart Component*
- *Smart Date & Time*
- *Smart Popup*
- *Smart Inline Action*
- *Smart Action Headitem*
- *Smart Browser Switch Headitem*

The Site Options

Skipping over a few tabs brings you to the Site options. This area contains three powerful additions that allow you to work in groups, no matter where in the world you're located. These options will be discussed in more detail in Chapter 9. Figure 1.8 previews them:

- *Design Section*—Gives you the ability to organize your site for greatest effect. A representation is shown of all parent and children pages. In the Design Section window, you also have the ability to change the relationship between pages (to make a child page a parent or *vice versa*).

- *Design Group*—If you are working as a team stationed in various locations around the planet, you can use this aspect of the program to put your site together while allowing team members access to the files to modify, add to, or make changes within the design prior to putting it online.

- *Design Annotation*—This option gives you the ability to create notes for others to read and react to. You can also make notes to yourself. This tool is handy if you're the head of the design team and you need to coordinate numerous people who each have their separate design functions.

The QuickTime Options

This new QuickTime options area of GoLive greatly expands upon the tools that you found in GoLive 4. With the proper use of these additions, you can dramatically increase your workflow. Figure 1.9 shows you what they are. These QuickTime options will be discussed in greater detail in Chapter 7:

- *Picture Track*
- *Generic Filter Track*

- *One Source Filter Track*
- *Two Source Filter Track*
- *MPEG Track* (Macintosh only)
- *SWF Track*
- *3D Track*
- *MIDI (Music) Track*
- *Streaming Track*
- *Folder Track*

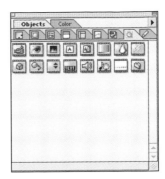

Figure 1.9
These tools will become indispensable if you ever need to
create multimedia files.

Ch-Ch-Ch-Changes...

Now it's time to take a deep breath because, if you thought what you've read
so far is the end of the differences between version 4 and version 5, hold onto
your hat! Here is a quick overview: Nearly every window palette has added
features or is modified to combine elements that were once scattered among
the different screens or the pull-down menus of version 4. It really is a good
idea to activate each of the windows to see how they were modified; just pre-
tend that you're a world explorer, discovering new lands and new opportunities
where once they didn't exist. It's worth the effort, and it's a great time saver
when you're ready to get down to the business of Web design.

The View Controller Window

Now turn your attention to the View Controller window, which is shown in
Figure 1.10. By default, this window is grouped with the Inspector window.
When you begin working in the document window, the View Controller gives
you numerous expanded design control. You can control the visibility of items
on the page and assign link warnings and numerous other attributes. Throughout the book, and especially in Chapter 15, you'll discover the power of this
particular window. Once again, depending on your work habits and your screen
real estate, you can undock the View Controller window to place it where it
will work best for you.

Figure 1.10
Determining how you view your
layout becomes much easier with
the View Controller window.

The Transform Window

New to the Transform window is the Z-Order Option, which you can see in
Figure 1.11. This new option allows you to reassign forward and backward
placement of your images. If you are using layered documents that have trans-
parencies assigned to them, you can now move these elements in front of or
behind other screen elements to make your design more effective. The "Z"
denotes depth, a term used in 3D modeling and measurement.

Figure 1.11
The new Z-Order Option gives you even greater control of your Web design, especially when working with "depth."

The Floating Boxes Window

Figure 1.12 shows another window new to GoLive 5—the Floating Boxes window. In previous versions of GoLive, after you placed a floating box into the document, you had to click on the box itself or on the small yellow floating box indicators handles to activate them. These extra steps could be a difficult prospect when you had an image in the box, because—unless you were careful—you might select the image, rather than the floating box that you originally intended to select. GoLive 5 now offers the Floating Boxes window that shows each box as its own layer, much like the layers in Photoshop, Illustrator, and other programs.

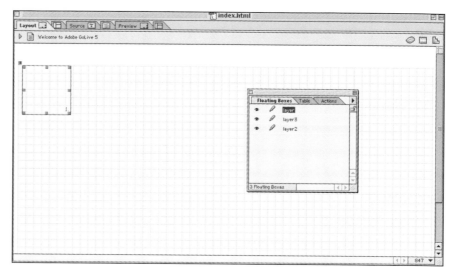

Figure 1.12
The new Floating Boxes window offers you greater ease in working with and modifying floaters on your page.

By clicking on the small arrow in the upper-right corner of the box, you gain other options to help you control your *floaters* (my term, not Adobe's). As you can see in Figure 1.13, these options help you manage the look of the floaters as you reposition them, whether floaters can overlap, and whether the boxes align themselves with the layout grid.

The Table Window

Another area that has received a great deal of attention is the Table window. Creative options abound in this area, as you can see in Figure 1.14. When you place a table element on your workspace, you get a double-tabbed palette that gives you control over almost every aspect of your table. Your options include:

- *Select*—This gives you precise control over each individual frame or row of frames, as seen in Figure 1.15.

Figure 1.13
You now have greater control of the various Floating Boxes, thanks to the expanded options in the Floating Boxes window.

Figure 1.14
You get greater control over the frames in your tables in GoLive 5.

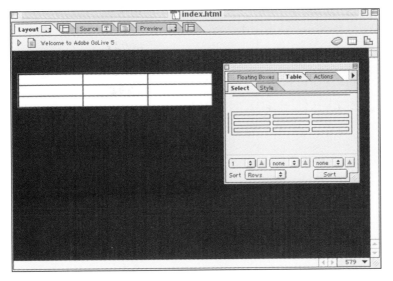

Figure 1.15
Here, you select basic options for the tables.

- *Style*—This lets you assign colors to the table's individual frames or framesets, as well as create your own color scheme for them, as seen in Figure 1.16.

You'll explore designing pages using tables in Chapter 4.

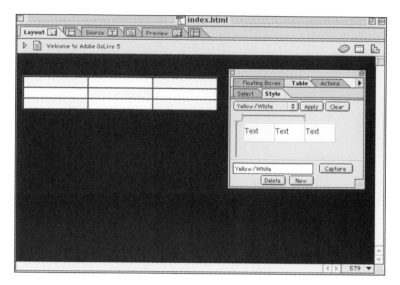

Figure 1.16
Adding color to your tables is now a cinch.

The Actions Window

In GoLive 4, Actions was tied in with the Inspector window. Figure 1.17 shows how it now has its own place on the screen. This is handy because, if you create a number of different actions on a page, the act of jumping back and forth among the tabs becomes tedious, to say the least. With the Actions window self-inclusive, you have the freedom to handle all the linking and basic setups in one window and to easily move over to the Actions window.

The Inspector Window

To see another side to the Inspector window, look at Figure 1.18. You'll see that it is now divided into a series of sub-tabs to help you organize your work. The following list describes the use of each of these tabs:

Figure 1.17
The Actions window has moved away and is now in its own window.

- *The Basic tab*—Gives you access to the controls for the various Objects on your page.

- *The More tab*—Gives you expanded control of your Objects.

- *The Link tab*—Gives you the same options as in previous versions.

Coming Almost Full Circle

This brings us around to the Site window itself. As anyone who has used versions of CyberStudio or GoLive 4 knows, this is probably the most important screen in the entire program.

The Site Window

Figure 1.18
The new Inspector window and its layout.

Figure 1.19 shows just how different and user-friendly this window has become. Split into two segments with myriad tabs to access different options, this window gives you, the designer, total control over your work. With a single click of a mouse, you can find out where link errors or other errors exist in your document. You can also access advanced workgroup tools, such as WebDAV (for more information on WebDAV, see Chapter 11). As with all tabbed windows, you can "tear" that particular section off to make it a self-contained floating window, if you want.

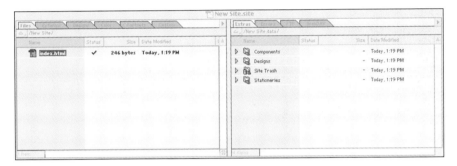

Figure 1.19
The expanded Site window with its multiple tabs helps you expedite your creative flow.

Let's take a little extra time to tour the options in this window because, as I just stated, this is probably the most important screen in the application. It's also another example of just how much more powerful GoLive has become.

Note: WebDAV is an acronym for Web Distributed Authoring and Versioning.

The Left Frame

In version 4, the left side of the Site window had only one screen. As you can see in Figure 1.20, the following six tabs now let you move between various elements of your site, so materials are more easily found and identified:

- *Files*—Gives you access to your various pages.

- *External*—Shows all of the files that are stored in an external folder or drive.

- *Designs*—Gives you quick access to layout designs for your site.

- *Colors*—Stores any special color groups assigned to your designs or Cascading Style Sheets (CSSs).

- *Fontsets*—Tracks any specialized fonts you may be using that are not normal to the Web, but that need to be accessed by visitors.

- *Custom*—Lets you store snippets of code for later use.

The Right Frame

Figure 1.21 shows the right side of the Site window, which contains the following tabs:

- *Extras*—The options in this tab show the various folders in which you will store your Web site's elements. This includes areas to store any components in your design (these areas are discussed in greater detail in

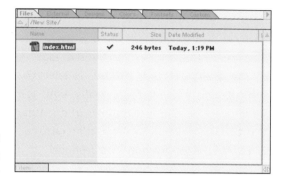

Figure 1.20
The Tab sets that are available on the left side of the Site window.

Chapter 5), designs (discussed later in this chapter), trash (kind of self-explanatory), and Stationeries.

- *Errors*—Helps you identify any set up links that haven't been assigned yet, image or motion files that haven't been assigned when an Options place-holder is in place, or other problems on your page. It's the perfect way to keep track of yourself as you build the site.

- *FTP*—Gives you the ability to choose which files you want to upload and/ or replace via File Transfer Protocol (FTP).

- *WebDAV*—If you are working with development groups in different locations around the city, country or world, this is the area you'll access. WebDAV is much like the FTP area for more specialized modifications. Again, you'll learn more about WebDAV in Chapter 11.

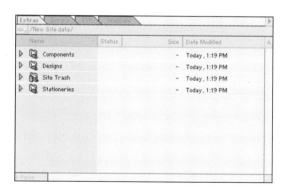

Figure 1.21
The tab sets that are available on the right side of the Site window.

Coding Capabilities

Until now, you've seen the modifications, additions, and reordering of the most visible aspects of GoLive 5. But wait; there's more. Although you've just taken a quick overview tour of the main work area of the program, it's important that you know where to find other options and tools and to see how some of them have changed.

A Site with a View

New to GoLive 5 is the capability to view both the page layout and the source code at the same time. In earlier GoLive versions, you had to build a page on the Layout screen (that is, a WYSIWYG screen) and then you had to select the Source tab to view the code (which you can still do, if you really want to). Figure 1.22 shows just how easy having access to both windows at one time makes your design work. This change allows you, as a designer and/or a scripter, to modify effects, placement, and more while receiving instant feedback.

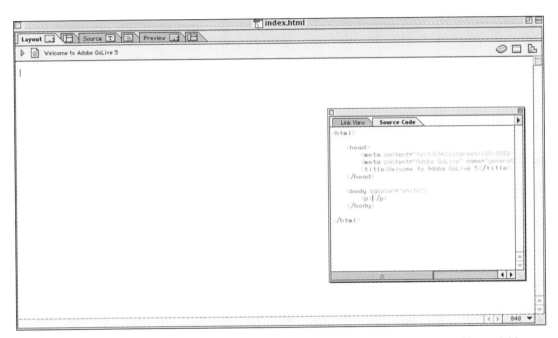

Figure 1.22

Now you can view both your page layout and the source code for the various elements at the same time.

Full Circle

For those of you who enjoy fiddling with those codes, but you still prefer to build in another editing environment, GoLive 5 has incorporated a new feature named *360Code*, a scriptwriter's dream. With 360Code, you're can write your codes—whether in JavaScript, FileMaker, CDML, XML, ASP, or ColdFusion—in any script editor that you choose without worrying about how the revised code will integrate into your design. GoLive won't alter the code at all, so "What You Write Is What You Get"—or WYWIWYG. (By the way, if anyone comes up with a cute—and socially acceptable—pronunciation for WYWIWYG other than wee-wee-wig, let me know.)

Also, the Markup Tree window shown in Figure 1.23 offers a new HTML navigational tool that shows the hierarchical positioning of any selected object that you place on your page. So, if you have elements that show up in numerous places—for example, in a paragraph, body, and HTML element—you'll get extra visual feedback to help identify your composition.

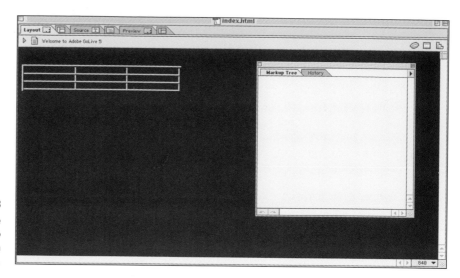

Figure 1.23
The addition of a Markup Tree palette gives you the ability to quickly see an element's use in your site design.

The Search Is On

Finding specific coding in your site just became easier. Figure 1.24 shows the new Find dialog box for HTML searches. When you select Find from the Edit menu, a tabbed box appears on screen, giving you access to specific styles and elements to search for. By selecting the Element tab, you can type in a specific HTML code and GoLive will find it for you.

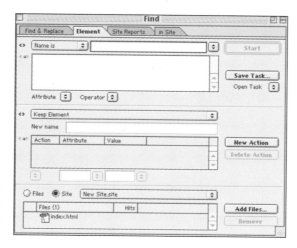

Figure 1.24
The new Element option in the Find dialog box gives you the ability to search for specific HTML codes on your page.

Improved Productivity

To complete this overview of the new GoLive 5 features, here are a few other enhancements to GoLive that will surely make you want to dive right in to update your existing site and to start creating even more sites (whether or not you have ideas for them):

- *CSS enhancements*—This feature allows you to drag and drop a style from one sheet to another, drag a style from the layout window directly into the HTML code and have it generate that code instantly, and import style sheets from predefined outside style sheets and turn them into useable embedded styles in your design.

- *Improved color placement*—Simply click on an element, bring up the Color palette, and any changes are instantly applied.

- *History palette*—As with other Adobe products, this palette tracks each step of your work so that you can go back (up to 20 prior steps) later and reverse changes to your project.

- *HTML storage*—Now you can store HTML snippets for later use using a drag and drop method.

- *Greater QuickTime interactivity*—Features enhance QuickTime authoring tools that are discussed more fully in Chapter 7.

- *Integrated site reports*—Provides you with the capability to print reports that include file information, errors, objects, links, and other items you specify.

- *Dynamic links*—Provides you with a way to visually design database content and e-commerce functions.

- *Customization tools*—Can't find a feature you need? GoLive offers a *Software Development Kit* (*SDK*) that allows you to write scripts to expand the program's capabilities through plug-in architecture.

Moving On

As you can see, GoLive 5 isn't your mother's Web design program. The changes that Adobe has made to GoLive 5 make it an almost entirely new program, albeit one that will be familiar to everyone who has used any Adobe product on the market.

It's now time to explore these new features by getting in there and using them. Take a moment, let all the intriguing changes sink in, and then read Chapter 2 and begin getting your hands dirty as you start working with one of the most exciting new aspects of Adobe GoLive 5—the Smart Objects.

Chapter 2

Exploring the Smart Tools

Modifying your artwork to satisfy clients or your own design sense has become about as easy as it gets, thanks to the inclusion of Smart Tools. Not only has GoLive gotten "Smart," it has made sure other programs have gotten their design degrees, as well.

Get Smart

Creating graphically enticing Web sites has always required a symbiotic yet segregated relationship among numerous programs. A designer needs libraries of programs to make everything work—like Photoshop to prepare photographic elements, Illustrator or Freehand to create vector art and text that follows along paths to add interest, a library of clip art to help draw original images, and plug-ins to help expedite the generation of complicated special effects within these programs.

Here's the scenario: You've spent dozens of hours creating complicated graphic elements for your or your client's new Web site. You've built logos, scanned in photographs, and modified them until you were completely satisfied. Then you saved your work in a Web-safe format, such as JPEG, GIF, or PNG. With great pride, you unveiled your Web design masterpiece to the client, and—as it always seems to happen—they wanted modifications made to some of the images. Yet, you had to flatten the images and (as always seems to happen) the layered files are nowhere to be found. This means you have to re-create images from scratch, adding hours to a job. Thanks to the inclusion of Smart Tools, this no longer needs to happen.

Smart Tools allow you to save your files in their native format—.psd for Photoshop, .ai for Illustrator, .liv for LiveMotion—and import them directly into GoLive, where they will be translated into Web-safe files. Until you upload your Web site to your Internet service provider's (ISP's) staging area, the links to the original files will be there. By double-clicking on the image on the GoLive workspace, the application the image file has created will be launched, along with the raw file, where you can make the appropriate changes. After you are finished making changes, the file automatically updates on the workspace—a cool and wonderful timesaving feature that will quickly become indispensable to you.

Note: This area of GoLive is memory intensive because it ultimately runs more than one program at a time. We have arranged with Crucial Technology (**www.crucial.com**) for a special discount on memory upgrades for both Macs and PCs. You can find details in the Memory Discount folder on this book's companion CD-ROM.

The Class Comes to Order

As you can see in Figure 2.1, Smart Tools have their own distinct look on the workspace. This workspace is very different from other tools in your arsenal. When you import a file, be it Photoshop, Illustrator, or LiveMotion, an icon for that program appears in the bottom-right corner of the placeholder.

Figure 2.1
The Smart Tools placeholders have their own distinct look to make them easily distinguishable from other placeholders.

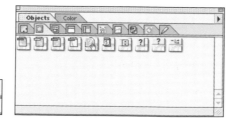

A New Family Member

LiveMotion, by the way, is Adobe's newest program that is the company's answer to creating Shockwave format animations for the Web. You can download from Adobe's Web site. The benefit to LiveMotion is its intuitive interface that closely follows the Graphic User Interface (GUI) design in the rest of Adobe's product line. This interface reduces the learning curve for LiveMotion, so that you'll find yourself creating basic animations very quickly.

You can select from numerous Smart Tools, but the ones you'll more than likely find yourself working with the most are the Photoshop, Illustrator, and LiveMotion (if you have this program) tools.

How the Smart Tools Work

Here's a brief summary of how the Smart Tools work. Instead of placing your flattened Web-ready image onto the workspace, Smart Tools create a link to the file that you choose. When you select, say, a layered Photoshop image, GoLive creates a Web-ready flattened file, but retains the link to the layered file. If modifications need to take place, you can access the layered file and have a new GIF or JPEG created that replaces the old one instantaneously.

To get a better feel for this, and maybe cut down on some of the confusion that this convoluted description might have caused, you'll begin by building an image in Photoshop and then make some basic modifications to it after you've placed it on a Web page. If you're familiar with Photoshop's layers, you might want to skip ahead to the section, "Using the Photoshop Smart Tool." First, review the finished layout prior to doing this so that you can have it ready for importing.

Before You Begin

Create a new site in GoLive 5. Name the site whatever you want, although for the purposes of this book, you may want to call it PshopCh02. Now create a media folder where you will store the interim image files that will be created when you link to the layered images. You will also want to create a folder inside the main site folder where you will store the main image files you will create. In this way, you will have an easily accessible area where the files can be saved. Call it MasterImageFiles.

> **Note:** The following steps can be accomplished in any version of Photoshop that you use. It is not version-specific, although it's advisable to have either a fully working or a demo of version 5.5 or 6.

Create a Layered Photoshop File

You can find the elements you'll be working with in the Chapter 2 folder on this book's companion CD-ROM, in the subfolder titled "PShopElements." Follow these steps to create the file:

1. Open Photoshop and open the following Photoshop files: ByDesign.psd, GRFX_Pencil.psd, and Paint_Drop.psd (see Figure 2.2).

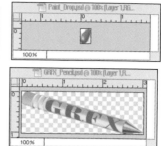

Figure 2.2
The three master files that will be used to create the layered image.

2. Create a new document approximately one inch larger in both height and width than the ByDesign file (5.986 inches wide by 2.819 inches high), so that you have some room to maneuver the elements.

3. Drag the elements from the other three files onto this new window, as seen in Figure 2.3. This is the initial look for the file, but some modifications still need to take place.

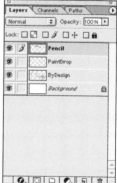

Figure 2.3
The finished layered logo layout.

4. With the Layers palette open (Window|ShowLayers), rename the layers ByDesign and Pencil, respectively. Then duplicate these two layers and place them as you see in Figure 2.4.

5. After you make sure that the Preserve Transparency box at the bottom of the Fill screen is checked, fill these duplicates with black. Add a Gaussian Blur to each of these layers (Filter|Blur|Gaussian Blur), assigning a radius of 2.0 pixels to each layer's image. Set the Opacity of these layers to 70%. Arrange the layers as you see in Figure 2.5, and then save the file as Layered_Logo.psd.

In the past, you would have had to save this file as a JPEG, GIF, or PNG image before you could import it into GoLive. This is no longer the case.

Figure 2.4
Duplicate the ByDesign and Pencil layers.

Using the Photoshop Smart Tool

Now that you have your layered file created, it's time to import it into GoLive. Doing so automatically creates what is called a Smart Link. To import the layered file, take the following steps:

1. Open GoLive. If you have not changed any of the default settings, a new document will open. Drag the Smart Photoshop Tool onto the workspace.

2. If you're familiar with previous versions of GoLive, you'll see in Figure 2.6 that the Inspector window's controls have changed dramatically. Under the Basic tab, you select the file you want to import using the Source selector. Use the browse button to navigate to your saved Photoshop file. When it is chosen, the Save For Web screen comes up which is exactly the same kind of screen that you get in Photoshop or ImageReady. Change the settings to what you see in Figure 2.7. When the file is opened, you are asked to specify the target file (see Figure 2.8). Place this new file into the media folder you created. The file is immediately placed on the page. Notice the logo is in the bottom right of the image placeholder (see Figure 2.9). Because this is a Photoshop file, the Photoshop logo is displayed. If you were using the Illustrator or the LiveMotion Smart Tool, you would see the respective program file's image.

Figure 2.5
Arrange the layers as you see here to complete the logo. This layered file will be the one imported into GoLive using the Photoshop Smart Tool.

Figure 2.6
The new Inspector window controls.

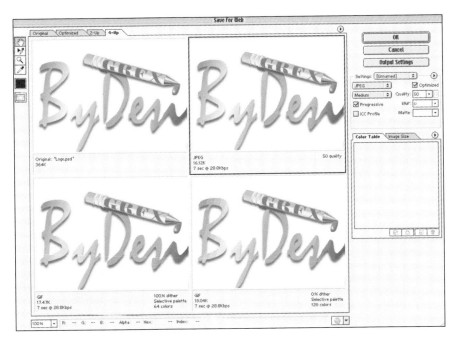

Figure 2.7
The Save For Web screen and the settings to be used for the logo file.

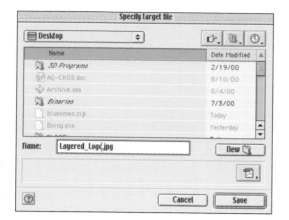

Figure 2.8
The Specify Target File screen,
asking where you want to save
the modified image.

Figure 2.9
When an image is placed into a
Smart Tool placeholder, the
program's icon is shown to help
you identify the creation program.

3. It's now time to modify the file and see just how powerful Smart Tools really are. First, you will make the paint drop a bit longer. Double-click on the image and watch the magic happen. Adobe Photoshop is automatically started, and the original layered file is opened.

4. Select the Paint Drop layer, choose Edit|Transform|Scale, and extend the paint drop so that the bottom is closer to the "i" in Design. You also need to change the drop shadows for the logo and pencil to 60%. Quit the program and choose OK to save the modified file.

5. You'll immediately see your updated image in GoLive. Figure 2.10 shows the modified files on the GoLive workspace, with the distinctive Smart Tools icon showing in which program the master file was created. You can now officially say, "Ooh! Ahh!"

Hey—You Flattened My Image!

The procedure you just went through assumed you wanted the Photoshop file to be flattened—merging the various layers into one—creating what is virtually a non-modifiable, finished image. However, let's say you have worked on a file that has numerous layers and you want to get mucho creative in how that

Figure 2.10

After completing the Web optimization process, you'll immediately see your modified image in GoLive.

image is displayed. What does "mucho creative" mean? You have just spent a lot of time building an image that has four layers, and you'd like to have those layers fly in separately to form the final image. Okay, you can do that. This, by the way, is where the true power of GoLive's import features shines.

Prior to this version of GoLive (in what seems like a totally different century, which… oh yeah, it was a different century), doing what you're about to do would have meant saving each layer as an independent Web-ready file. This onerous procedure has become a thing of the past. Now, you merely import the layered image into GoLive and do your creative magic.

Retaining Layered Photoshop Files

To import a layered Photoshop file that retains its layers, follow these steps:

1. Place the SumoBabyNoText.psd (see Figure 2.11) file from the Chapter 2 folder on your desktop or in your GoLive site folder. Then open GoLive and create a new page.

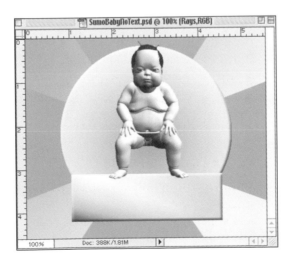

Figure 2.11

A baby only a mother (or fellow sumo wrestler) could love.

2. Choose File|Import|Photoshop As HTML (see Figure 2.12) and select the SumoBabyNoText.psd. Following this step, from the Browse For Folder dialog box, select a folder in which you will store the file. This creates a document that preserves the layers in your PSD file. It literally turns each layer into its own standalone file (see Figure 2.13). You will be asked to choose a folder in which to place the file, so choose the media folder in your Web site file.

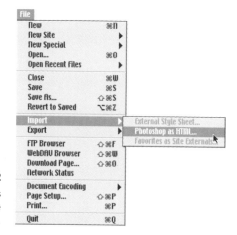

Figure 2.12

To import a Photoshop with its layers preserved, use the Photoshop As HTML command.

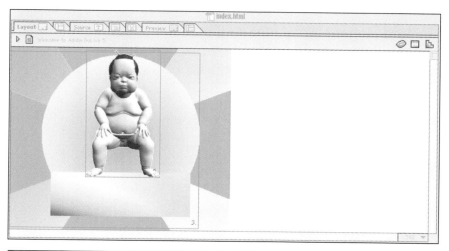

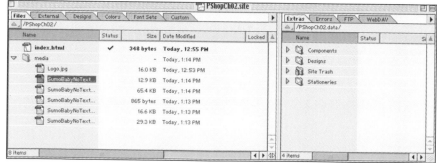

Figure 2.13

The Photoshop As HTML files inside the media folder and seen as separate layers on the workspace.

3. As with importing a file using the Photoshop Smart Tool, the Save For Web screen comes up for each layer. For the background and the bar layers, save as a JPEG image using the same parameters you did in the previous section of this chapter. For the sun rays, the sun and the baby layers, choose GIF and make sure that Transparency is selected (see Figure 2.14).

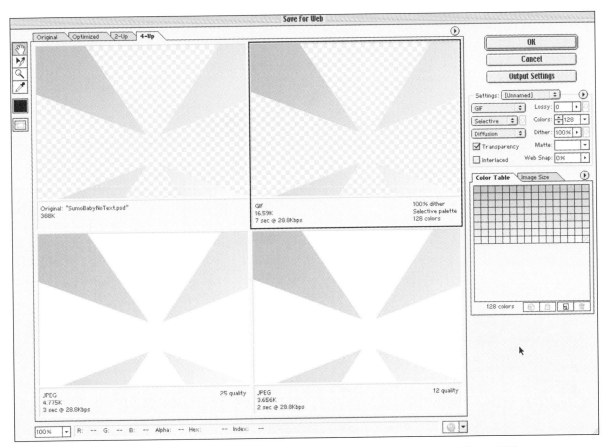

Figure 2.14
The rays layer (seen here) as well as the sun and baby layers should be saved as GIF files with Transparency selected.

4. While these different layers are being imported, they are automatically placed within a Floating Box, as you can see in Figure 2.15. This situation is wonderful because you can immediately begin to animate each layer in any way you desire.

Layer Shortcut

If you have a layered file in which each layer will be saved as a GIF with transparencies, just hold down Command|Ctl when accepting the settings. All layers will be assigned the same settings as the background layer.

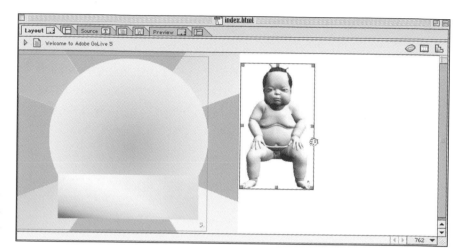

Figure 2.15
Each of your Photoshop layers is now situated in a Floating Box ready to be positioned.

Note: Animating Floating Boxes is discussed in greater detail in Chapter 6. At the end of this chapter, however, I'll begin whetting your appetite for layer animation that uses this Sumo Baby file.

Cutting Up in Class

"Okay, Mr. Author. This is all well and good," I can hear you say, "But I've got this awesome image file that I sliced up in Photoshop and ImageReady, and even assigned some button actions to it. What can Smart Tools do for me in this case?" I'm so glad you asked that, oh intrepid and far-sighted Web designer. It's one thing to build pages with lots of movement or static images, but Photoshop 5.5 and 6, with the inclusion of ImageReady, allow you to build files that are sliced and have rollover code assigned for use in Web programs. Of course, GoLive also supports importing these functions.

Sliced images really help the whole process of loading by cutting up a larger file into smaller, more manageable segments, like those shown in Figure 2.16. Like a puzzle when put together, these slices reveal an entire picture. You can also assign actions and links to each slice for navigation purposes. Let's look at how this works.

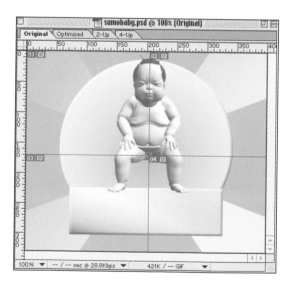

Figure 2.16
Creating sliced files expedites image-downloading time when a visitor with a slower Web connection views your Web site.

Working with Sliced Images

After you've created a sliced file, bring it into GoLive in the following manner:

1. Place the SumoBabySliced.psd file into your MasterImageFiles folder. Create a new document in GoLive and move a Photoshop Smart Tool placeholder onto the workspace. Click on the Browse button in the Source menu inside the Inspector window and locate the SumoBabySliced.psd file.

2. Figure 2.17 shows the first dialog box that appears. In this Save dialog box, you assign where GoLive will create a ".data" folder. This folder stores the HTML source codes for the slices as well as sliced image.

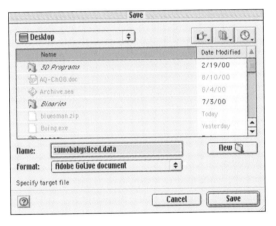

Figure 2.17

The options that appear when importing sliced files with HTML code already assigned.

3. This time, the Save For Web screen shows the sliced file (see Figure 2.18). In the Output Settings screen (which you can access by clicking on the Output Settings button), you have numerous controls for saving your sliced images. Figures 2.19 through 2.22 show, respectively, the HTML, Background, Saving Files, and Slices setting screens. Here is, in order, what each does:

   - *HTML*—In this setting screen, you can set up the HTML snippets for each portion of the image files; what type of Head Tags will be assigned, attributes, and more. You can also embed CSS information.

   - *Background*—Here, you can choose a background image to be assigned to the sliced file (if one is not already included in the design). For example, if the orange background were not a part of the SumoBabySliced.psd file, you could assign one that will load when the file is accessed.

   - *Saving Files*—This control gives you control over how each slice is named and configured. In the event that you see an error, you can modify each slice by using this screen and the pop-up controls (see Figure 2.23). You can also set up system compatibility, file storage, and copyright embedding with this setting screen.

- *Slices*—This setting screen enables you to modify the default names of each slice.

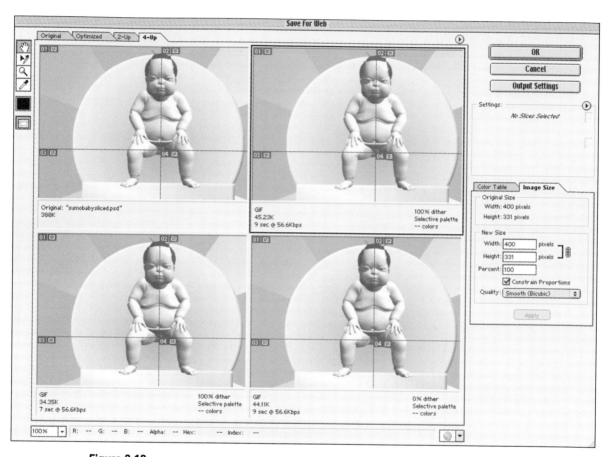

Figure 2.18
The Save For Web screen and how the sliced image appears.

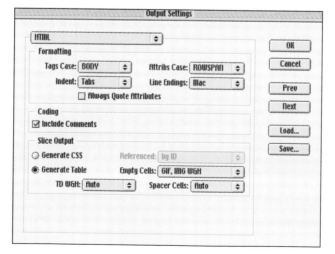

Figure 2.19
The HTML Output Settings screen.

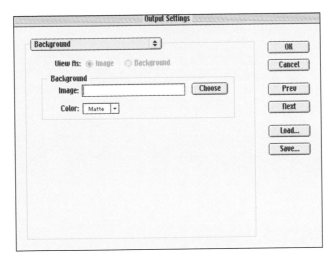

Figure 2.20
The Background Output
Settings screen.

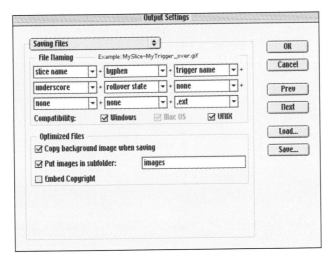

Figure 2.21
The Saving Files Output
Settings screen.

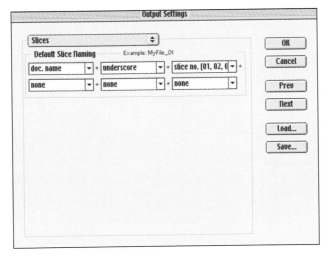

Figure 2.22
The Slices Output
Settings screen.

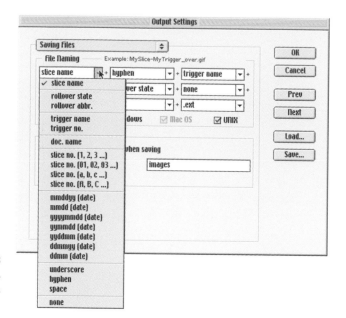

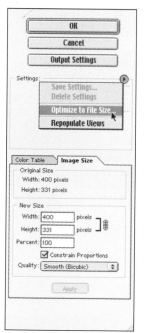

Figure 2.23
The pop-up selections for one section of the Saving Files Output Settings screen.

4. There are other controls at your disposal when you use the Save For Web screen. These controls include the Settings feature that, by selecting the arrow button to the right of the Setting header (see Figure 2.24), you can access the Optimize To File Size screen shown in Figure 2.25. You can then choose between various setting options to make sure that your image slices will load as quickly as possible.

5. After the file is imported as shown in Figure 2.26, you can modify each slice, as you normally would using the Inspector palette.

Other Class Members

This is only the start of what you can accomplish using the Smart Tools. Adobe Illustrator has one that gives you unlimited control over your design work. Suppose that you've created a series of vector graphics that originally fit the color scheme of your overall site design, but, after building the site, you decide to change the look of these graphics. It's now a simple procedure to refine the file.

Figure 2.24
The Settings pop-up choices, with the Optimize To File Size setting selected.

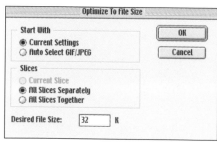

Figure 2.25
The Optimize To File Size screen.

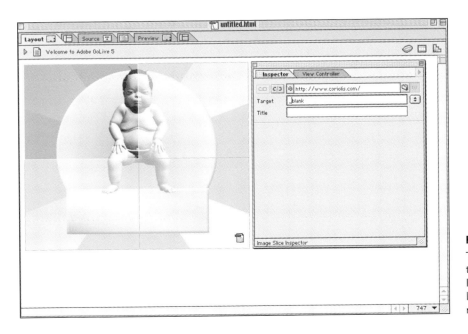

Using the Illustrator Smart Tool

Such is the case with the drop of paint coming out of the tip of the pencil in the logo. You can modify the shape and color of this graphic without leaving GoLive and immediately see how the new look fits in.

Note: The Illustrator Smart Tool only works with Illustrator 9. A demo of the program is available from Adobe's Web site.

Follow these steps to modify the graphic:

1. Open a new document in GoLive and place a Smart Illustrator placeholder on the workspace.

2. Create a link to the paint drop file in the Inspector window by clicking on the Browse button.

3. Figure 2.27 shows that, once again, the Conversion Settings dialog box will open, offering choices for Web modification of the files. Save the file as JPEG (High). The Illustrator image is converted and displays on the workspace. As you can see, some extraneous elements exist that aren't needed (the two crosshair symbols in the lower left of the image). You need to remove them, and you will want to place the pencil and the paint drop in their final positions.

Figure 2.27
As with the Photoshop Smart Tool, Web conversion settings for the Illustrator file are handled within GoLive.

4. Double-click on this image to open the original Illustrator file in Illustrator 9. Remember, what you see on the workspace is the converted file, but a link to the original is retained. Illustrator will start, and the original vector artwork will open.

5. Select the two crosshairs and then delete them. Next, move the pencil over the paint drop, as shown in Figure 2.28, and extend the paint drop itself so the bottom of it is closer to the "i".

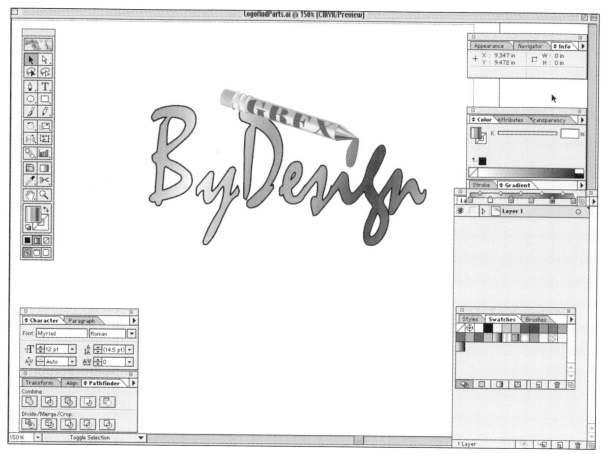

Figure 2.28

Modification of the Paint Drop is handled in Illustrator.

6. After you make the change, save the file, close Illustrator, and (as you can see in Figure 2.29) the changes are automatically updated in GoLive.

Note: You need to select both the filled and the outline for the paint drop because they aren't grouped.

Introducing SVG

While we're on the subject of vector graphics, note that a new standard has been set by the World Wide Web Consortium (W3C) called Scalable Vector Graphics (SVG). You are probably starting to see more and more of this technology on the Web. SVG is incorporated in the newest version of Illustrator (v9); if you're using Illustrator 7.x or 8.x, you can download an SVG plug-in from the Adobe Web site.

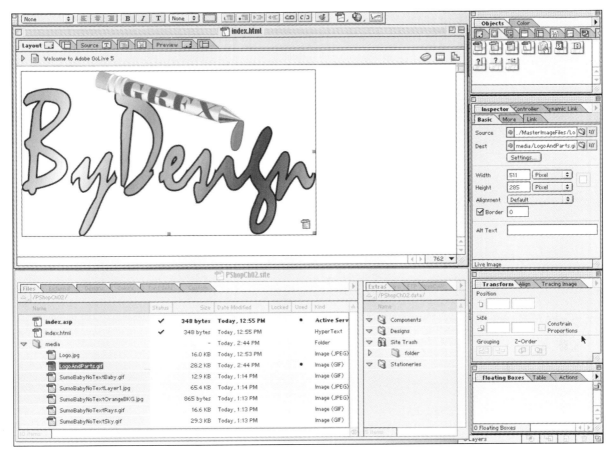

Figure 2.29
The changes you made to the Illustrator file are immediately updated and represented on the workspace.

In a nutshell, SVG is XML-based, which is the standard for the new version of HTML, and is for the most part compatible with all the new, emerging Web technologies. This also means that you can literally write HTML-like scripts without ever opening a program, such as Illustrator or Freehand; you only need to write out an SVG script and place it on your page. When working within Illustrator and saving in SVG, a dialog box like that in Figure 2.30 gives you a series of added options to take advantage of this format.

SVG gives you, the Web designer, the ability to create interactive files for use on the Web. This can include giving visitors the ability to scale your images,

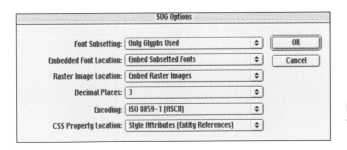

Figure 2.30
The SVG dialog box and its options.

Note: To learn more about scripting for SVG and to see sample scripts, go to **www.w3.org/Graphics/SVG/Overview.htm8**.

move them around the screen, and much, much more. Additionally, because these are vector graphics, no loss in resolution will occur; the edges of your objects will remain crisp and sharp, no matter what their size.

For those of you who are like me and are allergic to writing code, Illustrator, as mentioned earlier, lets you work in familiar territory—that of graphic design—generating the code without writing it. We'll explore SVG, how it looks and works, in Chapters 8 and 15. Scalable Vector Graphics could well become the hottest addition to your Web arsenal. For now, however, you'll want to go to the Web site listed in the preceding note and get a true feel for what SVG will mean to Web development and developers in the near future.

To import an SVG file, take the following steps:

1. Place the LogoAndParts.svg file from this book's companion CD-ROM to the media folder of your site. In the Basics area of the Objects window, drag the SVG element onto the workspace as you see in Figure 2.31. Then, following the usual procedure to link to the file, you need to link to the LogoAndParts.svg file.

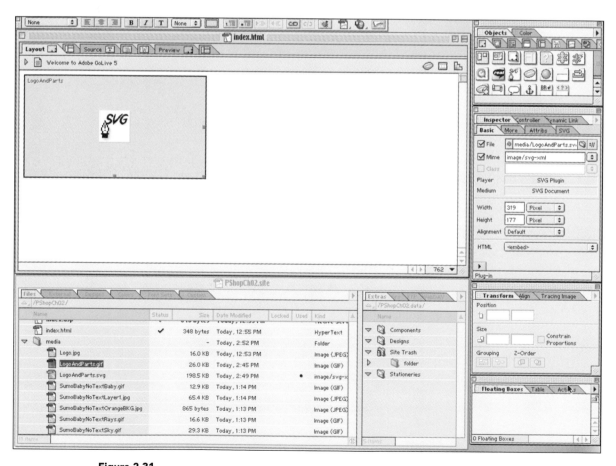

Figure 2.31
The SVG placeholder on the workspace.

2. Non-compressed SVG files aren't displayed on the workspace when you are in Layout mode. You get an image similar to what you see in Figure 2.32, with the file name and the SVG logo displayed. To see the image itself, select Preview (see Figure 2.33).

Figure 2.32
The way a non-compressed SVG file is displayed on the workspace in Layout mode.

Note: You cannot select or work with a compressed file on the workspace. To make any modifications, you need to first deselect Use Compressed SVG and then turn off the arrow button.

Figure 2.33
The non-compressed SVG image can be viewed when in Preview Mode.

3. You can change from non-compressed to compressed mode, and see your SVG file while in Layout mode by doing the following:

• Select the SVG tab in the Inspector window.

• Select the Use Compressed SVG option and click on the arrow button at the bottom right of the window (see Figure 2.34). Wait a few seconds as GoLive reformats the image. After reformatting is complete, you'll be able to see the SVG file on the workspace (see Figure 2.35).

4. You can still make modifications to the file while you are in Compressed mode via the Inspector window, assigning link attributes in the More section (see Figure 2.36), or giving other attributes to the file in the Attribs section.

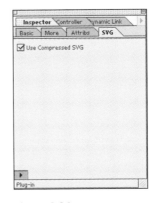

Figure 2.34
The Inspector window set up to change the SVG file into a viewable compressed file.

Figure 2.35

The SVG file seen in Layout mode on the workspace.

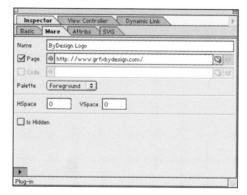

Figure 2.36

Changes to the Compressed file in the More section of the Inspector window. A link has been created by selecting Page in this area.

Notice the difference between an SVG file and the translated Illustrator 9 file you created previously in this chapter. The SVG colors are more vibrant. Because SVG is becoming a Web standard, the file sizes remain small, which allows for quick uploading for the designer (and, subsequently, quick downloading for the surfers who arrive at pages that contain these SVG files). The image quality, however, being more saturated, will really be impressive to those who haven't seen SVG images before.

Riding the Shockwave to Success

LiveMotion is Adobe's newest Web-creation family member. It allows you to create high-quality animations and save them in the Shockwave (SWF) format. GoLive provides you with a LiveMotion Smart Tool so you can create animated banners, interactive games, or other similar files. LiveMotion can also be used to create extended rollovers and interactive elements for your site. If you haven't already done so, install the demo of LiveMotion after downloading it from Adobe's site.

Importing a LiveMotion File

Working with and importing LiveMotion files is a breeze. Here's how:

1. If you haven't already done it, start LiveMotion and then open the Logo_Animation.Liv file in the Chapter 2 folder on the companion CD-ROM. Figure 2.37 shows the first frame of the logo we have animated. This is an eight-second, 640x480 pixel animation.

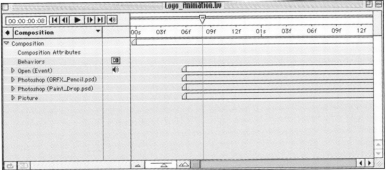

Figure 2.37

A screen for an opening animation created in LiveMotion.

2. If the TimeLine isn't visible, go to TimeLine|View TimeLine or use the Command/Ctrl+T key combination. Move the triangle back and forth along the TimeLine, as shown in Figure 2.38, to see what elements are there and to get a general feel for the animation.

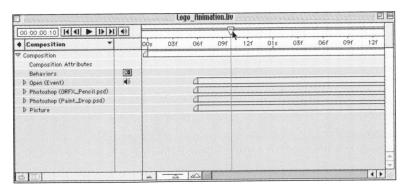

Figure 2.38

Move the TimeLine indicator back and forth to get a rough estimation of what the animation does.

3. Save this file to your desktop (or to the folder in which you keep your GoLive master files), then open GoLive 5 and create a new document. Drag the Smart LiveMotion placeholder onto the workspace and, as shown in Figure 2.39, set the parameters of the placeholder to the LiveMotion file's dimensions in the Smart Image Inspector window.

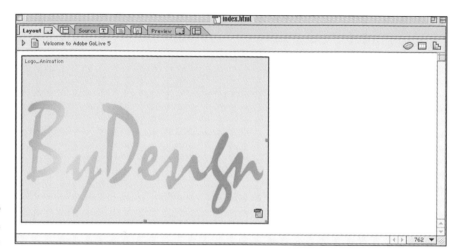

Figure 2.39
The LiveMotion placeholder set to the dimensions of the actual file.

4. After you set the LiveMotion placeholder parameters, you need to link to the Logo_Animation.Liv file. GoLive will launch LiveMotion and automatically save the file in the Shockwave format, as you see in Figure 2.40.

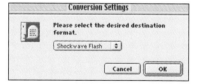

Figure 2.40
GoLive automatically saves the master LiveMotion file as a Shockwave file after the original is imported.

5. In the case of LiveMotion files, you need to save the modified document in your GoLive site folder. Select that folder and then click on OK when this screen comes up. This works like the other Smart Tools: If you want to modify a LiveMotion animation after you've already placed it, simply double-click on the appropriate screen on your workspace, and GoLive will launch LiveMotion.

Smart Tools: The Final Exam

As you can see, with the addition of Smart Tools, the process of building original sites has become much easier because you're no longer locked in to working with unmodifiable files. Your creative options have expanded dramatically with these tools, and the expanded design options allow you to modify your sites in a way that would heretofore be, at the least, pretty darn difficult—even impossible—to accomplish. You're also able to share your original files with other members of a design group (if you're part of one), who can then make changes to files that were impossible to make in other versions of the program.

Creating a Splash Screen

Let's return to those days when you would go to a Web site and, upon entering it, would find it filled with logos, links to other pages and sites, a bio, and some general information. Of course, many of these pages ran on and on for what seemed forever. If you've ever tried to print them, 25 or 30 pages used up your ribbons (remember those wonderfully noisy dot-matrix printers?) or guzzled your ink or toner cartridge with no regard to the expense of replacing them. Then again, to actually get to the point of printing the page meant waiting an interminable length of time for the entire document to load.

On today's Web, it seems that every Web site you come across has introductory splash screens—those single-image (mostly static or animated logo) pages that let you know when you've surfed to the right place. Usually the Web site tries to wow you with a flashy introduction reminiscent of a movie trailer prior to the start of the feature. Well, that's what you're about to create. However, instead of using a program such as LiveMotion, Macromedia Flash, Director, or Fireworks, as many of today's site designers do, you're going to build it with a layered Photoshop image brought into GoLive, and you're going to let the program do all the animation work. The Photoshop (as well as the Illustrator) Smart Tool is so powerful that its usefulness is best shown in conjunction with GoLive's animation capabilities.

I want to focus on the Photoshop Smart Tool when creating this splash screen for a simple reason. It's common practice to build an animation (be it a Shockwave or GIF animation) with a secondary program. What's not so commonplace is the ability to animate layered files without using one of these outside programs. So, to best show off the Smart Tools capabilities, designing an animation using what will probably become one of the most used elements will give you the strongest sense of what can be accomplished.

One Last Note before the Exam

One main design factor to remember when putting your page together: It's wonderful having a 17-inch or larger high-resolution monitor (1024×768, 1152×870, and so on) with high-speed Internet access via cable modem, DSL, or LAN. But the plain truth here is that the average monitor size is only 15 inches (especially now with the heavy sales of iMacs, which have built-in 15-inch monitors), and the average connection speed is between 33Kbps and 56.6Kbps. Keep this in mind as you move into personal, freelance, or full-time Web development.

Design Your Site with Everyone in Mind

You all have experienced sites where you not only had to scroll down, but you had to scroll across, as well. Although many of you have a 17-inch monitor set at a resolution of 1152×870 or higher, the average monitor size is 15 inches. The effective viewing surface of these smaller monitors equates to an area of approximately 13.5 inches. Imagine what it's like with a 13-inch or smaller screen!

The best way to avoid this "oversized page/undersized monitor" problem is to design a Web site from the ground up for a final viewing area of 640×480. Put it together, however, on a workspace that's 800×600. In this way you will know that everything you have worked on—whether it's an animation or a cutesy little rollover effect—will be seen as it was meant to be seen on any size monitor.

Note: Due to bandwidth limitations, a 56.6 modem doesn't actually receive at 56.6Kbps. Usually the fastest reception is in the low- to mid-40s.

Note: We'll go over all of the Design functionalities in greater detail, starting in the next chapter. So, consider this your introduction to the Design feature.

PROJECT 2.1 Smart SATs—Setting Up the Workspace

In this section, you explore methods of creating the first page of a Web site by working not only with the Smart Tools you've explored in the first part of this chapter, but also by using the upgraded Design features that allow you to build Web sites without actually creating them. What does this mean? How can you build a site without actually creating it? Actually, the answer is really quite simple.

Consider the Design area shown in Figure 2.41 as a sheet of paper. You lay out your initial design using this area, but instead of having a representative diagram, you have a fully functional site to work with before you ever save anything for uploading. This feature lets you incorporate the Smart Tools, see how they work, and make sure that you're happy with the outcome of their use. Then, only after your Web site is set up exactly the way you want it do you actually save the site in its final form.

Additionally, if you're part of a design team scattered here and there in your state, across the country, or around the world, the Design feature gives you the flexibility to work with others via the Internet. Anyone in your workgroup can modify the Web site via a private server or FTP area where the images and pages can be shared. It's an exciting and powerful way to make sure that all your elements are working properly. Then, when you premiere your new or modified site, it's as impressive and trouble-free as you can make it.

Using the Site Design Window

Follow these steps when working with the Design window:

1. Create a new site (File|New Site|Blank). Create a folder in which to place all the files and click on Choose. Now select Design|New Site Design. A screen similar to the one shown in Figure 2.41 will open. This is probably the most valuable real estate on the computer screen because, as you build the Web site, you can monitor the relationships between the pages you create—which ones link to which and how each page fits into the overall flow of the design.

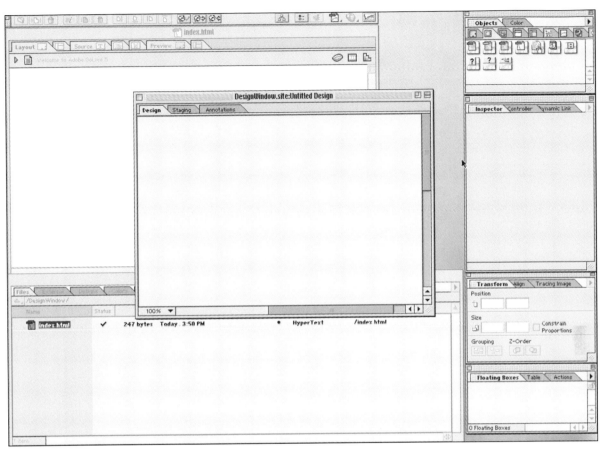

Figure 2.41
The Site Design window is an extremely valuable screen that allows you to oversee the functionality of your site.

2. Drag the index.html icon from the site management window onto the Design window. Figure 2.42 shows how this creates the beginning of your site tree with the index page as your anchor. From here, all subsequent pages will branch out with their link relationships represented.

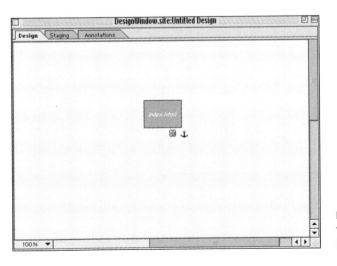

Figure 2.42
The anchor page in the Design Layout window.

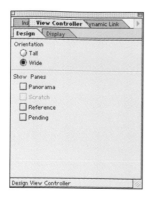

Figure 2.43

You can modify the elements that are shown in the Design Layout window by using the Inspector palette. With a little bit of experimentation, you will discover the method that works best for you and exactly what information you want shown.

Figure 2.44

You can modify the way your pages are represented in the Design Layout window, too.

Figure 2.45

Through the Design Layout window, you can control numerous aspects of your site.

3. Use the Inspector palette to modify the look of the Design Layout window. Click on the View Controller tab. Figure 2.43 shows that, under the Design tab, you can set up the Design Window Orientation as Tall or Wide, and set whether the window is split into "panes" to show other advanced relationships. The Display tab opens an option (see Figure 2.44). You can change the shape of the Design Tree icons, the way the page labels read, and other aspects of the Design window look.

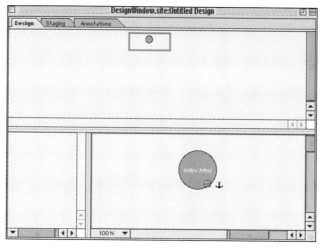

4. Figure 2.45 shows the controls under the Inspector tab. Clicking on this tab gives you control of the displaying of Design Tree object's name, target directory, file name (which is usually best to keep as index.html), and the title of the page.

5. Now that you have that out of the way, double-click on either the index.html icon in the site window or the icon in the Design window to open the blank page.

Import the Splash Screen Art

It's now time to import the layered Photoshop file. Because this will be part of your splash page animation, you'll use it as the base, and then import a Smart Object afterward. Set up site folders where you can store your various art elements and pages, which you'll do in the same way as in previous versions. Refer to the GoLive user manual if you need a refresher on creating site folders. You'll need the following folders: media, pages, and sumo. Store the SumoBabyNoText.psd elements in the latter folder.

Follow these steps:

1. With the workspace active, choose File|Import|Photoshop As HTML and then navigate to the folder where the SumoBabyNoText.psd file is located. Select this file. As each element is made Web-ready, you'll be asked where to save it. Put it in the sumo folder.

2. Import each layer in the following manner:

    -   *Background*—GIF/Selective/Diffusion, 100% Dither, 0% Web Snap,
        256 Colors.

    -   *Burst*—Same as Background, but select Transparency and Interlaced,
        as you see in Figure 2.46.

    -   *Sun & Sumo Baby*—Same as Burst.

    -   *Bar*—Go with the default setup.

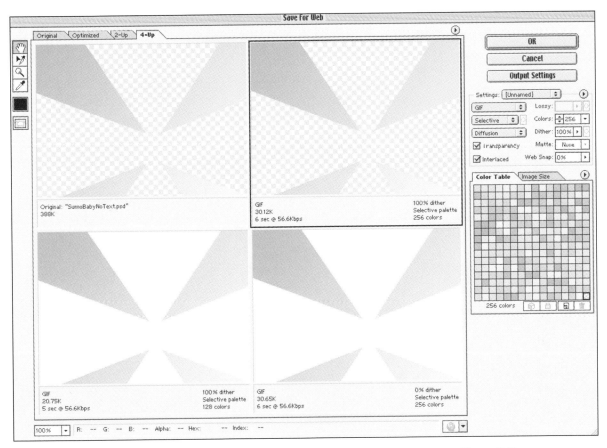

Figure 2.46

The Web-ready setup for all
the layers except Layer 1, which
has become your page's
background.

3. With everything in place on the page, select all the elements (except
    the background) by clicking on one of the floating boxes and using the
    Command/Ctrl+A quick key combination. Then center the layers using
    the Vertical Center button shown in Figure 2.47 in the Tools screen.

4. Once this is done, click anywhere on the background and then select
    the Sumo baby and drag him almost all the way off the left side of the
    screen. Figure 2.48 shows how your screen should now look.

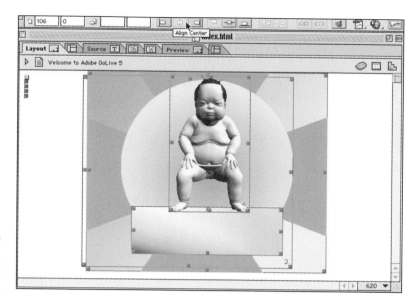

Figure 2.47
Use the Vertical Center button to center the floating boxes and the elements on the page.

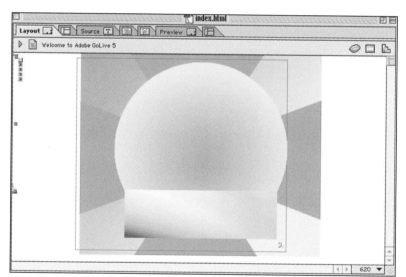

Figure 2.48
The very beginning of the splash screen animation.

5. Make sure that the Sumo Baby Floating Box is still active, and click on the Inspector tab on the Inspector palette. At the bottom of the screen, you'll see a section with an animation pull-down menu, KeyColor selector, and a Record button. You'll use these tools to set up the basic animation of the Sumo baby. Drag the Sumo baby around the screen in any manner you want, making sure that he ends up standing on the bar, as you see in Figure 2.49. (In this image, you'll also see how I set up mine to look like the little tyke is bouncing across the screen.) If you aren't happy with the path, simply move the element back into position, select the record option again, and move our rotund mascot around again. Press the Preview tab in the workspace window to see how your rough animation works out.

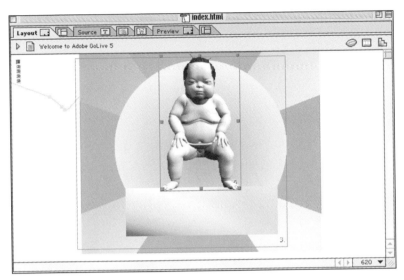

Figure 2.49
The Sumo baby has now moved into position and is poised to be joined by the "company" title.

6. Now you need to bring in the text. First, you'll need to place a new Floating Box from the Basic section of the Objects palette on the workspace. Then place the Smart Illustrator placeholder inside this Floating Box. Import the SumoTitle.ai file. The file is much too large for its final position. To fix this, click once on the bar to get the dimensions from the Inspector window. Now, you can do one of two things, change the dimensions of this file in the Inspector window or double-click on the SumoTitle Illustrator Smart Object file and resize the text to match in Illustrator 9. Make sure that you make the file slightly smaller than the bar so that text fits within the bar.

7. The animation for this file comes in from the bottom-left corner of the page, so repeat steps 5 and 6 to make this artwork fly into place, as you see in figure 2.50. I have included the saved GoLive 5 site file and added it onto this book's companion CD-ROM, in the EndOfCh02 folder.

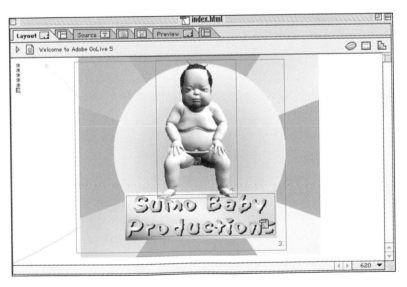

Figure 2.50
The way the Splash Screen animation should finish.

Moving On

One last reminder: A great feature of GoLive 5 is the ability to save your file without actually having created the site yet. You have the design and the elements, but you haven't "submitted" them as a site for actual use on the Web. This is actually a good thing, because you can really work on tweaking and modifying your Web-site design at this stage. After all the elements are in place and ready to go and you're happy with the design of your overall site, you simply submit it, and then upload it. This saves a lot of work if you're not one to use cascading style sheets or templates.

You've now created your basic animation. Strains of "Pomp & Circumstance" should be building in the background, and you should have your mortarboard in hand ready to toss into the air. In Chapter 6, we'll discuss in-depth how to actually modify the animation, and even make it a bit more interesting by working with and modifying each of the layers. For now, you need practice with your elements to become more familiar with the animation controls and the Design function. Then, after you show off your Chapter 2 diplomas (which, unfortunately, you'll have to create), take a look in Chapter 3 as you get hot and heavy into using frames in your Web site design.

Chapter 3

Frames and Tables

Use of frames and tables, along with forms—discussed in Chapter 4—and cascading style sheets—discussed in Chapter 5, are two aspects that Web designers either do well or poorly. Throughout this chapter, you'll get ideas and real-world examples of how to use these tools to make your site come together.

You've Been Framed

Almost everyone who has built any type of Web site has given frames a try. Usually, one frame spans the horizontal plane at the top and one frame flows in a vertical column along the left site; the remaining space fills a main screen where all the information appears. You can actually consider these as the first attempts at cascading style sheets because, once loaded, the top and side frames never change; only the content in the remaining frame does. Yes, it's a low-end idea of Cascading Style Sheet (CSS) technology; but remember, frames came along well before CSS and CSS1.

Unfortunately, many people began creating frames, and many "little" problems cropped up. Remember those wonderful "If you're stuck in frames, click here to break out of them" links? It often meant that the designer had to build the site twice—once for those who had the most current browsers and could actually see the frames, and once without frames for those whose browsers didn't support them (or for those who just didn't want the hassle). Yet, frames can be a strong design element in your site, and you can employ them without anyone knowing that you're using them.

To begin working with frames, set up a site with a navigation bar in one frame that is fairly small and out of the way, yet easily accessible. Create another frame that has your logo or name with a small Shockwave animation, and then create a main screen where all the information is displayed.

Frame Styles and Selection

Let's review how you set up frames within GoLive. The program comes with a set of frame templates (see Figure 3.1) that you can use and modify to your specifications. (Using frames does give you a little less design capability, as you're locked into the layouts provided.)

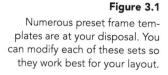

Figure 3.1
Numerous preset frame templates are at your disposal. You can modify each of these sets so they work best for your layout.

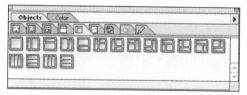

After you create your new site and the folders to store the files in, do the following to get started:

1. Click on the Frame Editor tab on the main workspace, as seen in Figure 3.2. Unless you're building your site within this area of the main workspace window, frame selection will not work.

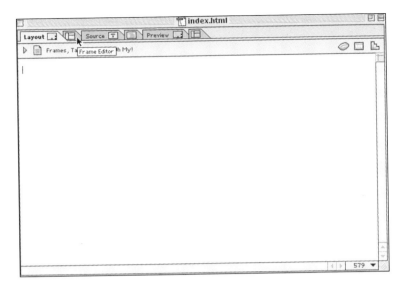

Figure 3.2
To use the frames function in GoLive, you need to go into frames mode in the workspace.

2. Select the frame set that has the lower frame running the width of the page and two frames in the upper portion of the screen. Figure 3.3 shows the frame set that you will be using. Drag this frame set to the workspace and then prepare to modify each of the frames to fit your layout needs.

You have the ability to name each frame to help you remember its contents. Each frame also has a set reference so that you can assign what files go where. Giving each frame its own descriptive name is extremely helpful, as you can see in Figure 3.4, as you set up your site, and especially as you set the parameters of each individual frame's element, which you'll do right now.

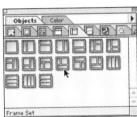

Figure 3.3
Use this frame set, the one to which the cursor is pointing to, for the file you are about to create.

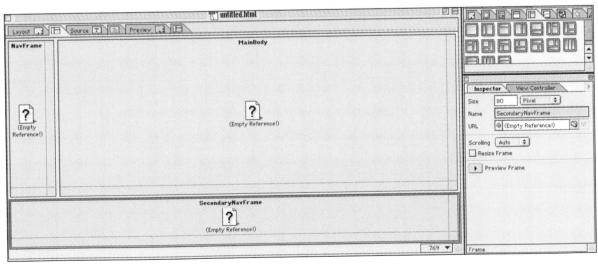

Figure 3.4
Each frame of a frame set can be named to help you remember what content should be placed where.

Frame Specs

At this point, you have some decisions to make. Should the frames resize automatically or remain fixed? What size should each frame be? Do you want borders to be seen, and if they are visible, how thick should the borders be? Which frames, if any, should have the ability to scroll?

A good rule of thumb to follow is to first determine the overall parameters of your site: 640×480? 800×600? 1024×768? Or should it be somewhere in-between? As I stated in Chapter 2, the standard monitor size at this time is 15 inches, so you should put your site together to fit comfortably into that screen size.

Frame Anomaly

I want to take a few moments here to discuss the way you can view frames within GoLive 5. First, you have to use the Frame Editor area of the workspace to view and work with the frames (see Figure 3.5). If you are in any other work area, you will not be able to comfortably build your page.

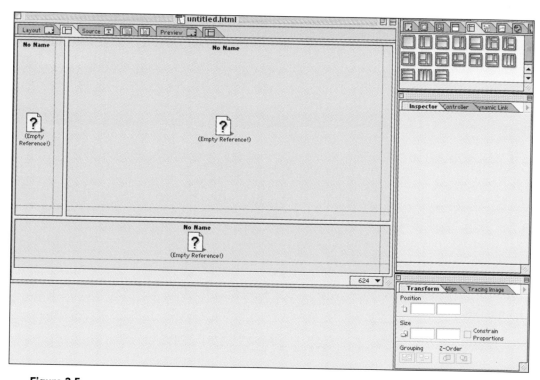

Figure 3.5

You should select the Frame Editor tab when you want to work with frames.

Second, you must have a Web browser set up to view your files. You will not be able to preview your changes unless you activate the Show In Browser feature. So, if you change the color of a border, for example, you will not see the change in Preview (see Figure 3.6); you will see it only via the assigned browsers (see Figure 3.7). You can, however, view the HTML file (see Figure 3.8).

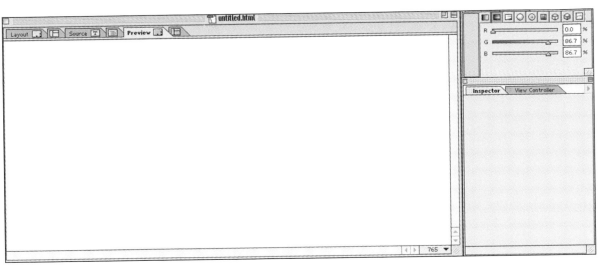

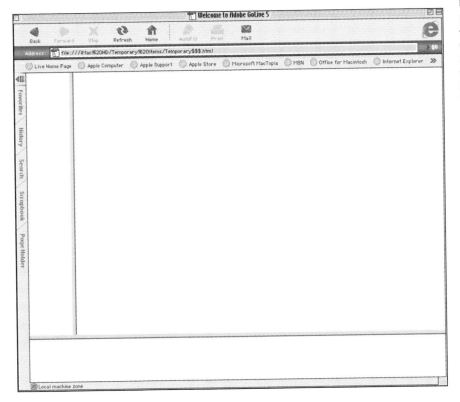

Figure 3.6
Frames, and modifications to them, will not be seen within GoLive's Preview window. This image looks like a blank workspace, but a frame set has been placed in the work area and been assigned a color (the RGB parameters can be seen in the Color window in the upper right).

Figure 3.7
By accessing the Show In Browser feature, you can see how the modifications you have made to individual frames and frame sets look.

Modifying Frames and Adding an Animation

Set up your frames so that they reflect the size of the artwork you have already created for the static screens. Image files have been created for you to use and they're available on this book's companion CD-ROM.

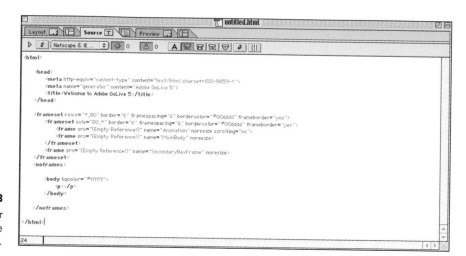

Figure 3.8
The Source tab lets you see your changes as they are made in the HTML script.

Here's how to modify the frames and add an animation:

1. Click once on the left-most frame. The Inspector window will display the basic parameter settings. Change them to the following, as shown in Figure 3.9:

   • Size: 80 Pixels

   • Name: Animation

   • Scrolling: No

   • Make sure Resize Frame is deselected.

   Select the Preview tab in the workspace window to see how your frames look.

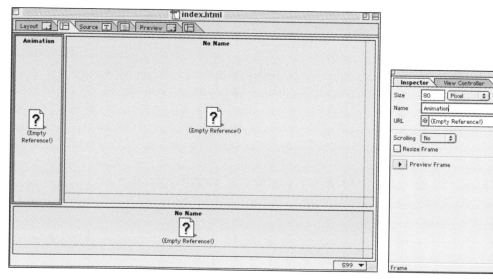

Figure 3.9
The left-most frame's parameters should look like this.

2. If you're using the gl5anim.swf file from the companion CD-ROM, drag it into the media folder you created for the site. Optionally, if you use the Point-and-Shoot tool, type in the location of the file in the text box, or click on the folder icon on the right of the URL field to create an outside link.

3. Set up the other frames as you see in Figure 3.10. Your main screen on the right should be titled "Body," whereas the lower frame that spans the width of the screen should be "Navigation Bar."

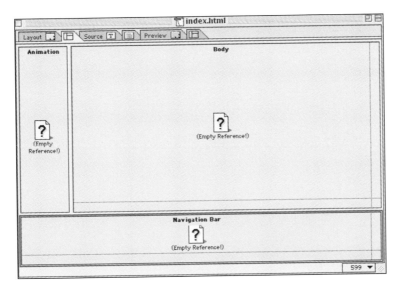

Figure 3.10
All the frames are set up and ready to be saved.

4. Reset the size of the Navigation Bar to 10 percent, as you see in Figure 3.11. Why do so? This allows you to define a specific size that will remain relative to whatever monitor size your visitor has. That is, the Navigation Bar frame will never appear larger than 10 percent of the overall screen size the visitor has assigned for their browser. So on a 14-inch monitor, the Navigation Bar will take up the same percent of browser screen space as it will on a 21-inch monitor.

Figure 3.11
Setting the Navigation Bar frame so that it displays at a percentage of the browser screen size.

The Navigation Bar Frame

Basic links will work just fine for this portion. We'll be looking at dynamic links and rollovers in later chapters. All we want to do now is expand on the information found in the *GoLive 5 User Manual* to help you create the best site you possibly can. So, you will create a new page and then link it to the Navigation Bar frame.

Basic links will work just fine for this portion. You'll be looking at dynamic links and rollovers in later chapters. Do the following:

1. Create a new page (File|New or Command/Ctl+N) and give it a name. Save this file to the pages folder in your Site Design window. Remember that, when you are setting up a new site, you are asked to where you want to save it. You need to create a root folder (or main folder if you're using a Mac) and then name the site folder inside of that. After you have done this, the Site Design window will be available (see Figure 3.12). If you haven't already created a pages folder to store extra pages associated with your site, do so now.

2. Click on the Navigation Bar frame to activate it. Notice the button with the spiral-like icon immediately next to URL in the Inspector window? This is the Point and Shoot button. When the cursor is over this button you press and hold down on the mouse button and drag the cursor to the file you want to link to. A "string" will extend from this button to the file. When the image you want to link to is highlighted, let go of the mouse button and a link will be established.

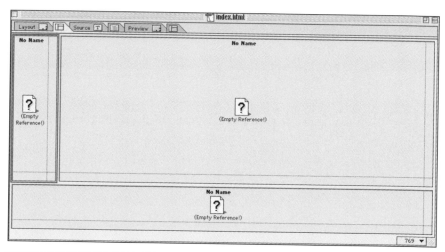

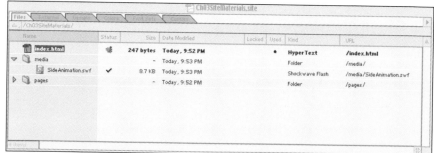

Figure 3.12
Your site's file window is available after you have created a new site.

3. Click on the Navigation Bar frame to activate it. Use Point and Shoot to create a link to the page you just created.

The Point and Shoot method is one of the great features of GoLive. Notice (in the field to the right of the URL heading of the Frame Inspector window) the button with the spiral icon (see Figure 3.13). This icon is the Fetch URL button. Click on this button and, without releasing the button, drag your cursor over the file that you want to select. When this file is highlighted, release the mouse button, and a link will be created, as is shown in Figure 3.14. This is the Point and Shoot method of linking to a file.

The Navigation Bar frame should now look like what you see in Figure 3.15, with a page icon replacing the question mark icon.

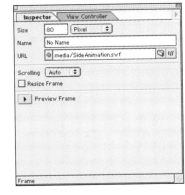

Figure 3.13
(Left) The button with the spiral icon on the left of the URL input field is the Fetch URL button. Use this to create a link to a file within your site folder.

Figure 3.14
(Right) A link has been established to the media file in the Site window.

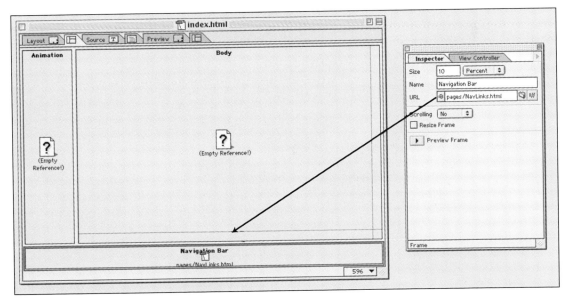

Figure 3.15
The Navigation Bar frame reflecting the addition of a link to your links document.

4. Using customary methods, that create a set of links, type in some link topics (either using the ones shown in Figure 3.16 or creating your own), and then save the site.

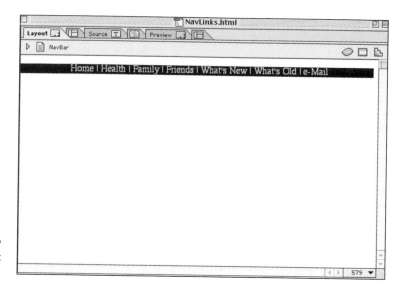

Figure 3.16
The link topics for this as yet unnamed site.

The Frames Inspector

Each of the frames, when selected, has its own inspector options so you have control over how the content appears, as well as the width and color of the frame borders themselves. This allows you complete flexibility if, for instance, you want to have a frame border separating the bottom portion of the screen from the top, while you have no frame border separating the animation area and the main page.

Click on the center of the frame to call up the options for the frame content, as seen in Figure 3.17. When you click on the border itself, the Inspector window reflects the current options for how the border appears. Figure 3.18 shows you the frame-specific controls.

Figure 3.17
Frame content is controlled from the expanded Inspector window.

Border Patrol

To get a feel for what you can accomplish, you're going to use the frames you've set up and modify them to fit the overall design. You want the left frame to have no border separating it from the top-right frame, and the bottom frame to have a border size of 6. Here's how to do it:

1. Click on the frame itself (not the interior section of the frame) to bring up the Frame Inspector window.

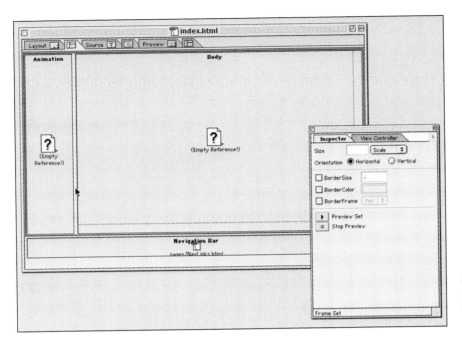

Figure 3.18
Stylize a border to fit your site design by clicking on the border itself.

2. Check Figure 3.19 as you modify this border. Make sure that the Horizontal Orientation is selected and set the Border Size to 0. Uncheck the Border Color. (Here, there is no border to colorize, it makes no difference if the Border Color button is checked or unchecked. In this case, I just left it active.)

3. If you have content in the frame you're working with, as well as the main content frame (what you've called the "Body frame"), you can select Preview Set by clicking on the Preview tab at the top of the workspace window to see how your design is coming along.

4. Select the bottom frame that contains the Navigation link set, and use Figure 3.20 as a guide. Keep the Size and Orientation as is, but change the Border Size to 6. Select Border Color, and click once in the color chip (or swatch, if you prefer) to the immediate right. This brings up the Color window (or brings it to the front if you have the palette group already open).

5. Figure 3.21 shows the color you selected based on the color scheme of the artwork used in the left frame animation. Because you want to stay as Web safe as possible, and you're not planning on preparing the page to be printed in a magazine or other high-resolution format, work in the RGB mode for consistency. Once you've input the RGB parameters, the change is instantly reflected on the workspace.

Figure 3.19
Border settings for the leftmost frame.

Figure 3.20
The Navigation frame setup.

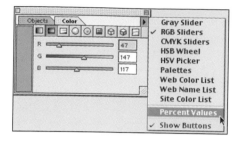

Figure 3.21
Use the following RGB percentage settings to set up your border color: R:47 G:147 B:117 The RGB value equivalent is R:120, G:255, B:255.

Turning Off Percentages

If you see your color values as percentages, make sure that Percent Values is deselected under the Color window's pop-up screen. On Macintosh computers, the Color window is initially set up to show color parameters as percentages (0 through 100%). It's more common to use color values. To change to value mode, click on the triangle pop-up in the upper right of the Color window and deselect Percent Values.

6. What would happen if you now changed the orientation of this frame? Click on it to find out, or look at Figure 3.22 to see. By working with the orientation controls, you can quickly modify the overall appearance of your layout. Now that you've seen the result—and if you have changed the orientation in your own files—click on the Vertical button to return to your original design.

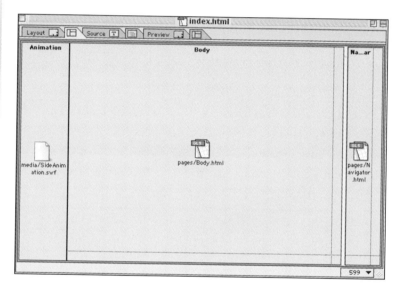

Figure 3.22
The results of changing the frame orientation of the lower frame.

Table Talk

As you are more than likely aware, using frames does have its limitations. Although you can create a contiguous look throughout the entire site without setting up a full cascading style sheet scenario, you still need other tools to give your site that unique and finished look.

When you put your site together, you'll certainly find times when you want to have exact placement of text in relationship to an image or a link. This really isn't possible to do in HTML, Java, or other scripting languages, at least, not without spending hours upon hours working on the code. Remember, HTML is not set up to give you controls like those in page layout. Additionally, unless you're very careful, the differences in the way competitive Web browsers work often change the way your final design is viewed. Tables can help you maintain a consistent look between browsers.

Tables have other uses, as well: Business sites, whether on the Internet or an intranet, can use tables to post spreadsheets; e-commerce sites can set up tables to act as columnar representations of their products, descriptions, and costs. Hobbyists can set up tables to hold photos and text for personal sites, as well as graphic representations of a family tree. By using tables in these instances, you can save your base layout (the blank table) for all the pages of your site, retaining continuity among the repetitive layouts.

As with anything, though, until you start using and seeing the potential for this feature, it initially looks like a bit of eye-candy—sort of like using your best china on a picnic. GoLive has always had strong table capabilities, and with this new version, they have become even more sophisticated. Throughout this section, you will discover the various ways tables can be modified and combined with frames to give your site an interesting look.

Setting the Table(s)

GoLive 5 gives you control over literally every aspect of tables, including the capability to add a different background to each cell. This feature can lead to interesting possibilities, especially when using sliced images.

Figure 3.23
The choices provided when placing tables on your workspace.

Here's a quick set of steps to help you see how it is done:

1. When you first create a Table placeholder on the workspace, you're greeted with a three-row by three-column grid. Let's change this right away. The Frame Inspector window seen in Figure 3.23 shows three tabs: Table, Row, and Cell. Each of these areas will become very good friends of yours as you build sites utilizing frames.

2. First, in the Table area of the Inspector window, select 2 for the number of Rows, while leaving Columns at 3. Change the Width of the table to 579 pixels and leave Auto selected for the Height. Finally, check the Caption box and choose Above Table. Your table will look like Figure 3.24.

This is all you need to do on the modifications. You'll notice, though, that you can choose a fill color in an area under each tab. Under the Table tab, choosing a fill color changes the background for the entire frameset. Under Row, the color affects only the cells in that particular row. And under Cell, the color changes only the individual cell. You could literally design a site and make it look like a patchwork quilt.

Generic Colorizing of Tables

Let's take a moment to go over changing table background colors. After you've gone through this short section, take one of your own bitmap images and, using the BgImage area of the Inspector, import your picture as the background.

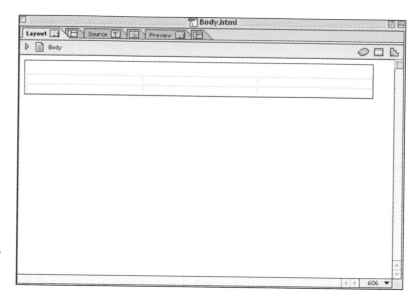

Figure 3.24

The table set up with a caption area selected.

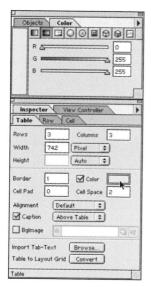

Figure 3.25

By assigning a new color and dragging it from the Color window swatch bar to the Color swatch window in the Table Inspector, the cells of your table are automatically updated to that new color.

To change the table background colors, take the following steps:

1. Click on the edge of the Table placeholder to activate it. When the entire table is selected, all cells will be affected by your changes, except in the cell header (if you have one). Change Rows back to 3 for this section.

2. Select Color and click on the color swatch button to make the Color window active. Change the color from white to something else (in my case, R:0, G:255, B:255). Drag this new color from the swatch column on the left of the Color window to the Color swatch window in the Table Inspector window. The change is automatically reflected on the workspace and in the color selector button in the Inspector window, as you can see in Figure 3.25.

3. Now select the middle row of cells by either pressing the Shift key while clicking inside each cell or by shift-clicking on the border of a row or column to select that entire group of cells, and repeat Steps 1 and 2 to change the color of the row to another color. (In my case, I made them as obnoxious as possible to see if I could induce a headache on the people who were looking over my shoulder as I was writing this.)

4. Finally, select the center bottom cell by itself and repeat Steps 1 and 2. You now will have a multicolored table somewhat like you see in Figure 3.26.

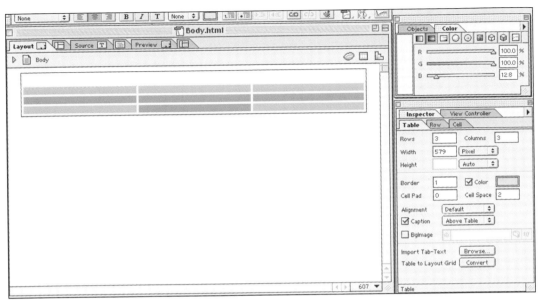

Figure 3.26
Multicolored backgrounds take mere moments to produce using the numerous tabs in the Inspector window.

Matching Colors from Images

For this exercise, you can either use the SmDragonTush.jpg image included in the Chapter 3 images folder on the companion CD-ROM, or one of your own. (Just be aware that this image has a much more intriguing name than what it really is.) Make sure that you place the image in the site's media folder before doing Step 1. Here's how to match the colors:

1. Delete the table on your workspace, create a new one, and from the Objects window, drag an Image placeholder into the Caption area of the table and center it. Create a link to the DragonTush.jpg or your own file. Figure 3.27 shows what your table should look like.

Note: Make sure that you hold down Shift when you select individual cells, just as when selecting multiple cells.

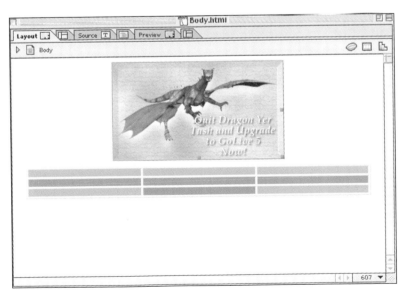

Figure 3.27
An image placed into the Caption area of the table.

2. Double-click on the image you just placed. Photoshop, or the program you used to create the file, will be launched. Sample one of the colors in the image—the orange-yellow in the case of the provided image—and write down the RGB settings. Also, get the RGB settings for the lightest instance of yellow in the image.

3. Close this program and go back to GoLive. Select the entire table and change the background to the orange-yellow color by imputing the RGB settings you just copied. Refer to Figure 3.28 for the color settings if you need to.

Figure 3.28
Use the RGB color settings you see in this image to match the dragon's background.

4. Select the middle cell only, and replace the orange-yellow color with the light yellow. Your final screen should look something like Figure 3.29.

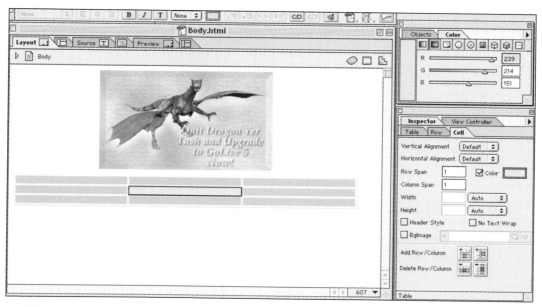

Figure 3.29
The modified table with color-coordinated cells.

Don't Go Overboard

I can pretty well guarantee that at some point in your design career, you'll want to stretch the boundaries, giving your friends, relatives, clients and so on a unique look. To do this, you want to use as many features of the program as you can. But as a warning, don't go overboard.

To use television as an example, you can always tell when a local station has gotten a new special effects toy or a new mixture of effects has been discovered—every promo, locally-produced commercial, and newscast will have that effect in there until it becomes a nuisance. Use effects not for the sake of effects, but because they enhance what you are trying to say.

Adding Content to Tables

As stated previously, you can add images to individual cells. You can accomplish this in one of two ways: as a standard image using an Image placeholder as you just did in the Caption area, or as a background image over which other information, such as text, can be placed. This can produce an attractive and complex design, if planned correctly.

Here, you will learn how to add images as backgrounds for your tables.

Picture This

Start by placing one individual shot into the table cells as a group. In these two examples, I recommend using the TableCellBKG.jpg and the series of sliced GIF files in the SlicedTableFiles folder provided on the companion CD-ROM. After placing these files into the appropriate areas in your site's folders, do the following:

1. Select the entire table, deselect Color, and check the BgImage box, as shown in Figure 3.30. Link to the TableCellBKG.jpg file and...that's it.

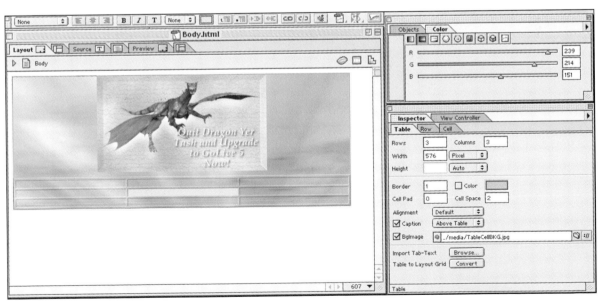

Figure 3.30
The table with a linked image as a background.

2. Now, highlight the image information within the BgImage selector box, delete the image by pressing the Delete key on your keyboard, and then press Return/Enter. Click on the upper-left cell to select it, and then go to the Cell Inspector. Under BgImage, link to the first image in the SlicedTableFiles folder. Moving left to right starting with the top row, repeat this process row by row for each subsequent cell until all nine cells are filled in, as shown in Figure 3.31.

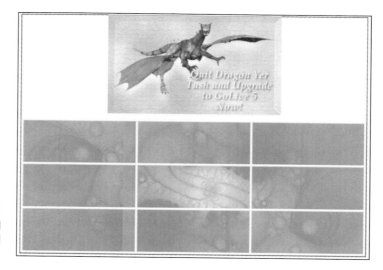

Figure 3.31
A sliced image, placed sequentially as background images in each cell.

3. Finally, fiddle (that's a highly technical term, found in the *"Dictionary of Highly Technical Image Editing and Web Design Terminology"*—to find out what it means, if you don't already know) with the cell width and the border width of the table to see what you like best.

You can use this technique as an image within a page representing a group of televisions showing a sequential video feed from screen to screen, or some other fun look.

Animate This

With the background image placed inside the individual cells, you'll next place a QuickTime animation in the center cell and then add some descriptive text to get a feel for how this can all be put together.

Here's how to do the animation:

1. Make sure that the BgImage checkbox is deselected. If this option is active, both the background image and the animation will be in the cell, which, at this point, you don't want. Then select the center cell of the table and place a QuickTime placeholder in it. Leave it positioned on the left, because you'll place some text immediately next to it.

2. Create a new file folder and call it "animations". Place the TheCurtainOpens.mov file into this folder and, with the QuickTime placeholder active, create a link to the MOV file. Figure 3.32 shows what happens in GoLive5 when you link to a movie: An image of the file appears, rather than the placeholder remaining as it was.

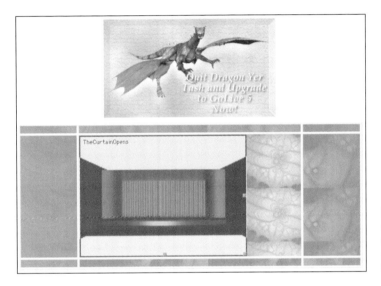

Figure 3.32
GoLive 5 now shows an image of the first frame of a linked movie, rather than retaining the generic QuickTime placeholder image.

3. Double-click on the MOV file to open the QuickTime editor and preview the movie, or switch over to Preview mode to see it play in your cell.

4. Write some sales-oriented text in the surrounding cells. Use Figure 3.33 to get a feel for how the text can be written and included into the cells.

Figure 3.33
The page with a table containing an image sequence placed in individual cells, a QuickTime movie, and text.

3.1 Create a Page with Frames and Tables

Now that you've experienced some GoLive table techniques, it's time to put all the skills you've just honed to good use.

The "Ain't GoLive 5 Fun" Home Page Initial Layout

Okay. Okay. I live in the southern region of the United States where "ain't" are a word. I realize "ain't" ain't acceptable grammar nearly everywhere else in the world, according to my English professors oh so many eons ago, but in this case, the aberrant word works for our purposes. Follow these steps to lay out your home page:

1. Create a new site with all the appropriate folders. Use the same frame set you worked with at the beginning of this chapter. If need be, refer back to the Frames area to get the setup parameters if you didn't save the site. You should duplicate what you created before.

2. Use the SideAnimation.swf file from the CD-ROM and place it into the left frame of the index.html page. Then save the file. (Always a good idea.)

3. Create a new page and save it to your pages folder with the name "link.html". Place a Layout Grid on the workspace and center it to the page using the Align Center button so it looks like Figure 3.34.

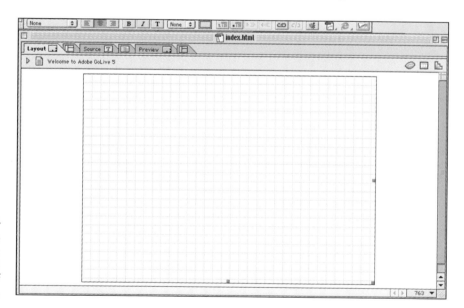

Figure 3.34
A Layout Grid is placed on the workspace and centered in preparation for adding and precisely positioning a series of Image placeholders.

4. Now place five Image placeholders at the top of the page and center them as you see in Figure 3.35.

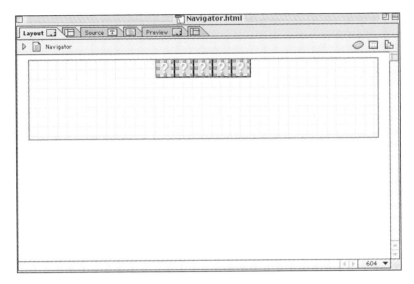

Figure 3.35
Positioning of the Image placeholders on the links.html page
you just created.

5. Link to the following files (from left to right):

- home.jpg

- info.jpg

- download.jpg

- adobe.jpg

- links.jpg

Make sure that the placeholders butt up against each other (using either the Left and Right arrow keys to move in grid space increments, or
the Option+Left Arrow or Option+Right Arrow) if they aren't already,
and save the page. Initially, if the Placeholders are more than a grid
space apart, you can use the arrow keys by themselves. To move placeholders pixel by pixel, you need to use the preceding key combination.
You will need to re-center the row of link buttons by shift-clicking on
the placeholders and choosing Align Center from the main toolbar (see
Figure 3.36). You can now save and close the page. If you closed the
index.html page, open it now.

6. Select the bottom frame and create a link to the link.html page using
the Point and Shoot button in the Inspector window. Now your page
should look like Figure 3.37. Once again, save your work and create a
new page.

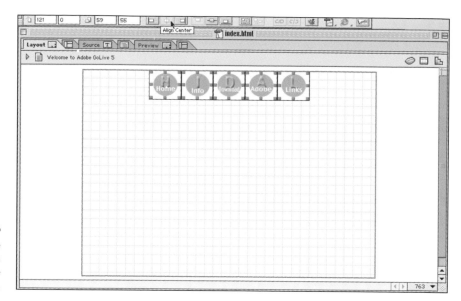

Figure 3.36
The Align Center button in the toolbar allows you to position multiple elements on the Layout Grid.

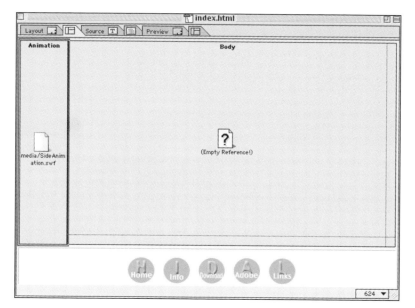

Figure 3.37
The home page with the left and bottom frames filled. You will need to have your workspace in Preview to see the bottommost images in your file.

7. Name this new page Body.html. Drag a table onto the workspace. Place the cursor on its right edge and extend the edge by dragging it to the right until it spans the width of the page.

The Body Beautiful

I know—beauty is in the eye of the beholder. But, because I'm beholdin' to you for buying this book, I guess that means I'm the beholder. Additionally, the body.html page that you're about to create is just about the most beautiful thing I've seen since the bearded lady at a small carnival in Ohio almost 35 years ago. Here's how to create that page:

1. Select the Table placeholder and set the following parameters so your Inspector window will look like Figure 3.38.

    - Rows and Columns: 2

    - Width: 577

    - Height: Auto

    - Caption: Above Table

2. Place a QuickTime placeholder in the Caption area and make sure it's centered. Link to the TheCurtainOpens.mov file so your screen now looks like Figure 3.39.

Figure 3.38
The setup for the table cells on your home page.

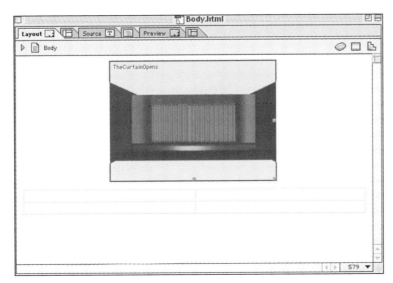

Figure 3.39
The curtain will open to greet visitors with a non-threatening sales pitch.

3. Here comes the fun part. Select the two right cells, and then place the cursor between them like you see in Figure 3.40. Hold down the Control key while right-clicking on a PC or holding down the mouse button on a Mac. This calls up the Cell Selection menu. (Ah—A hidden jewel.) Choose Merge Cells. The selected cells are now combined into one, while leaving the left cells untouched. Now your table should look like Figure 3.41. This will now become your text area.

4. For the left two cells, import the compguy.jpg and the SmDragonTush.jpg files.

5. In the combined right cell, type some appropriate text welcoming visitors to your GoLive 5 site and let them know just how proud you are to be using this cutting-edge program. Save the page and close the document.

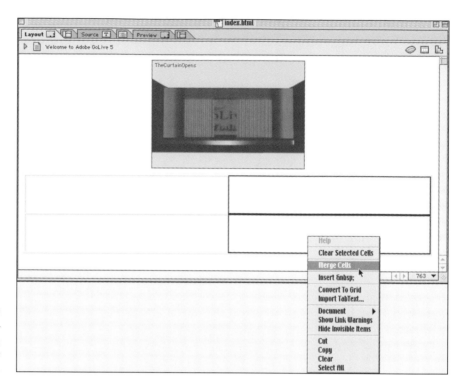

Figure 3.40
By using the Control key after selecting a column of cells, you can merge them into one by using a hidden menu.

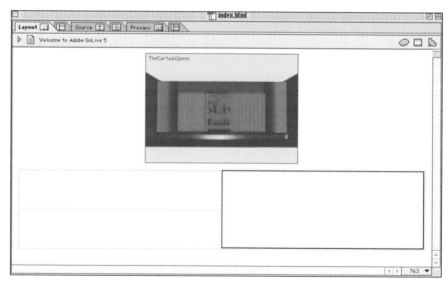

Figure 3.41
The table modified so two of its cells are merged into one while leaving the rest in their original state. The cells in this image are all selected so they can be seen more clearly.

6. Open the index.html file and create a link between the Body frame and the page you just saved. Select the Show In Browser button to open your default Web browser. If you haven't set one up yet, you'll be prompted to do this now. The selected Web browser will open and, like the example shown in Figure 3.42, you'll see your handiwork in all its glory.

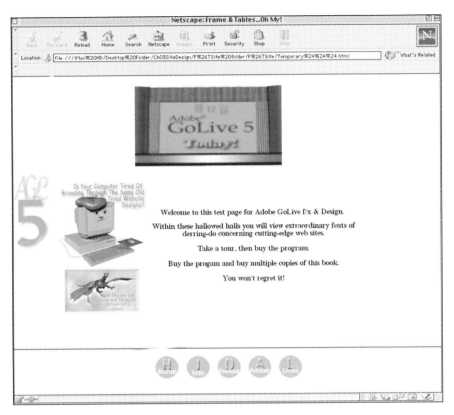

Figure 3.42
The home page design, employing frames and tables in its completed glory.

Moving On

In Project 3.1, you created a page using both frames and tables. What you didn't do was modify the borders for each. Take some time and do that now, experimenting until you find something that fits your individual creative style.

Consider how you could incorporate this combination into your own site updates and, when you've cogitated enough, head over to Chapter 4, where you'll get ideas on how to incorporate forms into your site structure.

Part II

Working with Advanced Features

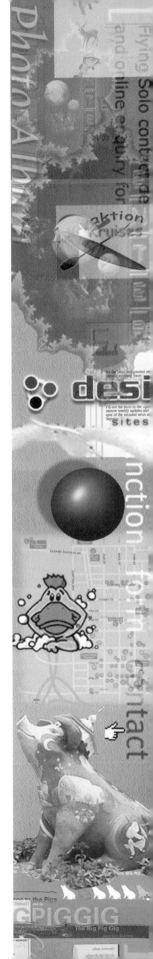

Chapter 4

Incorporating Forms

Adding forms to your site gives you the opportunity to solicit feedback, gather information for your company, and enter the Internet commerce arena.

It's all about information. You surf the Internet to get the latest tips and tricks for your favorite video games or software application. You can get news, reviews, and inside info on virtually everything that is of interest to you. You and your children can find information for school and/or work reports from literally everyone from renowned experts to armchair enthusiasts. Additionally, with only a few clicks of the mouse, you can subscribe to newsletters, daily stock reports, and even junk mail lists—all of which are delivered daily to your computer. Every time you fill out one of those Web questionnaires that so many companies include on their site, you're dealing with forms. So why should everyone else be gathering information but you aren't?

Forms: The Basics

Forms are tricky critters. You can design them, incorporate them into your site, and put them up on the Web with very little trouble. It's getting them to do what you want, however, that is a bit tricky.

Creating forms is really a two-part process. To make forms fully functional, you must have *Common Gateway Interface (CGI)* scripts on your server. These scripts take the information sent by a visitor and turn it into a readable form. This can be either by way of an email message or by a full-blown report that is stored in a special area that only you can access. Some servers, especially the free ones, don't give you the capability to place CGI scripts on them. Other servers may give you the option, but they make you either write the scripts or find someone who has them. Still others provide all the tools you need, making the process extremely easy. I'd better say it now: This chapter will not be dealing with CGI script creation. This subject is worthy of a whole other book. At the end of this chapter, though, I'll give you some Web sites that provide free or low-cost CGI scripts that you can download.

GoLive 5 provides some powerful tools that will help you create forms to do all the things I covered in the preceding paragraphs. You can create forms that incorporate text fields, radio buttons (those round selectors that seem to be pushed in when you click on them), checkboxes, and pull-down selectors, even password screens for sites requiring identification before access is allowed. Creative and judicious use of these elements can make your forms simple to fill out and—dare I say it—fun.

FORMulating Your Page

I just said that GoLive has a powerful set of form creation tools, so let's go over what is at your disposal. All the tools are housed under the Forms tab (the third one from the left) in the Objects window. Refer to Figure 4.1 as you work your way across, starting with the first element on the left:

- *Form*—This element literally tells a browser that this particular page, or portion of the page, is a form and then tells the browser where to send any information provided.

- *Submit button*—This element is fairly self-explanatory. Put this button at the end of your form for people to click when they're finished filling out the form.

- *Reset button*—This is another self-explanatory element. Place this button at the end of your form so that, in the event of a mistake, respondents can clear out all the information they just entered.

- *Button*—This is a multipurpose element, sometimes known as the *Universal Button*. You can assign HTML code to this button to customize its appearance.

- *Form Input Image*—Use this element to decorate your forms. It's a standard Image placeholder.

- *Label*—This element is to be used for HTML4-compatible Web browsers (so it won't work on previous browser versions). Use this one to identify the purpose of a button or text field.

- *Text Field*—Insert this on your page wherever you want respondents to fill in information, such as name, address, hair color, and so on.

- *Password*—Use this field when creating a password screen.

- *Text Area*—This element is a larger text screen that is commonly used for comment areas. This area allows text wrapping and gives the visitor a chance to give you a piece of their mind.

- *Checkbox*—This element is used to activate a particular choice to a multiple answer question, or to select particular options you offer.

- *Radio Button*—This element is similar to a checkbox, only it's circular, and the respondents can select only one radio button at a time.

- *PopUp*—This element allows you to enter various choices that are revealed when a visitor clicks on the element.

- *List Box*—This element is scrollable text box in which you can list different choices to be selected.

- *File Browser*—This element enables your visitor to search for specific items or key words on your page. The file browser selection is a must for Internet commerce sites.

- *Hidden*—As the name implies, this element allows you to add a non-displayable attribute to your form. You can then tell the browser what to do or send when that specific field or element is filled out or activated.

- *Key Generator*—For advanced users, this element can add security features to the visitor's transaction, whether it's supplying a password or sending credit card information.

- *Fieldset*—This element provides a separate area within the form where specific groups of elements can be stored (that is, an Options area that is set apart from the main information set). In version 4, this element was referred to as the Field Set & Legend tag.

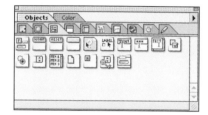

Figure 4.1

The Form placeholder elements in the Objects window.

As you can see, so many tools are available to work with to create forms that you can accomplish literally any design you like. When you combine these tools with other tools, such as frames or floating boxes, your forms page can take on some interesting and unique attributes.

Some of the previous information can be confusing. Usually, a specific group of form tools will be your everyday workhorses: Label, Checkbox and Radio Button, Pop Up, and so on. The more esoteric tools (or at least, the ones I consider esoteric), such as Hidden and Key Generator, will probably not become a part of your standard designs. It's great to know they are there, however, even if you use them in only one out of every ten sites you put together. As you become more adept at form creation and linking to CGI scripts, the more you'll want to accomplish. The tools are there, ready for you to implement them as your needs increase. (I'd rather have a number of options that I don't need at that moment as I learn a program, than to need tools that aren't part of the total package.)

Initial *FORM*ation

Now that we got all that fun stuff out of the way, it's time for you to build a form. We'll begin with a basic design and work our way through some more intricate ones. By the end of the chapter, you'll be putting other Web sites' forms to shame.

Basic Form Setup

Right now, you won't have to create a new site. Just open the program, and, if you haven't changed any of GoLive's preferences, a blank page should appear. You won't be saving this page as a part of a site. All you will do here is get a feel for working with some of these elements. You are going to link to the Feedback.jpg file:

1. Place a Form placeholder on the screen. You'll see a small icon and a box with a black border around it. Again, this element needs to be on your page so that the Web browser will recognize the page as a form (see Figure 4.2).

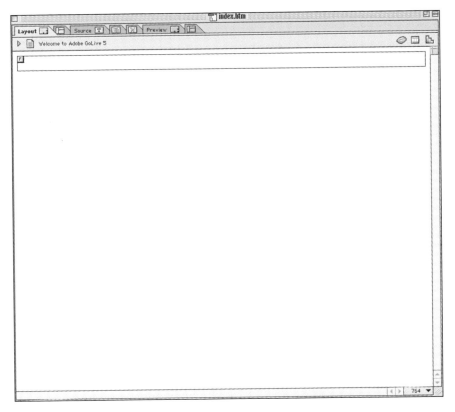

Figure 4.2
The Form placeholder on the workspace.

2. Click the Page icon in the Title bar of the workspace to activate the Page Inspector window. Instead of a plain white background, you could select a color by clicking the color option on this screen, or add the Feedback.jpg file as a background image. Activate the Image option and click on the folder button to the right of the link text field. Navigate to the folder where you placed the Feedback.jpg file. This is a 1024×768 image, so tiling will not be a problem for virtually 99 percent of your visitors.

3. Now, you're ready to start placing elements. I always like to have a Grid already in place on the screen so that I can move things around pixel by pixel, if needed. When you place the Forms element on a page, all other form elements should be placed inside the form itself. You can put non-form elements in here, too. In fact, as you can see in Figure 4.3, one Grid is placed outside and one inside the Form element.

Normally, however, just place everything inside the Form so that the entire page is read as a form. So, for this section, go ahead and place a Grid into the Form element.

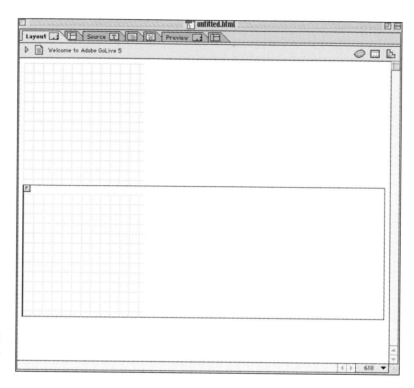

Figure 4.3
Two Layout Grids, with one inside the Form.

4. With the Layout Grid selected, change the Width and Height dimensions to 640×480 using the appropriate fields in the Image inspector.

5. This is just a basic form, asking for all the visitor's pertinent information. Before placing the form Text Box onto the page, place nine Layout Text Boxes on the screen, stacking them one on top of the other. Make them two grid units high and stretch each out to four grid spaces wide.

6. Make sure that the text is aligned to the left and type the following information into the appropriate text field:

   • Name:

   • Address:

   • Address 2 (Apt/Suite):

   • City:

   • State:

   • Zip:

Note: When you resize the Layout Grid from inside the Form element, the element will resize automatically to the new Grid dimensions.

- Phone:

- Fax:

- e-mail:

Your screen should now look similar to Figure 4.4.

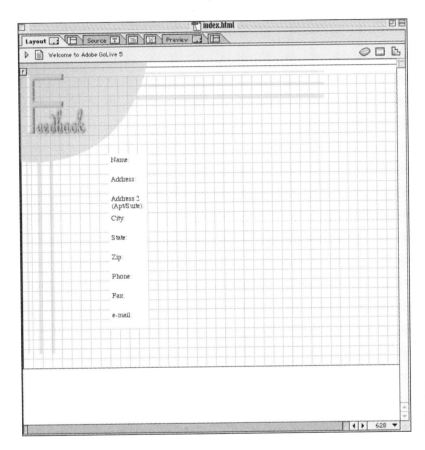

Figure 4.4
The Layout Text Boxes are set to identify the requested information.

7. Return to Forms in the Objects window and select the Text Field placeholder. Place a text field next to each Layout Text Box. Leave one grid
   space between the former and the latter.

You'll notice that the Text Fields snap to the nearest grid line and that you
can't resize the boxes vertically. That's okay. Normally, you would want to
center the Text Field with the Layout Text Box, but in this case, you won't need
to. The text was kept positioned at the top of the box, so the text fields line up
perfectly with the text.

8. Now, it's time to add the Submit and Reset buttons. Drag one of each
   from the Forms window to the bottom of the Layout Grid. You now
   have a choice: You can select both buttons by holding down Shift, clicking on each button, and then centering them to the Layout Grid by

clicking the Align Center button on the toolbar. Alternatively, you can align the Submit button along the left edge of the Layout Text Boxes and the Reset button to the right edge of the Text Field Boxes. I chose the latter for this example, as you can see in Figure 4.5.

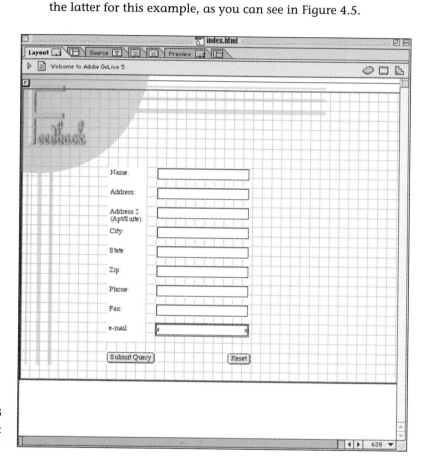

Figure 4.5
The final positions for the Submit and Reset buttons.

9. Suppose that you don't want to leave the word "Query" in the Submit button. To change the text in a button, select it and—in the Inspector window—click the Label checkbox and type a new name. Notice that when you select Label, the text in the button disappears and the button resizes. That's okay. Just type "Submit" in the Label field and it will resize itself to fit the text.

You're still missing something, though—some sort of informational text to let people know why they are filling out this form. Although your background screen says "Feedback" rather prominently, it's still a good idea to put additional lines of descriptive text to reinforce your form's purpose.

10. Place another Layout Text Box onto the Layout Grid, positioning it just below the lowest horizontal yellow line. Type something that explains the reasons why you want all this information and why it would be to

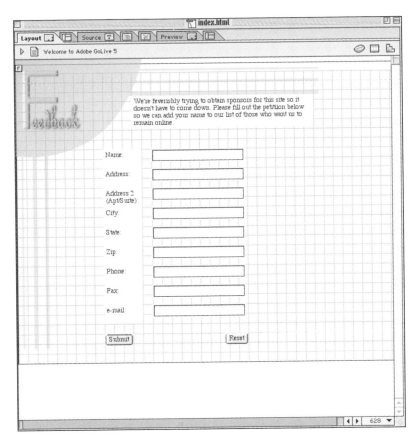

Figure 4.6
The finished form, complete with an explanation of the form's purpose.

a Web surfer's advantage to enter the data, as is shown in Figure 4.6. Now you've completed your form.

Did Something Go Amiss?

Before you do anything, switch over to Preview mode. Has something gone awry with the location of the different elements—especially the text just below the yellow bar? Notice that the paragraph has shifted upward and is now positioned over the horizontal bars. Figure 4.7 shows what happened to me, and what perhaps happened to you, too. In fact, I can almost guarantee it did.

Why did that happen? Take a good look at your page in the Layout mode. Notice how the F icon in the upper left corner has moved everything down a notch. Because this is an invisible element, when you switch to Preview or if you view the page using the Show In Browser option, all your elements are going to move up. Moreover, because the image you're using in the background is not affected by the Layout Grid, it doesn't move.

To fix this, move the topmost Layout Text Box down approximately one and one-half grid spaces. Now, use the Preview tab and look at your page. As you can see in Figure 4.8, it's aligned much better. You can also move the other elements down, but their new placement doesn't affect the overall look of the page.

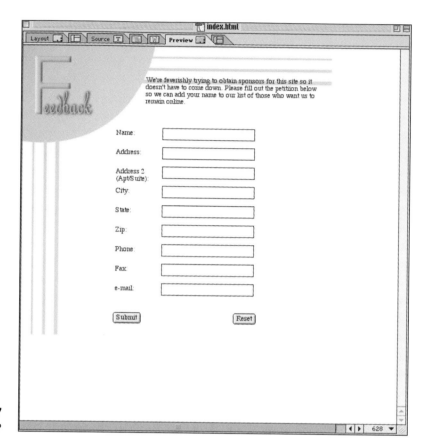

Figure 4.7
Now, why did this happen?

A *FORM*ula for Success

Well, that was a simple example of setting up a forms page that doesn't look like the norm. Think back and envision all the sites you've visited—sites where you filled out a form. Most of them were bland, right? In many cases (in my experience), the forms pages haven't even followed the overall format of the site—if a format was there to begin with. Often, a Web designer will simply put a form on a drab gray background, add a line spacer, and then inundate you with fields to fill out and questions to answer. These designers have lost their creative muse during the design process, or they have suddenly figured out how to put form elements on their pages and link them to a CGI script, so they threw together a quick page.

No quick pages here, my friends. You definitely want your form pages to have the same high-quality look as the rest of the site. If you remain committed to unity in every page of your site, it subliminally tells your visitor that you know what you are doing and that you will more than likely live up to what you are promising. To put it more succinctly, your site—and you—shows competence and integrity.

With rant number 5,235 out of the way, let's explore more ways you can incorporate forms with other elements in your toolbox.

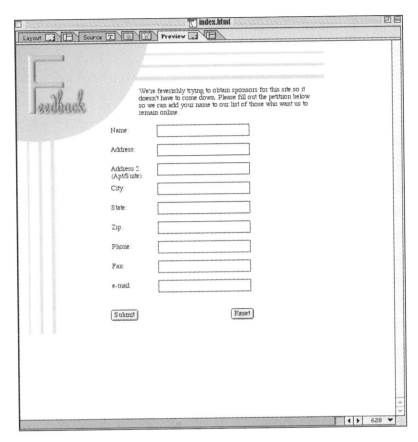

Figure 4.8
After repositioning the text block, the layout of the form is complete.

Using Tables in Forms

One way in which you can make your forms look different and better than the usual run-of-the-mill graybacked pages is by placing the elements into a Table placeholder. Tables add a lot to your design kit because they let you create new and exciting ways to lay out a page. In Project 4.1, you will examine a basic layout structure that uses the Table placeholder.

PROJECT 4.1 Building a Basic Table-Based Form

You need to create a contest entry page for a company named Kayaktion Kruises. You can see a color version of the page in the GoLive Studio section of this book. (What you'll create here won't be exactly like the example shown in this project.) For this project, you need the following image files from this book's companion CD-ROM:

- SideBarGroup.jpg
- Logo1.jpg
- Logo2.jpg

For this section, go ahead and create a site folder named Kayaktion, and place the three JPEG files listed previously into your site's media folder. After you do so, take the following steps:

1. Put a Form object onto your workspace and place a Layout Grid into it. Resize the Grid to 640x572.

2. Place an Image placeholder along the top left of the Grid and link to the SideBarGroup.jpg image. As you can see in Figure 4.9, this takes up quite a bit of screen real estate, but this isn't really a problem, as you'll learn in Step 3.

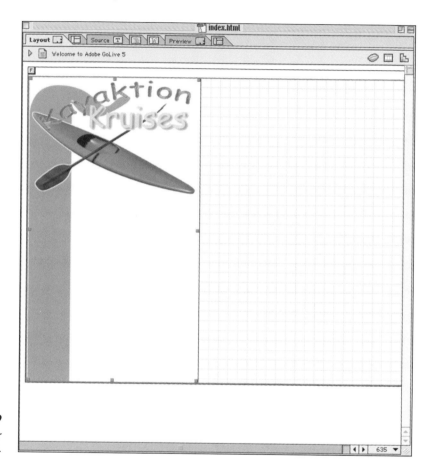

Figure 4.9
The logo image for Kayaktion Kruises.

3. Place a Floating Box (FB) onto the workspace. Although Floating Boxes are often used for holding text or images and animating them so the elements "float" around the screen, you will not be animating this floating box. Rather, it will contain your Table placeholder so that you can position it in a way that would otherwise be impossible. Before moving the FB into position, place the Table placeholder within it. Resize the Table width to 360 pixels in the Inspector window and change the Height to 220 pixels.

4. With the table resized, it will now be easier to position the Floating Box more precisely. As you probably have noticed, when you placed the

Floating Box onto the screen, all the elements moved to accommodate that invisible placeholder. Position the Floating Box so that it is one grid space over the bottom tip of the kayak image, and the center is two grid spaces to the right of the edge of the JPEG image, as shown in Figure 4.10.

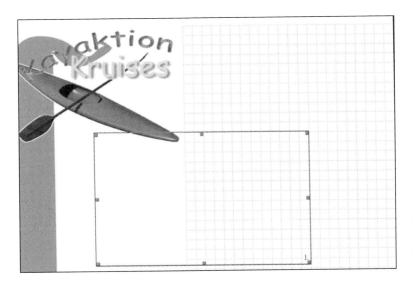

Figure 4.10
This is where you should position the Floating Box containing the Table placeholder.

5. You need one more Floating Box, which you'll place just under the word "Kruises" in the main logo. After it is in place, type "Win a Kayaktion Kruise Valued at $1,000!!!" Make sure that you place this Floating Box as you see it in Figure 4.11.

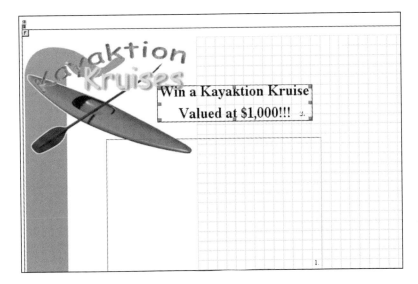

Figure 4.11
The final position of the enticement line so that it is in the correct location when you preview the page.

6. Place two Image placeholders at the bottom of the Layout Grid. Logo1.jpg should be linked to the left placeholder, Logo2.jpg to the

right. Position Logo1.jpg so it is flush against the left side of the Layout Grid and place Logo2.jpg in the bottom right corner of the Grid, as you see in Figure 4.12.

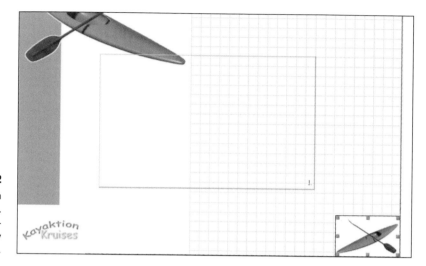

Figure 4.12

The individual logo elements, in place at the bottom of the page. These are not the actual positions of the images; rather, they are for placement purposes.

7. Finally, for this initial part of the layout design, place a Layout Text Box between the two logo elements and type the catch phrase: "A Kruise you'll never forget!" Make sure that the text is centered in the placeholder, and then center it between the two logo images by using the Align Center button on the toolbar.

You have created the basic layout. Notice how the Floating Boxes were used to place elements into positions they normally wouldn't go. You will work more with Floating Boxes in Chapter 6, and you will also learn how to animate them. However, now it's time to modify the table on this page so you can begin building your form:

8. Select the upper-middle and upper-right cells of the table: Click on one and then, holding down Shift, select the other. In Windows, hold down the Ctrl key and right-click the mouse. On the Mac, use the Option key while pressing and holding down the mouse button. A selection pop-up screen will appear. Select Merge Cells to turn the two cells into one.

9. Now, select the four cells beneath those two and merge them. Repeat this process for the two cells to the left of those. Your table will now look like Figure 4.13. At this stage, you're ready to add some content.

10. Click once in the upper-left cell and type the following: "Fill Out All Forms For Your Chance To Win". Center the text, and make it Bold and Size 5. You'll notice that as you typed this line, the cell resized.

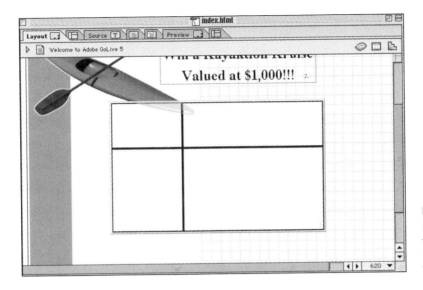

Figure 4.13

Merging the cells creates a table that looks like this. I've highlighted them so you can see them better.

You need to make it change back to approximately the width it was before. Activate the cell and change the width to 125 pixels in the Inspector window.

There is a difference in the representation of font sizes on the PC and Mac. Because much of this book was created using the Macintosh version of GoLive 5, when you work in Windows, your font sizes may vary from what you may see here. For this step, if you're working on a PC, you'll need to set the width of the box to 140 pixels, not the 125 pixels that the Macintosh uses.

11. In the upper-right part of the frame, you'll place the fields where visitors enter their personal information. First, type the following: "Name:", "Age:", "Daytime Phone:", "Evening Phone:", "e-mail:". Add a space and press Enter after each. Now your table will look much like Figure 4.14.

12. Place a Text Field next to each of these lines. Resize the fields and then save the file. Select the Preview tab. Notice how the text butts up against the cell borders. You need to change that so it looks cleaner. Select the entire Table element and, in the Table section of the Inspector window, change Cell Pad to 3. Now when you select Preview your layout should look like Figure 4.14. To finish, resize each of the Text Fields so each field fits on one line.

The bottom left cell in the table is where visitors will choose what trip package they would like to win. To set this up, type some explanatory information and then add a List Box.

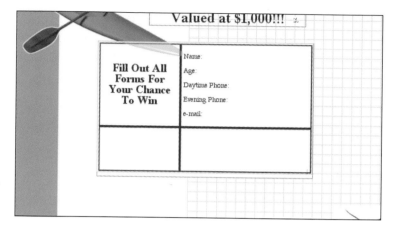

Figure 4.14
The Table prior to adding
text fields.

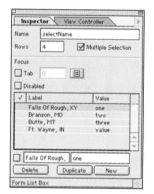

Figure 4.15
The List Box's Inspector window.
This is where you change the
information displayed in the Box.

13. Type the following, setting the text parameters to Bold and Center: "Tell Us Where You Would Like To Go". Press Return/Enter to add another line and then drag a List Box element into that cell. The associated Inspector window gives you the ability to change the text that is shown, and add extra lines if needed. Change the text in the following way:

    • Click on the word "first" in the list window.

    • Change the text to whatever you would like in the text fields that are activated. Whatever you type in the first text field is what will be displayed in the List Box. When you finish typing the information, either press Return/Enter or click on the next line in the list window.

    • Repeat this process for the next two lines (labeled "second" and "third"). When you are finished, your window should look like Figure 4.15, with the left fields containing the locations that will appear in the pop-up list.

    • To add a new line, click the New button on the bottom right of the Inspector window. As you add new lines, change the value to reflect their position on the list.

14. In the last frame, add a Text area so the entrants can talk you into choosing them. First, type: "Give Us A Reason To Send You There. Be As Creative As You Want." Center this text.

15. Now, add a Text Area element beneath this line. All that remains to do is to place the Submit and Reset buttons.

16. For this example, select the Table element and add a Caption area to the bottom. Place the Submit and Reset buttons in this area, and change their respective text to: "Enter Now" and "Let Me Start Over".

There you have it: A very different-looking entry form that is at once functional and somewhat pleasing to the eye (see Figure 4.16). If you want, you can play around with the positions of the various elements, changing the Table by adding another row and placing all the entry fields into the right frame. Everything's up to you and what you believe looks the best.

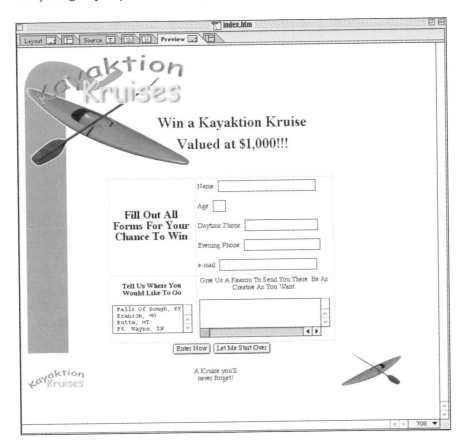

Figure 4.16
The final look for the Kayaktion Kruises Giveaway screen.

FORM Aide

Now that you've gotten a bit of hands-on work with some interesting and fun elements, and because the last one dealt with a kayaking company, you might as well stay with the outdoors theme. In this case, we'll use another fictitious company called—appropriately enough—The Great Outdoors. (By the way, if any of these company names I've come up with strikes your fancy and you want to use one as your company name, feel free. It's my little gift to you—just make sure that these companies aren't already in existence because things happen nearly as fast in the business world as they do in the computer industry.) The Great Outdoors (TGO) features clothing and sporting goods coveted by active sportspeople throughout a wide region of the country and, as your new client, they're counting on you to build a site that will bring the entire nation to their e-doorstep. In Project 4.2, it's definitely a case of "Today, the neighborhood; tomorrow, the world!"

PROJECT 4.2 Building a Basic Table-Based Form

For this project, you need to create some kind of form that gives the company a strong database of prospective clients. Of course, the way to do this is to offer free catalogs and incentives by having viewers fill out a form that you also placed on the Web site. With this in mind, you begin to work on a form that not only keeps with the advertising direction and brand recognition of the company, but it's also actually kind of fun to fill out.

You will use the following files in this project:

- OutdoorsLogo.jpg
- GrassyBar.jpg
- GrassyBarH.jpg
- Bass.jpg
- Bear.jpg
- Buck.jpg
- Hunt.jpg
- Fish.jpg
- Play.jpg
- Spacer.jpg

As always, these files—should you choose to accept them (sorry; couldn't resist)—can be found in the Chapter 04 folder on this book's companion CD-ROM. Again, you will create a new site titled Outdoors, place a Form element and Layout Grid on the index.html page, and prepare to get your hands dirty again.

Bucks and Bass and Bears—Oh My!

Look closely at The Great Outdoors page in the GoLive Studio section. This page will give you an idea of how this form page will look—although, once again, remember that the idea here is that you will strive to create something somewhat different, somewhat more "your own."

1. Resize the Layout Grid inside the Form element so it fills your workspace; it should fill your screen horizontally. Make the Height 1000. This gives you enough room to put all the elements you need on this page.

2. Place three Image placeholders on the Grid. These are used for the OutdoorsLogo.jpg and GrassyBar images.

3. Link these placeholders in the following manner:

   - *Top*—OutdoorsLogo.jpg
   - *Middle*—GrassyBarH.jpg
   - *Bottom*—GrassyBar.jpg

Now, your workspace should look something like Figure 4.17. Extend the GrassyBarH.jpg one grid space to the right, or in the Inspector window change the Width setting to 512 pixels. This change is a minor adjustment that won't affect the image quality; it will set the size to match with the next images you will add.

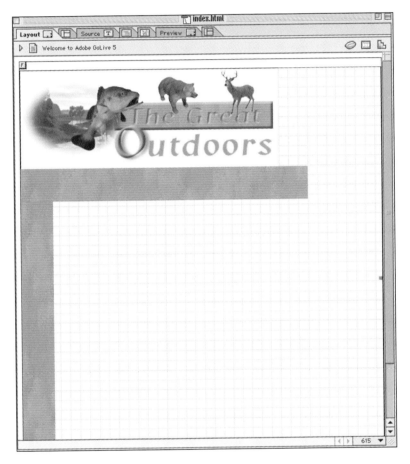

Figure 4.17
The graphic elements have been put in their places.

4. Position three more Image placeholders flush against the "The Great Outdoors" logo, as seen in Figure 4.18. Position a fourth Image placeholder against the right edge of the GrassyBarH image you just modified. Link the top three placeholders to these image files, respectively:

   - Hunt.jpg

   - Fish.jpg

   - Play.jpg

   If this were an actual site, these placeholders would be links to other areas of the TGO site.

Figure 4.18
Three Image placeholders positioned against the right edge of the company logo.

> **Note**: These three elements are large enough that they don't fit the grid proportions. This will make the other image placeholders snap to the next point, leaving a gap between each of them. You will need to use the Option|Ctrl+arrow key combination to move the images, pixel by pixel, so they butt up against each other correctly.

5. Link the last empty placeholder to the Spacer.jpg image and then move it into place beneath the other three images. Press Option|Ctrl+Up Arrow to move it flush against the bottom of the Play button. Change the Height setting of this image to between 18 and 23 pixels (depending on your system), then, move the GrassyBarH and GrassyBar images up until all these images are flush against each other. Use the Option|Ctrl+right arrow to move the buttons and spacer images so they are lined up with the right edge of the GrassyBarH image, as in Figure 4.19.

Figure 4.19
The final position for the graphic elements for The Great Outdoors site.

6. With everything in position, save the file. Place two Layout Text Boxes beneath the horizontal green bar. In the top box, type: "Your opinion is important to us." Make this text Bold, Centered, and Size 5. In the bottom box, type: "Please fill out the form below so we can keep improving to better serve you." Leave the text in its default state, but

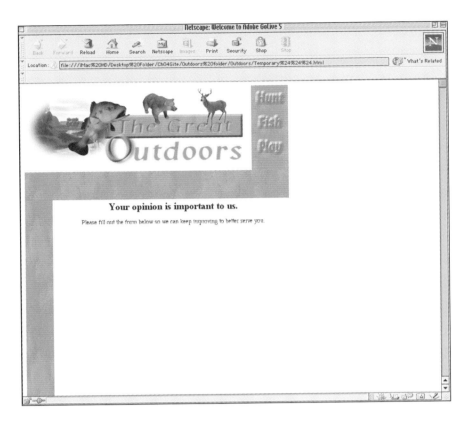

Figure 4.20
After placing the elements, the
first section of your survey page
should look similar to this.

make sure that it's centered in the box. Refer to Figure 4.20 to get a
better idea of how your page should now look.

7. To properly complete this page, you need to use a combination of
   Forms and Basic elements to lay out the survey. Begin by placing a Line
   element directly underneath the text boxes you just filled in. Add two
   more Layout Text Boxes beneath this line. Label the top Layout Text
   Box "Name:", and label the second one "e-mail:". Place a Text Field
   element next to each of these boxes. Place another Layout Text Box to
   the right of each and label them "Address:" and "City/State/Zip:". Add
   more Text Fields to complete this section. Finally, you need to work on
   the yes and no question area: "May we contact you regarding new
   specials as they become available?" Add the Layout Text Box, type this
   question in the Text Box, and place two radio buttons and label them
   "Yes" and "No", respectively, using a couple more Text Boxes.

8. Creating the second section of the survey requires the placement of a
   Table element underneath a second Line element. To set up the Table to
   meet your needs, do the following:

   • In the Inspector window, set Rows to 11.

   • Add a Caption area and specify Above Table.

**Image Placement
Anomalies**

There are times that, when
linking to an image, the resized
placeholder causes other
image placeholders to move
out of their positions. You can
move these errant placeholders back into place, or you can
position the unassigned Image
placeholders away from their
final destination, link the images to them, and then move
them into place.

In the caption area of the table, type: "I enjoy participating in the following outdoor activities: (Select all that apply)".

9. Now, you'll modify the table in the following manner:

   • Select the first ten cells of the left column and merge them.

   • Merge the middle and right cells in each row so they become individual cells.

10. In the large cell you created on the left, place an Image placeholder and link it to the Bass.jpg image. Then, in each of the 11 rows on the right of the Table, place a checkbox. Refer to Figure 4.21 for the selections to type in each row, or you can come up with your own text blocks that relate to outdoor activities. Make sure, however, that the bottommost cell gives your visitors a chance to enter their own suggestions.

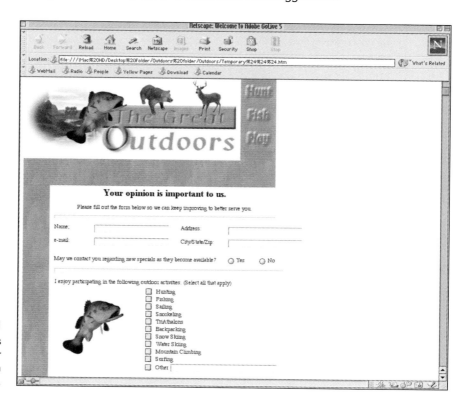

Figure 4.21

The first set of survey options along with a Text Field for visitors to give you feedback on their interests.

11. Now, you move to the third and final section of this page. Place another Line element below the last table you created, and then drag one more Table placeholder onto the screen. Define this element's parameters in the following manner:

   • Rows: 13, Columns 3

   • Caption Above Table

12. In the caption area type: "Please let us know how we can improve our online service."

13. Merge the first ten cells of the left column and put an Image placeholder in this area. Link it to the Buck.jpg.

14. Select the middle and right cells of the top ten rows and merge all of them. Inside of this, place a Text Area Box. Then, merge the two cells (middle and right) on the bottom row. Place a Submit button and rename it to Send Survey. Add a space and place the Reset button directly beneath the other one.

15. Finally, in what is now the third cell from the top in the left column, type "Thank you for your time." Your table should now look like the one in Figure 4.22. Your page should look much like the one shown in Figure 4.23.

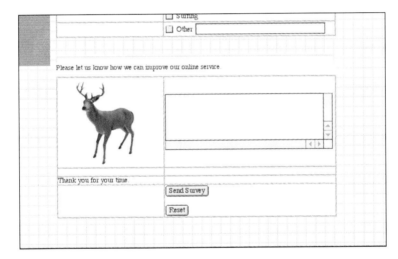

Figure 4.22
The second (and final) table layout for the The Great Outdoors survey page.

To close out this section, I want to give you one more idea. You can place background images in Table elements to give unique looks without deviating too much from the overall format of your site. I have added a couple of image files for you to use in the Chapter04 folder so you can experiment with doing this. They are BackgroundImageLG.jpg and BackgroundImage.jpg. Have fun using these files as you gain more experience with Form and overall Web design work.

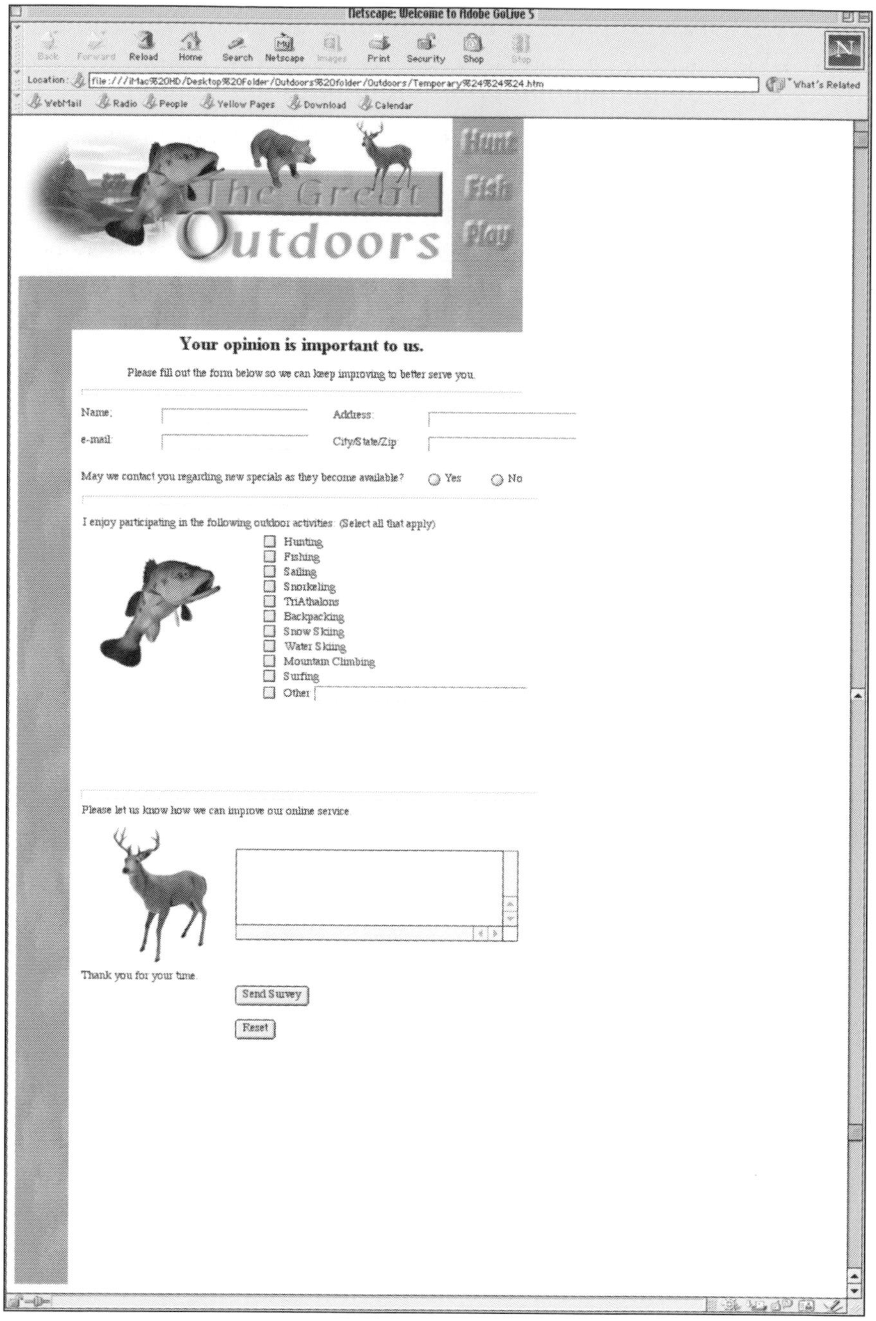

Figure 4.23

The survey page in its completed form. I have combined a couple of images so you can see how the entire screen looks. I also added an additional vertical bar, so the edge graphic continues the entire length of the page.

PROJECT 4.3 *FORM*ing a Master Plan

You've now built a couple of different pages using forms, and you have sat patiently through my little tirades regarding keeping a common look between pages. For being so kind, go ahead and create a two-page site; the first being a home page and the second being a form. This way, you can begin getting a feel for how you can make modifications to a basic design without veering too far off the design course.

Instead of working on another fictitious company's site design, I thought that, this time, you might enjoy using a real-world example. It's a site that I'm in the process of creating called (tentatively) The Coriolis Book Castle. I'm setting it up as an ancillary site that focuses on the Web and graphic design books the publisher of this book produces. Although not affiliated in any way with the company (heck, even Coriolis didn't know about this site until my editor read this section). I am in the beginning process of contacting some of the authors I know to provide some marketing materials to describe their books. Then links will be created to the Coriolis site where visitors can buy the book(s).

Note: You can see a more colorful version of the layout of the home page in this book's GoLive Studio.

The Initial Layout

This project will use the following files in its design:

- Header1.jpg
- GrassyBar1.jpg
- Cover1.jpg
- Cover2.jpg
- BackgroundImageLG.jpg

This will be a very basic design with modifications to be made later. Those changes will include the addition of advanced rollovers, the creation of which is discussed in Chapter 9. Here's how to get started:

1. After creating the Castle site folder and importing the image files you'll use, place a Layout Grid on the workspace. Position an Image placeholder in the upper-left corner of the Grid and link it to the Header1.jpg file.

2. Place another Image placeholder directly beneath the header image and link to GrassyBar1.jpg. Make sure that this image is positioned all the way on the left of the Grid. Notice that this image has three topic bars jutting out from it. These bars are labeled "New", "Hot", and "Buy". These topic bars will become specific links to those pages.

Create an Image Map

You can create an image map out of any placed image element very quickly within GoLive. This allows you to design a montage and then assign certain areas of that montage as links. In the case of the GrassyBar1 image, each of these reference bars will become a link:

1. Select the GrassyBar1 image and go to the Inspector window. Select the More tab and then activate the Use Map option approximately halfway down the window.

2. The toolbar (shown in Figure 4.24) changes to give you access to the tools to define the area that will become the hotspot. These tools are (from left to right):

- *The Region*—Allows you to select an individual hotspot area in an image that has multiple hotspots assigned to it.

- *Rectangle*—Creates rectangular or square hotspots.

- *Circle*—Creates oval hotspots.

- *Freeform*—Creates freeform hotspots.

- *Display URL*—Superimposes the selected hotspot and its associated assigned URL.

- *Frame Regions*—Toggles between showing and not showing a bounding box around each hotspot.

- *Color Regions*—Creates a colored interior to the hotspot for easier identification.

- *Select Color*—Assigns a color to the Color Regions option.

- *Bring Region To Front*—Changes the Z-Order of the hotspot. This is good for hotspots that overlap each other. This tool is also represented in the Transform window in the Z-Order area.

- *Send Region To Back*—Works in the opposite manner of the Bring Region to Front tool. This tool is also represented in the Transform window in the Z-Order area.

Figure 4.24

The Use Map feature in the Inspector window and the tools to create a hotspot. The creation tools themselves are accessible only in the toolbar.

3. Activate the Rectangle tool and drag a rectangular hotspot over each of the headings (New, Hot, and Buy). These areas can now be linked to specific pages on your site, or to other sites around the Web. When you go into Preview mode or view your page in a browser, your cursor will turn into a hand when it passes over your newly created hotspots.

4. To complete this page, refer to Figure 4.25 to place the rest of the Layout Text Boxes (5) and Image placeholders (2), plus one Line element positioned between the rightmost images so your window looks close to what you see in the figure. Save the index.html page and then delete everything, except for the Header1 and GrassyBar1 images, and the small text box directly beneath Header 1. In Chapter 5, you'll learn about creating style sheets, but for right now, use the Save As option from the File pull-down menu. Save this new page as Form.html and store it in your pages folder.

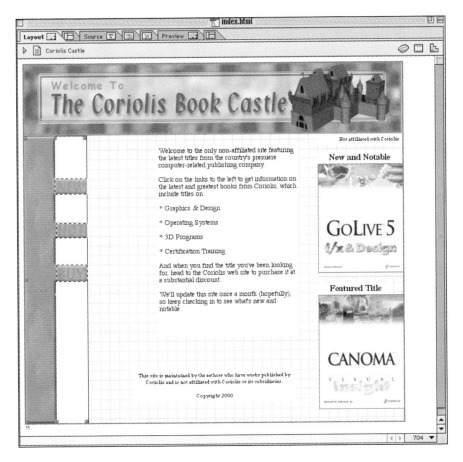

Figure 4.25
The final layout for the homepage of The Coriolis Book Castle site.

Create a Feedback Page

The form you'll create for this site is a feedback page. Here, visitors can select an author via a pull-down menu, ask questions or give comments on that person's particular book, and then send them via a special email account that will be set up. Therefore, this simple, yet eloquent page will be a very important addition to the site. Here's how to do it:

1. Place a Form element onto the new page. Select only the hotspots and the Grid and drag them into the Form area. Doing this will also move all the elements currently placed on the Grid.

2. Place a Table element on the page. The top of the Table should be positioned one grid space higher than the top of New, and two full grid spaces to the left of that GrassyBar1.jpg image. Set the height of the Table to 400 pixels.

3. Merge the center and right cells of each row. You'll place the Text Areas in these areas. The left cells will house that column's "topic" and pull-down menus. Your screen should now look like Figure 4.26.

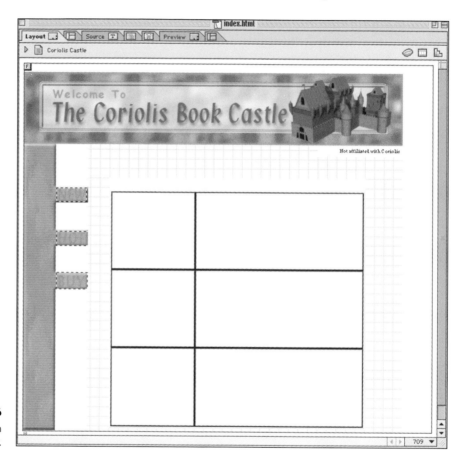

Figure 4.26
The Coriolis Book Castle form page is coming along nicely.

4. In the top right cell, type: "Send A Message". In the cell below that, type: "Ask A Technical Question". In the bottom right cell, type: "Give Your Opinion". Place a Text Area element into each of the right cells. Resize the Text Area elements slightly, and use the Align Right button on the toolbar to move them and the text against the right side of the cells.

5. Change the width of the left column of cells to 125 pixels. Just select one cell and change its width parameter to change it in all the cells of that column.

6. In the Caption area, type: "You've Got Our Ears. Talk To Us:", and make the text Bold and Size 4. If you want, change the color of the text.

7. In the upper left cell, add the text "Choose an Author", select all the text (Command|Ctrl+A), press Return/Enter, and then center the text. Place a PopUp element below the text. Now, turn to the Inspector window.

8. Notice that the associated Inspector window of the PopUp element looks much like the one for the List Box. Using the same method of changing the visible text, change "first" to "Name", and in the next label fields type in some names of authors you know and respect (for example, place this author's name at the top).

9. In the cell beneath that, type: "Choose a Title". Repeat the preceding steps, adding book titles into the Label area of the PopUp's Inspector window.

10. Now for that background image that you stored in your site folder. Select the Table element. In the Inspector window, select BgImage. You need to link to the BackgroundImageLG.jpg to place it into the background of the Table. This image adds a decorative quality to the page without being overbearing (which is the reason I added this step). Creating background images for use inside of tables is a wonderful option to remember.

11. The last steps are to add the Submit and Reset buttons, and change the Cell Border to 0. Figure 4.27 shows how this screen looks in Internet Explorer.

Final Comments

You probably noticed that no link was created to get from the home page to the form or *vice versa*. I did this intentionally; no, I didn't forget.

As you've discovered, creating forms can be as fulfilling creatively as any other aspect of Web design. I've talked to a number of people who build Web sites for a living, and they inevitably say that building a form is the most boring part of their day. However, it really doesn't have to be that way. With some planning and the knowledge of how to blend different elements in the GoLive toolkit, you can build forms within your sites that are anything but repetitive and boring.

As I mentioned at the beginning of this chapter, here's the list I promised. By visiting the following list of sites, you can obtain CGI scripts to make your forms work. In all, the following sites make a good starting point to begin your CGI scripts education:

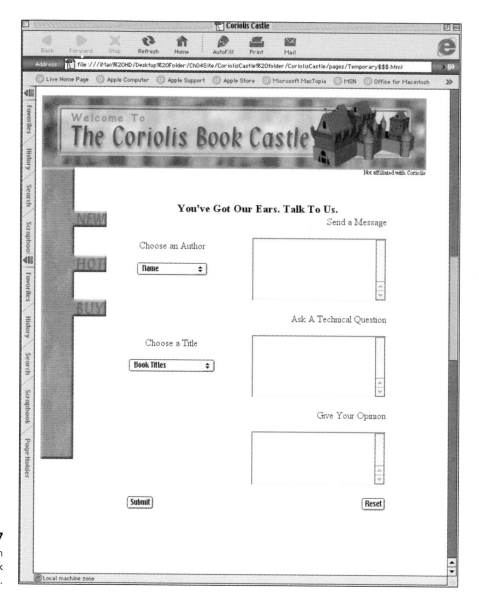

Figure 4.27
This figure shows the final Form screen for The Coriolis Book Castle Web site.

Free CGI Scripts
www.onlinebusiness.com/shops/_programming/BEST_CGI_Scripts.shtml

Matt's Script Archive
www.worldwidemart.com/scripts/

Dream Catchers Web Free CGI Scripts
http://dreamcatchersweb.com/scripts/

CGI Scripts Archive
http://best-of-web.com/computer/cgi_index.shtml

This list shows only a small sampling of what you can find. Some highly creative scripts are available that—as you search the archives—will definitely help get the ol' idea factory up and running.

Moving On

As you can see, there are a number of creative ways to use Forms within your site designs and various ways to fool the visitor into thinking you magically created a complicated page without using Forms. It can be fun to experiment and find new ways to incorporate this powerful design tool into your Web site layouts. Another exciting design element is Cascading Style Sheets (CSS).

In the next chapter, I'll demystify the ways you can use to set up CSS pages. I'll also give you the lowdown on what traps to watch out for when designing a Cascading Web site.

Chapter 5

Building Cascading Style Sheets

Continuity is the most effective means of getting your message to the people. Incorporating styles into a Web site is like creating style sheets in a word processor, and it gives you the same power to control the look of text elements throughout your site.

Continuity, Continuity, Continuity

If you're like me, as you create a Web page or a site, you often start looking for new ways to deliver your message. And, many times arise when you would like to take your text elements out of the normal HTML formatting limitations and give them a distinctive look. You may also want to easily re-create that look without having to go into the actual coding to change text parameters by hand. You're going to read a lot about continuity in these pages because, being an old ad man (*old* being the key term here), it has been driven into my skull that continuity is Rule #1 when it comes to corporate identity retention and maintenance. In other words, brand recognition.

Here's a short quiz for you that will help make my point. Don't worry—it's extremely easy and painless, and it won't be graded. (I always hated grading papers when I did part-time teaching at different colleges around the country, so I'm not about to do it here.) I'll give you some corporate symbols, and all you have to do is match the symbols to their company.

The Logo

1. Golden arches

2. A three-part red and blue globe with the product name cutting through the middle

3. A roaring lion

4. A tall, snow-peaked mountain with stars encircling it

5. Cinderella's castle

6. A colorful peacock

The Company

A. MGM/UA

B. Pepsi Cola Company

C. NBC Television Network

D. Walt Disney Company

E. McDonalds

F. Paramount Pictures

I think that for most of you, this brand-recognition test was extremely easy. The answers: 1-E, 2-B, 3-A, 4-F, 5-D, and 6-C. In most cases, these logos have been around your entire life, and you've committed them (involuntarily) to memory. You don't even need to see the name of the product; you just know what it is by the logo's color or shape. Each of these companies usually has a catch phrase (an identifying line) or music bite that pops into mind.

Where am I going with this? Again, remember that we're discussing the whole point of continuity. Each of these corporate entities has effectively placed their logo and, subsequently, their catch phrases, into the collective consciousness of the world. So let me bring this into the context of Web site design. I know we've all gone to Web sites where every page has a completely different look; a different background, a different layout, even a different set of fonts. It almost looks as if each page you're accessing is a totally different site; nothing ties everything together. By employing a cohesive look and feel through graphic elements and selective use of fonts and font layouts, you can still creatively change page design, while conveying the knowledge that the visitor is still on *your* site.

Incorporating *Cascading Style Sheets* (*CSSs*), commonly referred to as *Styles*, into your site design, lets you set up your site to have a contiguous look and feel, while allowing you to be creative in other ways. They effectively give you the ammunition you need to quickly and easily duplicate the look of text and the way paragraphs or blocks of text are displayed—all with a simple click of a button. Now, let's take a quick look at a basic example—simple text.

Simple Text

When you place text on a page, you can modify it only so much, because of the inherent limitations of the Web. As you all know, designing a Web page to be distinctive is not the same as working with a page-layout program, such as InDesign—you just don't have the nearly endless latitude. But, with cascading style sheets, whether internal or external, you have far more room to work because the formatting is not limited to the general HTML code like the rest of the e-world.

Figure 5.1 shows a page with three text boxes placed in a Layout Grid. The top box is the Header, the middle box is where the links are housed, and the bottom box has some engagingly informative text.

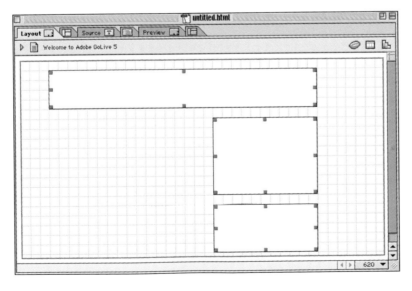

Figure 5.1
A sample home page with three text boxes placed into position.

The GoLive & PROSPER! Headline has been centered and the text is Bold and size 7, as seen in the toolbar in Figure 5.2. Figure 5.3 shows that, to change the size (which is the largest it can be using basic HTML limitations), you have few options. If you selected the Source tab on the workspace window or opened the Source Code window (Window|Source Code), you would see the following line of code:

```
<font color="#0033ff" size="7"><b>GoLive</b><b><i>&amp;</i></
b><b>PROSPER! </b></font>
```

Notice the ampersand within the line of code. I used HTML to italicize it to give it a slightly different look (this formatting is represented by the <i></i> brack-eting within the code).

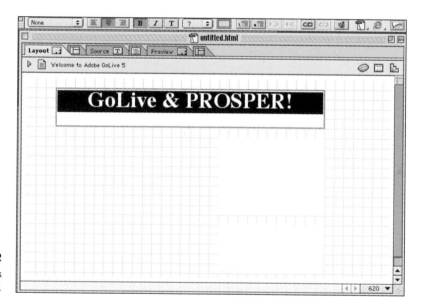

Figure 5.2
The basic HTML font parameters set up in the toolbar.

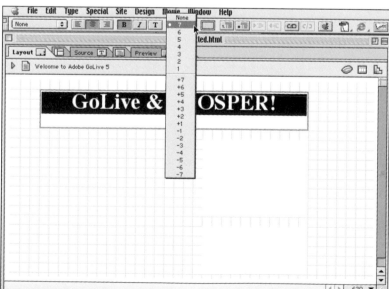

Figure 5.3
Text size choices from the pull-down menu in the toolbar.

For many, this would be adequate. Suppose that, however, you want the ampersand to really stand out—to be totally different than the rest of the headline. That's when you would incorporate a style sheet to change parameters to reflect percentages and point sizes for your fonts. So, "size="7"" could become "font-size=36pt" within the HTML script, giving you far more latitude in creating an eye-catching headline.

Pros and Cons

As with many situations dealing with today's Internet, you have to be careful when building sites that employ CSS technology. No two browsers see CSS in the same way because no uniform means of delivery exists. Even among the most up-to-date browsers, a style sheet can be reproduced differently. Nevertheless, they are the best choice for creating some uniformity in your pages.

Older versions of browsers (Netscape 3 and Internet Explorer 3 and earlier) won't be able to access CSS at all. In fact, depending on the type of CSS you assign to a page, you could literally (albeit inadvertently) cause a full system crash on your visitor's computer. So, I repeat, it's important that you warn people that they need the latest version of their browser of choice.

If this is the case, and CSS can cause complete system crashes in older browsers, then why use style sheets at all? Why not just write down the style parameters you created and re-create them by hand (as it were) on each appropriate page? Or why not create headline text in other programs, like Photoshop, Illustrator, Freehand, CorelDRAW, and simply use tables and frames to create a consistent style? First, it would add unnecessary time to your design efforts and, if you're creating a site for a client, it could raise the amount of money you agreed upon (causing the client to question your time management skills). Unless you are totally proficient at HTML scripting, finding the appropriate snippet of code in a dense page (one that has dozens of visual elements and myriad lines of text), can become a rather daunting task. Even with the source code window open as you build your page, keeping track of each line as it is generated and changing it immediately can get you out of that "design realm" that drives your creative muse.

However, a workaround is possible. It's right there, in the CSS lexicon of tools. You'll find out what that is shortly. (Aren't I a tease?)

Browsers, Browsers Everywhere

As you know, three main Web browsers serve today's surfing world: Internet Explorer (see Figure 5.4), Netscape Navigator/Communicator (see Figure 5.5), and AOL's proprietary Web browser, based on Navigator (which AOL owns). Regarding the first two browsers, the biggest difference is in the way they display fonts, with Explorer's base font size being larger than Communicator's. This difference can cause a discrepancy in the way text layouts are seen over the Web.

Figure 5.4
The splash screen for Microsoft Internet Explorer.

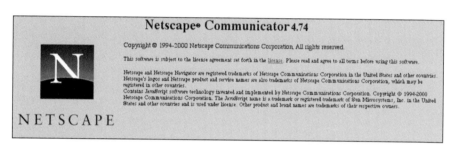

Figure 5.5
The splash screen for Netscape Communicator.

A fourth browser is the one used for people who own WebTVs. The WebTV display is based on Windows CE software and, because it's displayed on a television screen rather than on a computer monitor, some pages are reformatted in such a way that the design itself is reformatted into a more vertical display. Although WebTV isn't as prevalent as the previously mentioned browsers, it's still a factor to consider. If, for example, a friend has a WebTV, it might serve you to look at some familiar sites and see the differences in how they are displayed.

Also, new browsers are on the horizon. One company—Opera Software (**www.opera.com**)—is rolling out a competitive Web browser called, appropriately enough, Opera (see Figure 5.6). At the time of this writing, Opera is available for Windows, Linux, EPOC, and BeOS, and a Macintosh version is currently undergoing beta testing. Because my primary computer systems (and means for accessing the Internet) are Macs, I wasn't able to test this browser.

Another available browser that is designed to enable you to test many new developments in Web protocols and formats is called Amaya. It's available from the World Wide Web Consortium's (W3C) site (**www.w3.org/Amaya/**). So, if you are a Webmaster itching for the chance to experiment with cutting-edge technology before it becomes widely distributed, here's your chance. Amaya is available only for Win95/NT and Unix platforms.

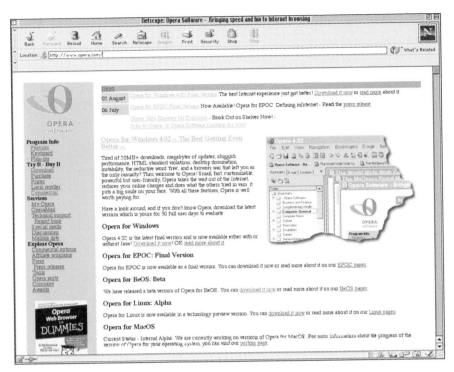

Figure 5.6
The Opera home page, featuring a new Web browser that looks to be fairly impressive.

Each Web browser can—and will—react differently to CSS, because no set standard exists for final display of this technology. Therefore, each Web browser has its own way of reading pages embedded with Cascading Style Sheet information. So, it's a good idea to have as many browsers as possible at your beck and call, so you can truly see how your work will be displayed to the widest possible audience.

CSS Tools

Take some time to look at the Cascading Style Sheet controls, so you can become familiar with them. You have a lot to go over in this area because setting up CSS forms can be, initially, a complicated procedure. You have many different control areas and two different style sheet formats from which to choose. So, the more familiar you become with the Inspector window and what you can do in it, the better off you are.

You can create a CSS form in two ways. The first method is found under File|New Special|Style Sheet Document (see Figure 5.7). This action defines an external style sheet. The second method is the Open CSS Interface, accessed by way of the last button on the right just above the workspace; it's the one that looks like a set of stairs (see Figure 5.8). This control defines an internal style sheet.

This probably is a good place to stop for a moment to define the types of style sheets that you can create, and to examine what makes a Cascading Style Sheet cascade.

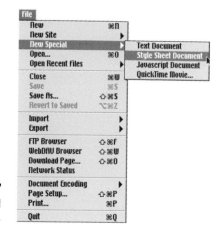

Figure 5.7

The path to creating an external style sheet.

Figure 5.8

Using the Open CSS Interface control, which looks like a set of stairs, lets you create an internal style sheet.

External Styles

As a brief definition, an *external* style sheet only controls text properties on a page or series of pages that have a common external style sheet attached to it. In a great sense, external style sheets are much like styles or templates you create in a word processor. As you develop your pages and create text styles using the CSS controls, you will always save these files to the external area of your site.

Internal Styles

Internal style sheets control the overall look to a page. An internal style sheet only affects the page it is linked to (or controls). These styles are embedded in the Head section of your page.

Inline Styles

An *inline* style is added to an internal style sheet *as a modification* for specific elements. By being able to add sub-styles directly into a style sheet, you are able to accomplish the cascading effect, with different elements taking on different attributes based on a hierarchical structure discussed a little later in this chapter.

Cascading

This is a fundamental setup for CSS1 technology implemented and approved by the W3C. Cascading applies to the capability to add various style sheets with varying style elements to one document, creating a cascading effect in which one style can override another based upon a hierarchy.

Granted, these are extremely simplified definitions, but even attempting to fully define these could take up many more pages than I'm allotted for this book. If you want to delve deeper into CSS history, a good place to begin your search is the W3C site at **www.w3c.org**.

External Tag Selectors

When you create an external style sheet, a set of three Tag Selectors appears in the toolbar. From left to right in Figure 5.9 these selectors are: New Class Selector, New Element Selector, and New ID Selector. When you choose one of these selectors, the Duplicate (+) button becomes available (far right). In the case of an internal style sheet, you also have access to the New Style Sheet File button (the stair icon).

Figure 5.9

The Tag Selectors tools that become active when you create an internal and/or external style sheet.

Basic CSS Setups

It's almost time to get your hands dirty by creating a couple of style sheets. Before you start, however, it's important that you review how a style sheet is defined. A style sheet can be internal (placed into the Head section of a page) or external (saved as a file that is accessed, or referenced, from your Web page).

You need to be aware of and comfortable with certain elements of style sheets as you start incorporating CSS into your designs. These are as follows:

- *Classes*—The most common use for these is to give warning notes or special message elements a distinctive look. Classes work on unlimited numbers of elements. They also only work with CSS compatible browsers. This means that older browsers might not read the page or, in the worse case scenario, your CSS page could cause the program or even the visitor's system to crash.

- *IDs*—The same as classes, only IDs work with a specific element of your page, whether a paragraph or selected text elements. The ID is a good tool to use for a catch phrase to give it a distinctive look from the rest of the text on your page.

- *Tag Selectors*—A true workhorse of an option and the potential savior I mentioned earlier in the chapter. Tag Selectors are placed in the Head section of your page and let you format said page as a CSS, while acting as a content delivery police officer. In other words, they make sure that your page content remains intact, even if your site is accessed through a non-CSS compatible browser. This is one element you'll want to use every time you have CSS elements embedded on your Web site.

Note: IDs have some problems that make them more troublesome than they are possibly worth. Because of the unresolved differences in CSS technology, to make IDs work, you have to do some hand coding in the Source view to actually use them on your page. So, unless you are adept at HTML, you might want to shy away from this CSS element until the technology is more defined.

Hierarchical Considerations

Cascading Style Sheets have a strong hierarchical structure. As you create your sites and add CSS to your design tools, you will need to remember this structure so your pages turn out as expected. The structure, in rank from bottom to top, is:

- External

- Internal

- InLine

So, if you have an external style sheet assigned to a page, then add an internal style sheet to the same page and have different settings assigned to text elements, the internal style sheet's structure will override the external style sheet's. If you have an inline style (.class) inside your internal style sheet structure with different text parameters, the inline style will override the internal style sheet's text styles.

Think of this structure in this way: You're on a boat in the middle of the high seas. A storm comes up and, before you can get under cover, you're soaked. That's your external style sheet affecting your page. As the storm increases, the sea gets a bit rougher and waves lash against your boat, making it pitch drunkenly in the water. That's your internal style sheet taking precedence over the external. Water starts filling the hold, causing the boat to sit lower, the waves crashing fore and aft, causing the boat to react sluggishly as you try to maintain course. That's your inline style sheet.

Okay, so it's a slightly horrific visual for a hierarchical description, but I think you get the general idea. The bottom line to proper understanding of style sheets is, as you add elements to the style sheets, remember that one can override the other, causing your carefully mapped out styles to take on a different look altogether.

Create an External Style Sheet

It's time to get used to really setting up a style sheet now. Remember, an external style sheet needs to be saved into your root folder. For the setup, create a new site and add a new folder to it (Site|New|Folder). Name this folder "Pages". Create two new pages (File|New or Cmd/Ctrl+N) and give them any name you want. Save them into the Pages folder. With no pages open at this point, do the following:

1. To create an external style sheet, select File|New Special|Style Sheet Document. An untitled.css window like the one in Figure 5.10 will open.

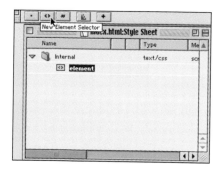

Figure 5.10
The Style Sheet Document window where your different styles will be listed.

2. For the purposes of this demonstration, create a new tag using the New Element Selector in the button toolbar at the top of the screen. This will create a new style listing in the Style Sheet Document window, as seen in Figure 5.11. With the element tag selected, rename it Body by either highlighting it in the style-sheet document or in the Name field of the Inspector window.

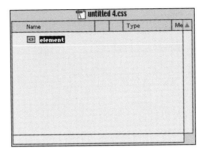

Figure 5.11
A new Tag element has been added to the untitled internal style sheet.

3. If it's not already, open the Inspector window. You now have numerous style options from which to choose (see Figure 5.12). The different tabs, as would be expected, give you various options for creating your style.

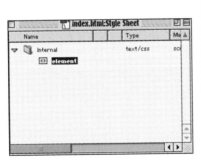 

Figure 5.12
The Inspector window associated with the Style Sheet Document window gives you everything you need to create site-specific styles.

From left to right, these tabs are:

- *Basic* (see Figure 5.13)—Names the style and shows any modifications made to it via the other tabs.

- *Font* (see Figure 5.14)—Assigns various font styles, such as italicized text, font family, color, and more.

- *Text* (see Figure 5.15)—Changes the properties, such as line and character spacing, alignment properties, and more.

- *Block* (see Figure 5.16)—If you are creating a style for a block of text (a paragraph, for example), this lets you set the parameters for how that block is displayed, including visual and non-visual elements of the block, as well as floating properties.

Figure 5.13
The Basic CSS Selector Inspector window.

Figure 5.14
(Left) The Font CSS Selector
Inspector window.

Figure 5.15
(Center) The Text CSS Selector
Inspector window.

Figure 5.16
(Right) The Block CSS Selector
Inspector window.

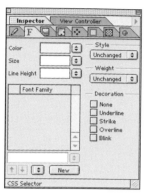

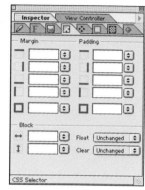

- *Position* (see Figure 5.17)—If you have floating boxes with elements inside, this area lets you change the floater's properties. Floating elements must have some kind of formatting assigned, such as position, clipping behavior, and so on.

- *Border* (see Figure 5.18)—Chooses border properties around blocks of information associated with that style.

Figure 5.17
(Left) The Position CSS Selector
Inspector window.

Figure 5.18
(Right) The Border CSS Selector
Inspector window.

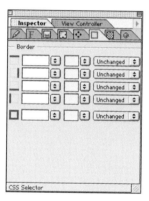

- *Background* (see Figure 5.19)—These controls work with blocks associated with the style. You can place an image or background color for that particular block.

- *List & Others* (see Figure 5.20)—If you are using bullet points or other formatting properties, this area gives you control over the bullet's appearance and even allows you to assign a custom image as a marker.

In the case of the element you just created, select the Basic tab. This time, name the element CatchPhrase and press Return. The new name is reflected in the SSD window. The large text area in the Inspector will list all of the properties assigned to that particular tag.

Figure 5.19
(Left) The Background CSS Selector Inspector window.

Figure 5.20
(Right) The List & Others CSS Selector Inspector window.

Assigning Properties

You want to give your catch phrase a distinctive look to make it stand out from the rest of the text on your page. This phrase is part of your logo, so you also want it color coordinated to your artwork, because it will appear on every page, or in specific places throughout your site.

A *catch phrase* is that one-word or one-sentence description that captures the essence of your company or project. Think of the line "The choice of a new generation". You know exactly what product that refers to without having the product name or logo attached to it. In my company's case, I use the phrase "Helping your company grow...ByDesign!" because the name of the company is GRFX ByDesign. I can use this in many different situations, with or without the logo.

For this section, you'll create a header for a GoLive page, using the phrase "GoLive 5 & Prosper":

1. With the Body tag (which you named "CatchPhrase") selected, choose the Font tab in the Inspector window. If the Body tag isn't already selected, click once on its name in the style-sheet document. A full set of style options appears, giving you great flexibility over the look of your catch phrase.

2. Set the Font parameters up as follows (refer to Figure 5.21) by either using the pop-up menus where appropriate, or selecting them with the checkboxes:

   - Color: Maroon
   - Size: 15 point
   - Line Height: Leave as is
   - Style: Italic
   - Weight: 500
   - Decoration: Underline

> **Note:** To get more detailed information on these tab elements, refer to the user manual, which provides more descriptive detail than I can here.

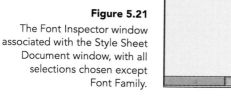

Figure 5.21

The Font Inspector window associated with the Style Sheet Document window, with all selections chosen except Font Family.

3. I purposefully left the CSS Selector Inspector's Font Family area untouched—until now, that is. To select a font or a family of fonts, either use the up/down arrow button below the Font Family screen to select the GoLive internal font families, or use the New button to select a font from your system. For this particular walkthrough, use the Font Family pop-up. In this pop-up menu (the up/down arrows button), select Courier New, Courier, Monaco or a similar font family, if this particular font is not available (see Figure 5.22). The fonts will now be listed in the Font Family area. Select Monaco, similar to the listing shown in Figure 5.23.

Figure 5.22

(Left) A list of available font families is displayed using the font selector button.

Figure 5.23

(Right) All fonts in a font family are listed individually in the Font Family area of the Inspector window.

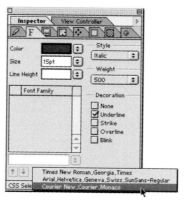

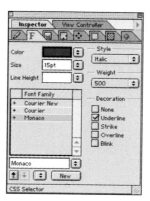

4. Select the Basic tab in the Inspector window and see how your changes are reflected in the information panel.

5. Now, select the Text tab and set Vertical Align to bottom, Font Variant to Small Caps, and Alignment to Right (see Figure 5.24). Leave the rest alone.

You have effectively just created a style sheet that will display anything you write on your pages to a large, italicized, maroon text. Next, you need to save your work.

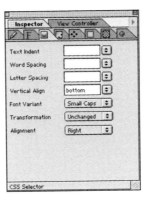

Figure 5.24
The Text area with parameters set for the alignment and style of the text display.

Saving the External Style Sheet

After you've made all the necessary changes to the style, save it into the site folder. Make sure that the untitled.css window is selected. Now, take the following steps:

1. Select Save (or use the Command/Ctrl+S key command). The Save As screen appears with the .css classification already added (see Figure 5.25). I named this style sheet TextTest.css.

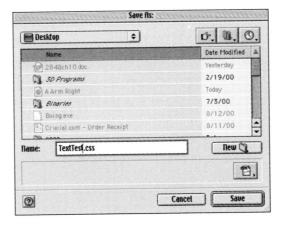

Figure 5.25
The Save As screen with the .css classification already added.

2. Notice the GoLive icon button at the bottom right of the Save As screen. The one you see in Figure 5.26 is the Mac position. Click on this button and choose Root folder (or simply Root, if you're using the Windows version of the program) from the choices (see Figure 5.27).

3. Select Save. GoLive will automatically place you into the root area of your site folder (see Figure 5.28).

Figure 5.26
(Left) Use this button to tell
GoLive how and where you want
to save the new style sheet.

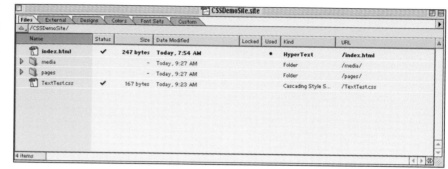

Figure 5.26
(Left) Use this button to tell
GoLive how and where you want
to save the new style sheet.

Figure 5.27
(Right) The list of choices on
where to save the external
style sheet.

Figure 5.28
The TestText.css file is accessible
via the Site window.

Assign the Style to a Page

You can use two methods to assign an external style sheet (ESS) to your pages.
This first section discusses one way. In the next section, I'll show you how to
assign the ESS to multiple pages:

1. Open your index.html page by double-clicking on its icon in the site
   window. Type some pithy phrase on the page. Figure 5.29 shows my
   screen prior to assigning the style sheet.

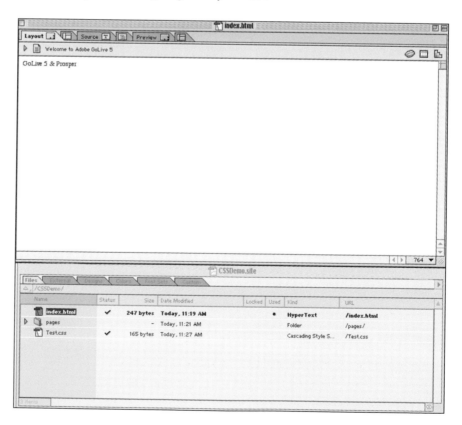

Figure 5.29
An index page with text ready for
the style sheet to be applied.

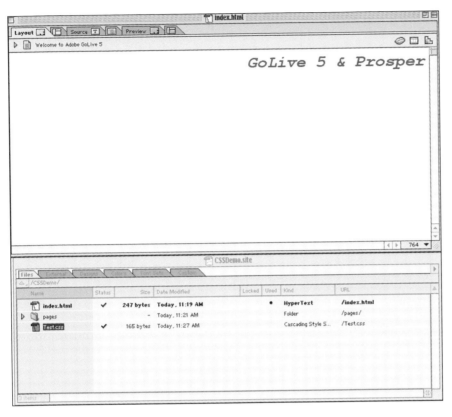

Figure 5.30
The Test.css file you created should appear similar to this in your site window.

2. In the site window, you'll see the Test.css page (see Figure 5.30). Select and drag this icon onto the Page icon in the title bar of the index workspace. The font parameters you set previously are automatically applied to your page.

Assign the Style to Multiple Pages

Using the first method, you could assign your external style sheet (ESS) to a page, page by page, until your entire site is linked to this CSS file. You could also assign the style to multiple pages at once, as follows:

1. Open each of the other pages you created at the beginning of this section. Type something onto each—either the same phrase as on the index.html page, or something different. Close and save these files without assigning the style sheet.

2. Shift+click on the two documents (seen in Figure 5.31, as Page1.html and Page2.html) to select both.

3. Notice the Inspector window. You now have a series of tabs, the last of which is Styles (see Figure 5.32). Select the Styles tab to reveal a large window where the style sheet(s) associated with each page will be listed after you link them. A path field and a number of presently inactive buttons at the bottom (see Figure 5.33) also displays.

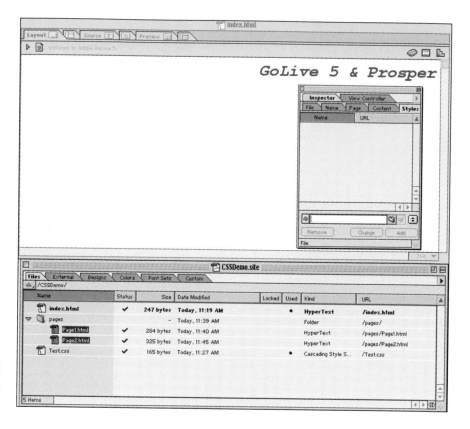

Figure 5.31
Both pages inside the pages folder have been selected and are ready to have the style sheet applied simultaneously.

Figure 5.32
The look of the File Inspector window when a page or multiple pages are selected.

Figure 5.33
The Styles area of the File Inspector window.

Figure 5.34
The link to the style sheet file has been created using the point and shoot method.

4. With the two pages still highlighted in the site window, use the point and shoot button (the one with the spiral icon) to set up a link to the Test.css file. Figure 5.34 shows the link that has been created, and the Add button active. You could also click on the Browse button to navigate to the Test.css file. But why do that? Point and shoot is just too much fun to use.

5. Press the Add button and your style sheet has been applied to each of the selected pages. Now open them to see how they look. Figure 5.35 shows all three pages of mine (index.html, Page1.html, and Page2.html), each of which now sports the same spiffy style.

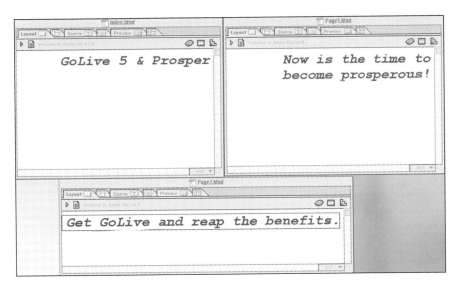

Figure 5.35
The three pages I created, each
with the same style sheet applied
to them.

Create an Internal Style Sheet

Internal style sheets are set up much in the same way as external style sheets, with one important difference: As you make changes, your page is automatically updated to reflect them, so you get instant feedback to your work. To demonstrate this feedback, try the following after you create a new site:

1. Open the index.html page and click on the Open CSS Interface button in the upper right of the workspace window (it looks like stair steps). This button opens the index.html:Style Sheet window shown in Figure 5.36.

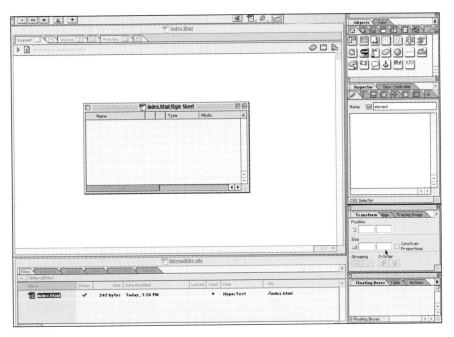

Figure 5.36
The internal style sheet
window associated with your
index.html page.

2. Add a new element to the style sheet by clicking on the New Element Selector. Once again, a tag element is placed in the Style Sheet window, but the folder associated with it is titled Internal, as you can see in Figure 5.37. This helps you remember what type of style sheet you are working on.

Figure 5.37

The element inside the Internal folder that has been created in your style sheet.

3. Rename the element Body. Now select the index.html page itself and type "GoLive 5 Web Design Wonderfulness" The tag element will look similar to the one shown in Figure 5.38.

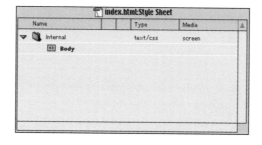

Figure 5.38

The renamed tag element.

4. Select the Body tag element in the Style Sheet window. In the CSS Selector Inspector window, choose the following parameters. As you make each change, you will see the text update immediately:

• Under Font, change the parameters to Color: Teal, Size: 50pt, Style: Oblique, Weight: 800.

• In the Text area, change Alignment to Center.

• Under Background, make the color Navy.

Pretty obnoxious looking, isn't it? Go ahead and change the Font color to Yellow.

The style you just created is linked to your index.html page so, when you save your page, all you're saving is the index.html.

Combining Internal and External Styles

You can combine both internal and external styles to your pages. One of the best examples for how this could work is to use the external style sheet to assign a background color or image and borders, and the internal style sheet to handle text size and format. Here's one possibility:

1. Create a new site. (I always like to have a fresh, unmodified page to experiment with.) From this book's companion CD-ROM, import the wavybkg.jpg file and place it into your media folder. Open the index.html page and then select File|New Special|Style Sheet Document to create an external style sheet file. Create a new element and call it Body.

2. Switch to the Background tab in the Inspector window and check the Image box. Use the point and shoot method to link to the wavybkg.jpg file (see Figure 5.39). The background image can now be used for any page you assign the .css file to. Save the style as background.css, making sure that you select the Root folder for the destination.

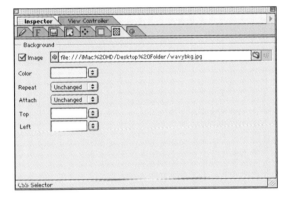

Figure 5.39
The expanded Inspector window, showing the path to the wavybkg.jpg image that will be used as a background on any page linked to the style sheet.

3. Click once on the index.html page in the Site window and link the page to the background.css file, using the method you learned earlier. Your page will now look like Figure 5.40.

4. Use the Open CSS Interface button to open an internal style sheet window. When you do this, the screen that appears has the external file already included. That's because your index.html page is linked to that style sheet, so it's viewable as part of the Style Sheet window.

5. Use the New Element Selector button to place a new tag in the style sheet. As you can see in Figure 5.41, this new tag is associated with an internal style sheet.

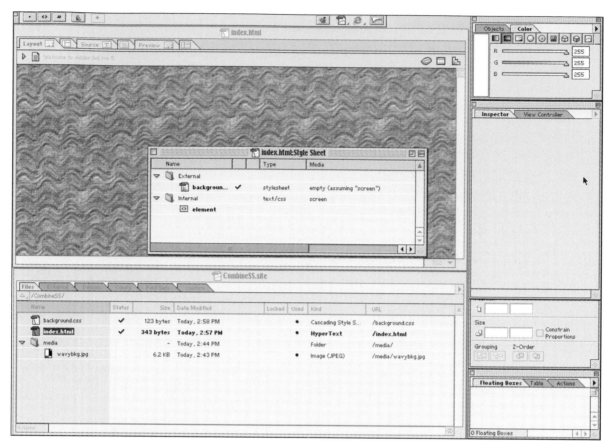

Figure 5.40

The wavybkg.jpg image as the background for the page you're creating.

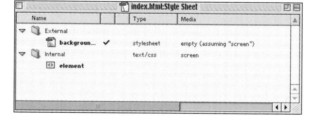

Figure 5.41

A new internal tag is added to the style sheet.

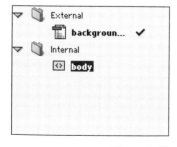

Figure 5.42

Any styles already assigned to your page will automatically be included in the Style Sheet window.

6. Name this element Body and then select the Font tab in the Inspector window. Change the parameters to the following:

- Color: Navy

- Size: 60pt

- Weight: 800

Switch to the Text tab and select Center in the Alignment pop-up (see Figure 5.42).

7. Type a headline. Figure 5.43 shows how your screen should look after you do this.

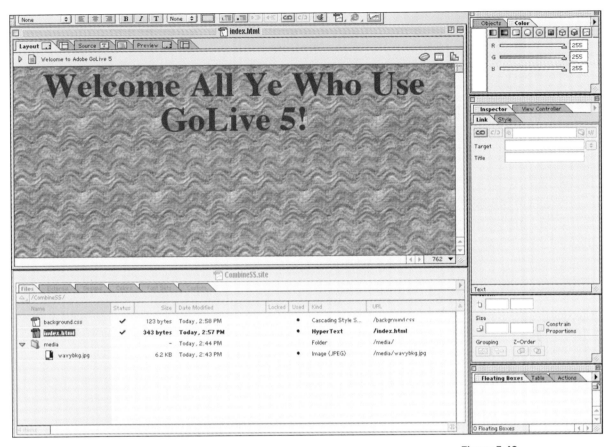

Figure 5.43
The finished page with a seam-less background assigned by way of an external style sheet and text size and position assigned by way of an internal style sheet.

You also can add class specifications to the internal or external style sheets that can be assigned to specific blocks of text or to singular letters. By clicking on the New Class Selector button with either an external or internal style sheet window open, you can, through the same methods outlined throughout the chapter, choose different text parameters and formats. Then, by selecting specific portions of the text on your page, you can assign those parameters. Additionally, depending on whether you are using and internal or external style sheet with the .class tag, those parameters will override others assigned to other style sheets.

PROJECT 5.1 Creating a Multipage Site Using CSS

In this project, you'll create a multipage site and incorporate style sheets to retain continuity between pages. These style sheets won't vary much from what you have done so far, but the process will, hopefully, give you a good idea of how creating a style sheet and utilizing it between different pages can really help speed up your creative process.

Build the Home Page

For this project, you will be using the whitebkg.jpg and GL5Alive.ai files from this book's companion CD-ROM. This background—as is the wavybkg.jpg

Figure 5.43
The finished page with a seam-less background assigned by way of an external style sheet and text size and position assigned by way of an internal style sheet.

image from the last section—are original backgrounds that you are free to use on any of your projects:

1. First, create a new site and call it GL5Alive. Also, create two new folders, pages and media, to store the appropriate files. These files include the two new pages you need to create (Page1.html and Page2.html), the whitebkg.jpg image, Look.ai, Links.ai, Reasons.ai, and GL5Alive.ai, the last four of which you will convert to GIF files using the Smart Illustrator tool.

2. Start with the index.html page. Create an external style sheet and place an element tag. Give this tag the name Body because, as mentioned earlier in the chapter, the element tag has to conform to standard head tag nomenclature, because it affects the entire page. (You also may have noticed that I frequently use Body as a tag name. I do this because it is extremely easy to get the style sheet to work when you are not an HTML programmer conversant in all the tag element names. When no other Body tags are inside a style sheet, I automatically use that name.)

3. Select the Background tab in the CSS Selector Inspector (I love that poetic play on words) window, select Image by clicking on the check box, and link to whitebkg.jpg. Now, select the Text tab and change the Alignment to Center. In the Font section, set it at 50 pixels Italic, and change the color to Blue. Save the file as pagebkg.css in your Root folder. Your Site window will now look like Figure 5.44, showing all the files at your disposal.

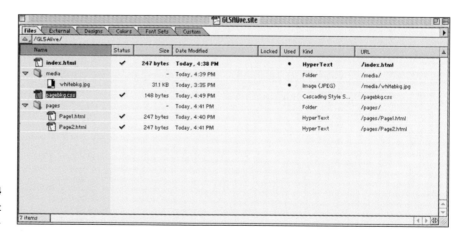

Figure 5.44
The Site window with the files that are included with your Web site.

4. Drag the pagebkg.css file onto the Page icon at the top of your index.html window. Again, this quickly creates a tag (shown in Figure 5.45) in the Head section of your page. You can also see this tag in the source code by selecting the Source tab in the index.html window (see Figure 5.46) to see how it fits within the code file.

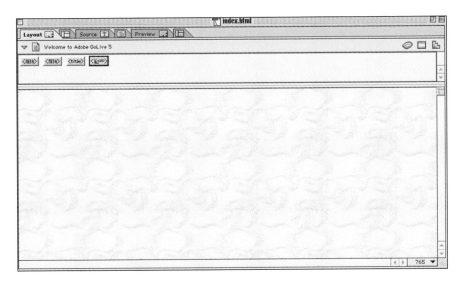

Figure 5.45
The tag element that has been placed into the Head section of your page.

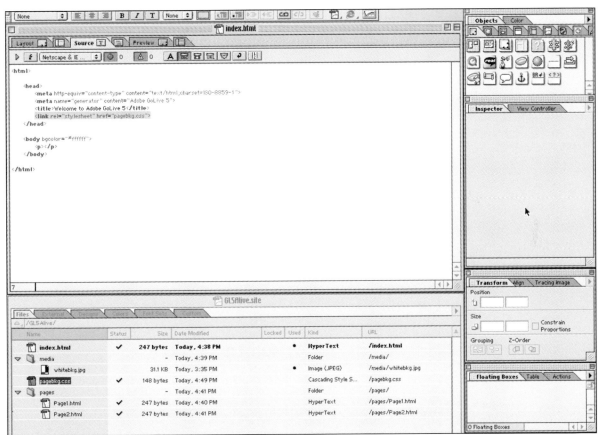

Figure 5.46
The tag element highlighted within the source code.

5. Returning now to Layout mode, place a Smart Illustrator placeholder onto the index.html page. Notice that because you assigned text to be aligned center, the placeholder also is aligned to the center of the screen (see Figure 5.47).

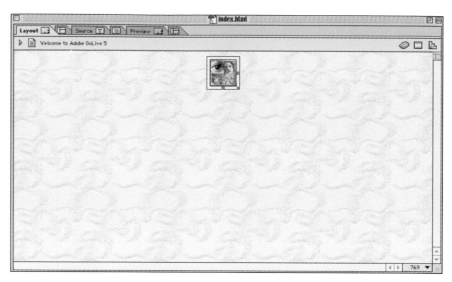

> **Note:** As a reminder, the Smart Illustrator feature works only with Illustrator 9. If you do not have this program, you can download a demo from **www.adobe.com/products/ tryaadobe/ main.html#illustrator.**

Figure 5.47
The Illustrator placeholder is automatically positioned flush center, affected by the style sheet parameters.

Figure 5.48
The logo needs to be in GIF format, so that a transparency can be assigned to the file. Select GIF from the list in the Conversion Settings window.

6. In the Image Inspector window, use the Source selector's Browse button to locate the GL5Alive.ai file. Choose GIF from the pop-up menu (see Figure 5.48) in the Conversion Settings window and click OK.

7. In the Save GIF window (see Figure 5.49), select GIF 128 Dither from the Settings pop-up so you have a clean logo. Click OK, and when you're asked to specify the target file, save it to the media folder you created.

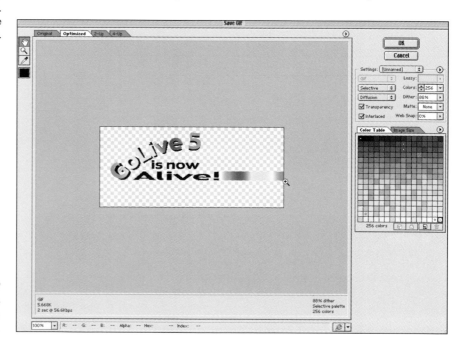

Figure 5.49
The Save GIF window. Use the settings you see here to save your file.

Assign the Style Sheet to Other Pages

You now have the index page set up. It's time to assign the pagebkg.css file to the other two pages you created. To do so, follow these steps:

1. Select Page1.html and Page2.html. In the File Inspector window, select the Styles tab and point and shoot to the pagebkg.css file in the Site window.

2. Click Add to assign the style sheet to those two pages. If you opened these two pages, they would have the same background and text set up as the index.html (or, as I'll call it from now on, the home page).

3. Repeat the steps in the previous section to create duplicate page layouts, so you have three identical pages.

Create Link Buttons and Add Text

Now you need to place the link buttons onto the page. These will be positioned on the left side of the screen. Being Illustrator 9 files, they will be converted to GIF images with a transparent background so the page background will show through:

1. Place a Table placeholder on the workspace. Set its parameters to the following:

   - Rows: 1
   - Columns: 3
   - Left Column Width: 139 pixels
   - Middle Column Width: 90 pixels
   - Right Column Width: 480 pixels
   - Vertical Alignment for all three columns: Top
   - Border: 0

2. Place three Smart Illustrator placeholders into the left cell of the table.

3. For the top placeholder, browse and convert the Look.ai file. The middle placeholder should be linked to Links.ai, and the bottom placeholder should house Reasons.ai. Your screen setup should look like the one shown in Figure 5.50. Make sure that you move the placeholders so they butt up against the bottom of the one above them.

4. Now it's time to add the text to the page. Remember, you already set up text parameters in the style sheet. Because the style is associated with the page itself, you don't want to put the text in a Text placeholder, but, rather, type it directly on the page itself. You can see the headline I wrote in Figure 5.51.

5. Inside the right cell of the table, type some introductory text. You will see this text in the same format as the headline text, but when it appears in your browser, it will not be seen with those parameters. Change the text setup to Bold, Center, Size: +3, and Color: Black. Figure 5.52 shows how this affects the cell text.

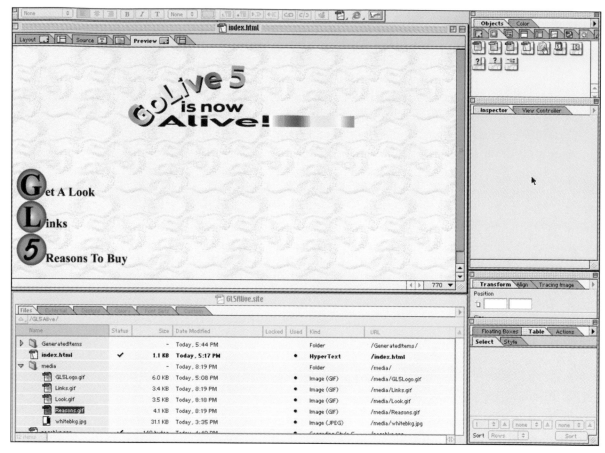

Figure 5.50
The button images converted and in position.

Figure 5.51
The headline I created for the page, reflecting the text parameters set in the style sheet associated with the page.

6. Create the following links for the image buttons in the left cell:

   - Look.gif to Page1.html

   - Reasons.gif to Page2.html

   The Links button doesn't have a page to link to right now. Feel free to create one if you like. Also, remember that you have assigned the pagebkg.css file to Page1 and Page2, so your background and font style will be the same as on this home page.

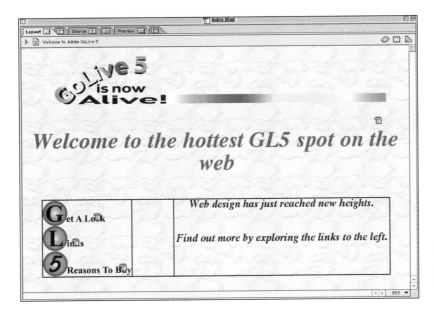

Figure 5.52
After changing the text parameters, this is how it will look in the
right cell of the Table placeholder.

When you build these next two pages, you can use the same techniques and ideas as outlined in the preceding steps, with the GL5Logo.gif file at the top, an appropriate headline beneath that, and a table element to lay out the rest of your page. On these subsequent pages, however, the Gl5Logo.gif can be placed into a standard Image placeholder, or you can use the Smart Illustrator tool to link directly to the .gif file. If you do the latter, any changes you might make later on to the GL5Logo.gif file will automatically be updated for all the pages where it exists. Figure 5.53 shows the completed site as you would see it in Internet Explorer.

Figure 5.53
The GoLive 5 Is Alive site, as seen
in Internet Explorer via the Show
In Browser function.

Moving On

As you learned in this chapter (although you worked with fairly simple style-sheet designs), the power and speed with which you can create a Web site that retains duplicate design elements, such as backgrounds and text styles, can really save a lot of time when you build Web pages.

In Chapter 15, you delve deeper into the use of CSS technology as you follow along with me to create an entire Web site, some pages of which will incorporate style sheets.

Chapter 6

Bringing Your Site to Life

With the help of programs such as Adobe LiveMotion, Macromedia Flash, QuickTime Pro, and RealProducer, you can add depth to your site. This chapter introduces you to these programs, as well as other production tools, and demonstrates the various creative ways you can utilize them in your designs.

It's Alive

Just like Baron Von Frankenstein (or is that Frahnkenschteen?), you probably get an indescribable thrill from seeing animations and videos that truly seem to live on the Web page. They load quickly and are wonderful pieces of eye candy that make your visitors want to delve into the furthest depths of your site. You probably all remember that first Web site you put together—you know the one—it probably had a logo you created, a few generic clip-art graphics that (as closely as possible) conveyed what was featured on your site, and line after line of text describing your thoughts on everything from family to world politics. Additionally, you hoped and prayed that the page actually showed up in the visitor's Web browser in a way that remotely resembled your vision, designs, and intentions.

These days, static pages filled with text are as verboten as driving 100 miles an hour through a residential neighborhood. Catching and holding the attention of your audience is becoming as difficult as taking a stroll from Great Britain to Canada. Now you need motion, interactivity, sound, dazzling effects, and eye-popping visuals. You need them to load fast and give instant feedback. Thankfully, a number of programs are available that are designed to help you do just that. And with the latest in Web programming, XML, and Scalable Vector Graphics (SVG)—the latter of which is featured heavily in Illustrator 9—it soon will make no difference how complicated your designs are, because they will remain small enough that even the slowest connections won't matter. Also, Adobe-backed updates to MetaStream (**www.metastream.com**), and Zap from Template Graphics Software (TGS) at **www.tgs.com** both create viewer-interactive images that can be rotated, zoomed in on, and even modified in realtime. It's an amazing time of change in the e-world.

Before you head into this chapter, one small caveat: You can have every hot program on the market in your design arsenal, but it doesn't mean that you must use all of them all the time. Be selective; make sure that your effects and animations truly convey your message without getting lost in a conglomeration of video sludge. Save some of your digital toys for other pages in your site; in this way, you can keep surprising your audience as they discover who you really are.

Choices, Choices

Shockwave files are, by far, the standard to create quick-loading animations to your Web site. The relatively small file size and the huge installed user base for the plug-ins make this format an extremely attractive choice. Up until a few months ago, if you wanted to create this type of file, you had only one program from which to choose: Macromedia Flash. This has changed. Now, a handful of programs enable you to create high quality Shockwave files. Each program allows you to not only create vector-only animations, but also to incorporate video and bitmapped images to build full multimedia for the Web. So, before incorporating them into your Web site, let's look at your choices for producing Shockwave files by company.

Note: Demo versions of all the programs discussed in this section are available on this book's companion CD-ROM or from the respective company's sites.

Macromedia

Your personal way of working will always determine which program to use if more than one competitive application is on the market. In the world of Web animations, however, Macromedia Flash has been around for the longest time. This venerable program, shown in Figure 6.1, started it all. And it's still the program that most Shockwave designers are using. To learn more about the program, you can visit **www.macromedia.com/software/flash/**. As of this writing, reportedly 195 million Flash Player users are surfing the Internet. If your browser doesn't have the Flash Player plug-in, it's available as a multiplatform free download at the preceding URL.

Figure 6.1
The program that started it all, Macromedia's Flash, now in version 5.

Another program from Macromedia is Fireworks, seen in Figure 6.2, introduced a few years ago. At its most basic, Fireworks (now in version 3) is to Shockwave animation as ImageReady is to bitmap graphic optimization. This means that in some ways, Fireworks can be viewed as somewhat redundant to Flash, but it offers features that really speed up your workflow. It also works seamlessly in conjunction with Flash (as ImageReady does with Photoshop), making the two programs virtually indispensable. Visit **www.macromedia.com/software/fireworks/** for more information.

Figure 6.2
Macromedia Fireworks, another strong Shockwave production tool.

Director has long been the choice for creating interactive CD-ROMs and presentations, but with Director 8 (D8) Shockwave Studio seen in Figure 6.3, it's becoming the Lamborghini of multimedia design. I say "the Lamborghini" because its initial price may seem daunting, but if you're looking for a program that will do what you need for Web animations, plus have uses beyond the Internet, this is about the only sensible choice out there. D8 Shockwave Studio comes packaged with Director and Fireworks 3. For more information on Director 8 Shockwave Studio, go to **www.macromedia.com/software/director/**.

Figure 6.3
Director 8 Shockwave Studio is the high-end choice for not only Shockwave production, but also for interactive presentations for CD-ROM, DVD, and more.

Adobe

Adobe's LiveMotion, seen in Figure 6.4, released in June 2000, is the new kid on the block. It's a powerful program that fully integrates with the other Adobe production tools, such as Photoshop and Illustrator. Its strong suit for many people is its very familiar user interface, because it follows the GUI structure of Adobe's other products. It will also be the program I'll work with the most throughout this chapter because of GoLive 5's Smart LiveMotion tool. To get more information on LiveMotion, visit **www.adobe.com/products/livemotion/main.html**.

Prepare To Be Shocked

Later in this chapter, you'll explore the video production tools available to help you create quickly accessible multimedia on your site. But for now, you'll begin creating a Shockwave splash screen for your site. Again, this chapter deals with the basics of Shockwave presentations. Myriad great books on the market deal specifically with each program just mentioned. Check the Coriolis Web site (**www.coriolis.com**) for the latest titles.

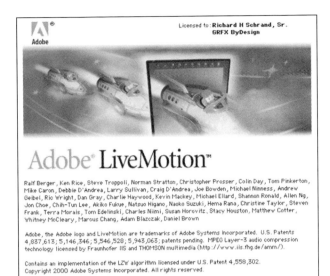

Figure 6.4
LiveMotion is the newest production tool for creating Shockwave animations.

Creating a Multimedia Welcome Screen

I'm sure that you all want to start working on the projects by now. Well, your wish is my command, dear reader. In this first section, you'll use LiveMotion to create a Shockwave animation. You'll need either your own files to work with, or if you want to use the ones shown here, you can copy the LiveMotion folder (located in the Ch06 folder on this book's companion CD-ROM) to your desktop. If you don't have the program already, download the LiveMotion demo from Adobe's Web site.

PROJECT 6.1 Build a LiveMotion Animation

First, you need to create your base animation. Figure 6.5 shows a frame from the animation I created that you'll be placing in GoLive. If you use Macromedia Flash, you can use the files provided to create the same animation.

Prepare the Document

You'll start this project by preparing the document. To do so, take the following steps:

1. Select File|New (Cmd/Ctl+N) and create a screen that is 640×480 pixels. Deselect Make HTML, and make sure the Frame Rate is set at 15fps—a good speed for smooth motion over 33.6Kbps and 56Kbps modems. Figure 6.6 shows how your setup screen should look.

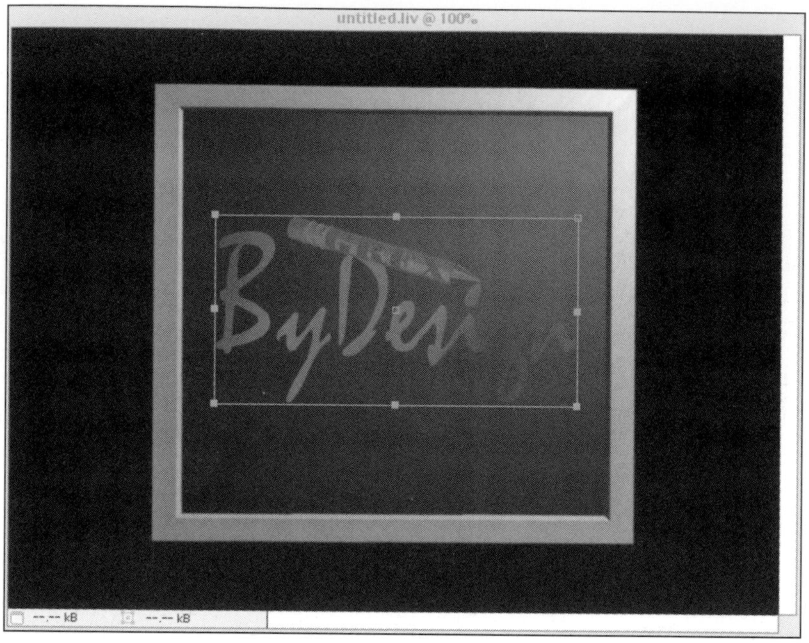

Figure 6.5
A frame from the LiveMotion animation you're about to create.

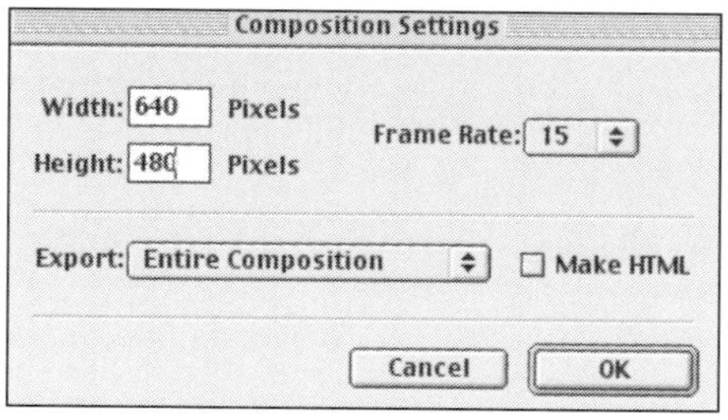

Figure 6.6
Setting up a new project in LiveMotion.

Note: The various palettes under the Windows pull-down are listed in their initial groupings. You can modify the groupings by tearing a tabbed menu and placing it in another window or an entirely new grouping.

2. After clicking the OK button, make sure the following screens are open:
   - The TimeLine window (TimeLine|Show TimeLine Window or Cmd/Ctl+T)
   - The Color, Properties, Object Layer, and Layer group windows (found under the Window pull-down menu)
3. In the Color palette, select black; using the Paint Bucket tool, fill the screen with black, as is shown in Figure 6.7.
4. Import the ByDesign.ai file (File|Place or Cmd/Ctl+I) from this book's companion CD-ROM and position it close to the center of the screen. The placed file is automatically added to the TimeLine. Set the time of the animation to 10 seconds by dragging the right side of the ByDesign layer's bar to 10s, as Figure 6.8 shows. Leave the Time Scrubber control (the downward pointing triangle at the top of the TimeLine screen) at 00s.

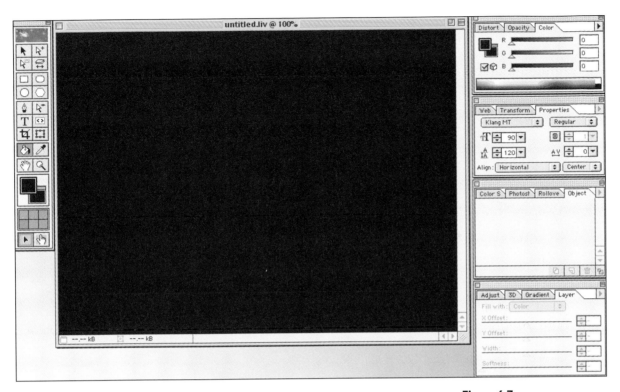

Figure 6.7
The base look for the animation.

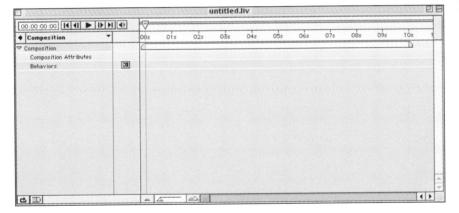

Figure 6.8
Setting the initial animation
length to 10 seconds.

5. Place the following files on the TimeLine in this order:

    - CenterFrame.jpg

    - PaintDrop.ai

    - GRFXPencil.ai

    - OpenAudio.aif (or .wav if you're using a PC)

    Because the audio file is just under 27 seconds, drag the Composition
    time bar out to match with the ending of the OpenAudio file. Press the
    spacebar to hear the audio. The screen should now look like Figure 6.9.

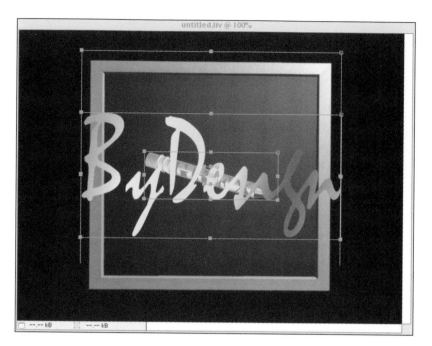

Figure 6.9
The elements are in place. Now they just need to be resized to fit in the frame.

6. Select each layer and change its dimensions by dragging on any of the solid control points (upper- and lower-left and lower-right) so that the elements fit into the frame. Retain their ratios by holding the Shift key while resizing. Figure 6.10 shows the final positions for each of the layers.

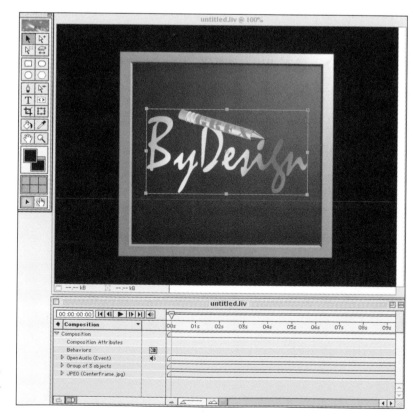

Figure 6.10
The final positions for the elements.

7. Select the ByDesign.ai, PaintDrop.ai, and the GRFXPencil.ai files by holding down the Shift key and clicking on the elements in the workspace or on their names in the TimeLine. Choose Object|Group or (Cmd/Ctl+G) to group them together. This new group is now listed in the TimeLine as Group of 3 objects, seen in Figure 6.11. By clicking on the arrow to the left of this, you expand the file to see the individual elements and their controls, seen in Figure 6.12.

8. Select the GRFXPencil.ai layer, expand the Transform controls associated with this layer, and click on the stopwatch icon next to Object Opacity. Bring the Opacity window to the front by clicking on its tab next to the Color palette tab, and set the Object Opacity to 0. Figure 6.13 shows the screen prior to changing the opacity of this layer. Next, perform the same process to the ByDesign.ai layer and the PaintDrop.ai layer, so that the only information seen on the workspace is the CenterFrame.jpg file.

Figure 6.11
Grouping layers results in a layer called Group of 3 objects. You can rename this (as with all layers) to help you manage your files.

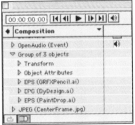

Figure 6.12
After layers are grouped, click on the expander arrow to see each one listed, so you can modify each element separately.

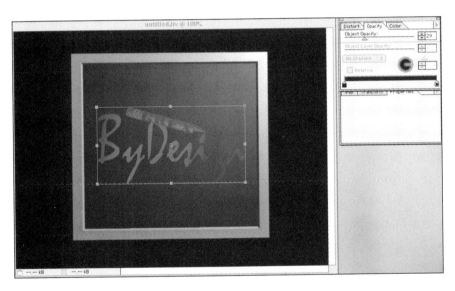

Figure 6.13
For the beginning portion of the animation, the logo and pencil will be transparent. Here is the pencil portion of the logo prior to having its opacity set to 0.

9. Select the CenterFrame.jpg layer, and move it as close to the edge as you can while holding down the Shift key to constrain the movement. Then, using the up arrow on your keyboard, move it totally off screen.

10. Move the Time Indicator to 10s (10 seconds), and expand the CenterFrame.jpg and the Transform Options. Click Position. A keyframe is created at the 10s mark as seen in Figure 6.14. Now, move the TimeLine indicator to 15s. Move the frame back to the center of the screen by using the down arrow on the keyboard. Now, you can press the Home button on your keyboard or slide the TimeLine indicator back to 00s, press the spacebar, and watch your screen move into place.

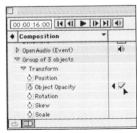

Figure 6.14
When you click in this box, a checkmark appears, letting you know that a new keyframe has been set.

11. At 16s, open the Group of 3 Objects|GRFXPencil.ai|and ByDesign.ai|
     Transform, as well as the PaintDrop.ai|Transform layer. In any of
     these, select Object Opacity by clicking on the stopwatch icon. If this
     is the first time you are setting a keyframe, this will cause one to auto-
     matically be created. If you have other keyframes in the same effects
     area (such as Opacity) already, click on the box to the right of that
     effect to set a new one, as seen in Figure 6.14. Place the TimeLine
     indicator at 16s/6f (16-seconds/6 frames)—or you can refer to the time
     readout in the upper-left corner and move the TimeLine Indicator to
     00:00:16:06, click the checkmark boxes again to set a new keyframe,
     and change the Opacity setting to 100. Repeat this procedure for the
     PaintDrop.ai file, too.

You've now created an animation where the frame slides onto the screen and
the logo quickly dissolves. This is one animation layer for the home page you're
creating. Save your file as Ch06Splash.liv; you'll be using it later in this chapter.

Create Basic Rollovers

You can set up both basic and advanced rollovers directly within GoLive. The
method of doing this has changed a bit; what used to be called the Button
Image placeholder is now the *Rollover placeholder* and it's located under Smart
Tools in the Objects window, as shown in Figure 6.15.

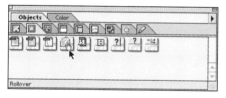

Figure 6.15
The Rollover placeholder is now
located under Smart Tools in the
Objects window.

In this section, you'll build a basic rollover. (Advanced rollover creation is ex-
plained in Chapter 8.) All the files for this section are contained on the
companion CD-ROM as GIF files. These files are:

- BaseButton.gif

- 3D.gif

- Books.gif

- Home.gif

- Links.gif

Using techniques you worked with in Chapter 3, you'll now build your page:

1. Create a new site, as well as a media folder to store the GIFs in.

2. Open index.html, rename it if you wish, and then drag a Table place-
    holder onto the window. The initial settings you need are shown in
    Figure 6.16.

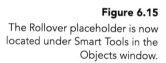

Figure 6.16
The table set up for the
rollover buttons.

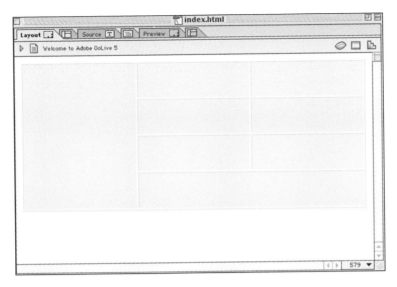

Figure 6.17
How your table should look following the combining of cells.

3. Using the technique you learned in Chapter 3, combine the cells of the left-most column. After that, combine the bottom-center and bottom-right cells. Your table should now look like the one in Figure 6.17. I colorized the cells so you could see them better in this image.

4. The GIF buttons provided are 1″ by 1″ (or 72 pixels wide and high). Modify the width of the left cell to reflect this size by selecting Pixel in the Width control and typing in "72". Refer to Figure 6.18. You don't have to worry about the height, because the Image placeholders you're about to place will automatically be sized to the image.

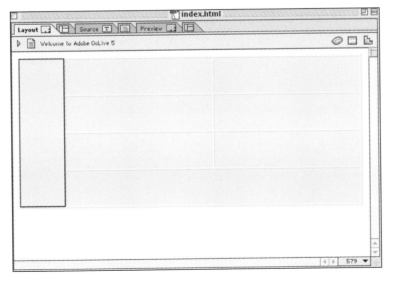

Figure 6.18
The left cell should be the width of the images you're using, in this case, 72 pixels wide.

5. Drag four Rollover placeholders into the vertical column you created, then create links to the BaseButton.gif for each of them. BaseButton.gif is the original image visitors to your site will see. You'll be setting up each of these image elements as rollovers; when the visitor places the cursor over a particular button, it will change to show which area they'll be transported to.

6. You should set the Table Border to 0, so no visible dividers are in your final page. Once you have this set up, your workspace will look like the one in Figure 6.19. If you select Preview, you'll see no visible border between the cells, just like in Figure 6.20.

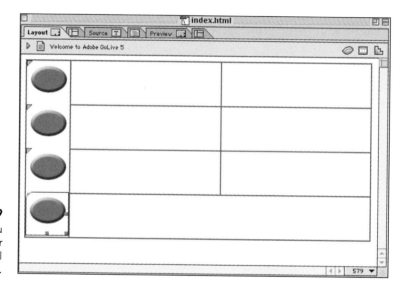

Figure 6.19
While in Layout mode, if you have selected a width of 0 for the borders, your screen will look like this.

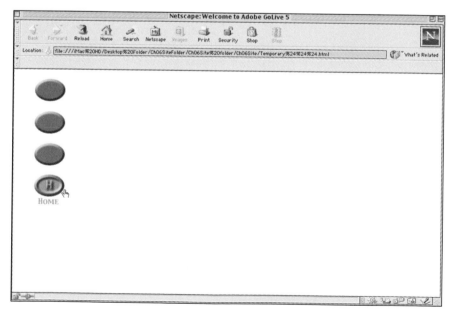

Figure 6.20
In Preview mode, you'll see how the page will look when it's on the Web.

7. Select Layout *again*, and the topmost Image placeholder. In the Rollover Inspector, rename each of the buttons (if you haven't already) in this order:

    *   3Dlink

    *   BooksLink

    *   Links

    *   HomeLink

8. With the 3DLink image chosen, select Over in the Inspector window and link to 3D.gif. Repeat this process for each of the other rollovers. When you select Preview, you will be able to run your cursor over the buttons and have them change to reveal what they link to, as shown in Figure 6.21.

Figure 6.21
A look at the results of the rollovers just created.

Adding Video to Your Site

Video production on the computer is H-O-T these days. It's propelled the iMac into one of the hottest computers on the market. But it has been problematic, to say the least. A high quality video can take up tons of space on your server—not to mention your hard drive—and it historically takes an inordinate amount of time to load. Those with slower modems and the patience of Job have enjoyed some rich experiences, but after a while, even those people tend to avoid unnecessary waits like the plague. Streaming video has helped this greatly. And with products like Media Cleaner Pro (**www.terran.com**), the size of video files can be reduced dramatically with little to no loss of quality.

It's been said that each of us has a story to tell. Thanks to the new video revolution, we're going to see more and more of these stories being produced. Digital cameras are coming down in price. The latest computers come equipped with RCA inputs (the kind that accept those common red, white, and yellow audio/video cables used with every VCR on the market), or SVHS video cables.

If you have an older Macintosh computer, companies such as Global Village produce a wonderful video input device called *VideoFX*, which connects directly to a USB port (see Figure 6.22).

XLR8, a subsidiary of Tripp Lite, produces the InterView (**www.xlr8.com**), seen in Figure 6.23, which (again through the USB port) lets you record video and stereo audio at a much lower cost than buying a video card.

Basically, two powerhouses exist now that can provide you with streaming movie files, and both are extremely popular: QuickTime and RealVideo. Both of these provide you with editing capabilities, and the means to set your files up to be streamed; the former has QuickTime Pro (**www.apple.com/quicktime/**) and the latter, RealProducer (**www.real.com/**). Both are low-cost, standalone applications (under $150) that provide you the means to create video presentations

Figure 6.22
One way to import video to your older computer is with the VideoFX unit. This is made expressly for the Macintosh computer. To learn more about this product, visit the Global Village Web site at **www.globalvillage.com/ products/videofx-info.html**.

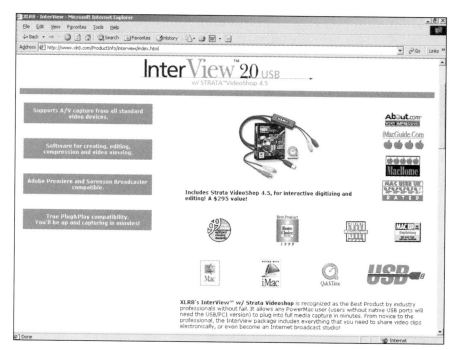

Figure 6.23
Another low-cost but high-quality alternative to a video card is XLR8's InterView dongle, which imports both video and stereo audio.

for the Web. Also, their free viewers have put them in virtually every Web surfer's hands over the past years.

Because video production is so popular these days, it's not surprising that GoLive 5 has its own online video editing. Using the QuickTime format, you can bring your own pre-produced QuickTime files in, or feed raw video and audio into the QuickTime Editor and produce your movies without leaving GoLive. We'll take a look at that now.

The QuickTime Editor

In a way, the QuickTime Editor is its own standalone entity. It's not accessible through the Objects window. All those QuickTime editing icons you see under the QuickTime tab work only with the editor itself, and not by dragging them onto the workspace. Now, take a few minutes to look at accessing the QuickTime Editor and to learn where the tools you can use are located.

1. To access the QuickTime Editor, choose File|New Special|QuickTime Movie. The screen seen in Figure 6.24 appears, asking you to set the parameters for the file you're about to create. Leave these settings as is and click OK.

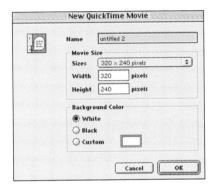

Figure 6.24
The QuickTime Editor is accessed via the File menu.

2. Notice the following changes in GoLive. The toolbar at the top of the screen has changed, as shown in Figure 6.25. These new tools are (from left to right):

   • Show Movie Window (which should be grayed out right now, because a movie window is open already)

   • Show TimeLine Window (go ahead and activate this now)

   • Export Movie

   • Export Track (audio)

   • Make Movie Streamable (mucho importante)

   • Position/Resize Track

   • Skew Track

   • Rotate Track

   • Lock Track

   • Unlock Track

   • Bring To Front

   • Send To Back

The Inspector window (shown in Figure 6.26) has also changed, allowing you control over various aspect of the video, and to give you information about the video you're creating. Under the Annotation tab, you can place any of the credits for the video.

Figure 6.25
The tools you need to create and save your QT files are located above the workspace in the toolbar.

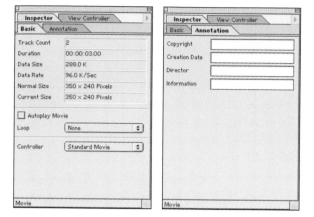

Figure 6.26
The newly redesigned QuickTime Inspector window.

3. The TimeLine window has all the tools you'll need to create videos. Here you control the length, types of edits, even create viewer interactive elements. Figure 6.27 shows the basic setup of the TimeLine window, which follows the standard Adobe format. If you're familiar with programs, such as Adobe Premiere or AfterEffects, you're going to feel right at home here.

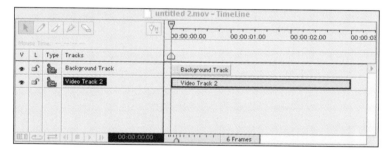

Figure 6.27
The QuickTime Editor's TimeLine window.

Create a QuickTime Video

Next, you'll create a small banner for the bottom of your open screen; an out-of-this-world recommendation for the services the company provides. Use the QT file Alien.mov on the companion CD-ROM for this example:

1. In the setup window, use the pop-up list to select Other, and change the Width/Height parameters to 350×150 (the dimensions of the Alien.mov file). Make the background black by selecting it from the list.

2. Open the TimeLine window and drag a Video Track placeholder onto the TimeLine. It will appear below the Background Track. This window displays the various layers of your movie in a descending order, so the Background will remain in the top position, with all subsequent layers

placed beneath it. When you move the Video Track placeholder onto the TimeLine, it will automatically ask for your movie file. If one doesn't exist, the Track won't be placed. Navigate to your file to select it. The MOV file will be displayed in the workspace, as seen in Figure 6.28.

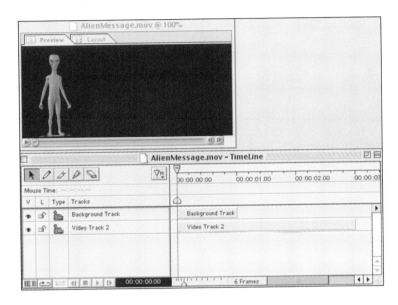

Figure 6.28
Our friendly spokes-alien video ready for editing.

3. Click once on the Video Track bar in the TimeLine area to highlight the layer and bring up the Track Inspector window seen in Figure 6.29. Here you can assign a name to the file, modify the timing, and set its appearance. (Refer to the user manual for detailed information on the various Mode settings.) Go ahead and change the name of the file to something more descriptive.

4. Our alien friend is mute. In fact, his entire race is telepathic and has no vocal chords. So, you need to create some text that will display that paraphrases the glowing praise for your work. Select the Text Track and drag it to the TimeLine window. Open the track's layer by clicking on the pointer to the immediate left (see Figure 6.30) so you can place the text. You might also want to give the Text Track a more descriptive name by typing it into the text field in the Inspector window.

5. Select Create Sample in order to add text to your file. You'll find this in the upper-left corner of the TimeLine window—the one with the pencil icon. Select it and then, starting at the 1-second mark, create a track in the Samples layer of the expanded Text Track. Figure 6.31 shows the appearance of the TimeLine and Inspector windows once you have created this track.

Figure 6.29
GoLive's Video Track Inspector window is filled with powerful controls to help you create exciting QT videos.

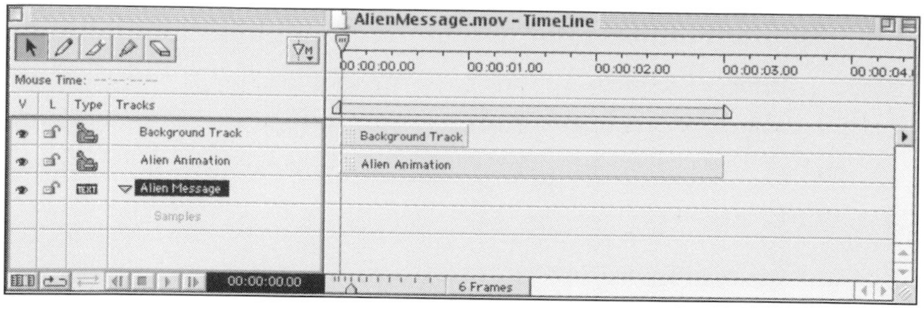

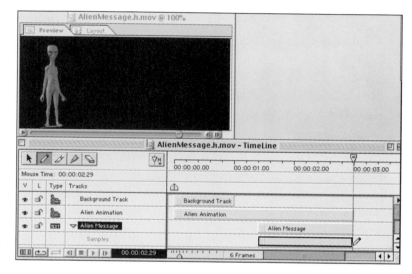

Figure 6.30
You need to expand the Text Track in order to add text and text effects to your movie.

Figure 6.31
Create Sample is used (in this instance) to assign an area where the text will appear.

6. Type your message in the window and work through the various palettes to set the properties (color, display style, scrolling, and so on), and the layout, where you definitely want to select Anti Alias to give smooth text. If you'd like, you can assign a mouse action, making the text a link to another page in the site or to another site altogether. Do this in the same way that you would create any link.

7. Now that you're finished, select Make Movie Streamable from the toolbar at the top of the screen and save it to your media folder within your site folder. Now it's ready to be placed on the home page.

Note: You need to create a new site, and you need to use either the files you created during this chapter or the ones from this book's companion CD-ROM.

PROJECT 6.2 Splish Splash

You've created a number of elements for your splash screen. Now it's time to bring them all together into one cohesive presentation. In this section, you'll combine not only what you have produced in this chapter, but draw upon other techniques you've learned in previous chapters. You might consider this a mid-term. Then again, you might not—especially if you hated school.

Here's how to create the presentation:

1. Once you have your site folders set up, and all the elements are in the appropriate site folder, double-click on the index.html icon to open the index page. Drag a Table placeholder onto the workspace and set it up in the following manner:

   - Rows: 4

   - Width: 576

   - Height: 250

2. Modify the table cells so that your elements will fit the overall design of the page:

   - Select the top three cells in the left column and merge them. Change the width of this column to 72 pixels. Set the Vertical Alignment to Top and the Horizontal Alignment to Center.

   - Select the three cells on the bottom row and merge them. Again, set the Vertical Alignment to Top and the Horizontal Alignment to Center. Change this new cell's background to black.

   - Select the six remaining cells (middle and right columns) and merge them. Your table will look like Figure 6.32.

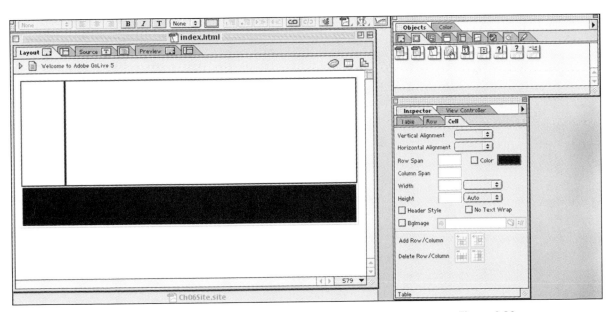

Figure 6.32
The modified table ready for specific content to be added.

3. Place your first Rollover placeholder into the left column and link it to the BaseButton.gif image. Repeat this process three more times until you have four BaseButton images in the column. As long as you have left the Height field set to Auto, the Table will resize to fit the buttons.

Now, add their rollover states in this order:

- 3D.gif

- Books.gif

- Links.gif

- Home.gif

4. Now, drag a QuickTime placeholder from the Basic placeholder set into the lower horizontal cell. Make a link to Alien.mov. Your page should now look like Figure 6.33.

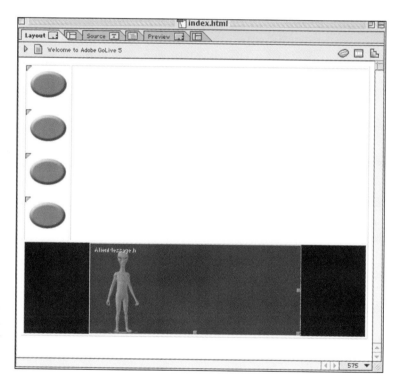

Figure 6.33
A look at the site design at the 3/4 mark. You need to add only one more element to finish the basic layout.

5. Drag an SWF Placeholder (it's the one that looks like a puzzle piece with a lightning bolt crossing over it) into the large cell group. Link this to Ch05Splash.swf file. As long as you set Auto for the dimensions of this cell group, it will expand to the SWF file's size.

You now have the basic setup for the page. Use the Show in Browser command to see how your page looks within your browser. Again, it's a good idea to have all the major browsers installed in your system so you can make sure your efforts will be displayed correctly in each. It might take up a little more room on your hard drive, but if you have room to spare, it's best to do this.

Add More Elements

A number of *dead spots* are in the SWF file—areas that have nothing going on. These are perfect spots to place some additional text information that flies across the screen. You'll do this with *Floating Boxes*:

1. Place the first Floating Box (FB) over the SWF placeholder. Click once inside the FB and type in some sort of descriptive term. Position the box at the top of the workspace directly above the left side of the SWF frame. Refer to Figure 6.34 for positioning.

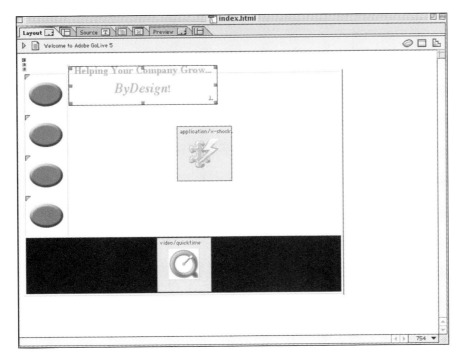

Figure 6.34
The starting position for the first Floating Box.

2. Add another Floating Box and type in another word or phrase. Place this one to the right side of the workspace aligned with the bottom of the SWF cell.

3. Now, add one last Floating Box and repeat the previous process, placing this one in the upper-right corner of the workspace.

4. Select the TimeLine Editor. Because your SWF animation is 16 seconds in length, with the frame dropping in at 8 seconds, extend the length (seen in Figure 6.35) to 8 seconds for each Floating Box element. Now, for fear of upsetting you, save your file.

5. Create the following animations (what I'll call a *fly-through* from here on):

   • Move the leftmost Floating Box straight down (hold the Shift key while moving it to constrain the movement), so that at 2 seconds it's positioned near the center left of the frame. Move it from this point off to the right of the workspace, so it disappears at approximately 4 seconds.

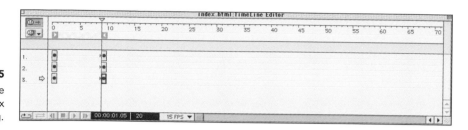

Figure 6.35
The TimeLine reflecting the change in the Floating Box animation timing.

- Start the upper-right fly-through at 2 seconds and move it close to the center of the SWF cell. Have it fly off to approximately the position where the first Floating Box started. It should be off screen at 6 seconds.

- The final Floating Box (the one positioned off the right of the workspace) should fly in at 4 seconds, move into position so its right edge is against the right edge of the SWF cell (as seen in Figure 6.36), and then move straight up the right side until it disappears from the screen at 8 seconds.

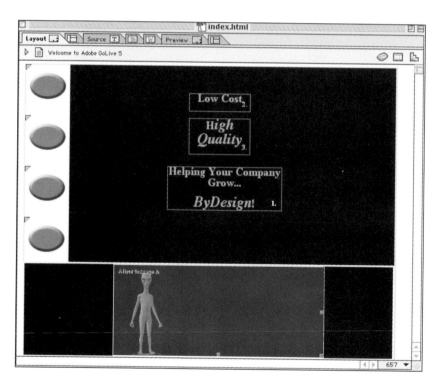

Figure 6.36
The final positions for the three Floating Box animations. A finished animation for you to look over is provided on this book's companion CD-ROM.

That's it. You now have an open splash screen that is a bit different than many you see on the Web. You can use the table as a template for the rest of your site if you'd like, leaving the rollover buttons in a set location, while changing the content of the large cell group. You can set up the bottom area to contain different banner messages or sponsor links. You can also use it to display special messages or, if you are creating a Business to Business (B2B) site, you can place special discounts or important product information inside.

Moving On

As you can see, employing numerous objects within your designs can provide you with highly stylized site designs that will set you apart from other Web designers. A little forethought and planning can go a long way. Plus, it ultimately keeps you sharp and fresh as you work out new and exciting ways to display your message(s).

What you accomplished here was just an overview, a tease as it were, for what can be done in GoLive, especially with the QuickTime Editor. In Chapter 7, I'll take you on a tour of all those wonderful QuickTime tools to help you get a better understanding of how you can create intricate, yet quickly loading, QT movies.

Chapter 7

Using the QuickTime Editor

GoLive's on-board QuickTime editor has been upgraded substantially, offering numerous production elements that will help you make great streamable videos for your site.

Production Notes

It has been said that artists work from a deep-seated need to excise internal demons. These demons can be the pressure you feel when you know you absolutely, positively have to do something, or else you're simply going to burst. Whatever the cause or the driving force behind the creative personality, if you've got it, you know you absolutely have to use it. In my case, this overpowering need to create was assuaged over the past almost-30 years in the broadcasting industry. Now, my creative releases are writing books like the one you now have in your hand, or finding new and intriguing ways to incorporate video, audio, and 3D imagery into—well, into something.

Suffice it to say, this chapter is probably going to excise some of my demons and provide you with laughs galore. It is definitely going to be a study in embarrassment for me because of the elements that will be used throughout. I will be using a very old video clip of myself looking like a fool while playing a game of 3-on-2 basketball against members of the Harlem Globetrotters. Of course, it was an extremely fair game, with three of the Globetrotters going against the interviewer and me. And I was the one faced with trying to defend against a 7'1" giant, as you can see in Figure 7.1. This piece aired on the ABC television affiliate in Cincinnati, Ohio, way back around 1975 when I was 17.

Figure 7.1
A still from the video you'll be using in this chapter, circa 1975.

So, with that out of the way, look at what you have. In the Chapter 7 folder of the companion CD-ROM is a raw QuickTime (QT) file titled "TallTale" in both StuffIt and Zip versions. Use this one if for no other reason than to laugh yourself silly. Or, if it becomes too much for you to take, use any old QuickTime file you might have lying around. But be forewarned, the screen captures in this chapter could well send you into spastic fits of hilarity and make you wonder if the author of this book has any sense of pride left in him.

Pre-Production

First, take a moment to go over these basics of video production.

Whenever you begin to build any type of video, whether it's used as streaming media on the Web or as a part of a resume reel, you probably do some pre-production work to help expedite your workflow. Figure 7.2 shows a raw example of a storyboard and a cut sheet. Many of you probably know what the storyboard is used for: You graphically map out the different shots you want so you know what you need to shoot or create for your video. The cut-sheet logs the footage you shoot so you know where on the tape your video is, its length, and so forth. These are indispensable tools you should always have nearby if you plan on producing any type of QT media.

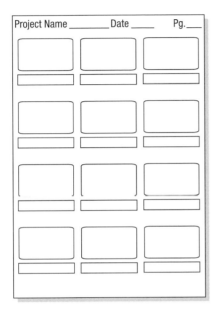

Figure 7.2

Samples of storyboard and cut-sheet designs.

Also, remember that QuickTime files that contain video and audio can become very large very quickly. It's not uncommon for a raw QT movie file to be hundreds of megabytes in size. So you'll need to have plenty of memory and storage space to hold the raw video and audio elements. We have arranged with Crucial Technology for a discount on memory upgrades to help with the latter; you'll find information on this on the companion CD-ROM in the memory discount folder inside the demos folder.

Note: A superb book that goes over these pre-production tools and more is Doug Kelly's *Character Animation In Depth* published by The Coriolis Group's Creative Professionals Press.

Finally, you also have to be aware of copyright laws and the use of non-original pre-recorded material if you plan on using a cut from your favorite album as background music. A good starting point to become familiar with the national and international copyright laws is **www.copyrightlaws.com/**, which deals with the new digital property regulations.

So, with all that in mind, it's time to start working with GoLive's QuickTime editor. If you have experience with creating QuickTime movies in prior editions of GoLive or CyberStudio, you're going to find a lot of new features in version 5. These include the following:

- New Objects to add functionality to your movies

- An expanded Movie menu

- A toolbar that adds even more functionality to the Movie menu

- Multiple undos

- Preview and Layout tabs incorporated directly into the Movie Viewer window.

- A redesigned TimeLine window (formerly known as the Track Editor)

- An extended track and Sample track editor

- More tracks to choose from and incorporate into your file

- The ability to import layered Photoshop files

> **Note:** A special note here: The PC and Macintosh versions of GoLive differ in the Track Options. QuickTime does not support MPEG video in the Windows version, so that particular tool is not available in the PC version of the program.

Video Production—The Setup

It's now time to quit discussing and start doing. If you are going to use my embarrassing TallTale video, copy it onto your hard drive now. If you're using a video of your own, make sure it's easily accessible. Again, what I'll be describing from here on pertains to the TallTale.mov file.

Begin by opening GoLive. Select File|New Special|QuickTime Movie and create a screen that is 320×240; name it whatever you want (as long as it isn't TheAuthorIsAFool or something equally derogatory). Make the background black and then click on OK.

Using the toolbar immediately below the pull down menu and above the movie viewer window, use the Show TimeLine Window button to open the TimeLine. After positioning the Objects and TimeLine windows, you should have a screen that looks somewhat like Figure 7.3. The Background Track is at this juncture the only element in the TimeLine. From this point, you'll be using various Objects throughout this section.

Build the TimeLine

You'll be working in layers, and each element and Object is present as an individual layer on the TimeLine. The first items that you will add are the various elements that make up the video. Start with a base file, in this case the QuickTime footage, and take these steps:

1. Drag the Video Track Object from the QuickTime tab in the Object window (top row, leftmost icon—it's the one whose icon resembles a video camera shown in Figure 7.4) directly beneath the Background Track layer.

2. Figure 7.4 also shows the newly added track and its related Inspector window. As you create different layers, the TimeLine can get filled pretty quickly, so it's important to get into the habit of naming your tracks. Give this track a new name in the Title field of the Inspector window. This change is reflected in both the layer and TimeLine of the TimeLine window.

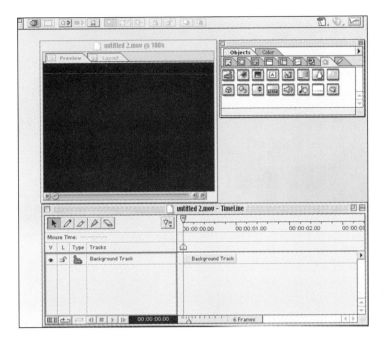

Figure 7.3
The initial screen setup for this chapter.

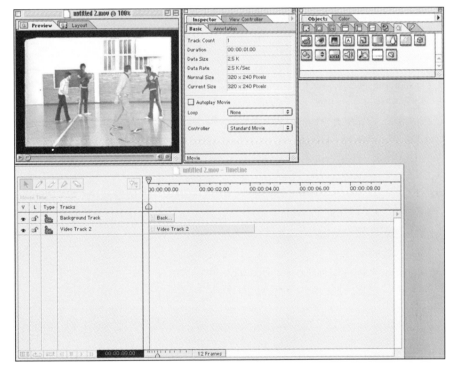

Figure 7.4
The Inspector window associated with the Video Track Object. If you're used to GoLive 4, you'll see many additions to these control options.

3. Now, take a moment to see what controls are available to you in the Inspector window. In the Start Time and Duration fields, shown in Figure 7.5, you see the length of the file you just added, its position on the workspace, the size of the workspace, and the way in which the video will be presented in the Mode pop-up. Leave everything as is in this section.

Figure 7.5

The base Inspector controls, including the Start Time and Duration fields, which indicate the element's length.

4. Next you'll add the following elements to the TimeLine so that everything is in place for editing:

- A Picture Track. Rename this Open_BKG.

- A Generic Filter Track.

- A Text Track.

Saving QuickTime Files

It often takes some time to build a QuickTime movie, just as it does creating images in other programs such as Photoshop, Illustrator, or Freehand. So, you should save all your work on a regular basis. When you save a QuickTime movie on which you're working in GoLive, it will be saved as a regular QuickTime file. The best thing to do is to save this file in the main folder that you previously set up for your Web site.

A couple of things to remember when saving a working file:

- Do not save it in any format that is a final render. In other words, don't set it up for streaming or hinted streaming. Your files need to remain editable.

- Always save the file in the Adobe GoLive document format, as you can see in Figure 7.6.

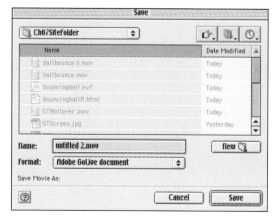

Figure 7.6

As you work on your QuickTime file, save it often in the GoLive document format.

Go ahead and save the file. You'll be coming back to it later in the chapter. For now, however, you need to work with individual QuickTime Objects so that you will get a feel for what they do. This following section is broken down into two portions—Video Filters and Audio Filters.

Video Filters

The Video Filters are "purty durn kewl," to use a friend's colorful description. Because you've already laid down a Video Track, this section goes on from there. This area focuses on the other Video Objects at your disposal that can enhance the production values of your files. This example uses the files that you placed in the folder GTSlideshow, and the GTScreen.jpg, TheGrandEmbarassment.mov, and GTScreenLayered.jpg files available on the CD-ROM. However, feel free to use other files, if you want.

The Video Objects include (starting at the top row, from left to right in Figure 7.7) the following:

- Video Track
- Picture Track
- Generic Filter Track
- One Source Filter Track
- Two Source Filter Track
- MPEG Track (Mac only - See the following note.)
- Sprite Track
- SWF Track
- 3D Track

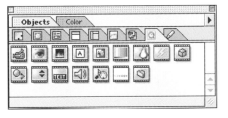

Figure 7.7
The Video Objects give you expanded control of your video effects.

Many of the effects filters work in a similar manner, so this section will not repeat itself here. Rather, after you work with one of the filters, you'll read how you can use other filter tracks, and which effects are available. Figure 7.8 shows how you can also see in advance in the Select Effect's preview window how a specific effect will look. The Embossing effect is shown here.

Note: The MPEG Track imports MPEG movies into QuickTime. Because it is Mac-specific and PC users do not have this option, this chapter omits discussing MPEG Track. Mac users are advised to work with the MPEG Track on their own.

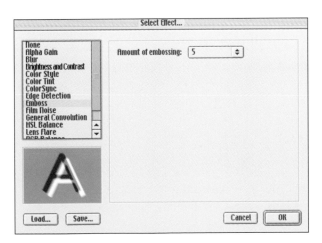

Figure 7.8
In each effect filter's Select Effect screen, you can see how your effect will look by watching the preview window in the lower left side of the user interface.

I purposely left the HREF, Chapter, and Text Tracks out of this listing because they don't necessarily fit into this category of the definition of video tracks. Additionally, because you have already worked with the Video Track feature, I'll start with the next in line, the Picture Track.

The Picture Track

This Object is perfect when you want to create a static (or non-moving) startup or end credit background, or to create a video slide show. If you do the latter, you will place various Picture Tracks onto the TimeLine and then change their positions along this window.

To create a slide show, do the following:

1. Create a new QuickTime Movie, open the TimeLine window, and place the first Picture Track Object there. Click once on the track to open the Inspector window. Rename this GT01, and then select the Images tab.

2. Select Import and navigate to the first image in the GTSlideshow folder. When the Compressions Settings dialog box appears, select Best Depth and change Quality to Best. The still picture is now imported.

3. Return to Basic and, in the Duration area, set the end time to 00:00:04.24, as is shown in Figure 7.9. The TimeLine will then extend to reflect the change in length.

> **Note:** You should get into the habit of placing files into specific folders so that you can find the files more easily. In the case of the Slide Show project, you will want to create a folder named GTSlideshow or something similar.

Figure 7.9
The Object's overall time changes immediately when you set a new Duration length.

4. However, you want to do a slide show, don't you? To do so, add a new Picture Track to the TimeLine. Call this one SlideShow, then go to Images in the Inspector window.

5. Select Import and, after navigating to the GTSlideShow folder, click on Add All. The result of this selection is shown in Figure 7.10. Select Done, and make the Compression Settings identical to those shown in Step 2.

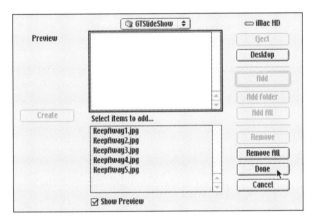

Figure 7.10
When working with the Picture Track, you can create a slide show by adding all your elements at one time.

6. In the Images area of the Picture Track Inspector, select a Slideshow Time Interval from the pop-up menu (for this example, I chose "3 sec", as you can see in Figure 7.11), and, if you want it to loop, enter the total number of repeats that you want.

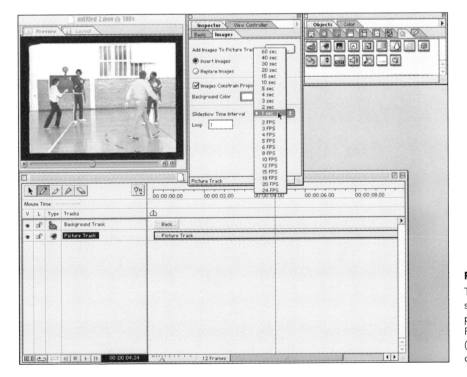

Figure 7.11
The overall duration of the slideshow is set by using this portion of the Picture Inspector. For this example, it shows 1 sec (one second), which will be changed to 3 secs for this project.

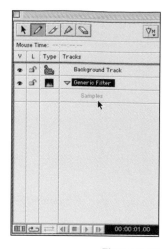

Figure 7.12

Assigning filters to the Generic Filter Track is accomplished by expanding the filter's name in the TimeLine to reveal the Samples layer.

As you can see when you play back the slideshow animation you created, three seconds is a long time between changes. Play with the timing some to find the speed most comfortable for you. To do this correctly, you not only need to set up the speed of the Slideshow Time Interval, you also need to set the Duration under the Basic section of the Inspector window.

The Generic Filter

The Generic Filter comes with three rather cool effects: Cloud, Fire, and Ripple. These effects interact with the video or pictures you have placed. By employing the Mode control in the Inspector window, you can give each effect a different appearance. Because the slide show we just created is so hot, it seems appropriate to use the Fire filter:

1. Place the Generic Filter Track onto the TimeLine. You can rename it, especially if you'll be combining different filters in your video. In Figure 7.12 you'll notice an expansion triangle next to Generic Filter. Expand it to access the Samples layer, which is where you'll create the filter effect.

2. Figure 7.13 shows the Create Sample selector in the TimeLine window. When you use this selector in conjunction with the Samples layer, you literally draw the length of time you want the filter to appear in the Samples TimeLine. Drag the cursor along the TimeLine to create this layer and, if need be, modify the length by clicking on either the start or end point.

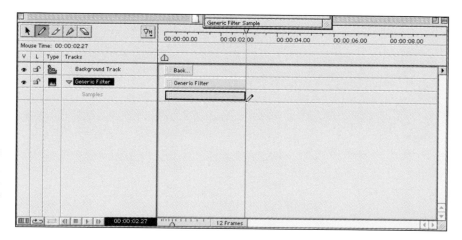

Figure 7.13

The Create Sample option in the TimeLine allows you to set the start and end points of your effect by dragging through the Samples area.

3. Select this newly created layer and choose Select to open. The Inspector window changes to what you see in Figure 7.14. You can now select from any of the three available filters.

4. Choose Fire, and set it up as you see in Figure 7.15. Play around with the settings to see how they interact with the filter so you can make this effect look the way you want.

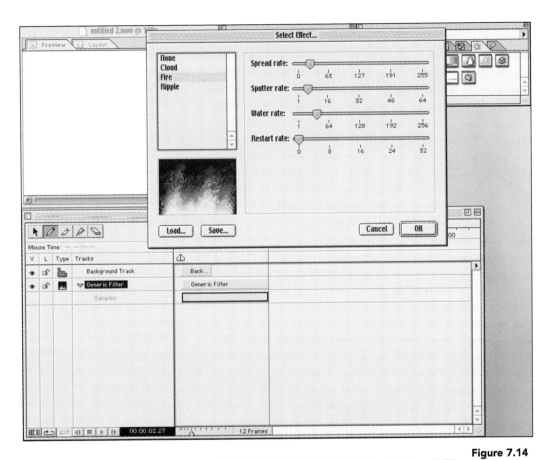

Figure 7.14
The new Samples layer you
created and its associated Select
Effect dialog box.

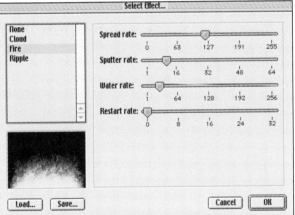

Figure 7.15
Such a hot video lends itself to
the Fire effect. Use these parameters to create a blaze similar to
the one I created.

5. Finally, after you've set up the parameters for the fire, click on the Generic Filter level to make it active. In the Inspector window (see Figure
   7.16), change the mode to Straight Alpha. This action turns the black
   area into a *chroma key* (a transparency), leaving only the flames to
   burn into your footage.

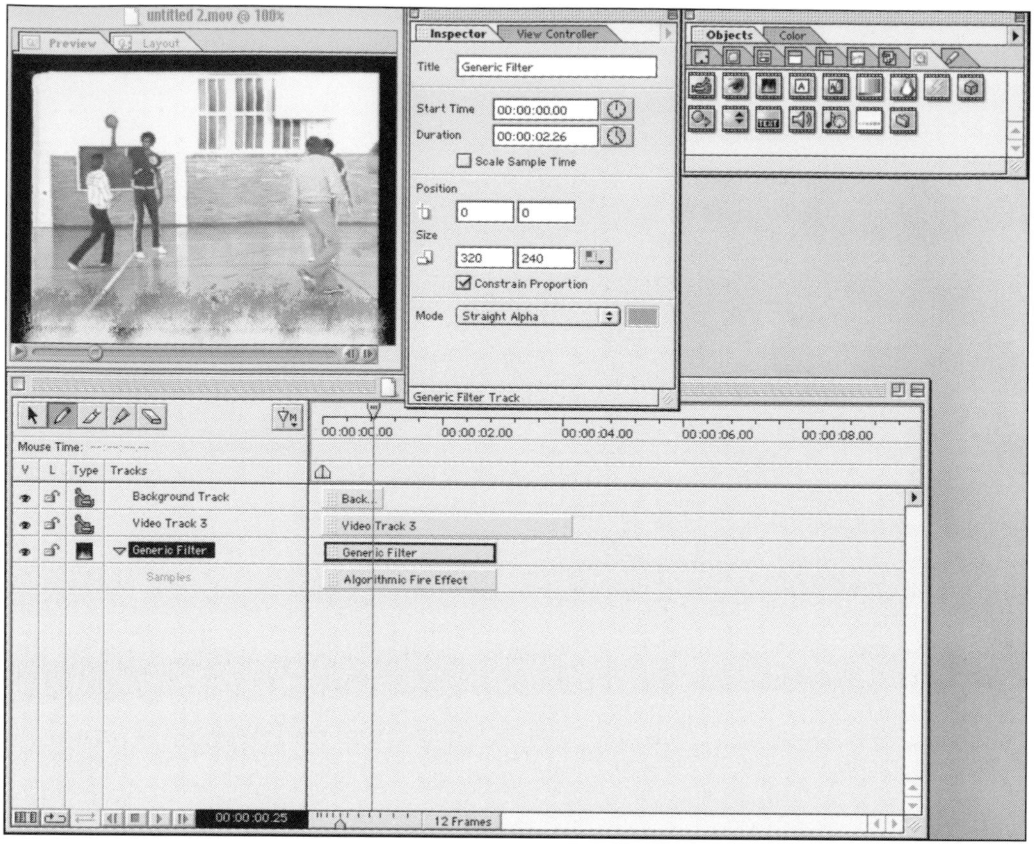

Figure 7.16

Use the Straight Alpha mode to create a chroma key effect that masks out the black areas of the fire effect, allowing the video below the effect to show through.

The One Source Filter

This is definitely one of the more fun tracks to work with because you can choose from so many possible effects. Because this filter works so much like the Generic Filter for its setup, it's best that you explore the various ways this filter works within your composition. Figure 7.17 shows the Select Effect screen, and the following list shows the filters now at your command:

- Alpha Gain
- Blur
- Brightness and Contrast
- Color Style
- Color Tint
- ColorSync (Mac)
- Edge Detection
- Emboss
- Film Noise
- General Convolution
- HSL Balance

- Lens Flare
- RGB Balance
- Sharpen

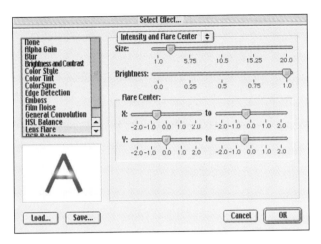

Again, these filters—in conjunction with the One Source Filter Track in its In-spector window—can give you some interesting looks. It's best to play a bit with these filters using the same method that you used with the Generic Filter Track: Walk through these filters to find the effect you like best.

Note: You'll find detailed definitions of items such as Alpha Gain, ColorSync, and others in the QuickTime section of the *GoLive User Manual.*

The Two Source Filter

The Two Source filter is designed to work with more than one video track. It creates wipes and effects from one video source to another. The following list shows the possible choices you have:

- Alpha Compositor
- Chroma Key
- Cross Fade
- Explode
- Gradient Wipe
- Implode
- Iris
- Matrix Wipe
- Push
- Radial
- Slide
- Wipe
- Zoom

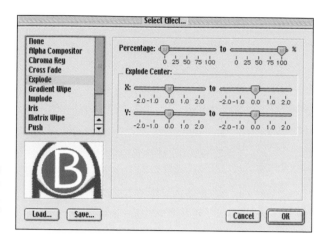

Figure 7.18
One of the two Source Filter effects, shown halfway through its move in the preview window of the Select Effect screen.

Figure 7.18 shows the halfway point of the Explode effect, and the controls at your command to modify it. Now, it's time to move to the Sprite Track.

The Sprite Track

The Sprite Track is fairly complicated. This one adds really amazing interactive capabilities to your QuickTime movie. This Track lets you literally set up hotspots in your final file that people can click on to go to other areas of your Web site. You can also import layered Photoshop files so that different behaviors can be assigned to different layers. The layers in the TimeLine are shown in Figure 7.19.

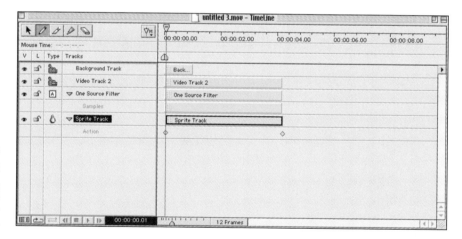

Figure 7.19
The Sprite Track allows you to not only import flattened image files, but also to work with layered Photoshop files. You can manipulate each layer individually.

Working with the Sprite Track adds a new term to your GoLive vocabulary—*image pool*. You must have elements in this image pool before you can assign interactive content to them. An image pool element can be virtually any photo format (JPEG, PICT, TIFF, and so on) because it is being added into a QuickTime file. This file will eventually be set up for the Web (as a QuickDraw GX file if you use a Mac, or as a QuickTime image if you are running Windows). As you work with it, you'll find the Sprite Track an extremely versatile tool that can enhance your QuickTime movies.

Now, you'll explore this tool by creating a QuickTime rollover. You need both a layered Photoshop file and a nonlayered file for this section. To create the QuickTime rollover, take the following steps:

1. Create a new QuickTime file in GL5 and accept the default parameters. Open the TimeLine and place a Sprite Track; expand it by clicking on the arrow next to its name.

2. Navigate to the folder in which you've placed your two images by selecting the Images tab in the Inspector window. Make sure that Import Multiple Layers is selected, as is shown in Figure 7.20. (For this example, I used the GTScreenBkg.jpg and GTScreenText.jpg files.) Highlight the first file and click on the Add button, then select the next image and do the same. Click on Done. When the Compression Settings screen comes up, make sure that Best Depth is selected in the pull-down menu and set Quality to Best. The files will now be listed in the Images portion of the Inspector window, as shown in Figure 7.21.

3. With the Sprite Track still selected, switch to the Sprites area of the Inspector window. In the Add New Sprites field, enter 2. This action creates both the Sprite 1 and Sprite 2 layers within the TimeLine and also a keyframe, represented by a diamond. Use the Create Sample tool to set another keyframe at the end of your rollover animation. For this example, I gave it a 4-second in length, as shown in Figure 7.22.

4. When you click with the Inspect/Move/Copy tool on the keyframe indicators, the Sprite Sample Inspector window appears. As you can see in Figure 7.23, you set the actions for your rollover animation here, just as you would when creating other types of rollovers. However, with the QuickTime rollovers, you can create any number of keyframes and

Figure 7.20
The Images section of the Inspector window. You can choose whether to have the Sprite Track recognize layered Photoshop files by activating the Import Multiple Layers option.

Figure 7.21
The files you selected are listed in the Images area of the Inspector window.

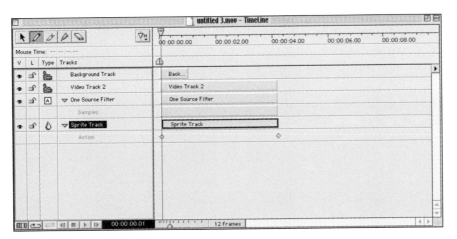

Figure 7.22
Assign a time for the animation. If you don't do this, the results of combining the interactive elements of the movie you're creating will not be accomplished when the file is viewed on the Web.

Figure 7.23

Create QT rollovers, using the same method that you would use to create static rollovers.

Figure 7.24

Using the Status text box, you can assign a message like this one, which will be revealed in the Web browser when a particular action occurs.

assign different actions throughout the animation. You could, for example, assign music to start when the visitor moves the cursor over the screen on one Sprite Sample. Another action you can make could assign the visual reveal.

5. Use the second Sprite Sample to create your reveal. You'll notice you can also change the look of the cursor when certain actions occur by using the Cursor pull-down menu. In the Status area, type a message that will be revealed in the message area of the Web browser (at the bottom bar, as is shown in Figure 7.24).

This process is simply a basic walkthrough of what you can create for interactive QuickTime elements. In my opinion, it is probably one of the most exciting areas of animation development offered in any package… anywhere. You can use layered Photoshop files, SWF files, and many others elements to build extremely complex animations. With some experimentation, you can even produce elements that have never before been seen on the Web.

Use caution, however. You don't want to create a movie that is so large that it takes forever to download. For example, the movie you just created has a final size of about 920K. If you start adding audio and other effects, you could end up with a file that pushes the low- to mid-megabyte range, which on a slower connection could take a Web surfer with a 56Kbps modem a seeming eternity to load.

The SWF Track

You can build SWF files in LiveMotion and import them into your QuickTime movie, as shown in Figure 7.25, and still retain all of the information stored in the files. The technique for importing Shockwave files is the same as outlined in the "Sprite Track" section of this chapter. You can use the SWF Track to import background animations and then add other effects. I included an SWF file in the Chapter 7 folder, so feel free to play around a bit with different options.

If you don't have a copy of LiveMotion, you can download the demo from the Adobe Web site (**www.adobe.com**). If you've ever considered creating Shockwave animations, I highly recommend that you purchase this program.

The 3D Track

Use the 3D Track to incorporate a QuickDraw 3D image into your movie. Like the SWF Track and others, when you place a 3D Track into the TimeLine, you'll be asked to find the file you want to add (see Figure 7.26). If you are into 3D modeling—or at least have one of the major 3D packages (such as Amapi 3D, Bryce 4, Carrara, Pixels:3D, or LightWave), export your creations in the 3DMF

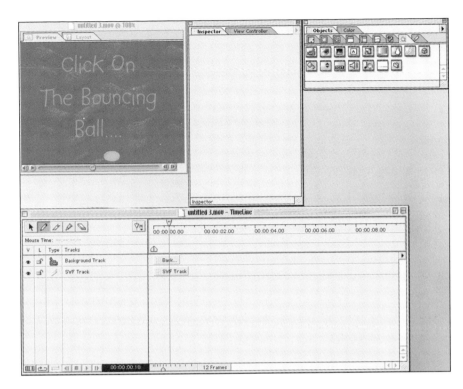

Figure 7.25
An SWF (Shockwave) file placed
into the QuickTime movie.

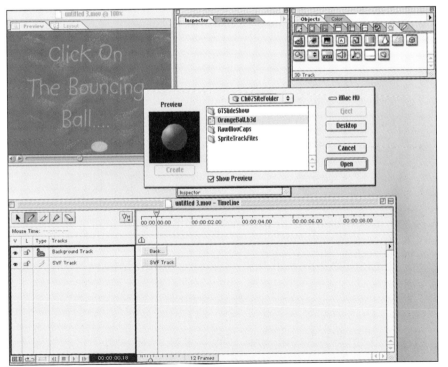

Figure 7.26
When you place a 3D Track onto
the TimeLine, you're automatically
prompted to assign a 3DMF file.

format. Unfortunately, 3D Studio Max, the most popular PC-based 3D appli-
cation, does not support 3DMF export because this is a Macintosh-only format.
You have basic control over 3D Track elements accessed through the Inspector's
Mode menu.

PROJECT 7.1 Build a Multifaceted QT Movie

Now that you've gone over the basics of building a QuickTime movie within GoLive, it's time to put your knowledge to good use. Because you'll be working with audio files in the following chapter, here you'll focus only on creating a QuickTime movie that uses video, different Track elements, and ends with an interactive screen that will transport your fascinated visitors to another location on the Web.

Placing Elements

Start by creating a new QuickTime movie with the same dimensions (320×240) that you used throughout this chapter. It doesn't matter what background color you've chosen, so when the setup screen appears, just click on OK. Save this QT file as HGVid.mov. To get everything started, place the following files (in the TimeLine in the order listed), and position the elements as stated:

1. *Video Track*—Select the TallTale.mov file for this section and rename it in the Inspector window. Move the starting point of this video to approximately 02-seconds by dragging the TimeLine indicator to that spot.

2. *Picture Track*—Place this Track at the starting point of the movie and select the GTScreenBkg.jpg image. Extend the length of the file to overlap the beginning of the Tall Tale Track so it looks like Figure 7.27.

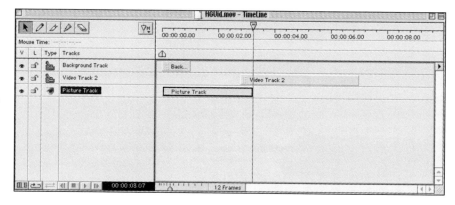

Figure 7.27

After adding the Picture Track, extend it so it overlaps the Video Track in the TimeLine. This is called Pad, giving you time for a transition from one Track to another.

3. *Two Source Filter Track*—Move the time indicator to the beginning of the Tall Tale Track. Use the Create Sample tool to draw a Sample starting from the beginning of the Tall Tale Track to the end of the Picture Track. This sets the timing of the transition you'll be creating from the former to the latter Tracks. Your TimeLine should now look like Figure 7.28.

4. *Text Track*—Move the TimeLine indicator back to the start and place a Text Track Object. (We'll discuss the Text Track shortly.) You'll be creating text that will appear during the start of the movie a little later in this section.

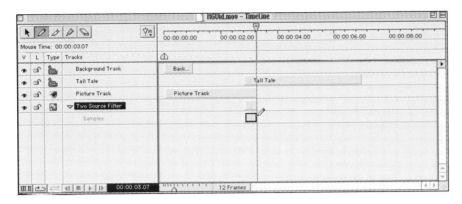

Figure 7.28
A look at the TimeLine, with the Two Source Filter Track in position to create an effect between the Video and Picture Tracks.

5. *Sprite Track*—The video will end with a rollover link to the Harlem Globetrotters' site. Place this Track into the TimeLine. Import the GTScreenBkg.jpg and GTScreenText.jpg files. Make sure that the beginning of the Sprite is placed close to the end of the Tall Tale video and that it extends beyond the end of the video.

6. *Duplicate the Picture Track*—Hold down the Option/Ctrl key and drag the Track layer beneath the Sprite Track. Make sure that only this new Track layer is selected, and move it to the beginning of the Sprite Track. Shorten the length until it's even with the end of the Tall Tale Track.

7. *Two Source Filter Track*—Place another TSF and, set it up to coincide with the duplicated Picture Track that you just created and the end of the Tall Tale Track.

Remember that, as you are building your QT video, the various elements that you use will be placed in a descending order. If you're used to layers in Photoshop or in other programs where each new layer is "placed" above the preceding layer, the QT-building process can be at first confusing.

Your TimeLine should now look like the one in Figure 7.29. Note the positions of each Track in the hierarchy (left side of the TimeLine) and in the TimeLine itself.

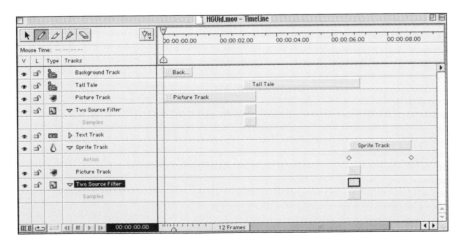

Figure 7.29
The TimeLine with all elements (or Tracks, to be precise) in place.

Figure 7.30

The Text Inspector gives you an area in which you can type your text and perform the initial setup for the way it's displayed in your movie.

Create an Opening Message

Now it's time to work with the Text Track. Move the TimeLine indicator back to the beginning and select the Text Track element. To create the message, take the following steps:

1. The text should begin at the start of the video and end just before the transition between the Picture Track and Tall Tale Track happens. Expand the Text Track and, with the Create Sample tool, create a Samples Track in the TimeLine. Notice the changes in the Inspector screen (see Figure 7.30). It's in this window where you'll create your text. If you desire, you could even turn the text into a hyperlink by assigning an action to it. For now, however, you're not going to do that.

2. Select the text you just typed and go to the Movie pull-down menu at the top of the screen (see Figure 7.31). Select Movie|Text. You now have all the controls that allow you the size of your font, the font style, color, and so on. Make your changes; then, go back to the Inspector window.

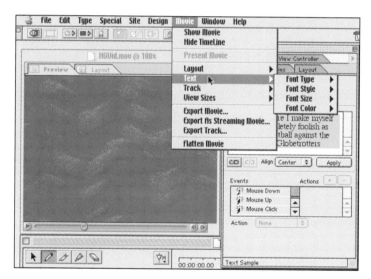

Figure 7.31

Change the font style and color by using the Movie pull-down menu at the top of the screen.

3. Choose the Properties tab and choose Scroll In to have the text come in from the bottom of the screen. If you want, you can also have it Scroll Out by selecting that option.

4. Select the Layout tab and make sure that you have Anti Alias and Transparent selected. You can also add a drop shadow to the text.

5. Click on the Text tab to return to that area, select Center and then Apply. If you play your video now, the text will flow in as you can see in Figure 7.32.

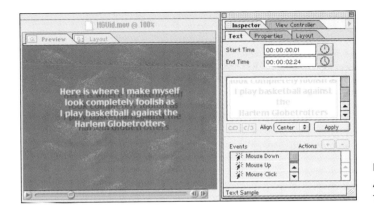

Figure 7.32
A look at the text, halfway through its move onto the screen.

Transitions

Now you're ready to set the transitions for both of the Two Source Filters (TSF). First you will create a transition for the uppermost TSF, and then a transition for the second one you placed:

1. Select the first Two Source Filter Track and go to the Inspector window. Figure 7.33 shows this window, where you see two new pull-down menus—Source A and Source B. In these menus, you will assign which Track is which for the transition.

2. Activate the TSF Samples layer and, in the Inspector window, choose Transition from Source A to B. Press the Select button and select a wipe from the Select Effect screen. Figure 7.34 shows a Horizontal bow tie Wipe with a Border width of 3 pixels, Soft edges, and a Border color of Orange.

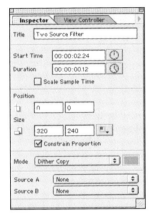

Figure 7.33
Assigning the Source elements in the Two Source Track Inspector window is accomplished with the Source A and Source B pull-down menus shown at the bottom of the window.

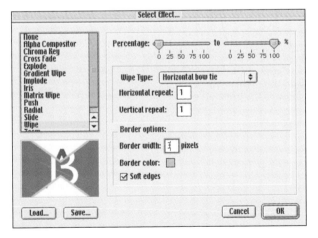

Figure 7.34
The first transitional effect chosen for the video.

3. With the transition effect set up, choose the second TSF in the TimeLine. Make Source A the Tall Tale Track and Source B the second Picture Track in the list. Repeat Step 2 to assign a new transition wipe. Make this new wipe different from what you've used previously (such as the horizontal bow tie wipe used in the preceding example), so that the viewer will not know what to expect.

The Sprite Track

Using the techniques you learned previously in this chapter, set up the Sprite Track to create a rollover. When the movie ends, the visitors to your site will be able to move their cursor over the screen to reveal the message. You also want this portion of the video to act as a hyperlink to another location. To do so, take the following steps:

1. Select the Text keyframe (or the bottommost layer's keyframe if you didn't assign a new name to the layer). By selecting this, changes you make to the text will be in effect throughout the animation.

2. In the Over portion under the Basic tab, change the Cursor from None to Pointing Hand, and then type a message in the Status box, similar to the one that you see in Figure 7.35.

Figure 7.35

In the Sprite Track Inspector, you can assign the rollover effect all the way, even to how the cursor will look when the user passes it over the QT window.

3. Go to the Actions screen, choose Mouse Click, and press the plus symbol next to Actions at the top of the window. From the Action pull-down menu, select GoTo URL. In the Link box, enter a location. In the example I created here, it's **http://www.harlemglobetrotters.com/**. In the Target window, either type "_blank" (without the quotation marks) or use the up/down arrow button to select _blank from the list. This step tells the visitor's Web browser to create a new, blank window in which the location will be displayed.

Finishing Up

Now only saving the QuickTime movie you just created and placing it onto a page remains to be done. Create a new document, drag a QuickTime object onto the workspace, and link it to your new movie. Then, use the Show In Browser button to open your browser and watch the movie play. At the end, move your cursor over the screen and press the mouse button. Your Web browser will open a new, blank window and connect to the URL you assigned.

Moving On

This chapter merely touched on the myriad possibilities for QuickTime production. Rarely, if ever, do you see a QuickTime file that is as intricate as the one you just created, and even more rare is the QT file that takes what you've just learned and expands on it. Go wild and have fun in creating original QT files for Web distribution. However, beware of the file size as you create your movie; the one you just created, when saved as a streaming file, comes in at approximately 2MB, a bit larger for the PC file. This is without audio, which will, of course, add more to the final file size. When creating larger movies, consider saving them as hinted streaming files; they store the full file on your server, while only displaying a visual link to that file.

And speaking of audio, read on. Chapter 8 details the ins and outs of working with audio.

GoLive 5 Studio

This studio showcases world-class sites built using GoLive's exciting features as well as several of the projects in this book.

The Slide Show Auto Action
You can use GoLive to combine action elements for your site. This layout was created as a potential site to be maintained by authors to help promote their books. The cover images incorporate the Slide Show Auto action, which is covered in Chapter 7.

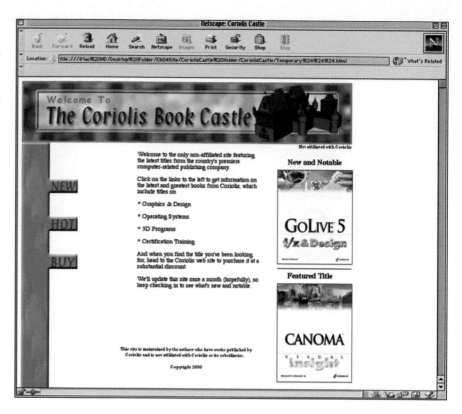

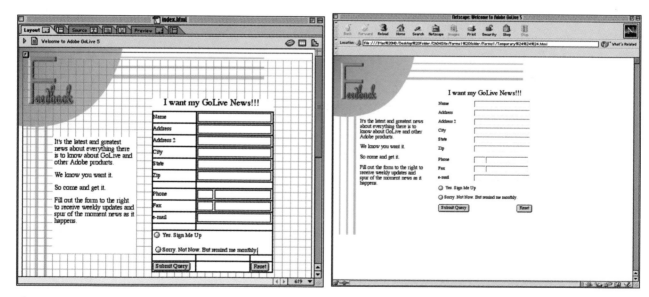

The Form Tool
Forms are becoming a staple of Web site design. Not only can you build great looking forms using only the Forms tool, but when you employ other design elements, you can control every pixel. You'll discover how to create forms for your sites in Chapter 4.

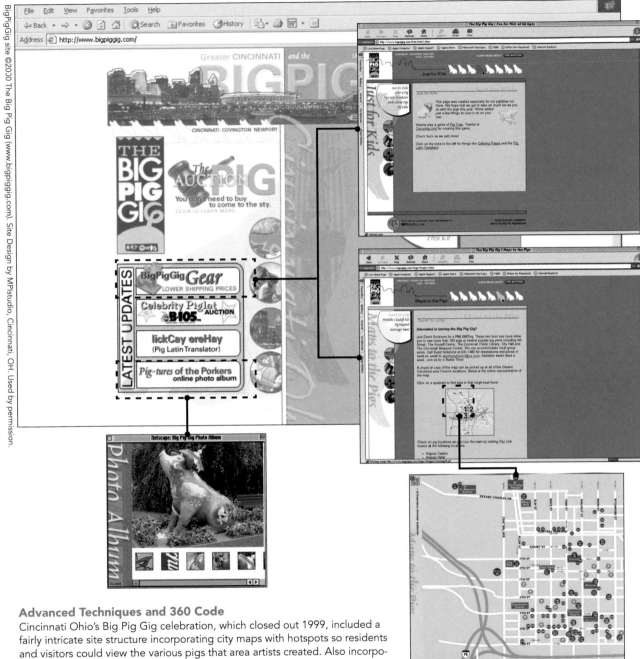

Advanced Techniques and 360 Code

Cincinnati Ohio's Big Pig Gig celebration, which closed out 1999, included a fairly intricate site structure incorporating city maps with hotspots so residents and visitors could view the various pigs that area artists created. Also incorporated on the site were advanced rollovers and games for younger visitors. Techniques employed on this site are discussed throughout the book.

Luckily for the creators of the Big Pig Gig site, GoLive has incorporated advanced scripting capabilities such as 360 Code, which allows designers and programmers to work together more efficiently. Changes may be made to portions of HTML code that, when brought back into GoLive, allow for seamless Web site updates without affecting any other portion of the page. You can learn more about 360 Code and other site-management tools in Chapter 11.

```
image1off = new Image();
image1off.src = "images_s/snav1.gif";
image2off = new Image();
image2off.src = "images_s/snav2.gif";
image3off = new Image();
image3off.src = "images_s/snav3.gif";
image4off = new Image();
image4off.src = "images_s/snav4.gif";
image5off = new Image();
image5off.src = "images_s/snav5.gif";
image6off = new Image();
```

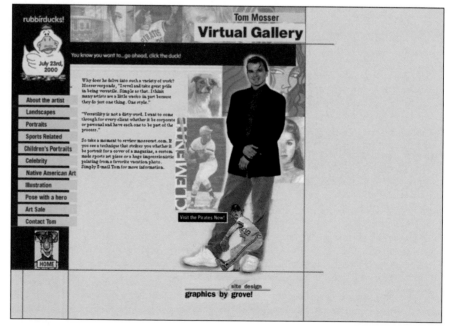

Using Graphics for Impact

Good use of creative graphics can really catch your visitors' attention. The top image shows an example of a whimsical site created by graphics by grove (www.graphicsbygrove.com) to promote an art exhibit. The firm took their creation a little further and also created the home site for the featured artist (bottom).

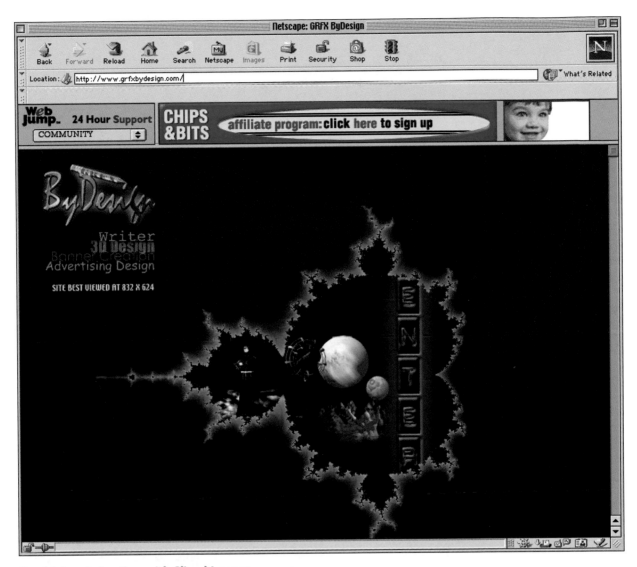

Combining Animation with Sliced Images

You can combine animation and sliced image files. Slicing is a technique used to break up large images into smaller ones in order to create more manageable parts. This image shows an earlier version of the author's home splash screen. The logo and text in the upper left corner of the screen is an animated GIF created in Headline Studio. The Mandlebrot fractal is a sliced image laid over a duplicate image that was placed as a background screen. The Enter strip is a rollover button that takes the visitor to the first page of the site. The pros and cons of this layout are discussed in various chapters throughout the book.

Subtlety

Rollovers don't have to be large and gaudy. Subtlety can make a Web site fun to visit because you never know what you'll find. On this site, **www.out.to/**, the hotspots aren't readily apparent. Moving your cursor over (or clicking on) the red bars, however, makes interesting changes occur on the page.

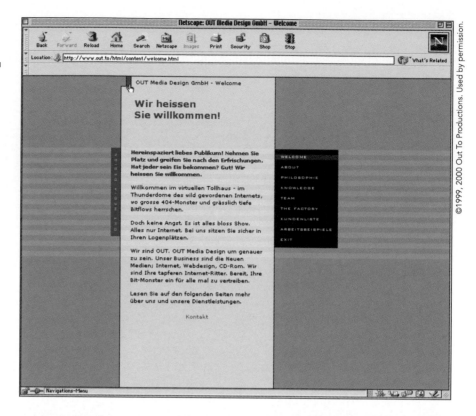

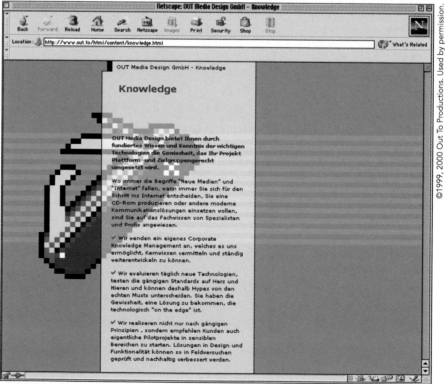

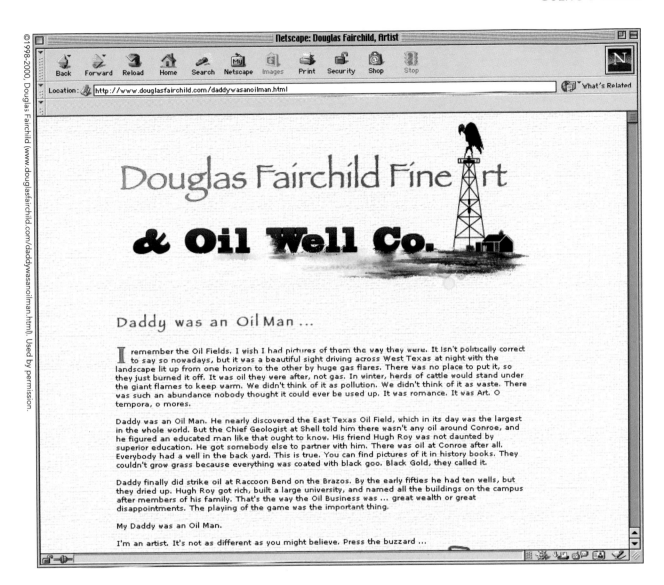

Daddy was an Oil Man ...

I remember the Oil Fields. I wish I had pictures of them the way they were. It isn't politically correct to say so nowadays, but it was a beautiful sight driving across West Texas at night with the landscape lit up from one horizon to the other by huge gas flares. There was no place to put it, so they just burned it off. It was oil they were after, not gas. In winter, herds of cattle would stand under the giant flames to keep warm. We didn't think of it as pollution. We didn't think of it as waste. There was such an abundance nobody thought it could ever be used up. It was romance. It was Art. O tempora, o mores.

Daddy was an Oil Man. He nearly discovered the East Texas Oil Field, which in its day was the largest in the whole world. But the Chief Geologist at Shell told him there wasn't any oil around Conroe, and he figured an educated man like that ought to know. His friend Hugh Roy was not daunted by superior education. He got somebody else to partner with him. There was oil at Conroe after all. Everybody had a well in the back yard. This is true. You can find pictures of it in history books. They couldn't grow grass because everything was coated with black goo. Black Gold, they called it.

Daddy finally did strike oil at Raccoon Bend on the Brazos. By the early fifties he had ten wells, but they dried up. Hugh Roy got rich, built a large university, and named all the buildings on the campus after members of his family. That's the way the Oil Business was ... great wealth or great disappointments. The playing of the game was the important thing.

My Daddy was an Oil Man.

I'm an artist. It's not as different as you might believe. Press the buzzard ...

Subtle Rollovers

An example of how Douglas Fairchild creates unexpected rollovers on his sites. In this case, the vulture is the rollover button. Notice the change in the bird's head between the top and bottom plates.

Using Shockwave

The home page (or splash screen) for the author's client, Summer Of '66, a Broadway-style musical that played in Myrtle Beach, SC. The logo is a Shockwave animation in which the sun rays rotate and the dancers sway to the beat of the streaming audio track of "I Love Beach Music." The Enter button is a rollover. You learn how to import Shockwave animations in Chapters 2, 6, and 12. GoLive's audio capabilities are covered in Chapter 8.

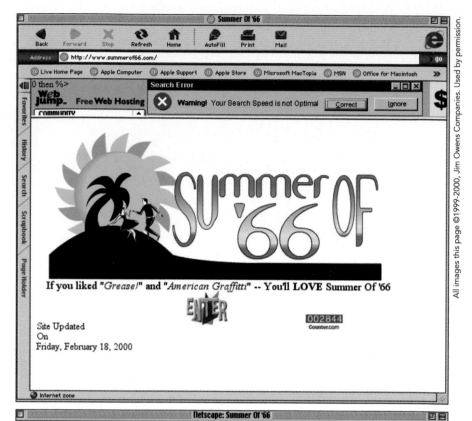

Creating Rollover Buttons out of Graphics

After clicking on ENTER on the home page, you will see the first page of the Summer Of '66 site. The backdrop beach scene is a JPEG image placed as a BgImage on the page. The transparent white box in which the Summer of '66 logo and text are positioned is a separate image; all the navigation buttons are rollovers. See Chapters 6 and 9 for more about rollovers.

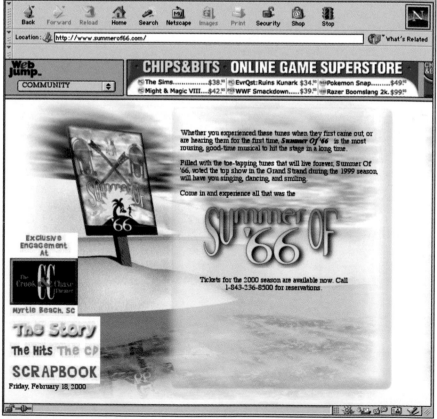

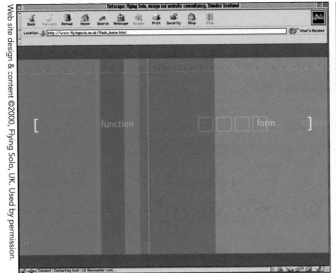

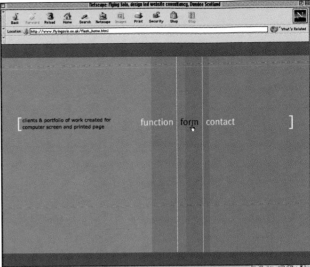

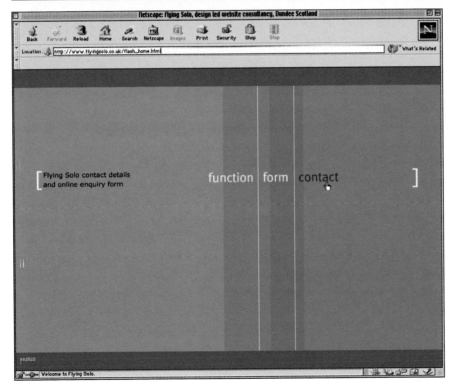

Flash and Shockwave

Here is an interesting example of how to bring a site to life. Shown here are three screens from the Flying Solo site (**www.flyingsolo.co.uk**) where even the thumbnail images are Shockwave animations. Employing Flash files extensively, every page of this particular Web site is animated and has many DHTML features. Ways to bring a site to life are discussed in Chapter 6. Shockwave files are discussed in Chapter 2. Macromedia Flash is discussed in Chapter 13.

Site Backgrounds

This site, designed by Koch Creative Services for a subsidiary of Koch Petroleum Group, L.P., is a great example of how to employ interesting background imagery to tie an entire project together. This background image sets the tone for the site and is used throughout each page of the site. Images on the home page (top) have been sliced to allow a site to load faster. The download page (bottom) uses pop-up menus to the optimum, allowing visitors to choose the screen resolution most suitable for their monitor. Sliced images are discussed in Chapter 15. Pop-up menus are discussed in Chapters 9 and 15.

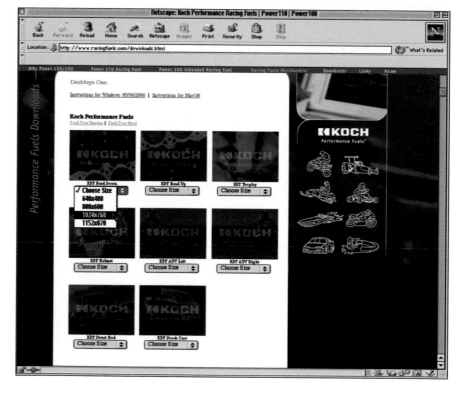

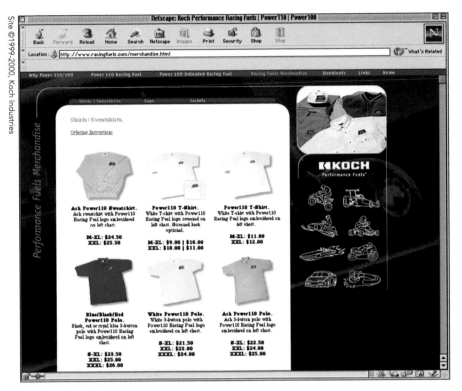

Online Interactivity

Two design examples for online product information. This site presents an online catalog featuring, in this case, the company's shirts.

The bottom image shows us an visually interesting way of providing free downloads to site visitors. See Chapters 2 and 15 to learn more.

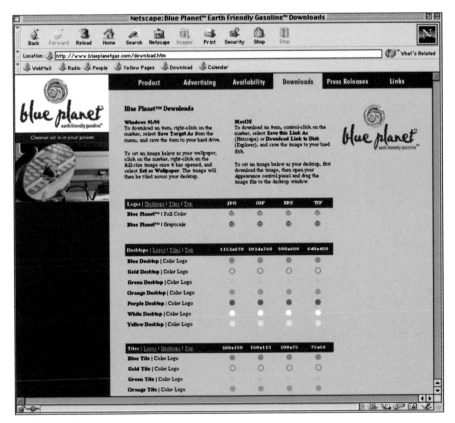

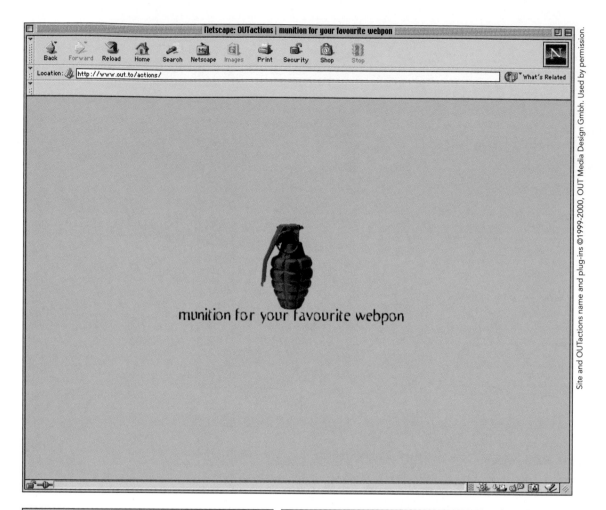

An Explosive Effect

An extremely fun three-way rollover using the Main/Over/Click function. This is featured on the OUTactions site (**www.out.to**). There are sample OUTactions provided by Oliver Zahorka discussed in Chapter 12.

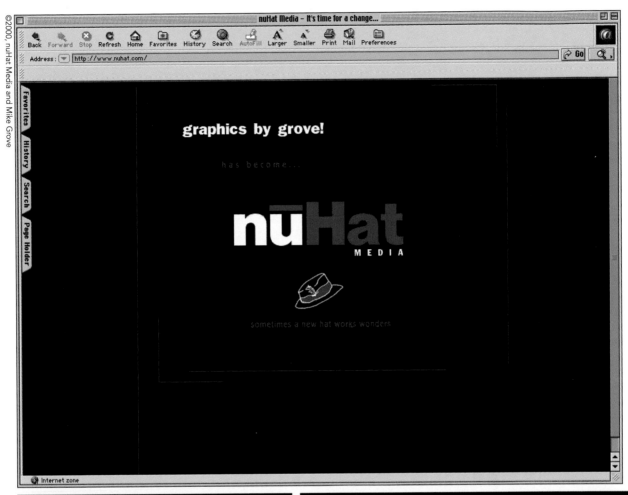

A New Name Equals A New Look

After changing his company name, a new look was called for. Utilizing GoLive's DHTML capabilities, remote rollovers that incorporate multiple images for each are used to show off the company's work. DHTML is covered in Chapter 2.

Table Of Contents

Two views of the Table of Contents page featured in Chapter 15. Notice the starburst next to the cursor. You learn how to create an effect where an image follows the movements of the cursor. You'll also learn how to control the area of movement so that the images are confined to certain coordinates of a Web page.

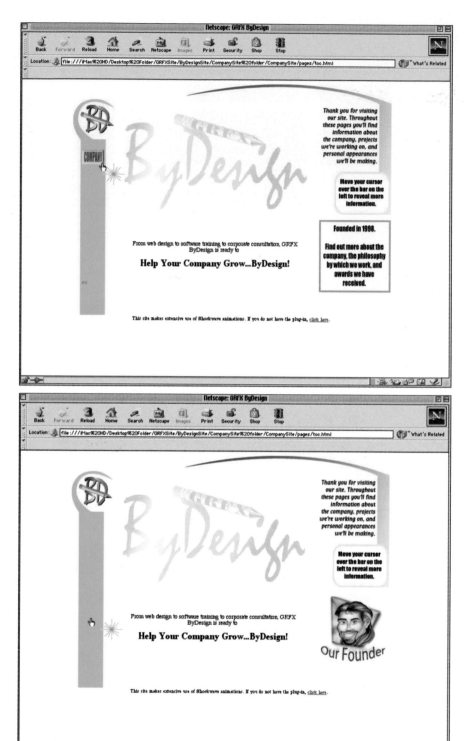

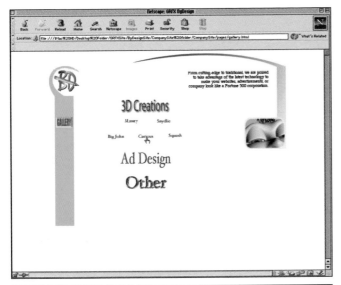

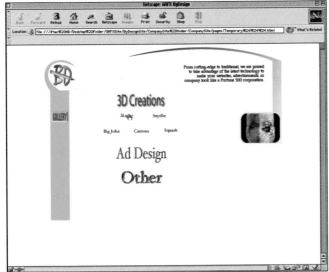

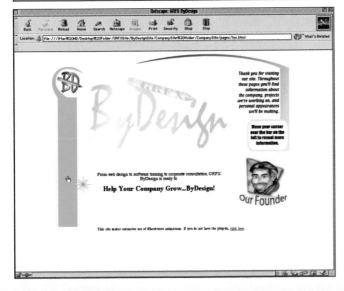

Rollovers at Work

An example of a remote rollover (DHTML) technique you will work on in Chapter 15. As a visitor moves their mouse over the topics, an image appears in the view screen on the right side of the page.

Creating Streaming Media

Using GoLive's internal QT video editing controls (discussed in Chapter 7) or importing pre-built animations compressed with programs such as Media Cleaner Pro, you can build fast-loading movie files for your site.

Textures

Here's a sampling of the seamless textures included on the companion CD-ROM. All textures were created using ArtisSoftware's TextureMagic Pro. Each texture is royalty-free and ready for you to use as backgrounds on your Web sites.

Chapter 8

Fun with Sonics

Audio is becoming a big part of Web content since the advent of high-speed connections, such as ADSL and cable modems. Numerous software packages can help you create streamable audio to enhance your sites. In this chapter, you'll get an overview of audio creation do's and don'ts that will help you create high-quality, quickly loadable audio files for your site.

Prelude

This chapter isn't so much a hands-on, how-to set of tutorials as much as it is an overview of what concerns to be aware of and how to save audio files that you create. Its importance is that it discusses the production concerns that you need to be aware of and understand when creating audio content for the Web. These concerns include copyright information, where to get the latest updates to the codes (which are being revised almost as quickly as Internet technology is), and the best ways to save your files for the easiest retrieval.

This chapter also gives you a quick rundown of audio editing and creation software that is available for PCs, Macs, and both. Due, however, to the vast differences in audio manipulation programs—some edit only existing files, some let you create original audio files, and some give you the capability to import your video files in order to synchronize your audio while the video is playing—it's almost impossible to create a hands-on walkthrough for sound file editing. Therefore, this chapter is written primarily as a reference tool, a guide to help you define your needs.

Playing to the Senses

Today's Internet is playing to two of our senses—sight and sound. I envision the day when you'll also have the ability to feel and smell content as well. (I try not to picture the day when taste is added to these files, because the thought of having to put my tongue against the monitor is a bit... disconcerting.) As technology advances, it becomes easier to deliver high-quality video and audio to Web surfers around the world. At this stage, however, it is extremely important to be able to create files that will quickly load and play back in the way you intended. Later, you will learn why you need to consider this load and playback precision.

First, let's return to the early days of the Internet, when Web pages were made up strictly of text. For those of you old enough to remember, do you recall how awesome it was when pictures were added to these pages? Do you remember the excitement you experienced when you saw your first clip art image that, more often than not, had nothing to do with the content of the site? It didn't matter, did it? It was just too thrilling to see a picture on a page. Shortly thereafter, photographs began to appear, then video, and with each advance you were more than happy to wait 10 or 15 minutes for these files to be read into the page through your speedy 9600baud modem.

Fast forward to the present. It seems like everyone, whether on dial-up modems or running with high-speed ADSL or cable modems, is complaining about how long it takes to load a page. Additionally, if you're like many other people who are discovering the excitement of providing video over the Web (either embedded on your page or available for download with a simple hyperlink click), you're probably searching for more effective and time-efficient ways to make this content available to those who access your pages.

In Chapter 7, you discovered how to edit QuickTime videos from within GoLive. Although this method is extremely efficient for creating high-quality, "streamable" content, remember, however, that you were working on silent video. To make your work memorable, you have to play to the ear as well as to the eye. Therefore, if you're not already doing so, you'll eventually want to edit audio or to create your own sound files to augment your work.

Sounds Good

As you plan your multimedia content, you have to make a couple of decisions regarding the way your audio will be played back: Figures 8.1, 8.2, and 8.3 show typical computers and speaker setups for each of these sound options.

- *Will it be a mono file?* Plenty of computers still don't have built-in stereo speakers. Additionally, a number of WebTV owners have their boxes hooked up to mono TV sets. The nice thing, however, is that creating in mono really doesn't matter, except for the size of the created file. Mono provides the smallest file you can create, and it will be the format that you'll use if you're providing voice-only content.

- *How about stereo?* For several years now, most new computers have shipped from the factory with stereo speakers, either built-in or external. You definitely don't want to ignore this quickly growing group. Most affordable audio editing packages support stereo.

- *Is SurroundSound a viable option?* SurroundSound is growing by leaps and bounds. Many computer systems offer SurroundSound packages that contain five speakers (a left- and right-front, a left- and right-rear, and a center channel). The standard two-channel surround provides a rear channel track in mono only, and the 5.1 channel surround supports stereo through the rear speakers. (The .1 in 5.1 is the center speaker channel.)

Almost as many audio editing programs as multimedia producers are on the market. These programs are either cross-platform (for Windows 95/98/ Millenium and NT/2000, Linux, Mac, and so on) or platform-specific. However, not all are equal. This is definitely one of those cases where the more you spend, the more functionality you get. Two wonderful audio editing programs that won't destroy your budget are Sonic Foundry's Sound Forge for Windows (see Figure 8.4) and Bias, Inc.'s Peak 2.10 for the Mac (see Figure 8.5).

Figure 8.1
Computers prior to 1998 often came with a single built-in speaker.

Figure 8.2
These days, literally every computer, whether desktop or laptop, comes with built-in stereo speakers.

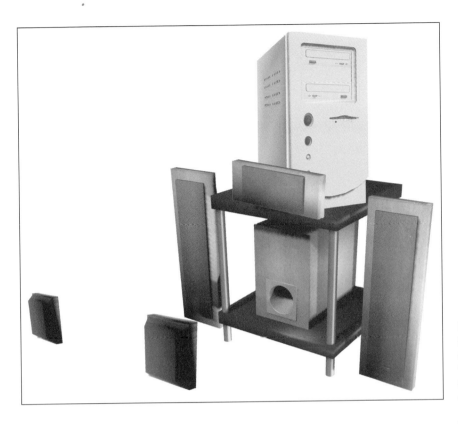

Figure 8.3
SurroundSound, either 2 channel or 5.1 channel, is really taking off for multimedia purposes with surround speaker packages available for many computers.

Legalities

Now, for an extremely important part of learning about sound: lawyers. Remember that when you work with any type of copyrighted material, you need to get permission to use it, or you could possibly face embarrassing (and potentially financially ruinous) legal action if caught. I definitely don't recommend using copyrighted music for use on a Web site or especially for distribution. In addition, this area is growing extremely murky when it has to do with the Internet, because you are not only broadcasting this music in one geographical location (and even if you were, copyright law would still apply), you're literally broadcasting it to the world. While the attorneys and the courts busily work to smooth out new e-laws concerning copyright, your best bet is not to use copyrighted material on your Web site.

A number of sites provide the latest laws pertaining to copyright and copyright infringement. These include the following:

Figure 8.4
Sonic Foundry's Sound Forge software is a great audio editing program for Windows.

- CopyrightLaws.com at **www.copyrightlaws.com**/—A great site, with information, links, and other help. This Web site also includes a link to Canadian copyright law pages.

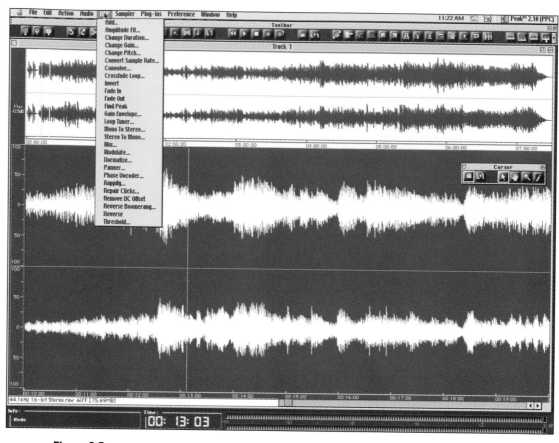

Figure 8.5

If you use a Mac, Peak by Bias, Inc., is a full-featured audio production tool.

- US Copyright Office at **http://lcweb.loc.gov/copyright/**—This is the Library of Congress's U.S. Copyright Office site. An excellent resource of almost everything you need to know, from copyright basics to International copyright law.

- The Copyright Website at **www.benedict.com/**—This site attempts to deliver practical and relevant copyright information of interest, whether you are a surfer musician, content provider, and so on. Launched on May Day 95 (which makes this site a Web institution), this site seeks to encourage discourse and invites solutions to the myriad of copyright tangles that currently permeate the Web.

- **www.eff.org/pub/CAF/law/ip-primer**—This online document is a copyright primer.

Note: the CAF in this link must be ALL-CAPS.

The latter is an article titled "An Intellectual Property Law Primer for Multimedia and Web Developers." It's well worth your time to print it out and keep it handy in case you have any questions. Dozens of other sites are available as well. You need only do a search for copyright laws to find other Web sites that may answer your questions.

Numerous packages are available commercially that include music pieces for use on the Web. Most of these packages come in CD-ROM sets that include sound effects, musical *stingers* (short music bursts), and a few longer clips. When you buy one of these packages, make sure that it clearly states that all the files are royalty-free; otherwise, you could run into problems with the distributors and end up having to pay a usage fee for the material.

You can easily argue that, with MP3 becoming so popular and many record companies jumping on the download bandwagon, it should be all right to use any music you want at any time. Nevertheless, this isn't true. If the record companies license their music for download, that's one thing; to lift a soundtrack from that download site or from an album for personal use without at least giving the copyright information (artist, date, album title, record label, and so on) is stealing.

Audio Production Tools

If you are musically inclined, you can create your own music by using various packages with prices that are geared toward everyone from the novice to the high-end professional software packages that almost write the tunes for you.

Windows Software

Sonic Foundry is among the most prolific publishers of this type of software. Included in its audio production tools are the following:

- *ACID Pro 2*—Geared toward professional computers, ACID Pro and the other ACID products are loop-based programs that employ what the company calls *paint and play* technology. Music can be created in 8-, 16-, and 24-bit files. Figure 8.6 shows an example of the ACID Pro screen layout.

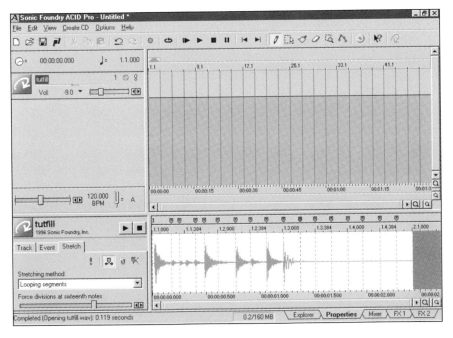

Figure 8.6

A look at the layout in ACID Pro 2. You can assign each audio track a different color for quick reference.

- *ACID Music 2*—This software package is a lower priced and not-quite-as-full-featured version of its big brother. ACID Music 2 supports 8- and 16-bit audio files.

- *ACID DJ, Hip-Hop, and Rock (all version 2)*—These are specialized music creation packages.

Sonic Foundry also produces other audio and audio/video editing packages that, like Acid Pro 2 are filled with features found in extremely high-end programs that are far more expensive. The following packages are included in their lineup:

- *Sound Forge 4.5*—As you can see from Figure 8.7, Sound Forge is an in-depth audio and video creation package, specially designed to create productions for multimedia and the Web. Figure 8.7 shows the basic layout of the program's user interface. It can also be used to create broadcast-quality videos. When Sound Forge is used in conjunction with ACID Pro, Windows users have one heck of a powerful multimedia arsenal.

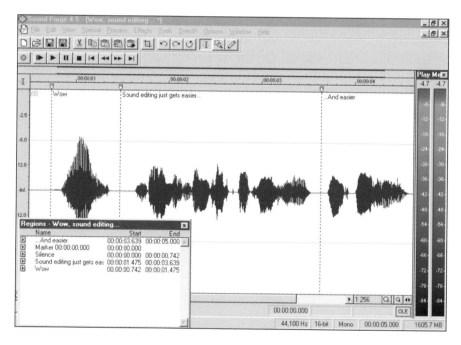

Figure 8.7

A look at Sound Forge's main audio window, where you can make notes as to what the wave-form represents audio-wise, and the Regions screen.

- *Sound Forge XP*—This XP package (see Figure 8.8) is the light edition of Sound Forge, designed specifically for Web-file production. It doesn't have all the bells and whistles of its big brother program, but if you are just starting in Web media production, this program is a great entry-level tool.

Figure 8.8
The Sound Forge XP splash screen. The user interface is almost identical to that of Sound Forge.

- *Vegas Video*—Here's the big boy of Sonic Foundry's programs. Vegas Video (see Figure 8.9) is a professional high-end audio/visual (A/V) production tool that lets you create multimedia for the Web, for CD and DVD production, and for broadcast. The interface shown in Figure 8.10 is extremely easy to work with, with numerous tabbed areas that give you access to other production elements (see figure 8.11).

Figure 8.9
The Vegas Video splash screen.

Sonic Foundry also produces extras for these programs that help you manage the audio quality of your files when producing them for the Web. These products include:

- Noise Reduction

- Stream Anywhere

If you are using a Windows-based system and want to move into the audio and A/V realm, I highly recommend that you try these programs. You can find out more about Sonic Foundry's software (and you can download demos) from the Web site **www.sonicfoundry.com**.

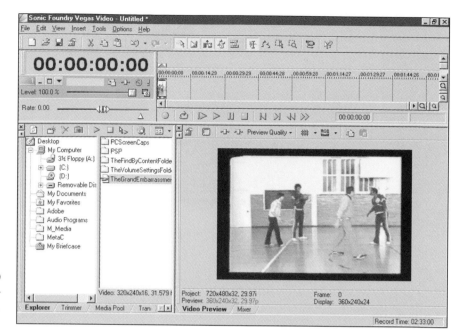

Figure 8.10

Putting audio to my very embarassing video (discussed in Chapter 7).

Figure 8.11

A close-up of Vegas Video's timeline, zoomed out to show both the video and audio layers of the production.

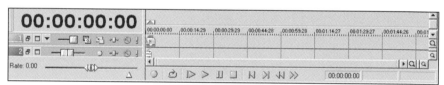

Cakewalk (**www.cakewalk.com**) produces another set of high-end audio editing tools. Their products include the following:

- *Cakewalk and Peavey StudioMix*—This package has eight independent control modules that can be assigned to each track of your mix.

- *Cakewalk Home Studio 9*—This Windows 95/98/NT 4 product is a powerful, entry-level software package that lets you create 256 virtual audio tracks.

- *Cakewalk Pro Audio Deluxe 9*—This package features everything in Home Studio 9, and adds in The Musician's Toolbox III, which is a two-CD-ROM set of MIDI and audio files, as well as other useful tools to help you learn to create your own music.

- *Cakewalk Pro Audio 9*—This package features 32-bit real-time effects processing, waveform editing, and DirectX audio plug-in support, among others.

- *Cakewalk Pro Suite*—This Windows 95/98 package features virtually everything from all the other packages, and it adds in extra files to help you create ear-catching music. Figure 8.12 shows some of the Pro Suite features.

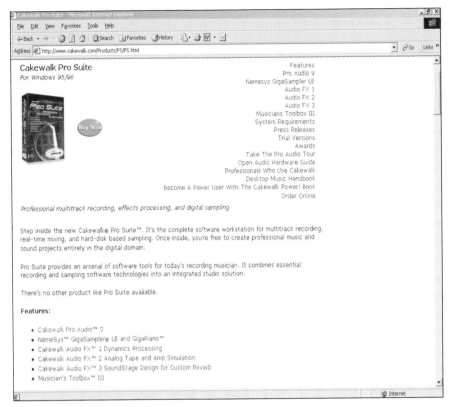

Figure 8.12
Cakewalk's premiere audio package, Pro Suite.

Windows and Mac

My first experience with computer-based audio editing outside of the broadcast environment was with Cubase, **www.cubase.com**, a very deep and highly professional tool that has been around for a number of years (see Figure 8.13). Cubase VST 5 is intense and is definitely *not* for someone who wants to get right in there and, within minutes of installing the software, create their own music. Cubase has an open architecture that allows you to add plug-ins to extend the functionality of the program. I definitely recommend this application for intermediate to advanced musicians and songwriters looking for a truly high-end production tool. You can download demos of VST/24 for Windows and Mac from the Cubase site.

Macintosh

As I mentioned previously, Bias, Inc. produces a program called Peak 2.5 for the Mac (see Figure 8.14). It's a highly sophisticated audio-editing package, with a simple user interface that belies a sophisticated set of tools. Peak has everything that a Macintosh user could want when editing sound files, and as a bonus, it's available at a quite reasonable price. You can get more information on this program at **www.bias-inc.com**.

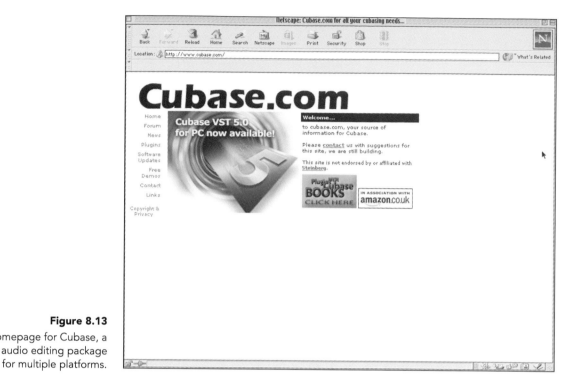

Figure 8.13
The homepage for Cubase, a high-end audio editing package for multiple platforms.

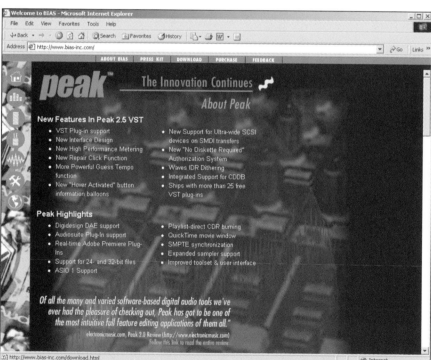

Figure 8.14
The peak Web site, showing the list of features.

A number of other high-quality programs for both platforms are available in retail outlets and from the Web. Additionally, you will find many newsgroups on the Web that focus on audio editing in general and on specific audio packages in point. Do some research prior to buying; it's the best way to find the one that most closely fits your way of working.

Working with Waveforms

With that out of the way, let's look at how you can prepare audio files for importation to GoLive. When working in an audio environment you'll be dealing with *waveforms*. A waveform is a visual representation of the audio file, showing the flow of the music in peaks and valleys as seen in Figure 8.15.

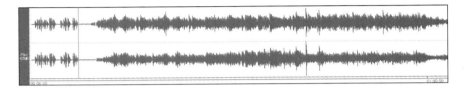

Figure 8.15
An audio waveform as seen in Bias, Inc.'s, Peak 2.1 program.

Single-Track Music Editing

To get a feel for how you work with these types of files, load the OpenTheme audio from the companion CD-ROM in the format appropriate for your system: AIFF for Mac, WAV for PC, or, if you use RealProducer, I also included an RM file.

1. In many cases, the initial view of a waveform is rather crowded, but visual clues help you know what you are hearing. The high points are representative of higher audio levels as music builds or, for example, the sharp strike of a cymbal. The low points are where the music fades or grows softer.

2. Refer to your audio editing software's user manual to find out how to zoom in on the waveform. As you do this, the peaks and valleys become more separated, as shown in Figure 8.16, so you can begin to see each beat of a drum or each representation of voice or individual instruments.

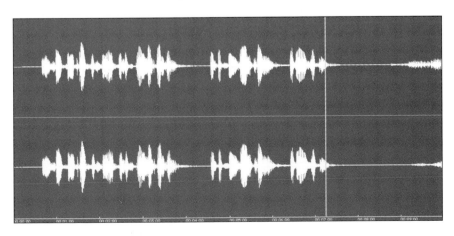

Figure 8.16
The highs and lows in waveform editing. Watch closely as the "playhead" moves across the waveform so that you can begin visualizing how it corresponds to what you hear.

3. By selecting areas in your waveform, you can copy and paste sections of music in order to create your own unique sound file. Additionally, through your audio application's various menus, you can fade your audio in or out to make smoother transitions. Figure 8.17 shows a Fade In effect for the OpenTheme audio.

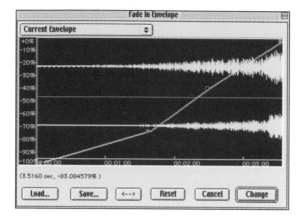

Figure 8.17

After you edit your audio, you'll want to create a fade in so the start of the music isn't so abrupt.

Efficiency Is the Key

As you become more proficient at audio editing, you'll begin to create multiple layer files that take up more and more space due to their ever-increasing length. It's a natural part of creative advancement: You'll want to use all your tricks to create that ultimate aural and visual presentation. As the complexity deepens, however, the size of your files increases exponentially. Consider that, in raw form, a five-minute piece of music can be hundreds of megabytes (see figure 8.18), and that's even before you add video.

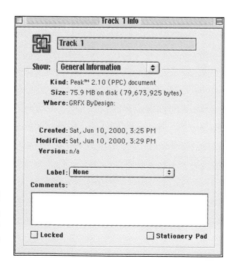

Figure 8.18

The Info screen associated with the raw music file. Notice how large this file has grown prior to compressing it.

Saving your files on CD-ROM or DVD for presentations, this is usually no problem unless you don't have enough memory in your system. But, how do you save files for the Web? Well, as you all know, even a 1-megabyte file download can be tedious. Compression technology for both your video and audio needs is out there to save your, and your visitors', sanity.

Compression Software for Beginners to Professionals

Media Cleaner EZ, Media Cleaner 5, Media Cleaner Pro, and the recent Media Cleaner Compression Suite (**www.terran.com**/) are very high-end compression tools that not only safely and efficiently compress your files, but they also allow you to save them in virtually all of the popular Web formats: QuickTime, AVI, RealMedia, MP3, and more. The simple-to-use interface shown in Figure 8.19 literally guides you through the entire compression process. Available for both Windows and Macintosh, you can download a demo of Media Cleaner Pro from the Terran Web site.

Compression software uses small programs called CODECs, which are specific algorithms that tell the software how and what type of compression and decompression of your files should happen. QuickTime employs various CODECs, including Sorensen, that come free with the program. Other CODECs can be purchased to add flexibility to your work. Among the most common CODECs are:

- Sorenson Video, for high-quality Web video

- RealVideo G2 with SVT, the main video CODEC for RealVideo

- MPEG-4, which—again—creates high-quality Web video

- JPEG, for photographic images

- QDesign, for high-quality QuickTime 3 audio for the Web

Note: The Codec Central URL is a shortcut that will automatically take you to the appropriate area of the Terran, Inc., Web site.

You can visit various Web sites to learn more about CODECs; however, a good first-stop site is **www.CodecCentral.com**.

So, why is there all this talk about CODECs? Understanding exactly which CODEC works for which media type that you are saving to (QuickTime, RealVideo, MPEG, AVI, and so on) will help you save files in a more efficient and high-quality manner. A bonus is that, because GoLive comes with the QuickTime Editor, when you save files for the Web, many of these CODECs are already at your disposal. Additionally, after you save the QuickTime file, you can open it in a program like Media Cleaner or RealProducer (**www.real.com**) to save in other formats for your multiplatform/multiplayback Web environment.

Aural Awareness

Another aspect of Web-based audio you need to be aware of, and one that Web designers overlook, is the sampling rate. You don't want to bog down your Web site with files that are far too complicated for the delivery system. From this point on, most of this caution refers to stereo files, although the information also pertains to saving mono and surround files.

Sample rate refers to the number of samples/second at which the file is played back. The more samples, the larger the file; conversely, the fewer samples, the smaller the file. This is because the higher the sample size, or the accuracy in which a sound file is recorded, the higher the quality of that sound. We all want our work to shine, so the tendency is to save an audio file at its best sample rate.

Sample rates are broken down into two groups, bit size and kiloHertz (kHz). Bit size in the audio world is 8 bit and 16 bit, with kHz rates of 11,025, 22.050, and 44,100, as seen in Figure 8.19. The higher the rate, the better the sound quality—and, as stated before, the larger the saved file size. So, if you want to present your work in its best form, why not just save your files at the higher sampling rate?

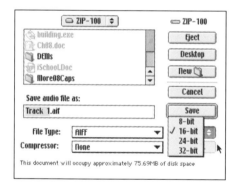

Figure 8.19
Sample Rate settings choices as seen in the Save options screen.

Sampling Primer

Save your files at the best rate for the particular medium in which they'll be played back. The Internet still has some growing to do before we see truly high-quality, hyper-fast access. In addition, remember, the average connection speed for most people is through a 56.6 kilobytes per second (Kbps) modem. Even this is not a realistic speed to consider because these modems are connected through what is quickly becoming an out-of-date delivery system. Normal phone lines cannot handle a 56.6Kbps flow. The highest throughput (the speed in which information is transmitted) is usually closer to somewhere in the low to lower-mid 40s. That means, for fear of stating the obvious, that your files are not being transmitted at the speeds you may think they are.

With this in mind, and with the knowledge that many people use the internal speakers that come with their particular system (which frequently do not produce the highest sound-production quality), why burden everyone with high sampling rates that won't play back at any higher quality, whether in 8-bit or 16-bit? Quick and efficient is the key.

As a general rule, save your audio file as an 8-bit, 11.025 or 22.050 file if it's going to be used on the Internet. If you're burning a CD-ROM or—if you can afford it—a DVD burner, save at the highest quality settings: 16-bit/44.100kHz. These delivery systems can handle the higher sampling rates without batting the proverbial eye, whereas the Internet can't.

Moving On

As you can see, you need to consider many things when working with audio and preparing it for insertion into a QuickTime, Real, AVI, or MPEG file. This chapter only touched the surface of the ultimate complexity, because using audio could easily be a book unto itself. Again, use this chapter as a reference point as you create and save files. As you become more adept at audio editing and, ultimately, audio design, you'll have a strong base from which to work.

In Chapter 9, you learn the ins and outs of working with DHTML and GoLive. You also find out about some of the tools you'll need if you want to avoid writing all that code!

Chapter 9

DHTML Techniques

It's one thing to create visual effects when a visitor's cursor moves over a link graphic; it's quite another to create fascinating animations and informational screens that appear when the same cursor moves onto a link. In this chapter, you'll discover the power of advanced rollover and Dynamic HTML (DHTML) authoring...without having to write a line of code (if you don't want to).

DHTML Demystified

So far, you've discovered a great deal of what GoLive can do with imported files. At this stage, you could create an extremely nice site, but you can do things through GoLive's controls that—especially for the intermediate user—have been hidden away inside those cool control panels. Well, now it's time to delve deeper into the subtle intricacies of Dynamic HTML and see how easy it is to get the effect you want with very little effort.

Now, you will move to the official definition of DHTML (Dynamic Hypertext Markup Language). It was dubbed by Netscape and Microsoft to refer to Document Object Models (DOMs), Cascading Style Sheets (CSSs), and client-side scripting in order to make a Web site more interactive. This means that current versions of Communicator and Internet Explorer can read this type of coding, which definitely makes your job as a Web designer much easier. You don't have to overly worry, for example, that your effects won't show up correctly in competing browsers, although it is still a good idea to view your work in as many browsers as is practical prior to uploading it to your Internet Service Provider (ISP). (Consider it an ounce of prevention.)

Before you start leaping into blocks of code, however, take a moment and learn the official definitions of the following two important parts of this puzzle:

> **Note:** If you do any Java scripting using VBScript, be aware that this form of scripting is only recognized in Internet Explorer. JavaScipt, on the other hand, is recognized by both; this is why GoLive's internal script engine uses the latter.

- *Document Object Model* (*DOM*)—This defines properties of various elements on an HTML page; it also includes the methods assigned in the script. You can look at this as the images affected by your scripting.

- *Cascading Style Sheet* (*CSS*)—This was discussed in Chapter 5. As a refresher, a CSS allows you to simplify your page designs to set formatting and text properties for consistency between your pages.

What's interesting is, according to the World Wide Web Consortium (W3C), that DHTML is not a Web authoring standard; the reason for this situation is that no standardization of the DOM has yet been formalized. CSS and JavaScript, on the other hand, are standardized. Therefore, in a way, DHTML is still in its formative stages.

A Personal View of DHTML

In a way, I might be considered a rogue when in the way that I look at DHTML versus standard HTML. Purists will definitely find fault with my view; but then as with many things in life, we all look at things in the way that best helps us differentiate between what can often be fine points of distinction.

I tend to view HTML as the base code that defines the layout and structure of the site, from image placement to link information. I view almost anything that veers from this norm—user-accessed pop-up screens, animations, floating boxes (FB), and so on—as DHTML.

Getting a Feel for DHTML

Before we go any further, I need to remind you of what I said in the introduction: I am not a script writer. My mind does not associate various symbols or codes with anything that can be accomplished on a Web site. Therefore, with that said again, let's move on.

One of the most basic forms of DHTML creativity is the *advanced rollover*. To clear up any confusion, some people call it a *remote rollover*. Advanced rollovers are those actions that affect what is displayed on the page, while not directly affecting the area where the action was produced. Say what? You'll create one in this chapter, so you'll need a better feel for what I'm talking about.

The MorphMammals Rollover

In this demonstration, you'll use images from the Images folder in the Chapter 9 file on this book's companion CD-ROM. This is a set of files for a new (albeit fake) comic book series called *MorphMammals*. The lead character is Holly Days who, through some extraordinary circumstances, has gained the ability to change into various mammalian forms. In this example, you'll set up a page where visitors can see what creatures she can become:

1. Create a new site and a folder in which to store the various visual elements of the page. The elements you need are as follows:

   - MorphMammals.jpg

   - ChangingShape.jpg

   - Holly, Ani, Gurl, and Ali.jpgs

   - Morph0.jpg

   - Morph1, 2, 3, & 4.jpgs

2. After adding a layout grid to the page, place two Image placeholders and four Rollover placeholders along the left side of the screen. Position the Rollover placeholders between the two Image placeholders. Your screen should now look like Figure 9.1. Create links to the images in the following order:

   - Image placeholders: MorphMammals.jpg and ChangingShape.jpg

   - Rollover placeholders: Holly.jpg, Ali.jpg, Ani.jpg, Gurl.jpg

   After you have assigned the images to the appropriate placeholders, place another Rollover placeholder onto the screen. This placeholder will be the one that reveals the different characters as visitors place their cursor on their names.

> **Note**: In the Inspector window, you will only use the Main Image link. The Over and Click Image links aren't necessary for this project.

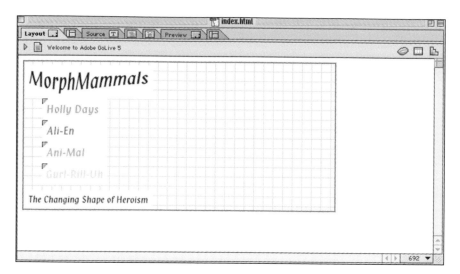

Figure 9.1

The initial placement of the first Image and Rollover placeholders.

Figure 9.2

Preparing for the action that will happen when the cursor moves over the first name.

3. Position the Rollover placeholder centered and to the right of the images you just placed on the page. Create a link to Morph0.jpg. Yes, it's a completely white image. This is done for reasons that will become obvious as you move further into this project. At this stage, though, you need to give this image a name to differentiate it from the other images already placed. In the Name field of the Inspector window, call it baseImage or something similar.

4. Time to make those name images do their magic. First, select the Holly Days Rollover placeholder and in the Actions window select Mouse Enter as seen in Figure 9.2. Click on the + button. Press the Action button and choose Image|Set Image URL. Figure 9.3 shows the added selections that appear. In the Image pop-up menu, select baseImage. This tells the program that, when the cursor is away from this particular Rollover placeholder, your white image should be active. Now link to the Morph1.jpg file in your media folder.

5. You're not done yet. If you checked out your work by either selecting Preview or accessing the Show In Browser feature, you would be able to move the cursor over Holly Days to reveal her picture, but when you moved the mouse away, her picture would remain. That's because you haven't told the program what to do on Mouse Exit. With Holly Days still selected, choose Mouse Exit. Repeat Step 4 and link to Morph0.jpg. This tells GoLive that, when the cursor leaves the area of that particular placeholder, the white screen should return.

Repeat these steps for the remaining Rollover placeholders, assigning the correct image for each Mouse Enter action. Remember that the baseImage must be set for each of the rollover elements for this to work. When you preview the rollover in your browser (again, using the Show In Browser feature), you will see the appropriate image appear and disappear when you move your cursor over the names.

Multiple Rollovers

Having an image change when the cursor moves over it is a cool effect, and one that is the basis for every other rollover effect you can create. However, now you're ready to take it just a step farther because, as you're aware, you only used the baseImage in this example. Now you'll create a multiple rollover effect using the same file. Go ahead and save this page and then drag the images from the Images2 folder into your site's media folder. Then take the following steps:

1. Start with the Holly Days name. Activate it by clicking on it and, in the Inspector window, select Over by clicking on the question mark icon.

2. Next, you need to link to Holly2.jpg. To do so, click on the checkbox below the Image row and link to it using either the point-and-shoot method or the image-link button to the right of the image-text field. Repeat this process for each remaining name.

3. Use the Show In Browser link to view the page you just created. As you see in Figure 9.4, now when you place the cursor over a name, it changes along with the remote image.

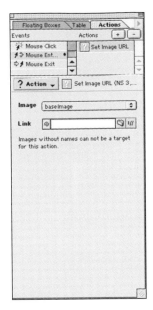

Figure 9.3
The expanded selectors in the Actions window.

Figure 9.4
An example of a multiple rollover.

Discovering Hot Tools for DHTML

Now that you have discovered one of the powerful options inside the Actions window, it's a good time to go over other functions available in this area. Although this hasn't changed much at all between versions 4 and 5, if you're like me, you have overlooked some of the most interesting features available within the program. As we explore some of these, you won't need to create a new site. Just create a new page not associated with a site and make sure the Actions window is open so that you can play a little bit.

Figure 9.5

The Actions window, which holds many advanced controls for DHTML and other Web site creativity.

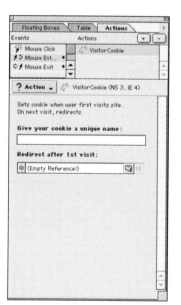

Figure 9.6

Frequently, a GoLive action has a descriptive paragraph to help you determine its use.

The Actions window, seen in Figure 9.5, holds a plethora of cool tools to be associated with the mouse click, entry, and exit. Although the actions are the same for each, it's how you use each action that gives it a unique result. I won't go into great detail on each of the items (you can review them in the GoLive User Manual), but I'll do my best to flesh a few of them out so you can get a better feel for how they work.

Each action is grouped under specific headings. These are as follows:

- ActionsPlus

- Getters

- Image

- Link

- Message

- Multimedia

- Others

- Specials

- Variables

Many times, when you select an Action, a description of what that action does is provided (as seen in Figure 9.6). This can help you choose the most appropriate action for what you want to accomplish. Of course, you won't want to use every action on every site you design; knowing what's available, though, gives you the power to create specific actions appropriate to your client's or your personal site.

With these actions, you can set cookie parameters, force windows to be resized, assign sounds to be played or multimedia scenes to start, even set up links to sites that will only be active at specific times of the day or night. Many of these may not seem useful to you at all, but if you consider how quickly the Internet is changing, those actions you might not see any use for now might very well become a big part of your future designs.

Now, it's time for you to examine the use of the TimeRedirect action. You can find this tool under the ActionsPlus heading. As you can see in Figure 9.7, TimeRedirect is designed to redirect a visitor to another location, depending on the time parameters that you set up.

So, what can the TimeRedirect action be used for? Consider this possible scenario: Your client is a retail store whose weekly sale changes on Fridays at noon, Greenwich Mean Time. The thought of being in the office and replacing one page with another at a specific time each week for the rest of your 20-year contract is about as appealing as diving into a vat of boiling baby oil. With this option, you can redesign the page, upload it when you want, and then set the time that particular page's link will actually access it. When you think about it, you'll see that this is a cool function.

Therefore, to put things into perspective, if an action or feature does not immediately jump out at you as being useful, take time to think it through. You can draw from dozens of available actions, and each of them has the potential of serving your purpose very nicely.

DHTML and the Floating Box

In your travels through the world of the Web, think back: How many times have you seen images floating across the screen? Sure, plenty of sites have featured text moving from one side to another, but rarely did you see an image flying around from point to point. I'm not sure why the Web is this way, other than it takes some extra planning to make everything integrate correctly. I also know from personal experience that this is a technique that takes a bit of time to perfect. However, once you get the hang of this, you can really have some fun.

You also need to be aware that this technology can only be viewed in the more recent browsers—4.x and later. Anything older than 4.x probably won't support this option. Additionally, I've found that, in some cases, the 4.0 versions of browsers don't always show your floating box animations, either. Therefore, it's an excellent idea to warn your visitors that they need the latest and greatest version of their particular browser to get the full benefit of your work.

Follow the Bouncing Ball

This exercise will make a ball bounce across the screen. You'll use a background image and the ball files located in the Images 3 folder. This will be a quick walkthrough before moving on to something more involved:

1. Create a new site. In the media folder, place the files MountainRange.jpg and BallLayer.psd. Click the Page icon next to Welcome to Adobe GoLive 5 to bring up the index.html Inspector window. Change the background color to black. Just beneath the Color checkbox is an Image checkbox. Activate it at link MountainRange.jpg to make it a background image.

2. Drag a Floating Box placeholder onto the workspace and position it to the left of the screen in the black area of the mountain range. Place a Smart Photoshop placeholder inside the Floating Box and link to the BallLayer.psd file. It will automatically open the Save For Web screen, where you can set up your file's parameters (see Figure 9.8). Set this up the way you want.

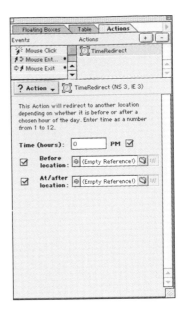

Figure 9.7
The TimeRedirect action has great uses for B2B or commercial sites.

Note: The MountainRange.jpg file will tile on the screen. This image, therefore, will repeat itself to fill all the background area in your Web browser. Don't worry about this right now; you'll discover ways to offset this later in the chapter.

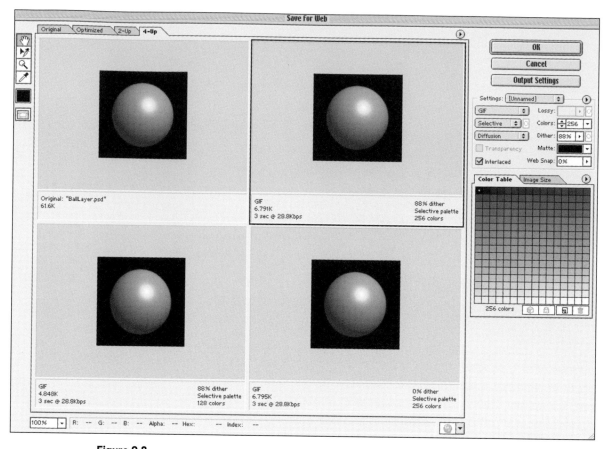

Figure 9.8

The Save For Web screen that appears when you place an image into the Smart Photoshop placeholder.

3. After you have set the image parameters and closed the Save For Web window, it's time for you to animate the ball. Here, this ball will bounce from screen left to screen right. Select the Open DHTML TimeLine Editor window by clicking on the filmstrip icon in the upper right of the index.html window. Position the Floating Box where it is just barely accessible on the left side of the screen.

4. Select the first keyframe. Activate the record option by clicking the Record button in the Inspector window. Move the Floating Box in a bouncing fashion from the starting point to a comparable ending point on the right side of the workspace window. If you want the animation to loop, make sure that your animation is selected in the TimeLine Editor and select the Loop button at the lower left of the TimeLine Editor window. If you want it to loop (to go first from left to right and then from right to left, *ad infinitum*), select the Palindrome option directly to the right of the loop button. Figure 9.9 shows the TimeLine Editor with both the Loop and the Palindrome options activated.

5. Select the Preview tab to watch the animation you just created.

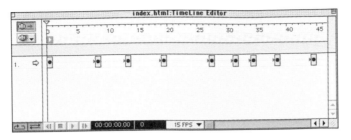

Figure 9.9
The animation set up to loop. The Loop and Palindrome options in the lower left are a dark gray, showing they are active.

As you see, it is quite easy to create a DHTML animation with the DHTML TimeLine Editor. You'll have also noticed upon placing the Floating Box that a small yellow square appeared on screen. This square is the *Floating Box marker*. As you grow more adept at Floating Box DHTML animations, you'll want to add a few boxes on the screen for more intricate effects. For each Floating Box, a yellow marker will appear. Click on the appropriate marker to activate that particular Floating Box; it's the easiest way to navigate between multiple FBs.

Working with Multiple Floating Boxes

Returning to the MorphMammals files in the Images folder, you'll now create a new site and folder to store the JPEG files. The difference here is that you will have your characters passing in front of and behind each other, as well as rotating, to add some extra interest:

1. Set up your page so it has a white background (if you didn't create a new site). Drag four Floating Boxes onto the workspace. Notice how each is numbered and is positioned next to its marker. The numbers can be rather hard to read, especially if you've been working on your site for a while and your eyes are beginning to gloss over. So, assign a background color to each box to make them easier to identify.

2. Click on a marker for the first FB you placed. In the Inspector window (seen in Figure 9.10), you'll see an area where you can assign a color (to the background) or an image to the background (BGImage). At this stage, all you want to do is color code the FBs. Assign different colors to each of the FBs.

3. Place a fifth FB on the workspace. This FB will become a text box after you have everything set up. That's right; Floating Boxes can also be used for text, giving you a full range of creativity in how you choose to display animations. Position this fifth FB near the center of the screen. Move the other FBs around it: You now have everything close at hand.

4. Click once in the Floating Box you just created (#5). A flashing cursor appears, letting you know that it's ready for text to be added. Type the following:

"MorphMammals
The Changing Shape of Heroism."

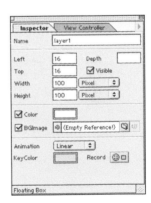

Figure 9.10
You can assign either background colors or background images to Floating Boxes.

Select the text (Command/Ctrl+A). Go to Type|Size|7 or, if you are using a PC, click the right button on your mouse. Change the text color to red by selecting the Color window and dragging the selected color from the long box on the left of the screen over the selected text. Make the text bold and centered. When you deselect the text, you'll see the other FBs behind it.

5. Move the other four boxes to the four corners (it doesn't make any difference which box goes where). Place an Image placeholder into each of these and then assign one of the JPEGs to each. Now it's time to animate the FBs.

6. Using the markers, select the first FB. If your screen is like mine, as shown in Figure 9.11, the markers are stacked above each other with the first Floating Box's marker at top. There's another way to select an FB; you can open the Floating Boxes window seen in Figure 9.12. Once in the Floating Boxes window, each box is listed as a layer. In this window, you can make each box visible or invisible by clicking on the eye icon. You can name each of these layers in the corresponding Inspector window.

7. Begin animating each FB by using the methods described in the last project. Be as creative as you like. When you're happy with the animations, save your file.

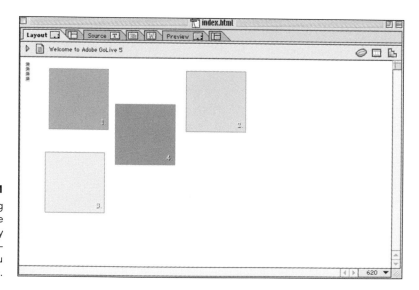

Figure 9.11
The markers for the Floating Boxes are stacked in this example (see upper-left corner). They could also be lined up horizontally, depending on how you placed them.

You can tweak your animation by selecting any keyframe in the TimeLine Editor and moving it to different locations along the TimeLine. Additionally, when you select a given keyframe (see Figure 9.13), more options become available in the Inspector window. These new options include the Left and Top coordinates of the particular Floating Box and Depth. Use these options to change the level (z depth) of the Floating Box, sending it behind or in front of other FBs it encounters. The number 1 positions the Floating Box as far back as possible, where the highest number in the number of layers you have will bring the Floating Box and its image all the way to the front.

Figure 9.12

The Floating Boxes can also be selected using the Floating Boxes window.

To clarify that a bit, because you have five different Floating Boxes in this file, typing "1" in the Depth box positions that FB behind all the other boxes, whereas typing "5" in the Depth box positions it in front of all the other ones. Now, it's time for you to give it a try.

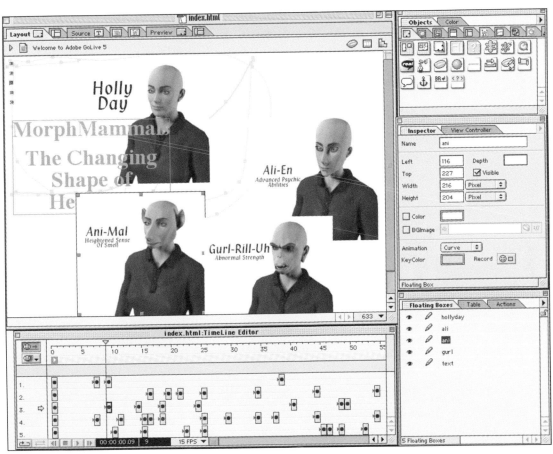

Figure 9.13

Selecting a keyframe in the TimeLine Editor activates more control options in the Inspector window.

Changing Depth

Moving a Floating Box behind or in front of another element is also referred to as *changing the Z position* of the object. This term comes from CAD and 3D applications where the X coordinate is the height of an object, the Y coordinate is the position along the horizontal (left/right) plane, and the Z coordinate is how close to or far back from the viewer an object is.

In the following exercise, you'll work with z depth, moving a layer behind another to create the feel of depth:

1. First, select the FB that contains the text. Click on the keyframe at the starting point (0) and enter the number 1 in the Depth box of the Inspector window.

2. Starting from Layer 1 and working down toward Layer 4, position as 2, 3, 4 and 5, respectively.

3. You can assign different positions for the layers at various keyframes, giving your movement extra impact as images cross over in front of and then slip behind each other through the course of the animation.

When dealing with multiple Floating Boxes, get into the habit of naming each layer so it's easily recognizable. This becomes imperative if you're working in a group situation where files are interchanged among different locations. Working in groups is discussed more thoroughly in Chapter 10, but suffice it to say if you are with a company that has its graphic department in one geographical location and your Web design division in another, keeping things as clean and specific as possible will make all of your lives much easier.

Also consider this: If you are building a personal Web site, it will take you anywhere from a few days to a few weeks to put it together. During this time, it is too easy to forget which FB is which. Giving each layer a distinctive name should be the first thing you do as you place content in there.

A Few More Samples

Okay, you've gone over a lot of information regarding putting DHTML options on your site. Next, you'll look at a few more examples of how DHTML can enhance your site presentation before combining the effects in a more complex way.

Secondary Info Screen

Have you ever entered a site where, once you started moving around, a warning screen came up? If so, then you've probably considered adding something like that to a site of yours. Here's how you can do it in GoLive 5:

1. Place a Rollover placeholder onto your workspace. Use one of your own image files, or use the Morph1.jpg file from earlier.

2. Open the Actions window and select Mouse Enter. Use the + button and in the Action pull-down, select Message|Open Alert Window. Figure 9.14 shows the Message field in which you can type whatever alert you feel necessary. Do not press Return/Enter until you are done. The text will automatically be formatted to fit the warning screen.

3. After that, open your page in your Web browser and see what happens when you move the cursor over Holly Days. Figure 9.15 shows the alert that I created as this example; the alert appeared as I moved the cursor over Holly.

Figure 9.14

Type the alert message you want to appear into the Message field.

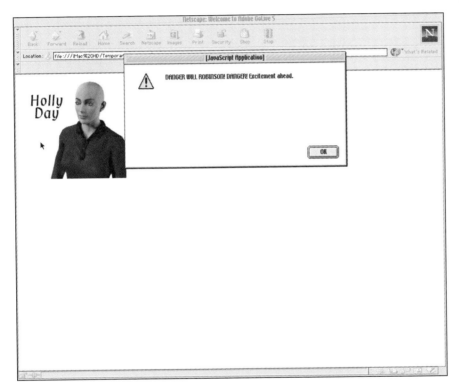

Figure 9.15

The warning screen comes up when you move the cursor over the image.

An Image a Day

You might also want to create an area where, each day, a surprise image appears during a certain rollover action. This is a fun way to keep people coming back, especially if you have a lot of artwork or images you want to show off. For this demonstration, you will use the Morph JPEGs mentioned previously in this chapter. You'll set this up in the same way you set up the previous remote rollover. To create the surprise image, take the following steps:

1. Place two Image placeholders onto the workspace and line them up next to each other. Put the Morph1.jpg file in the left-most placeholder,

and the Morph0.jpg image in the other. Change the name of the latter to Screen.

2. In the Actions window, select Mouse Enter and then ActionPlus|DailyImageURL. The screen you see in Figure 9.16 will appear. In the Image pop-up, select Screen. Then enter an image location for each day of the week. A visitor who moves their cursor over the leftmost image will be greeted with a new image each day.

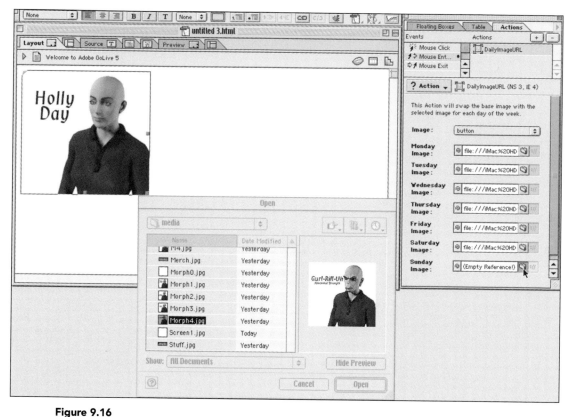

Figure 9.16

The DailyImageURL screen, where you can assign a different image to be displayed, with each image dependent on the day of the week.

The Active Site

Now you're ready to go ahead and put together everything you've learned so far to get a feel for how these tools can be employed in your site design. Not only will this following section review what you've already accomplished, but it will also add a few more elements that weren't covered yet. This site will be the first page of the new MorphMammals site. It will use the same files as earlier, plus image files in the Images4 folder from this book's companion CD-ROM. Before you begin, though, here's an idea of what you'll be building.

As was mentioned previously, MorphMammals is a new (and imaginary) comic book printed by a large conglomerate. It really doesn't need any more money, but figure it will make billions, not only on the comic itself, but also in all the ancillary materials such as toys, Halloween costumes, and so on. You have been hired by this company to create a site that draws upon all the fun and fantasy of the comic, while gently guiding the visitor to the sales section of the site. For this section, you'll only build the home page with all the effects active. You will be presenting this to the head of the conglomerate. Figure 9.17 shows the final layout of the page. So let's get started.

Figure 9.17
The final look for the fictitious MorphMammals site.

Setup

Create a new site folder called MorphMammals and a media folder. Place all the Morph JPEG files in the media folder, as well as the files from the Images4 folder. Now it's time to start designing. Take the following steps:

1. First, set the background image. Click on the Page icon and, in the Inspector window, activate Image and link to Bkg.jpg. This is a 640×480 pixel file. As you can see, the file is set up so you can add rollovers, text, and other placeholders.

2. Place a layout grid on the workspace and change the Width/Height ratio to 625×480 in the first two fields of the Grid Inspector window. Your screen will look much like Figure 9.18. (Placing the grid on the workspace helps in the precise positioning of the following placeholders.)

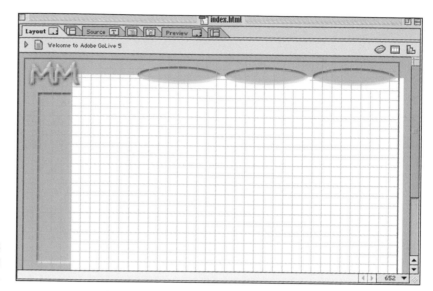

Figure 9.18
The background image and grid are now in place.

3. Place four Rollover placeholders horizontally along the bottom of the screen so your work looks like Figure 9.19. Then place three more Rollover placeholders inside the vertical depression at screen left, as is detailed in Figure 9.20.

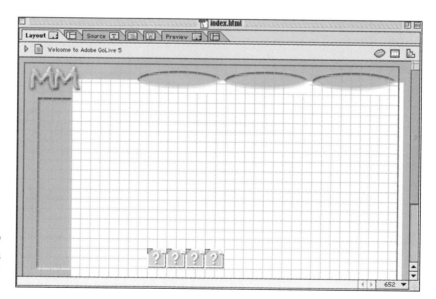

Figure 9.19
Four new Rollover placeholders are positioned horizontally at the bottom of the workspace.

4. Now, position three layout text boxes inside the ovals at the top of the screen, and position a Rollover placeholder near the center of the grid in preparation for adding content to it. (If you placed the Rollover placeholder in its final location along the right edge of the grid, when you linked to the image the grid would be resized to compensate.)

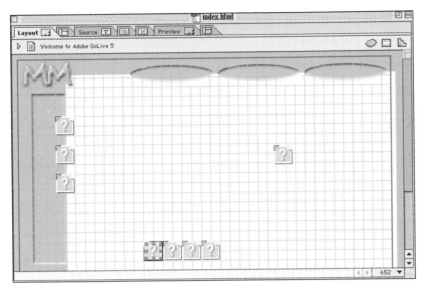

Figure 9.20
Now, three of the eight original Rollover placeholders are positioned at screen left.

5. Link to the following files (starting from screen left and moving around to the center Rollover placeholder:

   - ButtonUp.jpg (Main) and Charac.jpg (Over)

   - ButtonUp.jpg (Main) and Merch.jpg (Over)

   - ButtonUp.jpg (Main) and Stuff.jpg (Over)

   - Holly.jpg (Main) and Holly2.jpg (Over)

   - Ali.jpg (Main) and Ali2.jpg (Over)

   - Ani.jpg (Main) and Ani2.jpg (Over)

   - Gurl.jpg (Main) and Gurl2.jpg (Over)

   - Morph0.jpg

6. In the text boxes you placed inside the ovals, from left to right, type "Fast!", "Furious", and "Fun". Change the size to 5, make the text bold, and change the color to R204, G0, B204, and center. Hold down the Shift key and select all three text boxes. In the Align window, choose the alignment option that is third from the right in the second row. Your screen should now resemble the one shown in Figure 9.21.

Now take a few moments to make sure that all the rollovers are working correctly by selecting the Preview tab. Save the file, and then you'll start working on the first set of rollovers for your developing page.

The First Set of Rollovers

This first set of rollovers will pretty much duplicate what you did earlier. The main links will be the names at the bottom of the screen. Again, you will not

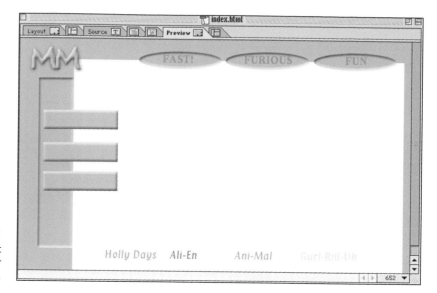

Figure 9.21
When you finish with this first section of the project, your screen will look similar to this.

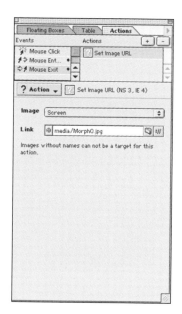

Figure 9.22
The Mouse Exit command and links in the Actions window.

only want to create the Mouse Enter, you'll also assign the Mouse Exit function as well. The following steps show how to do it:

1. Select the Holly Days rollover. In the Actions window choose Mouse Enter and set it up to reveal Morph1.jpg using the Set Image URL command. Don't forget to choose Screen in the Image pull-down menu. Then, select Mouse Exit and set up the command to return to the Morph0.jpg image. Figure 9.22 shows how the result should look.

2. Repeat this process for the rest of the rollovers along the bottom of the screen. Again, save the file then make sure all your commands are functioning correctly by choosing Show In Browser.

The Second Set of Rollovers

Now it's time for you to set up remote rollovers associated with the gray bars along the left side. These remote rollovers will be different than the last set: The information revealed will become a link to another page in the site, so you won't be creating a Mouse Exit event:

1. Place a Rollover placeholder approximately one-and-one-half grid spaces to the right of and one grid space above the top of the top bar. In the Inspector window, link to Screen1.jpg as the main image. Give it a recognizable name in the Name field.

2. Select the top-most bar (the one that reveals the word "Characters" when the cursor moves over it) and create the same Mouse Enter event you just created. In the Actions window, you need to link to the Info1.jpg file. Your work now should look like Figure 9.23.

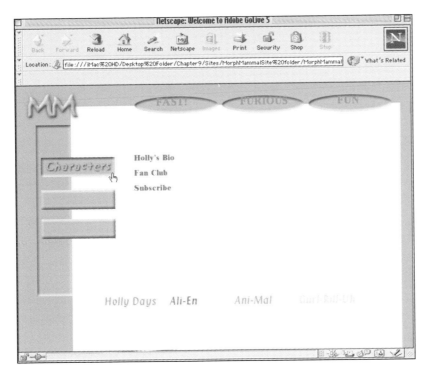

Figure 9.23

A second set of rollovers is being created for the three gray bars on the left side of the screen.

3. Repeat the above steps using the Info2.jpg file for the middle bar and the Info3.jpg file for the bottom bar.

Creating the Links

These bars are the actual links to other parts of the site, with the remote rollover reveals telling the visitor what they'll be accessing. Consequently, you need to set up the link information in the individual bar's Inspector window. Normally, you would assign the page the visitor connects to in the same way that you assign images, but because the only thing created so far is this home page, you'll fake it a bit:

1. Select the top bar. In the URL field of the Inspector window, type a URL. For the purpose of this project, just enter the URL of your favorite site (for an example of this, see Figure 9.24).

2. Repeat the process in Step 1 for the other two bars, once again typing the name of a remote URL.

Figure 9.24

Creating a link to a new page.

Bypassing Writing Extra Code

As you know, through the actions you have just taken, GoLive automatically writes the appropriate HTML script for you. In reality, you never have to access the source code if you don't want to. Sometimes, though, it's fun to just take a peek at the code that's been generated and try to figure out what it all means.

In the source file, the link you just created reads like the following:

```
<td width="112"height="118"colspan="3"rowspan="3"valign=
"left"align="left"xpos="176"><csobj w="90"h="90"t=
"Button"ht="media/Info1.jpg">
<a href=http://www.coriolis.com/target="_blank"onmouseover=
"CSAction(new Array(/*CMP*/'B58EC6E18'));RETURN CSIShow
(/*CMP*/'button2',1)"onmouseout=
"return CSIShow(/*CMP*/'button2',0)"onclick=
"return CSButtonReturn()"><img src="media/ButtonUp.jpg"width=
"123"height="32"name="button2"border=
"0"></a></csobj></td>
```

The only difference between this code and what you have just created is the "_blank" command near the middle, which tells the browser to open a new, blank window for that particular assigned link. So, if you wanted to add it into your existing code right now, you could do it by clicking on the Source tab in the workspace window, locating the appropriate code for that button, and typing that snippet into the proper place in the string.

However, if you're like me, this would be extremely painful. For those of you who enjoy working directly with HTML scripting, I salute you. Even after all these years of designing sites, HTML is not spoken here. Luckily for me (and possibly for many of you too), you can assign this command quickly without going through all of that coding.

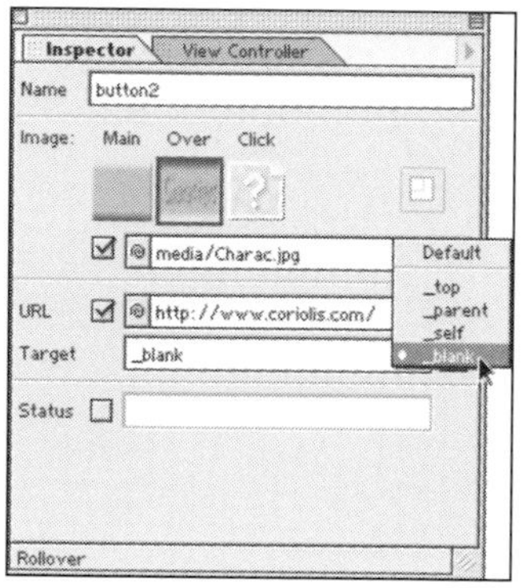

Beneath the URL field in the Inspector window is the Target field, as seen in Figure 9.25. You can either type "_blank" (without the quotation marks) in that field, or use the button to the right to select the link's target. GoLive automatically places that snippet of code into the appropriate HTML string so that, when the visitor clicks on the link, a new page opens.

Figure 9.25
The Target field lets you either type a target command or choose from a list of target options.

Finishing the Home Page

Getting back on track here, a couple of things are still missing—the logo and some text. You'll place those next and then admire your work. To prepare for some displacement of the objects already on screen, hold down the Shift key, select all of the rollover elements you created, and using the down arrow on your keyboard, move them down so they're out of the way, as in Figure 9.26.

To complete the home page, take the following steps:

1. Put an Image placeholder near the top of the workspace and link to Header.jpg.

2. See Figure 9.27 for placement of the logo, and then move the other elements back into place, as you see them in that image.

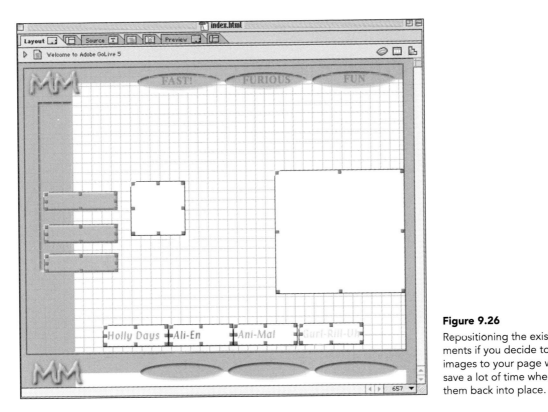

Figure 9.26
Repositioning the existing elements if you decide to add more images to your page will help save a lot of time when moving them back into place.

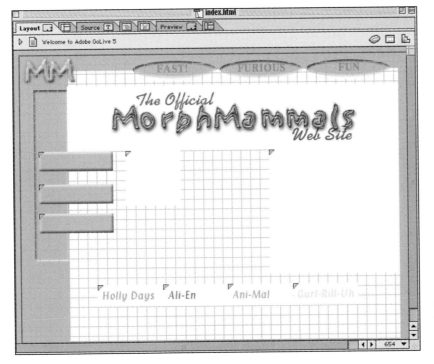

Figure 9.27
The final image and its rollover placement for the MorphMammals site.

3. Now you need to add some text. Place a Text placeholder on the workspace between the two remote rollover screens. Type some fascinating welcoming copy into the placeholder that will wow your visitors. As an example, you can read the copy I created in Figure 9.28.

Figure 9.28
Adding a welcoming message helps to fill in the empty portions of your page.

Moving On

As you can see, the potential for creating super sites with DHTML is not only fast, it's highly intuitive. You could even add a Floating Box in the blank area of the side indentation and have a ball or small images moving up and down as if they were perpetually bouncing off the bar and top edge. You could even have the logo fly in from off screen. Just remember: Keep it clean. The more you have going on in your design, the less impact your text will have. You need to find that fine line between an energetic visual approach and top-notch copy that enhance each other.

Another important area of Web-site creation is the actual layout of the site. By creating a site layout, you not only are able to see how many pages you'll need to create and how intricate the site itself will be, you'll be able to make sure that you don't forget to create pages that are important to the site's success. GoLive 5 gives you the ability to create the design layout directly inside the program so you can reference it at any time—without having to shift through reams of paper. In Chapter 10, you'll learn more about this great addition to the program, and you'll find out how it actually works.

Part III

GoLive and Other Products

Chapter 10

Site Design

Improved visualization tools give you the ability to monitor the interactivity between your pages and overall site designs. The customizable design interface also makes it a pleasant task to check for missing links. In this chapter, you will discover the power of this extremely useful tool.

Visualizing the Flow

We all have our own unique way of working; our own sense of what helps us stay on course during the creative process. Some of us use reams of notepaper to keep track of where we are. Others use their computer's Notepad program. Still others—and often I fall into this category—go with the flow and let the muse take them where it will. When creating a Web site, though, the importance of knowing the basic structure is one of the most important pre-planning processes you can undertake. An outline of the site (which pages link to which, what the topic and purpose for each page will be) is almost a necessity if you plan on bringing your vision to life. Yet, if your workspace is like mine—cluttered to the point of having to precariously position my coffee mug on top of an unstable stack of floppy disks—trying to keep your site mock-up handy for referencing is a very difficult task. So, to have a visual representation of my sites right on my screen as they are being built is like manna from heaven for me.

Creating Web sites is not unlike producing a magazine, television program, or movie, although the relationship between magazine publishing and a Web site is the most accurate. Publishers plan their pages down to the word count per page, where images and ads will be placed, and which pages reference which. It's an exacting process, but one that can produce award-winning publications. Publishers must also remember their mission. Uniformity in look and graphic design from page to page and month to month gives the periodical a recognizable image; a reader who buys an issue knows exactly what to expect stylistically and in the tone of the articles. Structuring your site should use the same principals, because you're really doing nothing more than publishing your vision and your ideas.

GoLive's *site design feature* is a fully interactive tool that helps you create that base structure. It is your *galley*, a term used in publishing for a set of pages that contain the basic page layout prior to adding the images and text. It is also your *galley proof*, showing you how the pages look prior to going to print (staging in the GoLive lexicon). Once you're happy with the layout, you produce the plates, which equates to saving the site design into the site folder and preparing it for transfer to the Web. The last step is publishing—putting your site on the Web for everyone to see.

The Site Design window is also customizable, allowing you to see different visual representations of the site structure that meet your specific needs based on screen real estate and eclectic preferences. What this means is, if you have a smaller monitor (14"-15") with a maximum 800x600 pixel screen resolution, you can change the graphical representation and window display setup of the Design window to better integrate into the available screen space. As you add more and more pages to your site, you have full interactivity with the

Design window workspace, allowing you to position the pages and display their relational links where they are the most effective. More possibilities exist, as you'll discover as you work through this chapter.

On the surface, the Site Design window looks much like the In & Out Links window, as you can see in Figure 10.1. But that's where the similarities end. The In & Out Links window merely shows the hierarchical structure of your site. You cannot move the icons around in the window for better reference; it's strictly a static display of your page and link structure. The Site Design window, on the other hand, is a fully interactive tool that you can use to modify your links and literally build your entire site layout. To understand this more fully, let's explore the Site Design window and its various features.

Note: When working in Site Design, set up your screen so that you can see both your workspace and the SD window. This allows you to modify your overall design, while still having the page you're working on open.

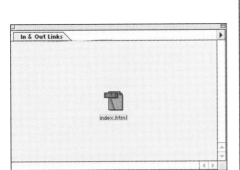

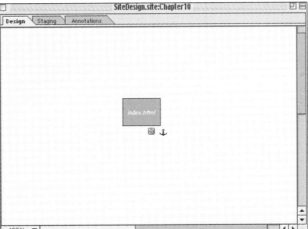

Figure 10.1

A comparison of the In & Out Links window and the Site Design window. Although extremely similar in appearance, the latter is used for full site creation.

How It Works

Understanding site design is good, but how does the site design area really work, and why would you want to use it? Simply put, you can build your entire site within this area, modify its setup, create or delete links from one page to another, and see how your actions affect the site in a temporary fashion. Usually, when you build a site, you're making design commitments that can be difficult to correct, because one change could affect a slew of other pages or links. Working in the site design area lets you experiment and hone your site until you're ready to tell the program that this is what you want. It's your interactive sketch and notepad, giving you instantaneous feedback on any modification actions you take.

It's yet one other thing. If you're like me, and you create sites that encompass dozens of pages, it's often difficult to keep track of which pages are finished and which still need work. With the site design's Staging window, you can get instant feedback; you see exactly which pages are finished and which still need more work.

Creating a Site Design File

Before working with the site design section, you need to create a design file. This is easily accomplished by doing the following:

1. After creating a new site as you normally would, go to the site window and click on the Designs tab.

2. Select Design|New Site Design. A page will appear in the Design Site window. You can change the name of this page immediately, or you can change it later by clicking once on the icon and typing a new name in the resultant Inspector window.

3. Double-clicking on this initial icon in the Design Site window opens the site design workspace.

This is a nice, easy process to get started, much like that of creating a new site. To view the Site Design window, double-click on the file you just named. You will now have a blank "staging area" where you can begin to create the site. When you work in the site design area, you basically work on a rough draft, never really creating a tangible file until you submit it. In a way, you can view the site design area as the area in which you create a site prototype, pending final approval, to be put on display.

Another important aspect of the screen you should be aware of is the way in which the toolbar has changed to give you special design controls. Three buttons (seen in Figure 10.2) are now available to you on the left side of the tool bar that, from left to right, check your design for any problems that might exist (such as bad image links), tell the program to submit the site, and recall the design you had just saved.

Figure 10.2
Three specialized toolbar controls appear on the left of the toolbar when you work in the site design mode.

You can create a fresh sight design by creating a new site in the normal fashion (File|New Site|Blank) that is anchored to the Site Design window, or you can import an entire site and anchor it. This latter procedure will turn the home/index.html page into the anchor page. I'll go over this page a little later. First, however, let's explore the Site Design window itself.

Navigating the Site Design Window

This window is set up to provide an efficient means of monitoring your site pages and their interactions with each other. The Site Design window is almost like an interactive quick-reference chart: After you get used to using it, it can save you an immense amount of time in finding that errant page that just doesn't want to appear when it's supposed to. The window contains three tabbed areas: Design, Staging, and Annotations.

1. *Design*—This is the graphical interface. Figure 10.3 shows how this window represents a site's structure by presenting you with a fully manipulatable representation of page linkage. You can also retarget links to modify the structure of your site.

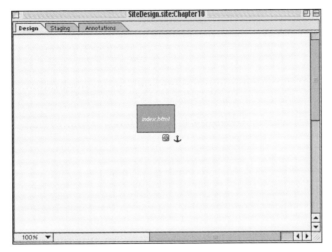

Figure 10.3
The Site Design window gives you a fully interactive graphical representation of your site structure.

2. *Staging*—This area lets you review precisely where you are in the design process. As you work on them, all files are grouped based on where you are in building the site, as seen in Figure 10.4, from Anchor Pages to Live Pages (those that have been completed), to Design Pages (those you are still working on).

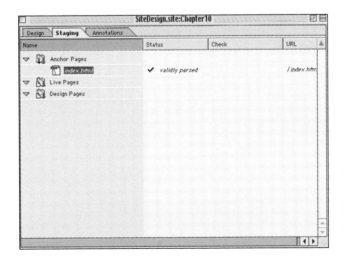

Figure 10.4
The Staging window area of the Site Design window gives you information on what pages have been finished and which still need to be worked on.

3. *Annotations*—If you create notes during the design process for other members of a design team, the team can easily refer to them in this area. Every annotation that you make is listed by subject.

The Site Design window also has a graphical representation in the main site design area. If it isn't already revealed, and your window resembles Figure 10.5, click on the small left/right triangle button in the lower right corner. (The area is highlighted.) This action splits this screen into two parts. Figure 10.6 shows the Site Design folder structure viewable under the Extras tab. This is another site management tool for you to use as you create sites.

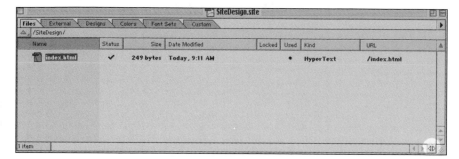

Figure 10.5

Expand the main site window to reveal the other informational tabs at your disposal.

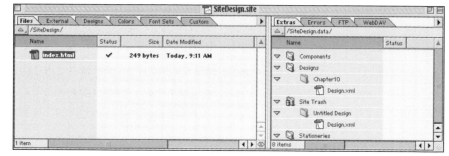

Figure 10.6

Another informational area for your design purpose is featured under the Extras tab in the expanded Site Design window.

Note: You can resize the frames by placing your cursor on the vertical separator and dragging it left or right until the frames are the size you want.

The design area of this window will probably be the one you refer to the most when in this mode. And, it's completely interactive. To find out just how interactive this area is, give the following steps a try:

1. Drag the index.html page icon from the main Site Design window onto the Design screen. A box will appear in the screen.

2. Place your cursor over the index.html box and drag it around inside the window.

As your site builds, being able to drag elements around becomes imperative to keep some semblance of order to your window. You'll see what I mean by that shortly.

Notice the two icons beneath the index.html element you just placed (refer to Figure 10.7). One icon should be familiar: It's the Point and Shoot button that allows you to select a link to an item in your site folder. The other icon, the anchor, indicates that the index.html page is the anchor page for the site—the one from which every other page builds out.

Controlling the Element Appearance

Right now, the index.html graphic representation is functional, but it sure is bland. A medium-gray square is not exactly what you might consider to be generally pleasing—you might like it or you might not. If you fall into the latter category, you can change it. To do this, take the following steps:

1. With the Site Design screen active, open the Inspector window and select the View Controller tab. This action brings up two more control tabs: Design and Display. Design controls the overall Site Design window display.

2. At this juncture, the orientation should be set at Wide as seen in Figure 10.8. In conjunction with the Show Panes area of this screen, you can set how your Site Design window structure will be displayed. Select Tall and Panorama to see how the look of the window changes.

3. If you move the icon in either of the newly created panes, that change of position will be reflected in the other.

4. Now select Reference and Pending. The Site Design window is now split into four elements. Switch the Orientation from Tall to Wide to see how that affects the display. These two additions give you added information regarding the structure of your site and, ultimately, can be saved out to PDF format or printed out, so the design and structure can be reviewed by other members of a design team.

5. Switch to Display and reference Figure 10.9. Here you can change the visual display of the icons, how the page labels are displayed, and the icons' size and color. For this section, change to Show Items As Ovals, keep the Item Label as it currently is, and change the color to red by clicking in the color chip box next to Item Color. Set the Frame Size to Wide. Your screen will now look like Figure 10.10.

As you can see, setting up this area is very simple. Its power, however, lies in its ability to help you visualize and oversee your site creation.

New and Existing Sites

As I stated a few pages ago, you can anchor a new or an existing site to the Web site design area. To anchor a page or site means that you submit it, or assign it, to the hierarchy you're creating.

The New Site

To create a new anchor page for a new site, take the following steps:

1. Create a new site and then double-click on the index.html file to open it. Make sure that the Site Design window is open, as well.

Figure 10.7
A close-up of the index.html element. The Point and Shoot control and anchor page icons directly beneath it give you a quick visual reference.

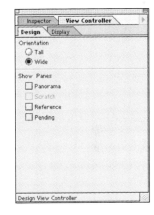

Figure 10.8
In the Design area of the Inspector window, you control the structural look of the Site Design window.

Note: You will not see an immediate change to the icon color until you click in any of the windows away from the icon itself. The standard color for a selected element is medium gray.

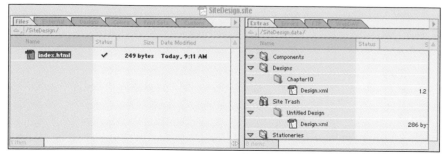

Figure 10.9

(Left) The Display area of the View Controller window gives you numerous options to control the look of the Site Display graphic representation.

Figure 10.10

(Right) After making some basic changes, your Site Display window will look like this.

2. From the main site window (shown in Figure 10.11), drag the index.html page icon onto the Site Design window where the anchor will be established. You know which page is the anchor by the anchor icon situated beneath it.

3. Pages that you create and link to this anchor page will now be reflected in the Site Design window.

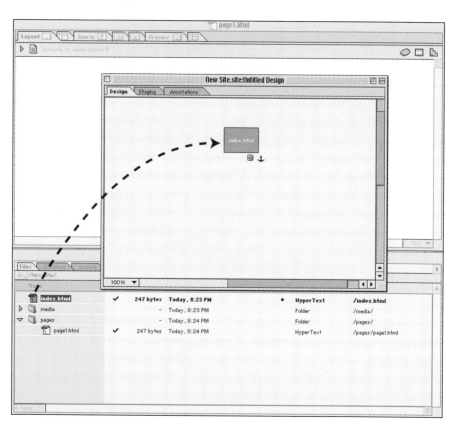

Figure 10.11

Dragging a page from the main site window to the Site Design window turns the page into an anchor from which all pages created from here on are linked.

An Existing Site

To create a site design for an existing site:

1. Open an existing site.

2. From the site window, drag the page you want as the anchor page (in most cases this will be your home page, but it could be any page within your site structure) onto the Site Design window.

The reason you would want to create a design for a set of Web pages within an existing site is to make hierarchical chains that allow you to work on specific sections of a site. It could almost be looked at (using the nomenclature of image-manipulation and vector-graphics programs) as *layering* your site. By telling GoLive that you want the first page of a specific section, an art gallery section, for example, you can modify that section with the design window without having to rework the entire structure of a site. These layers, or *sections* (as they are actually referred to), can then have their own subset of sections. Your design hierarchy will help you manage large Web sites by working within sets of pages.

Developing a New Site in the Design Window

So far, we've spent most of this chapter in discussion mode; now, it's time to actually begin work. Let's start building a Web site design, using a four-page site as an example. The pages that you create will contain no content for now. All you are doing here is becoming used to building a design hierarchy and seeing how you can modify that hierarchy. After you get a better feel for it, you can begin incorporating the design structure to build your sites.

Adding Pages

With the Site Design window open and your index.html page in the workspace, do the following to add pages to your design. For this walkthrough, you'll create the first child page (the index.html page being the parent from which all other pages cascade) and work a bit with the links:

1. To create the new page, click on the index.html icon in the site design workspace to make it active.

2. Select Design|New Page and, as you see in Figure 10.12, a new page is displayed. The new page has a green arrow going toward it from the parent and back to the parent, which shows its relationship to the index.html page.

3. This page is interactive. You can drag either icon to any other place on the workspace. When you do, the hierarchy indicator arrows will stretch, remaining attached to the pages, as you can see in Figure 10.13.

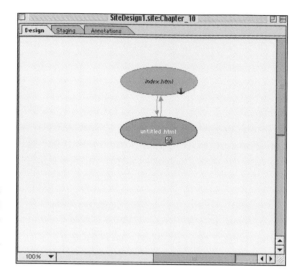

Figure 10.12

A new page has been created (untitled.html), and the Site Design window shows its hierarchical relationship to the parent page by the arrows between the icons.

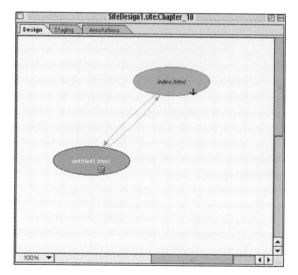

Figure 10.13

The hierarchical link indicators stretch or retract, depending on where you move a page icon.

4. You can also modify these link indicators. Simply click on one and a control point appears between the two arrowheads. Click and hold down the mouse button on the control point and change the curve of the link indicator. This procedure can be helpful when you get a fairly large number of pages in a site and the indicators start overlapping.

5. You've probably noticed the Point and Shoot control situated beneath the page icons if they are in their default square shape, or inside the page icons when you have a different display shape selected. We'll get to this control in just a minute. First, you need to create two more pages, the first page linked to the page you just created, and the second page linked from that page, so that your Site Design window looks similar to that shown in Figure 10.14. Note how each of these pages are linked to and from the previous one, with only untitled1.html being linked to the home page.

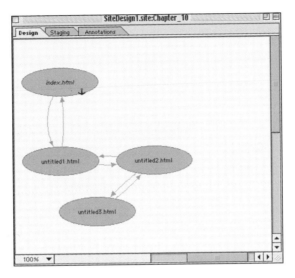

Figure 10.14
The site now has four pages associated with it, each linked from one to the other.

6. Change the links by linking untitled3 to untitled1 and untitled2 to the anchor page. This is where the Point and Shoot button comes into play. First, select untitled3 and use the Point and Shoot button to link to untitled1. Do the same from untitled2 to the anchor page. Notice that the links you just created are a different color than the color of the master links. This color difference indicates that you have a secondary hierarchical relationship between those pages. It also helps you recognize that fact more quickly.

7. Do a quick test. Move untitled3 to a point to the right of the anchor page. Notice how the link indicators move with it. Now, select the blue link from u3 to u1 and drag it out so it swoops around u2. Your workspace should look similar to Figure 10.15.

Note: During the course of writing this chapter, I deleted one of the pages, so the numbering of pages in subsequent images might be different than yours. Do not worry about this; use the images as a guide to the overall layout and design of your site.

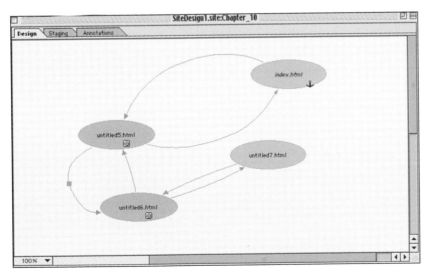

Figure 10.15
Links to and from one page to another can be changed to make the links more easily identifiable. You can rearrange the links to look like this image or in a layout position that you find the easiest to work with.

8. A last item: Go to the View controller window and, under Show Panes, choose Panorama. Change to Display. Click on the bottom portion of the Site Design screen and change the Zoom factor to 50%. The red box you see in the top window is a navigation area. This box represents the area you see in the bottom window. By moving it around, you can move around your workspace to focus in on a specific page.

So, there you have a general overview of the main features of the Design window. Now, it's time to put it to practical use.

PROJECT 10.1 Creating a Multipage Web Site

Switch your attention to the way you would turn the blank pages you've worked with so far into an actual Web site. Save your files before moving on from here because you'll be creating a multipage site via the Site Design window and then staging it for the Web.

Adding Annotations

The Annotations screen enables you to view any production notes you create either for yourself or for others. These notes can be anything from reminders of what you want to do with a particular page to full critiques of the design. Before you begin this process, let's set the scene. It's midnight. You have been working on your site for the past four hours. It's basically finished and you really want to keep going, but your eyes are blurring, you're constantly yawning, and you have to be up in five hours to head to the airport for a five-day business trip. As you look at your page, you see some elements you want to change, but you just don't have the strength left to do it right now. So you create some annotations to remind you of what you want to fix when you get your next chance to work on the site.

Creating these notes is done in the Design window, so set up a site design, and open the index.html page:

1. Use the following files to build a Splash screen:

    - Bleary.jpg
    - Bkg.jpg
    - Back.jpg
    - Home.jpg
    - Forward.jpg

    These are just basic image files, so no need for rollovers. Place the files on the workspace as you see in Figure 10.16.

Figure 10.16
The page design you've created with some glaring mistakes that need to be corrected.

2. I'm sure that you have noticed that the buttons are way too big. This is what your annotation will remind you about. When you return from your trip and open the Site Design window to work some more on your site, you'll remember what you wanted to fix on this page.

3. In the Objects window, go to the Site tab (which has the GoLive page icon) and select the Design Annotation element. Drag it onto the index.html icon in the Site Design window. Notice that the icon is highlighted. This highlight extends beyond the icon itself, indicating the area in which you can place the element to have it linked to that page.

4. Bring the Inspector window forward. It now has text fields where you can type a subject and the text, as shown in Figure 10.17. In this exercise, the Subject should be titled Mucho Importante. In the Text box, type "Reduce button sizes by two-thirds". If you want, you can have the Subject and/or the Text displayed by selecting the feature at the bottom of the Inspector window. You can also change the note display position in the design area by using the Position pop-up.

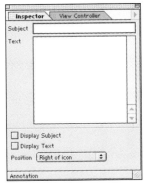

Figure 10.17
The Annotation Inspector is the area where you will type your notes, ideas, or changes that need to be applied to the page.

5. In the Site Design window, choose the Annotation tab. Your note is now displayed on that screen. As you add notes, they will be added to this area, so you have a quick reference for yourself or your team members.

Modifying Pages Via the Site Design Window

As I've already stated, you build your entire site structure within the site design area. But you also can go ahead and build the pages just as you would normally, only in this case, you do it via the site design workspace.

The Splash Screen

For this section you'll need the following files from the CD-ROM:

- boat.liv

- In1.jpg

- In2.jpg

- Sail1.jpg

- Sail2.jpg

Store these files in a separate folder inside your main site folder. Now, you'll begin building the introductory splash screen for the site.

1. If it isn't open already, open your saved site. If you did happen to close down before moving onto this section, click on the Design tab on the site window and open the Site Design window by double-clicking on the saved file. After the window is open, double-click on the index.html icon to open the page. From here you create your page design as you normally do.

2. Set up this page in the following manner:

   - Set the background color to black. Set the Text color to white, and Link to a yellow-gold.

   - Place a Layout Grid onto the page and resize it to 640x480.

   - Place a Smart LiveMotion placeholder onto the grid. It doesn't matter where you position it on the grid, because you'll center it after importing the file.

Note: If you don't have the LiveMotion program, you can download a demo from the Adobe site at **www.adobe.com/products/ livemotion/main.html**.

3. With everything in place, select the Smart LiveMotion placeholder. Use the Browse button (the one that looks like a file folder) in the Source field of the Inspector window to navigate to where you placed the boat.liv file. After you have linked to the file, you will be asked in which format you want to save the file (the only choice here should be Shockwave), and GoLive will automatically open the LiveMotion program. The file will be saved as an SWF file, and you'll be asked where to put it. Navigate to the NewFiles folder inside your site folder and save it.

4. Now center the placeholder on the Layout Grid using the Align Center button on the toolbar. Your page will look like Figure 10.18.

5. The other images are for two rollover buttons, one that will take you into the main site, the other to send them packing. So place two rollover buttons on the Layout Grid. In Chapter 9, you worked on creating rollovers using DHTML. In this case, these will be standard rollovers:

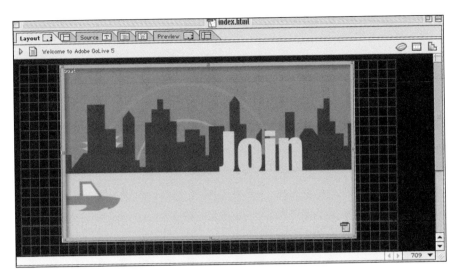

Figure 10.18
A Shockwave animation file created in LiveMotion is positioned
on the page. This is the first part
of the splash screen layout.

- In the left placeholder, link In1.jpg to Image: Main. The In2.jpg file will be linked to Image:Over. Leave the URL blank for right now. You'll be linking to Page 1 of the site in a little bit.

- In the right placeholder, link Sail1.jpg to Image:Main, and Sail2.jpg to Image:Over. In the URL field type in an address where you would like people who don't want to see your site to go. (Keep it clean, though. And don't forget to add "http://" when typing in the URL.)

6. So the placeholders can be in the same position for all of us, move the In placeholder so that its left edge is aligned with the left edge of the animation placeholder. Move the Sail placeholder so the right edge is flush with the right of the animation. Now, using the appropriate arrow keys, move the placeholders toward the center four spaces. The screen will now resemble what you see in Figure 10.19.

7 You need to have some sort of greeting, legal disclaimer, or "created by" text on the page. Place a Layout text box between the two rollovers, positioning it so it's slightly higher than center between them.

8. Finally, because it's proper Web site etiquette, create text links that corre-spond with the rollover buttons. To do this, place a Layout text box beneath each of the Rollover placeholders. Under the In rollover, type "C'mon In". Under the Sail rollover, type "Sail Away". Select the Sail Away text by clicking in the text box and using the Command|Control+A key combination. In the Inspector window, click on the Link button and type in the same URL you did for the rollover button.

Save your Splash screen, and then test it by activating Show In Browser. Unfor-tunately, at this writing, Smart LiveMotion files cannot be seen in Preview mode. So, to view the page accurately, do so in your Web browsers. (It's always

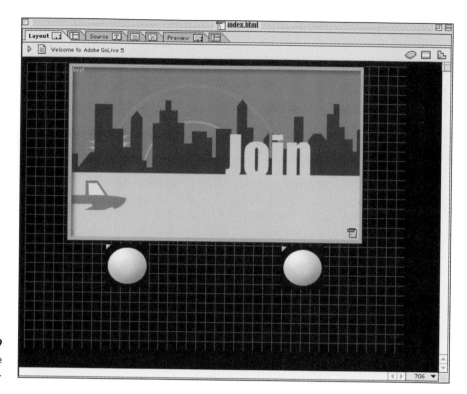

Figure 10.19
The Splash screen with the rollover buttons in position.

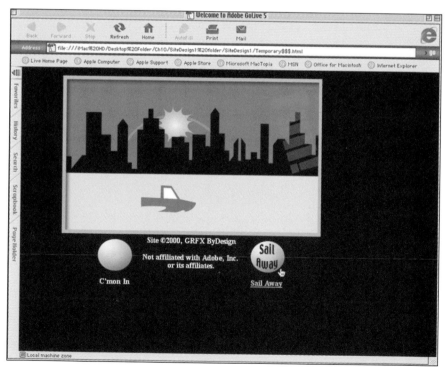

Figure 10.20
The finished Splash screen viewed in Internet Explorer 5.

a good idea to test your pages with, at a minimum, the two most popular browsers.) The splash will look pretty close to what you see in Figure 10.20. Close the index.html page and open the untitled1.html page by double-clicking its image in the Site Design window.

Build and Link to Page 1

After the page is open, place a Layout Grid on the workspace and resize it to 640x480. To complete this section of the chapter, you will need the following files:

- GoLiveHand.jpg

- GoLiveHeader.jpg

- NavButtons.jpg

This page will be simple—basically set up as an informational introduction of what will be found on the rest of the Web site. Although you won't type paragraph after paragraph, you will set up the page so the text will be positioned correctly. It is about as far from an award-winning design as Venus is from the sun, but it will serve its purpose for this exercise:

1. Put an Image placeholder in the upper-left corner of the Layout Grid. Then, place one four-grid block beneath it along the left-hand side and a third one to the first placeholder's right. The first Image placeholder will be linked to the GoLiveHeader.jpg file. Do this now.

2. The placeholder directly to the right is where the GoLiveHand.jpg file is linked. Make sure that the image is aligned with the top of the grid and that the left side is butted up against the Header image.

3. The last image to link to is the NavButtons.jpg file. As you can see, this is not set up to be a set of rollover buttons, it is intended as an image map. Each bar will be assigned a unique map that will then take the visitor to that particular page or site. So, now that everything is in place and looks like Figure 10.21, you'll set up the links.

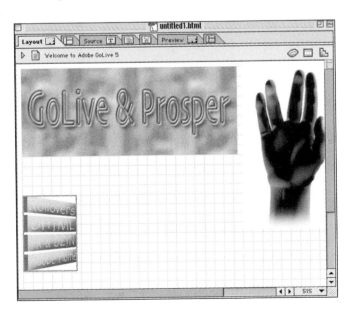

Figure 10.21
The position of the elements in this image is not critical, but it leaves plenty of room for text to be positioned later on.

4. With the NavButtons.jpg image active, select More in the Inspector window and activate Use Map. Go to the toolbar and select the Create Rectangle tool. Outline each of the bars like you see in Figure 10.22. You can use the Create Rectangle tool for this particular image because the elements are spaced closely enough that, while you can control bleed-over from one hotspot to the next, you don't have to worry if a portion of one of the hotspots doesn't totally cover the image.

5. Leave all the URL fields blank except for the bottom one (Adobe Home). Type "http://www.adobe.com/" in that field and, in the Target field, type "_blank" so that a new window will be opened every time you send your visitors to Adobe's site. Use Show In Browser to test the link and make sure that the new window opens as it should. If it doesn't open, ensure that you put the underscore before the word "blank".

6. Now, add two text fields—a horizontal one between the Header and NavButtons images and a vertical one between the NavButtons and GoLiveHand images. Figure 10.22 shows how these fields should be sized for this walkthrough.

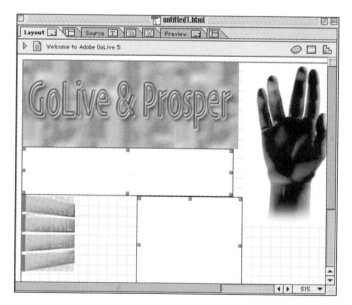

Figure 10.22
The text fields placed on the page are the last elements to be used on this page.

7. In the horizontal text field, use text that is Bold, flush left, and Size 6. Type a one- or two-line welcome. In the other text box, leave the text parameters at their default and write some sort of explanatory text.

8. With that page completed, you can now link the In rollover on the Splash screen to this new page. But, before you do, select untitled1.html (the page you just built) in the Site Design window and change its

name to Entry.html by going to the Inspector window and changing the name in the File Name field.

The Updated Site Design Window

If you look at the site window, you will notice a checkmark in the status area in the Extras window showing that the link is successful. But if you have the Site Design window set up as a single- or double-pane window (Panorama turned off or on), you will not see any difference from what you had before. Things have happened behind the scenes, however, that provide you with a wealth of information regarding your site design. Here is how to garner even more information when using the Site Design window while building your sites:

1. Select the Site Design window and go to the View Controller window (housed with the Inspector window).

2. Choose the Design tab and select Reference.

3. Select either the index.html or Entry.html icon in either pane. The Reference window shows the images that are associated with that particular page, as seen in the lower-left box in the window portion of Figure 10.23. When nothing is assigned to a page, such as with untitled2 and untitled3, the Reference window will be empty.

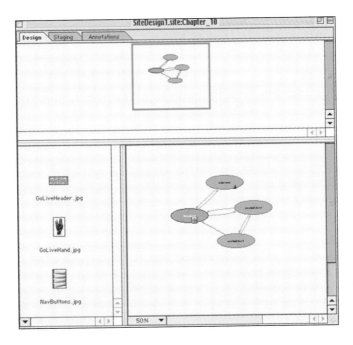

Figure 10.23
A look at the Site Design window with the Reference pane active. Any images associated with a selected page are shown here.

4. Deselect Reference and choose Pending. A pane is revealed that shows which pages have a relationship with the selected page, and whether a link has been made to one of these pages or not (see Figure 10.24). A page that has a relationship, but no link to the selected page, has a yellow triangular warning symbol in the lower-right corner of that page icon.

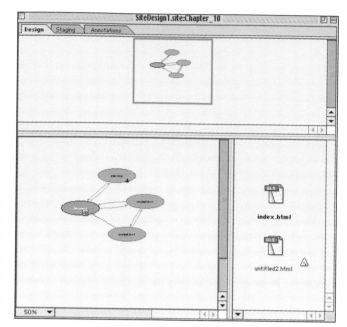

Figure 10.24

A look at the Site Design window with the Pending pane active. All pages associated with the selected page will be shown, along with a visual indicator (the yellow warning symbol) to let you know whether or not a formal link has been established.

Figure 10.25

By setting the Site Design window to Tall—the setting that is shown here—you can comfortably have all panes open at one time to keep track of your site setup.

Figure 10.26

A look at the Site Design window with all the panes open and the Orientation set to Wide. This makes for a very tough job in keeping your design in perspective.

Of course, you can have all the panes active at the same time, but it can get rather crowded. The best way to have the Site Design window set up if you want all views at one time is to set the Orientation to Tall. The Site Design window will look like Figure 10.25, which is far more manageable than what you see in Figure 10.26.

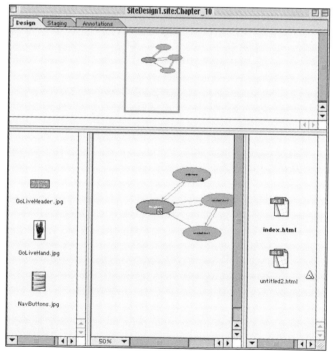

Errata

The Staging tab in the Site Design window gives you much of the same information the Pending window gives in the Design section. The information that you gather from this window (seen in Figure 10.27), however, is a bit more detailed. Here, you can find out if everything is set up and ready to be staged. If everything is set up properly, a checkmark and the note "validly parsed" appear in the Status area. If links are missing or have not been set yet, the triangular symbol and note "generic page" appear.

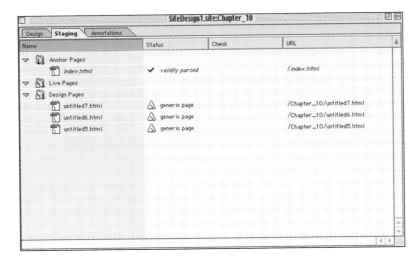

Figure 10.27
The Staging window gives you a quick reference to which pages have been completed, and which still need to be worked on.

Moving On

Employing the Web site design feature if you are working in a group is almost a *fait accompli*. For example, if you're responsible for placing the design elements on a page and then passing the files off to a Webmaster, it would be difficult for the Webmaster to set up the pages, reposition them in the site hierarchy, and literally tweak the site until it's perfect if the site has been laid out in any other way. This leads to the topic of working in groups and how GoLive and WebDAV make collaborative design efforts much more effective for the entire development team.

The Site Design window can also be an integral tool when working on design development in a team setting. In the next chapter, you'll discover the offerings in GoLive 5 designed specifically for group efforts and how efficient the group design process can be.

Chapter 11

The Creative Group Environment

The evolving face of Web production has seen changes in the way a Web site is created. Teams of designers, artists, and technical personnel often work together to create what you see on the Web. In this chapter, you'll discover the way GoLive 5 has positioned itself to meet the workgroup environment.

Producing Web Sites

If you have been keeping track of Web happenings over the past few years—and even the past few months—you know that what we know the Internet as now is not what we're going to be surfing in the next few years. The technology is advancing so dramatically that it is almost impossible for a single person to keep up with it all. Case in point: Until the beginning of this century, the hottest catchphrase in Internet content was *e-commerce*. In case you haven't noticed, I do not use this term within these pages. Companies are folding left and right that, less than a year ago, seemed destined to reach the stars. A recent casualty, Reel.com, handed off its e-commerce service to Buy.com. At the moment, the term "e-commerce" is almost considered a pariah within the community. This, however, can (and does) change on the flip of a bit!

A second case is the evolution of visual content delivery. HTML begat DHTML, CSS1 begat CSS2, graphic delivery is evolving into SVG technology, and the list goes on and on. How does one person stay on top of everything?

Unfortunately, it's literally impossible. If you spent all your time studying the latest changes and learning how to incorporate them into your site, you'd be spending 95 percent of your time doing the latter and only 5 percent actually creating content that is deliverable. So, the trend is now turning toward specialization. Individuals, each with their particular expertise, are being brought together or are forming their own companies to create cutting-edge Web sites as new technology arises. But with the Web, these groups could be spread out all over the world, with some people in the United States, others in Canada, Bosnia, and the UK—literally anywhere on the surface of the planet. The one aspect that hasn't changed in all the years of general Internet access is its capability to let people work together, no matter where they are geographically.

The Internet has brought us to the cusp of a new way of looking at the workforce. On the positive side, it has obviated the need for people to commute to a centralized office building for a specified number of hours per day. Anyone with a computer, a modem, and the right software can work from home just as efficiently (and, in some cases, even more so) than they would be from a cubicle on the 15th floor of a high-rise office building. On the negative side, it can force many people to work longer hours because escape from the job is no longer possible; it's nearby, 24 hours a day, seven days a week. For workaholics like me, this is pure bliss. For families of workaholics, it could spell the end of civilization as we know it.

The Workgroup Structure

Now, let's take a quick look at the structure of a Web design workgroup. Figure 11.1 shows a basic business hierarchy that would be a rudimentary workgroup.

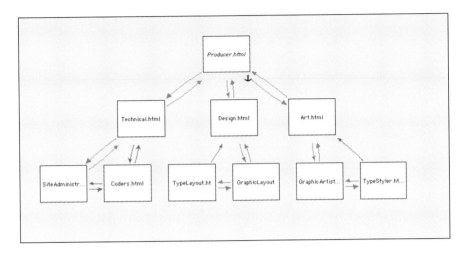

Figure 11.1
One possible Web-production group hierarchy. Some positions near the bottom of the chart could be considered as one, with a number of people responsible for both aspects.

Note: The image in Figure 11.1 also shows another potential use for GoLive's Site Design feature. The structure shown in the figure was laid out in this area of the program, which is why you see the HTML tags.

Here are the roles:

1. *Producer*—The role of this person is the lynchpin of the group. The producer ultimately gives the yea or nay on a particular design or layout. Often, this person is the go-between for the workgroup and the client and is responsible for keeping the project on time and on budget.

2. *Technical*—In a full business structure, this position would be listed as the Chief Technical Officer (CTO). This person is in charge of keeping up to date on all the latest technologies and making sure that his staff is trained properly. His or her department would consist of the programmers/coders who modify a site's HTML, Java, XML, and other technologies to ensure that the site is finely tuned. I use the title Site Administrator in this case to mean the person who's responsible for the day-to-day maintenance of the site.

3. *Design*—These people create the pages in site-design programs such as GoLive. The head of this department would be considered the Associate Producer. The Associate Producer works closely with the art department and the Producer to ensure that the site looks the way the client wants. This person's team may include a graphic-layout specialist to create the look of the Web site, and possibly a type-layout specialist, who chooses the correct fonts and their flow to augment the design.

4. *Art*—The head of this area would be considered the Art Director for a company. This person would oversee the creation of the graphic elements for the Web site. The head of the art department would command a small (or large) group of graphic artists who create the individual pieces of art and possibly a type styler (someone who has been trained to create new font faces for inclusion on the sites that the company designs).

What you don't see on the chart in Figure 11.1 are locations. The Producer could be in Silicon Valley (or in some similar high tech locale) at the home office of the design firm; the design and art department team might also be located at the home office, or they could be spread all over the world. Usually, the technical staff will also be at the home office, or wherever the server equipment is located, although the coders could be in Big Sandy, Montana or in Perth, Australia… they could be anywhere.

It's fascinating how the Internet has changed our world in only the last few years and how it has brought together so many disparate ideas. This "bringing together" has actually made for more creative environments because each of us—as individuals—can continue to grow in our artistic knowledge. As a manager, I encouraged creative discourse. As I told my employees, a bad idea just doesn't exist; although one particular idea may not work for an immediate situation, it could well be the right answer for the next project.

Bringing the Group Together

In Chapter 10, you went over the site design area of GoLive 5. By now, you have a solid idea of how to use this tool to design a site prior to staging it. However, how do you send the site around to everyone who needs to work on it? First, you can put the files on an intranet or you can send the files via email (if your ISP allows for large file transfers). You can use an FTP site to store and retrieve files, as well. This, however, isn't what this chapter's about (although the latter does fall into the last part of this chapter). You need to focus on GoLive's *WebDAV* feature. Unfortunately, you need to have a connection to a server that can handle WebDAV before you can employ it. That's why this chapter isn't going to be particularly long.

WebDAV

As I mentioned in Chapter 1, WebDAV stands for *Web Distributed Authoring and Versioning*. As an HTTP protocol extension, WebDAV gives you the ability to manage files directly on remote Web servers. If your server runs with Microsoft IIS 5, Apache with the mod_dav module installed, or Novell NetWare 5.1, you can use this technology to collaborate on Web-site creation. (By the way, Microsoft IIS 5 comes standard with Windows 2000. It is not included with NT.) In some circles, WebDAV is referred to as *Web Folders* because of its accessibility to geographically disparate team structures. Figure 11.2 shows this distributed model in a graphic representation.

WebDAV setups can have two areas, a file-storage area where the development team accesses the files, and a staging area where surfers can view the finished site. This is a great way for modifying a site and immediately changing the page without leaving the server.

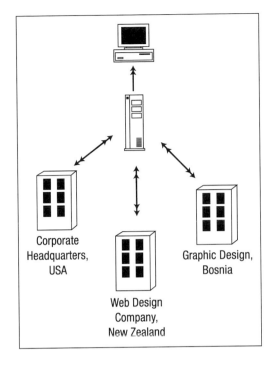

Corporate Headquarters, USA

Graphic Design, Bosnia

Web Design Company, New Zealand

Figure 11.2
A basic representation of WebDAV. Three companies share information on the same server, and their finished work is retrieved by a surfer on a home computer.

Unless you have access to a WebDAV server, this feature isn't going to be of use to you. That's why I have taken the liberty to set up one for this book so you can get a feel for how WebDAV can expedite your workflow. **Driveway.com**, an Internet storage provider (and more), has graciously allowed me to set up a book-specific site so that you can experiment with the WebDAV feature. I'd urge you—even if you aren't a part of a workgroup, but find yourself in need of storage space—to check out their service. It's a free service (for now—you never know what could happen as they catch on), and it works like a dream. You can find out more about their offerings at **www.driveway.com**.

Working with WebDAV

This upcoming section will start with the basics of getting GoLive's WebDAV feature set up, and connecting to the site. In this section I will give you the username and password, which is secret and under the protection of the Universal Password Security & Exchange Commission, so you are hereby sworn to secrecy. And if you believe this… . Seriously, the code you'll employ is for your use if you want to take advantage of this. It's really the best way I can think of to truly give you a way to really get a feel for how WebDAV works.

A couple of notes before getting your hands dirty. First, you must have a site file open to access the WebDAV controls in GoLive; you can't just open the program and log onto a server. Second, you have to set up the WebDAV parameters in a couple of areas. (Here's where you'll learn that super-secret username and password I told you about.) For this initial portion, you won't need to have a site file open:

1. Go to Edit|Preferences. Expand the Network option by clicking on the triangle next to the name and choose the WebDAV option (as seen in Figure 11.3). In the Windows version of the program, you would click on the plus sign.

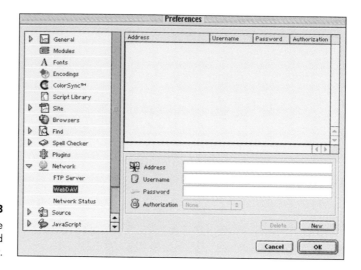

Figure 11.3
The Preferences screen with the WebDAV option selected and ready to be filled out.

2. You need to fill in the Address|Server, Username, and Password fields seen in the bottom-right quadrant of this screen, as well as set the Authorization. To do this, select New by clicking on the button and entering the following into the appropriate fields:

   • Address: **www.driveway.com/user.golivefx**

   • Username: golivefx

   • Password: anddesign

   • Authorization: Basic

3. Figure 11.4 shows how your screen should now look. Once you have filled this in, it will be stored in the program. If you add more addresses (i.e., you have several clients that you or your workgroup are building sites for; store them in separate accounts for easy retrieval), you will see them listed in the upper-right quadrant of the Preferences screen. When you're finished, click OK or press Enter.

4. Now, create a new site so you can set up the next section needed for WebDAV access. All you need is the Site window open; you don't need to open the index.html page.

5. Go to Site|Settings—which was, up to now, grayed out. Select the second choice in the list, FTP & WebDAV Server, by clicking on it once. Your (Site name) Settings screen will look much like the Preferences screen

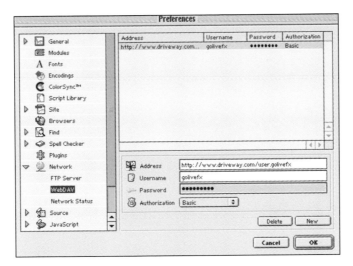

Figure 11.4
The WebDAV Preferences screen as it should look after you input the required information.

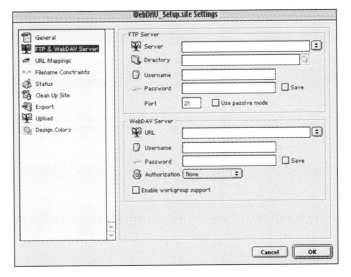

Figure 11.5
The WebDAV setup screen accessed by the Site|Settings command.

did, only it will also have FTP fields, as well. You can place your site's FTP protocols in that area. But for now, all you're going to focus on is the WebDAV settings in the lower portion of the screen (see Figure 11.5).

The reason you have to input your 'DAV settings again is that, when you tell the program to connect to a 'DAV server, it accesses this area to get the address. If you have more than one server listed, you'll need to come to this area prior to connecting to select the correct server.

6. It's fairly easy to set up the WebDAV area of this screen. Use the selector button to the right of the URL field to display the server list you input in Preferences (see Figure 11.6), and select the server you want to access. All your fields will be automatically filled in for you, as seen in Figure 11.7. If you're part of a workgroup, you'll also need to check Enable workgroup support.

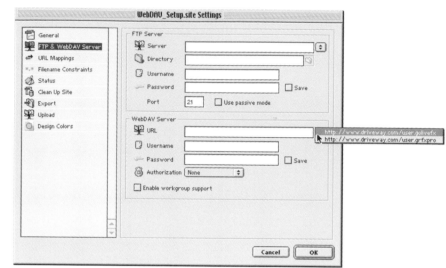

Figure 11.6

You can access a shortcut to setting up the Site|Settings parameters by using the pop-up button to the right of the URL text field. Any servers you have listed will be revealed. In this image, you can see my server listing as "grfxpro".

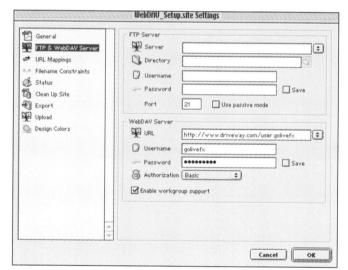

Figure 11.7

The Site|Settings screen is automatically updated after choosing the server by using the pop-up field. Make sure that you also activate Enable workgroup support.

Note: If you have more than one server, it's extremely important to use Site|Settings before trying to connect. This ensures that you're connecting to the server you want to be on, and not to a server you had previously visited.

Figure 11.8

The WebDAV Server connect/disconnect button on the toolbar (the button is not grayed out).

Connecting to the Server

Now, it's time to actually connect to the WebDAV server so you can get to the files I have put there. Use these steps:

1. You can connect in a couple of ways. The first is using Site|WebDAV Server|Connect. Also, a button is located approximately at the middle of the toolbar that's called WebDAV Server connect/disconnect. You can see this in Figure 11.8. Once you connect via either method, more WebDAV-specific buttons appear on the toolbar.

2. Figure 11.9 shows the new controls at your disposal. Starting with the first button to the right of the connect/disconnect button, these are:

   • WebDAV Synchronize All

   • WebDAV Upload Modified Items

   • WebDAV Download Modified Items

You'll also notice the WebDAV tab in your Site window has come to the front (see Figure 11.10). Here you can see the files, folders, and other materials within that area of the server.

Figure 11.9
The controls that become active when you log on to a WebDAV site.

Figure 11.10
The WebDAV area of the Site window shows all the elements stored on the server.

From this point, it's a matter of working on a file, uploading it to the correct area on the server, and giving others in the group the ability to review or modify the file at a later date. What you are also able to do, if the server has both a main site area (that which is accessible on the Web) and a private WebDAV area, is make modifications to your existing site and then immediately replace the old page(s) with the new. This is a wonderful site management tool you should consider using if your server has enough space on it, and it has WebDAV accessibility.

Note: I did not have the site files ready at the time of writing this chapter. When you connect to the GoLive book server area, the files you access will differ from the figures in this book.

Realizing that actual site pages are small (a few kilobytes, at the most), storage will only become a problem if you are extremely close to the storage limits because of all the image and multimedia files the pages link to. So, be aware of your ISP's maximum storage.

Synchronization

You need to be aware of another important area when using WebDAV, because you will more than likely encounter it the first time you log on. That is: *synchronization*. Synchronizing files can be done both on files you have open and those on the WebDAV server. If GoLive detects files that have been edited in either area, it will make sure the files are updated by synchronizing them. This is also a non-date or -time specific function. It's basically a function of differences in file content. So if a page or site has been changed, no matter when, it will be detected.

Community DAVelopment

Now that you've explored the WebDAV site set up for this book, you will have noticed that a site file was actually there. It has been set up specifically for you to work with in a community environment so you can work with files via this function. Here's what has been provided and the ways in which you can best utilize it.

The initial file is on the 'DAV site you've just accessed. So that all of you who have this book can benefit from this, two sets of master folders exist: one called

Original, the other called Modified. Modified is the area where you can work with files that others have changed by adding, changing, deleting, and basically practicing the uploading and synchronization functions. Original is where the starter file is located. All I ask is that you do not modify this file at all. Merely use it as a starting point to build a new site.

If you have set up your own WebDAV area with Driveway.com or another DAV provider, you can download this master file, upload it to your DAV server, and practice modifying the files on your own. Another way you can use this practice area is by getting with friends and colleagues and working as a team to create your own site starting with the Original file. Again, all I ask is that the Original folder remain pristine so everyone has the chance to use the original file as their starting point.

360Code

This feature allows a graphic artist to design a site, positioning elements exactly as wanted, and then send the HTML code to a programmer for modification. Any code the programmer writes to bring extra functionality to the site—DHTML, JavaScript, and so on—will be added without affecting any of the other code on the page. Then, the file can be re-imported to the site for safe, effective updating.

The Source Code Window

If you are adept at HTML, JavaScript, or other coding language, or if you work in a group that includes design and layout people, as well as script writers, the utilization of the Source Code window will become your new best friend. You can have both the workspace and Source Code windows open on your desktop and monitor the code for every change you make on your page. You can also send your page to the script writer at any location; he or she can open the Source Code window, make whatever changes and enhancements are needed, and send the page back to you with very little loss of time.

To give an idea of how smoothly working with the Source Code window integrates with your visual layout, you'll next create a very basic document and then make some modifications to it. Use the following image files for this example:

- EHI1.jpg
- EHI2.jpg
- EHI3.jpg

1. Set up a new site. Unless you already have the Web Color List selected for this window, you will need to do the following:

   - Go to the right-pointing arrow pop-up menu button to the right of the Color window.

   - Select Web Color List from the list of choices.

You now will see a multi-pane color chart, along with a Value field where you can add a specific color value. In the Color window, change the text color to #FF6600. This sets the text to a nice orange color. Figure 11.11 shows the color selector section to use when using values for color assignation.

2. Drag a Layout Grid and three Image placeholders onto the workspace. Link these to the three EHI graphic files and place them randomly around the lower two-thirds of the workspace, as in Figure 11.12.

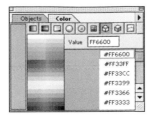

Figure 11.11
Use this color set to choose color using its value code. Either select a color from the color chips on the left, or, if you know the value already, type it into the Value text box.

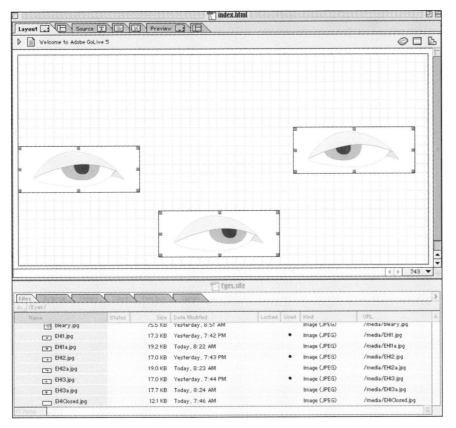

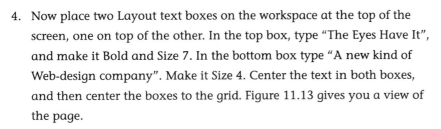

Figure 11.12
This is a rather paranoia-inducing screen for a fictitious Web design company.

3. Select the Grid and click the Optimize button in the Inspector window to fit it to the image edges.

4. Now place two Layout text boxes on the workspace at the top of the screen, one on top of the other. In the top box, type "The Eyes Have It", and make it Bold and Size 7. In the bottom box type "A new kind of Web-design company". Make it Size 4. Center the text in both boxes, and then center the boxes to the grid. Figure 11.13 gives you a view of the page.

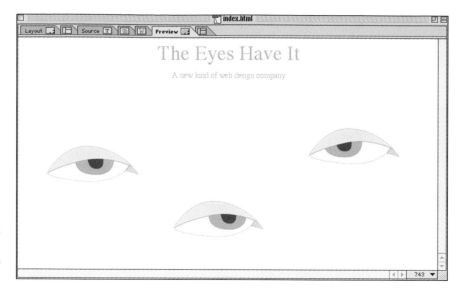

Figure 11.13
Here's The Eyes Have It splash screen, finished and ready to have its code modified.

5. Select the Source tab and look at the source code associated with the page. It's extremely short and succinct, because not much is happening on the page. Switch back to Layout mode and open the Source Code window (Window|Source Code), seen in Figure 11.14.

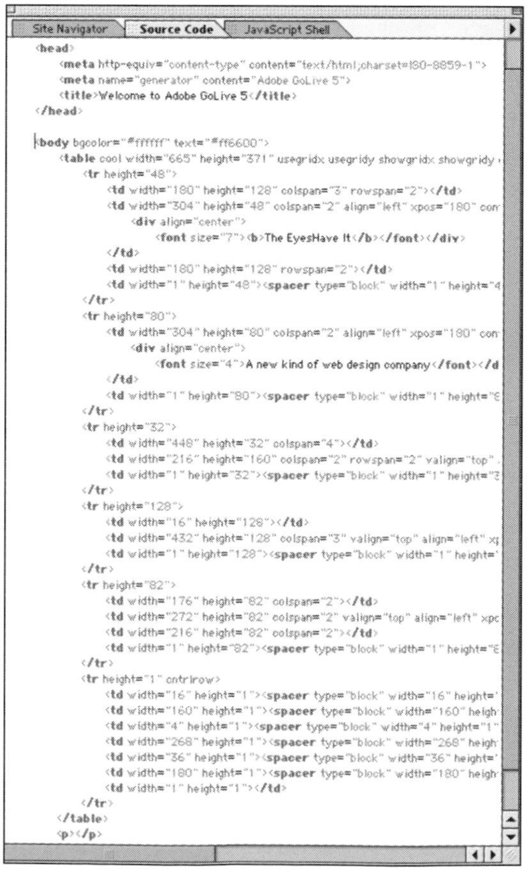

Figure 11.14
When the Source Code window is open while building your site, you can see the code generated for every change you make. Depending on your operating system, this window may look slightly different than in this image.

6. Change the source code in the Source Code Window. Where it says

```
<body bgcolor="#ffffff" text="#ff6600">
```

change it to

```
<body bgcolor="0066ff" text="#ff6600">
```

You have just changed the background color from white to a shade of blue (seen in Figure 11.15) that closely matches the color of the eyes. You will see the change when you switch the main workspace window to Layout view.

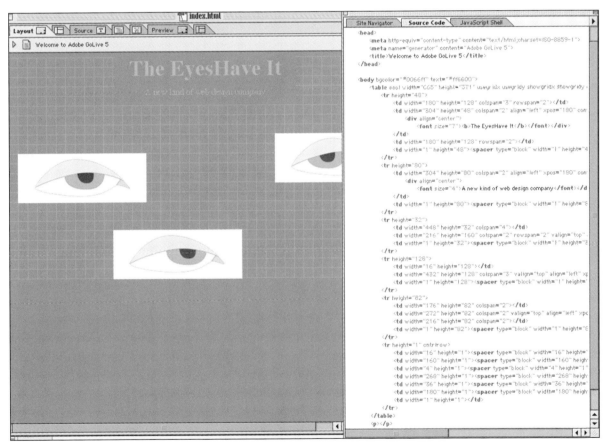

Figure 11.15

The new background color generated by changing the bgcolor value in the Source Code window.

7. This change is automatically reflected in the Source view of the Layout window.

8. If you usually write code in a program like BBEdit or FrontPage, you can copy this code to your other program, modify it, and then copy and paste the changes/modifications into the Source Code window as well.

This last step is an extremely simplistic example of taking the code outside of GoLive, modifying it, and bringing it back in without affecting the rest of the site. For Web groups building a page, the ability to send HTML wizards the source code for modification to (and, then to plug it back in via the Source Code window while knowing nothing else will be affected) is truly a best-of-both-worlds feature.

Other Workgroup Features

In this section, I'll look at some other features in GoLive that, in some ways, didn't fit anywhere else in the book. Although these features aren't necessarily workgroup specific, if you've been following my train of thought regarding a division between the layout specialists and the code-writing specialists, you will see why I've added these materials in this section. I have also provided a Word document and a SimpleText document containing the code for this homepage so you can make modifications to it and explore the 360Code and the following elements.

This section uses the Eyes site seen in Figure 11.16. As you can see, this site is made of standard image files and three rollovers. When a visitor moves the cursor onto one of the closed eyes, it opens and tells what section of the site the visitor will be taken to.

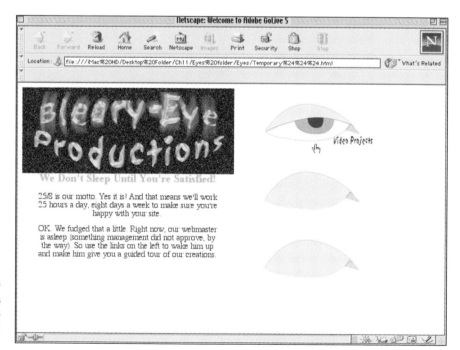

Figure 11.16
The Bleary-Eye Productions homepage with rollover links that make the eyes open when activated.

The Markup Tree

This is an HTML navigation tool that gives you the ability to reposition elements within the page's hierarchy. The screen, shown in Figure 11.17, gives a graphic representation of the elements contained in selected elements on your page. To get a better understanding of this, do the following:

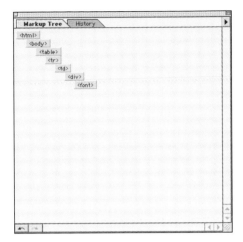

Figure 11.17
The Markup Tree window shows all the content associated with a selected element on your page. This is represented in a hierarchical manner.

1. Open the Eyes folder (provided in the Ch11 folder of this book's companion CD-ROM) and open the Eyes.site file. Open the index.html page and then go to Window|Markup Tree or use the Command|Ctrl+7 key combo to open the Markup Tree window.

2. Select any element on the index.html page. The hierarchy structure will expand and all the elements within that element will be highlighted.

3. Without deselecting the element you chose, open the Source Code window. The element and its contents are highlighted here as well, as you can see in Figure 11.18.

As you can see, this is an excellent way of finding the exact block of code you want to modify quickly and efficiently.

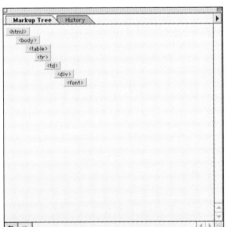
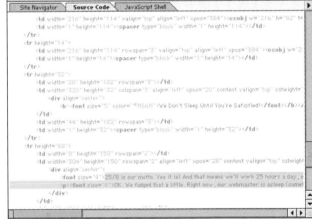

The Find Window

Another way team members or you as an individual designer can find specific code is with the Find window. For code warriors, this is a fantastic screen that

Figure 11.18
When used with the Source Code window, the Markup Tree can help you easily locate specific HTML elements on complicated pages.

can really expedite your HTML modification needs. To access this screen, choose Edit|Find (Command/Ctrl+F).

The Find window is broken down into the following tabbed sections:

- *Find & Replace*—This section (see Figure 11.19) is the default screen that appears when you first open the window. It acts like every other Find screen in other applications. Type in what you want GoLive to find, choose the parameters, click the appropriate button, and GoLive will find that particular entry.

- *Content*—Content (see Figure 11.20) gives you the ability to search for specific content in your site and then lists each match it finds in the large field at the bottom.

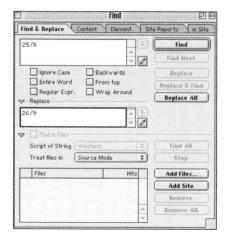
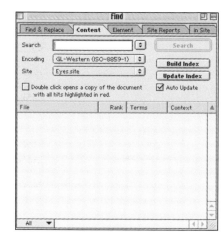

Figure 11.19
(Left) The expanded Find & Replace screen.

Figure 11.20
(Right) The Content screen within the Find window.

- *Element*—This screen (see Figure 11.21) allows you to search for specific HTML text using the HTML syntax rules. For individuals or team members versed in HTML, this is the screen you'll want to use when making modifications to a site.

- *Site Reports*—This section (see Figure 11.22) of the Find window is broken up into other subsections that allow the designers and management to monitor the entire site structure. It provides detailed reporting on dozens of site issues.

- *in Site*—This screen (see Figure 11.23) allows you to find specific information that would pertain to the entire Web site. This tool is used in the same way as Find & Replace.

The best thing to do is open an existing site and do specific searches using each of these subelements. The more you work with it, the better you'll become at knowing the best resource to use for your queries.

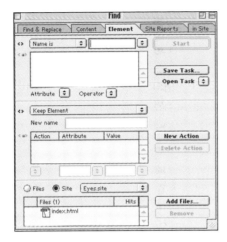

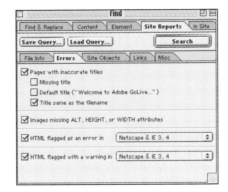

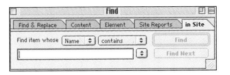

Figure 11.21

(Left) The Element window uses HTML syntax to find specific items in your code.

Figure 11.22

(Right) The Site Reports screen is invaluable to the Web site management team to keep track of each phase of site design. Here, the Errors subset is shown.

Figure 11.23

The in Site subset screen gives you the tools to find related elements within the entire site.

Final Elements

As you can see, myriad tools are at your disposal that streamline creating Web sites in a team atmosphere, just as various tools you can use to create elements for placement on your site(s). In the next two chapters, I'll introduce some of these tools, starting with the Adobe line of products. Then, I'll introduce other programs and resources, some of which you've probably heard of and some of which are totally new to the market.

Moving On

Now that you know how to modify your Web site designs (in a design group setting) by using the various HTML editing functions in GoLive, next, you'll take a break and look at the various programs that you can use to generate content for your sites. You'll discover ways to use other programs in ways you may not have considered because their stated purpose might differ from the way that I will suggest you use them. However, before you do this, Chapter 12 will help you get up to speed with Adobe's other products, including Illustrator 9, which is the only version of the program that works with the Smart Illustrator tool.

Chapter 12

Incorporating Other Adobe Products

Tight integration among the Adobe family of products
makes for a strong symbiotic tool set for creation of
high-end Web sites within GoLive.

Shake Hands and Come Out Creating

From photographic manipulation to professional vector graphic creation, the tools at your disposal for site element creation have never been stronger. Most professionals wouldn't know what to do without programs like Photoshop or Illustrator, both of which have been upgraded significantly during the writing of this book. These upgrades are more than incremental fixes; in the case of Photoshop, version 6 has almost been reinvented and comes with ImageReady 3, the upgrade to the powerful Web production utility program. Illustrator 9 adds so many powerful options designers and graphic artists have asked for over the years that its power is literally unrivaled. I know I'm sounding like an evangelist for these programs, but it really is amazing just how much things have been improved with these upgrades.

For those on a limited budget (and who isn't these days?), consider PhotoDeluxe 2 for the Mac, the PhotoDeluxe Home Edition for Windows, and Photoshop LE (which stands for Limited Edition) for both systems. The former two provide you with many tools and templates that help you create calendars, cards, flyers and more. For the hobbyist or the person who has taken on design tasks for their civic or church groups, these are the perfect, low-cost solution. Photoshop LE is, literally, the introductory-level edition of Photoshop. If you have whet your creative whistle on PhotoDeluxe and are looking for more challenges, Photoshop LE is the program that bridges the gap between hobbyist and professional quality image editing.

LiveMotion, Adobe's newest production tool, creates stunning Shockwave (SWF) animations (also known as *Flash animations*). Shockwave has become the defacto ruler of animation delivery over the Web because of its small file size and great creative power. Everything from banners to full-length cartoons is created and saved for Web distribution using this format. Also, most everyone who surfs the Web has the Shockwave player or plug-in on their computers. At last report, over 90% of Web surfers have this installed in their browser.

If you are interested in video production, Adobe's products include Premiere 5.1, which allows you to create broadcast-quality streaming video for the Web, as well as for multimedia presentations, film, video, and more. Add AfterEffects to this mix, and you have an extremely high-end suite of tools that gives you full Web content creation capabilities.

I also don't want to forget Acrobat and the resultant PDF files that can be displayed as Web pages or can be included in sites as downloadable files. PDF files, as I'm sure you're aware, are cross-platform compatible files that allow you to create complete documents with graphics, text, and even hyperlinks to locations on the Web.

In this chapter I'll give you an idea of how these tools interact with GoLive. You can either use the files provided on the CD-ROM in the Chapter 10 folder, or you can use your own.

Photoshop 6

Unless you are totally new to the world of image manipulation, this program is one you either have in your creative toolkit or have drooled over for years. In its newest version, 6, Adobe has upgraded many of the tools and made massive changes to the interface. The biggest change is the toolbar located at the top of the screen, which changes to give specific controls for the tool you have selected. In Figure 12.1, you see the toolbar associated with the Text tool, which I very purposely chose for this example to demonstrate how much the new version has improved.

Create the Logo in Photoshop

It used to be that to create anything but horizontal or vertical text, you had to use programs like Illustrator or Macromedia Freehand. Now, Photoshop gives you the ability to create text on a curve without having to use these programs or buy plug-ins. Let's take a look at this new addition to Photoshop and how text can be created that looks like it is following a path. To learn more about this new Photoshop feature, take the following steps:

Figure 12.1

Photoshop 6 provides an expanded text toolbar where you control all the parameters of your text.

1. Open the HomeSweetHome.jpg file into Photoshop 6. Select the Type tool and add the text "Home Sweet Home" above the porch image.

2. Resize the text so it closely resembles Figure 12.2.

Figure 12.2

Prepare to be amazed.

3. With the Text tool selected along with the text, select the "T" button on the right side of the tool bar to open the path modification options for the text called Warp Text. In this case, I have selected Flag from the pop-up menu (see Figure 12.3). Controls appear that allow you to control the horizontal and vertical warp factor. For this example, use the parameters you see in Figure 12.4. Figure 12.5 shows the final warp effect.

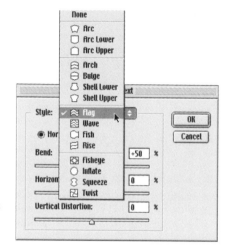

Figure 12.3
The text warping options you can select from.

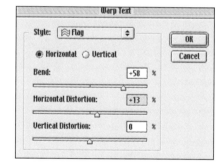

Figure 12.4
Use these parameters for the final text warp to achieve the look you want for this example.

4. After adding some more effects to the text and then creating a new layer that became the drop shadow, save the file as HSH1.jpg.

That's how simple it is to now create what I'll refer to as "text on a path" without the path. This is among the various warp effects available in Photoshop 6.

Combining Effects in Photoshop

You can easily and quickly achieve many more interesting and fun effects in Photoshop 5.x and 6 using the Layer Style blending options. If you haven't used them before, now is the time to do so. The Layer Style options are located by selecting Layer|Layer Style|Blending Options, which gives you access to all the individual built-in effects, or you can choose an individual effect from the submenu in the Layer Style pop-up.

Figure 12.5
The text has been warped using the Flag setting. This is something that could not have been done inside earlier versions of Photoshop without special plug-ins.

In this next section, you will explore some of these Layer Styles and how they can be incorporated into a logo design. This logo is for a fictitious company called The Glass Guru (see Figure 12.6), so you'll create numerous layers, each building upon the other, to give the logo a glass-like appearance. Afterward, save the file as a native PSD file (with layers preserved), so you can import it directly into GoLive and modify it layer by layer:

Figure 12.6
The logo for a fictitious company called The Glass Guru. This is the final look you will create in Photoshop 6.

1. First, select a good, thick font as shown in Figure 12.7. For this, I used one called Impact. It makes no difference what font you use, but the main things to look for are very few curlicues and thin ridges when doing work such as this. The fancier fonts make wonderful logos, but when you want to add some pretty strong effects to a font, the thicker and plainer they are, the better the finished product will look.

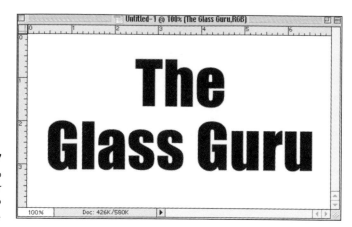

Figure 12.7
The font that will be used to create the logo. Use a similar style that is rather plain to achieve the best results.

2. Select the Palettes option from the top toolbar (see Figure 12.8). This opens the Text modifier window, where you can change the font style, leading, letter spacing and more. If you click on the Paragraph tab (see Figure 12.9), you have control over this portion of the design.

Figure 12.8
The new look for text control in Photoshop 6. The Palettes button on the far right of this bar opens the text parameter controls.

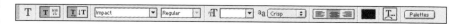

3. Duplicate this layer twice, so that you have three layers, plus the Background layer. Each layer, seen in Figure 12.10, will have a different effect added, each building and interacting with the other, to get the look you want.

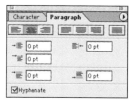

Figure 12.9
By selecting the Paragraph tab, you have all the controls for the overall settings of your text block.

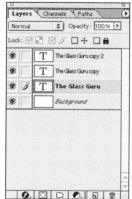

Figure 12.10
Three duplicate layers and the Background make up this project.

4. Activate the bottom-most text layer; this will become a drop shadow. Rasterize this layer (Layer|Rasterize|Type seen in Figure 12.11). Choose Filter|Blur|Gaussian Blur and set the Radius to 4. This creates a nice, soft drop shadow effect. Then, in the Layer's Opacity field, change the opacity of the blurred layer to 55%.

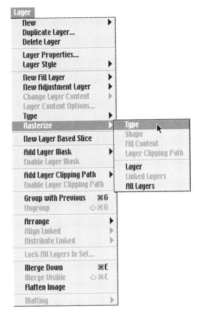

Figure 12.11
The path to rasterizing your text.

5. Lock the bottom-most text layer by clicking on the Lock button (see Figure 12.12). Then make the top-most text layer invisible by clicking on the eye icon. Now select the middle layer. Change the foreground color to white and the background color to R:1, G:19, B:253 (a deep blue). Using the Magic Wand, select the text, and choose Filter|Render|Clouds. As you see in Figure 12.13, you will be asked to rasterize the layer. If you do so, your text layer will look similar to the one shown in Figure 12.14.

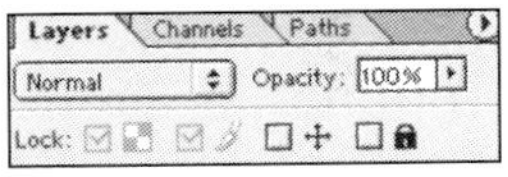

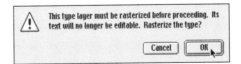

Figure 12.12
Locking layers in Photoshop 6 is now accomplished using the Lock commands just above the layer icons in the Layer window. You can now lock different aspects of a layer using this control strip or use the various Lock buttons to lock different aspects of a layer.

Figure 12.13
Before applying an effect to the text, you will be told to rasterize it if you haven't already.

This type layer must be rasterized before proceeding. Its text will no longer be editable. Rasterize the type?

Cancel   OK

Figure 12.14
The text with the final Cloud effect added.

6. From here, it's a matter of modifying each layer, giving each a distinct look to give the impression of looking like glass. Create one more text layer, make it the bottom-most one, make it a pure blue, and choose Filter|Render|Lighting Effects to set it up as you see in Figure 12.15.

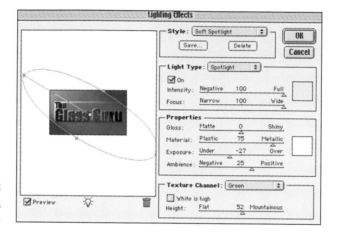

Figure 12.15
The bottom-most text layer's Lighting Effects settings.

> **Note**: I used a texture that I created using TextureMagic, discussed in Chapter 13. You can use any texture you'd like for this example.

7. For the next layer up, choose Layer|Layer Style|Blending Options. You want to create an Inner Glow, the parameters for which are shown in Figure 12.16. You will more than likely want to change the element's color (the radial button just beneath the Noise setting) to a light yellow like I did. Then, add Bevel and Emboss (see Figure 12.17), Contour (see Figure 12.18), and Texture (see Figure 12.19). Figure 12.20 shows what the layer should look like.

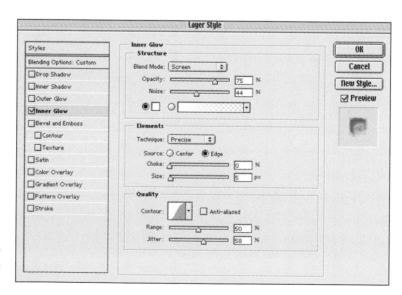

Figure 12.16
The Inner Glow settings for the second layer of text.

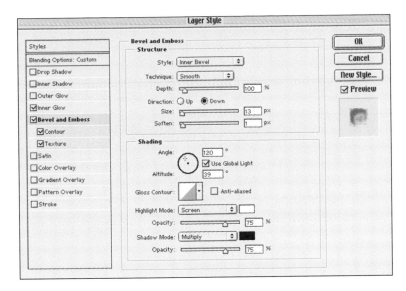

Figure 12.17
The Bevel and Emboss settings.

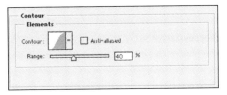

Figure 12.18
The Contour settings.

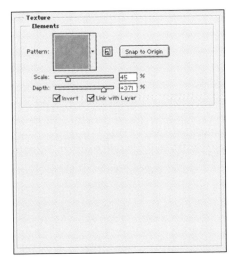

Figure 12.19
The Texture settings.

8. Make the top-most text layer visible and choose the Inner Glow settings seen in Figure 12.21, the Bevel And Emboss settings from Figure 12.22, and the Contour and Texture settings seen in Figures 12.23 and 12.24.

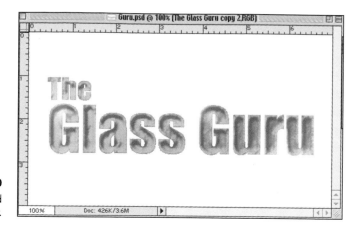

Figure 12.20
The final look for the second
text layer.

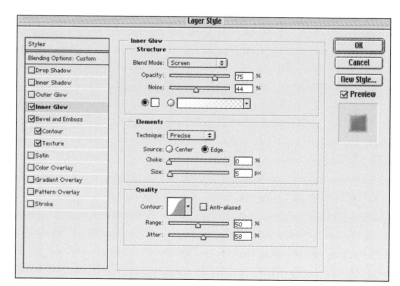

Figure 12.21
The top-most text layer's Inner
Glow settings.

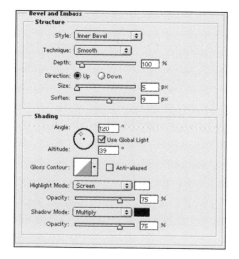

Figure 12.22
The top-most text layer's Bevel
and Emboss settings.

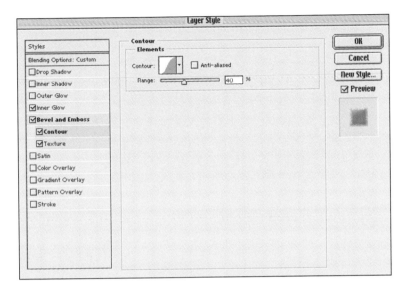

Figure 12.23
The top-most text layer's
Contour settings.

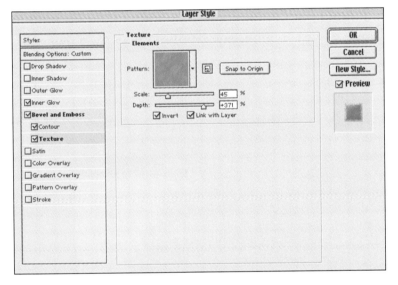

Figure 12.24
The top-most text layer's
Texture settings.

9. Duplicate the Background layer and choose Filter|Texture|Stained Glass. After you have applied the filter, select various random cells and fill them with washed out colors to give an artsy stained glass look to the layer, as in Figure 12.25.

10. Duplicate this layer and apply the File|Render|Lighting Effects you see in Figure 12.26. Once set, your layer will look like Figure 12.27. Move this layer behind the first stained glass layer. Make the Opacity of the top stained glass layer 91% and merge the two.

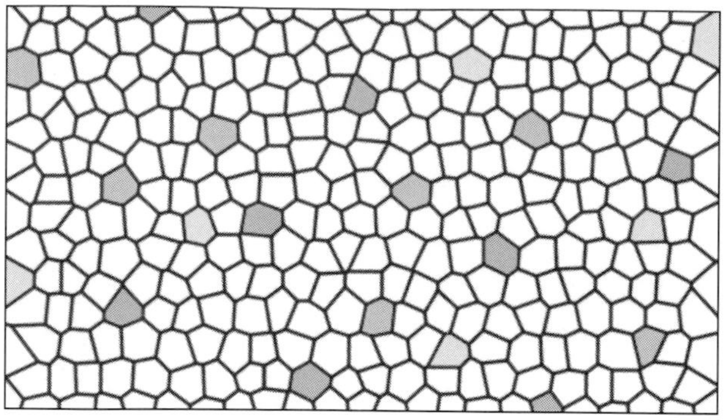

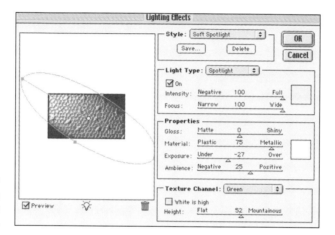

Figure 12.25

The Stained Glass filter applied to the duplicated Background layer, with random cells filled in with washed-out primary colors.

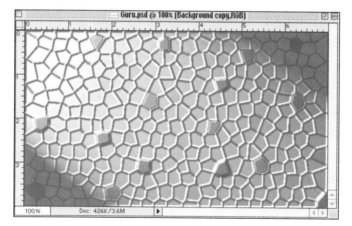

Figure 12.26

The Lighting Effects parameters used to create depth to the stained glass layer.

Figure 12.27

The final look for the new stained glass layer.

11. Set the following Opacity levels for the text layers, starting with the bottom-most layer and moving up to the top-most:

   • Bottom (The drop shadow layer): Unlock this layer and change the Opacity to 89%.

   • Third: 61%

   • Second: 56%

   • Top: 60%

Merge these layers (make sure to turn off all the Background layers first) by choosing Merge Visible from the pop-up menu in the Layers window.

12. Change the merged text layer's opacity to 83% and then open Levels (Image|Adjust|Levels) and the layer's levels, as you see in Figure 12.28.

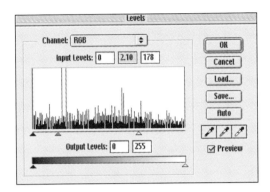

Figure 12.28
The text layer's appearance modified using the Levels controls.

13. Finally, merge only the stained glass backgrounds (leaving the main background layer separate) and change the Opacity to 89%. Your logo will now look like what you see in Figure 12.29.

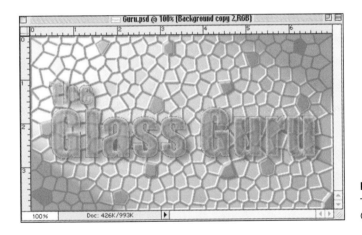

Figure 12.29
The semi-final look for The Glass Guru logo.

ImageReady 3

ImageReady started out as a standalone program, but was quickly paired with Photoshop because of its heavily symbiotic relationship with the latter. Photoshop 5/5.5 came with ImageReady 2. Photoshop 6 comes with ImageReady 3, and, like Photoshop, ImageReady has been expanded and improved to help you create advanced Web effects.

ImageReady gives you the ability to set any number of parameters for your file. In the case of HomeSweetHome.jpg you made earlier in this chapter, saved as one single file, it would take approximately 10 seconds to load (under

perfect conditions) on a 56.6Kbps modem. For this section, you will need to use the HomeSweetHome.jpg image, and slice it up into a series of smaller files that make up the final image, to save download time on the Web:

1. As in Photoshop 5.5, version 6 has a direct link to ImageReady 3 located in the bottom-right corner of the tool set (see Figure 12.30). When you click on this button, ImageReady opens so you can modify your Photoshop file. Meanwhile, Photoshop remains open as well so you can move easily between the two programs if you need to.

2. After ImageReady opens, use the Slice tool (third from the top in the right column of the toolbar) to cut the image into four separate images, like in Figure 12.31. Use the Slice Select tool (see Figure 12.32) to select each slice and rename each to something more fitting. (In my case, I named the slices hsh_01, _02, _03, and _04.)

Figure 12.30

The control to open ImageReady in the Photoshop Tools window.

Figure 12.31

The Home Sweet Home image cut into four slices in ImageReady 3.

3. Choose File|Output Settings|HTML and change the Settings choice to Include GoLive Code. Then go to File|Save Optimized As and give the file the name HSH.html. Change the other parameters to what you see in Figure 12.33.

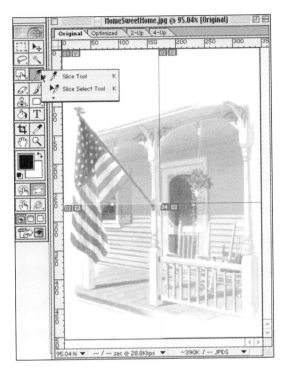

Figure 12.32
The Slice Select tool is located in an expandable toolset button. Press and hold on the Slice tool to reveal it.

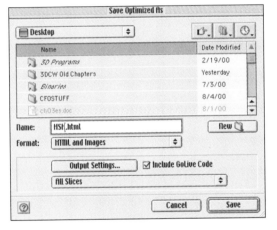

Figure 12.33
The Save Optimized As settings for the sliced image. Use these as you save the Home Sweet Home ImageReady file.

By saving your file only as images, you can create DHTML animations by using each section of the image, bringing it together to end the animation. Also, save the file as HTML and Images if you know you don't want to do any animation with the files.

4. Open the GoLive program and select File|Open and then navigate to the generated HTML file. Select it and choose Open.

5. The file that opens looks like Figure 12.34. Notice the "word balloons" that appear above and below the slices. Click on one of them and the Inspector window changes to give you information about the file (see Figure 12.35).

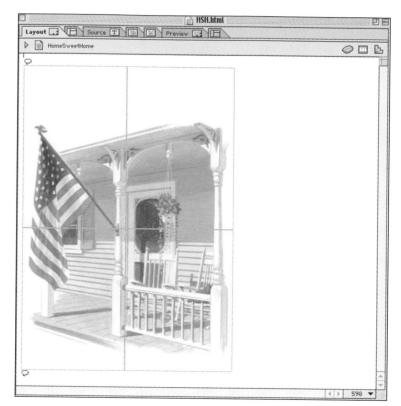

Figure 12.34

Information regarding the starting code and ending code are accessible through the word balloon icons above and below your image files.

Figure 12.35

You can see all information regarding the sliced image file in the Inspector window when you click once on either the top or bottom word balloon.

6. Also, switch to Source mode in the workspace window to see how your image is denoted in the HTML script (see Figure 12.36). If you had assigned rollover or other effects to any or all of the slices, you would see the code for that in this screen, as well.

The combination of Photoshop and ImageReady gives you the ability to create some extremely advanced Web features within a highly familiar environment. Then, you can tweak the subsequent file or add more features in GoLive 5. These programs are, literally, indispensable for the professional Web designer.

Illustrator 9

This upgrade to Adobe Illustrator occurred in July 2000 and has ushered in the beginning of a new era for vector graphic creation. With many new features added, Illustrator 9 is the must-have upgrade for any Illustrator user who has been putting off upgrading the program. Most of the changes are far from cosmetic (a concern many have with most upgrades for many programs). In the case of Illustrator 9, the implemented changes include many that are useful day-to-day design features that Illustrator users have been asking for. Some of the many changes that Illustrator 9 includes are briefly summarized in the following list:

Figure 12.36
The HTML source code with the ImageReady HTML automatically inserted. If you have rollover information assigned to a slice, it would also appear here.

- The capability to simplify a path while retaining the integrity of the image. This change reduces the total number of points along a path and results in smaller file sizes.

- The capability to view your designs as pixel-based images because when you are preparing files for the Web, your Illustrator files usually are going to be turned into JPEGs, PNGs, or GIFs. In this way, you can see how they will translate for the Web.

- A tool to instantly create drop shadows without having to use the blend tool.

- Shockwave and SVG file generation. In the former, you can generate a single file, a multiple animation file, or even files for each layer of your image. In the latter, you can create JAVA-based interactive elements directly in Illustrator and export them.

- New blending and transparency modes.

- Layer, clipping, and feathered masks and paths.

- Many new layer features that could take up a book all by themselves.

And this is just a taste of the many enhancements and changes that make up the latest version of this perennial program. Now, it's possible to do many things directly in Illustrator that were previously accomplished only by importing Illustrator files into Photoshop. Let's take a look at the new blending feature in Illustrator to get a taste for what it can do.

Build a Blended File in Illustrator 9

Prior to version 9, to build a blended file like the one you're about to create would have entailed keeping both elements separate, importing them to an image manipulation program such as Photoshop or CorelDRAW, and then creating a blend in the latter program. Here's how you can now do it directly within Illustrator 9:

1. Create a horizontal bar like the one in Figure 12.37. In this case, I gave it a light blue fill. Remove the stroke if you see one.

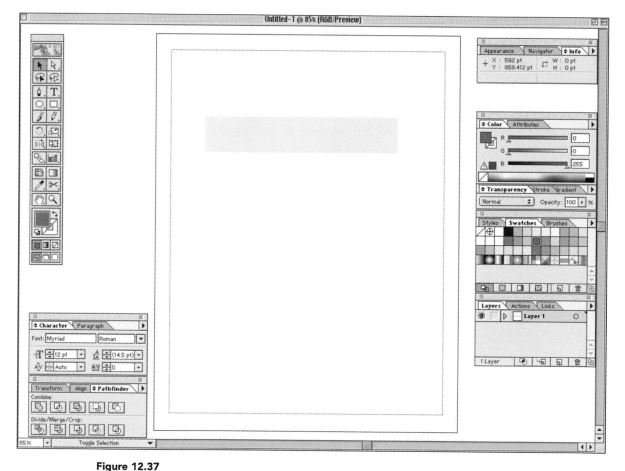

Figure 12.37

The bar created for the background of the Illustrator 9 blend function.

2. Copy the bar (Cmd/Ctrl+D) and paste it on top of the original (Cmd/Ctrl+F). Double-click on the Scale tool (seen in Figure 12.38), and select Non-Uniform. Change the Horizontal scale to 95% and the Vertical scale to 85%. Fill this with a deep blue color so your image looks like Figure 12.39. Then, select both elements.

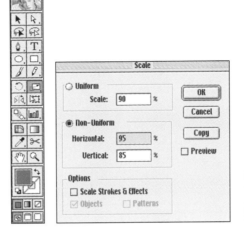

Figure 12.38
The Scale tool in the Tool palette along with its corresponding screen.

Figure 12.39
The two bars you created should look like this.

3. Double-click on the Blend tool (seen in Figure 12.40) to pull up the Blend Options screen. Make sure Smooth Color and the Align To Path Orientation are selected (see Figure 12.41) and click OK. Make the blend by clicking on adjacent corners of the two bars so your image looks like Figure 12.42.

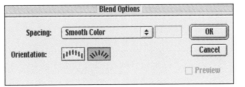

Figure 12.40
(Left) The Blend tool item in the Tool palette.

Figure 12.41
(Right) The Blend Options screen.

Figure 12.42

The two bars blended together.

4. Create some text (making it fairly large in size) and turning it into outlines (Cmd/Ctrl+Shift+O). For this example, I made the text white and turned off the stroke color. Group the outlines (Cmd/Ctrl+G) and move them into the bar, as seen in Figure 12.43.

Figure 12.43

The text positioned within the bar, ready to be made into a transparent object.

5. Now that the art is completed, take a look at the new functions in Illustrator 9. Figure 12.44 shows the new Transparency window, expanded to show the Options. As you can see in Figure 12.45, the controls in the pop-up menu reflect the controls found in Photoshop. Using the Opacity control, as in Photoshop, you can change the transparency of the text.

Figure 12.44

(Left) The new Transparency window, which has controls that look a lot like Photoshop's Layers commands.

Figure 12.45

(Right) Almost all of Photoshop's Layer options are present in the Transparency pop-up window. The only one missing is Dissolve.

Figure 12.46

The preview pane in the Transparency control screen shows your imported image.

6. Import a photo or JPEG image and place it over the bar you created. Notice how, in Figure 12.46, the image is now reflected in the preview pane of the Transparency window. You can now use any of the controls from the pop-up window to create the look you want right within Illustrator (see Figure 12.47).

These changes are also reflected in the Layers palette, where you now have added control over the various changes you make (see Figure 12.48). You can isolate sublayers, meaning you can make changes to individual levels without affecting other elements in the same layer. You can save these changes to create Shockwave animations or as separate files. It's really a cool tool that satisfies many creative needs.

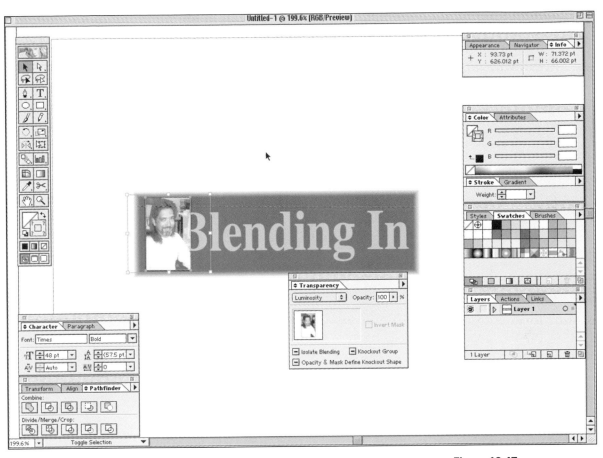

Figure 12.47
The JPEG image with Luminosity assigned to it. This has created an interesting look impossible to achieve in earlier versions of Illustrator.

Note: For more detailed descriptions of the new features in Illustrator, refer to the Illustrator 9 User Manual.

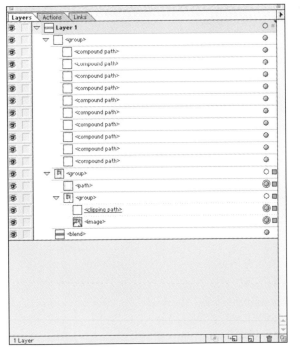

Figure 12.48
Expanded Layer options show sublayers that can be modified individually, copied, or grouped into new layers.

All you need to do now is save the file as an AI file and use the Smart Illustrator tool in GoLive. Chapter 2 showed you how to do that; you might want to refer to it again as you incorporate Illustrator 9 files into GoLive.

Other Adobe Products

Other programs are available that you can use to enhance your Web site designs. I won't go into detail regarding how they work; however, the following is a list of products you might want to consider using as your Web design prowess expands.

LiveMotion

This program is so integral a part of GoLive 5 that it has its own Smart Tool. As described in Chapter 2, LiveMotion (seen in Figure 12.49) is Adobe's newest product. It allows you to create Flash Shockwave files for Web site animations. The difference between LiveMotion and its competitors is LiveMotion's ease of use. If you are used to the Adobe interface, LiveMotion will make you feel right at home. Figure 12.50 gives you another look at the work area and the various design palettes.

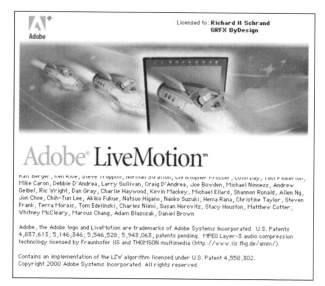

Figure 12.49
The splash screen for LiveMotion, Adobe's new Flash/Shockwave generation program.

At the time of this writing, LiveMotion was still in version 1. You can expect Adobe to upgrade the program, adding features and implementing more interactive elements, so that LiveMotion grows along with its sister programs.

Premiere

Premiere is, well, the premiere digital video editing package on the market. This powerful tool gives you everything you need to create high quality, professional movies. Your work can be saved for the Web as streaming video, or be

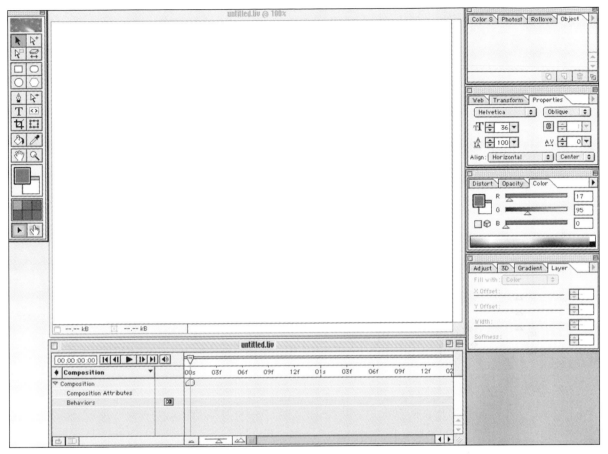

Figure 12.50
The LiveMotion user interface is designed to reflect the GUIs of Adobe's other programs, making it easier for you to jump right in and create.

output for video tape, CD, or film. Figure 12.51 shows the interface. As the bandwidth continues to increase and more and more people can access QuickTime and AVI files more efficiently, using programs like Premiere will become more and more commonplace. Consider this scenario: You can create an animation in a 3D program such as Poser, bring it into Premiere, and combine it with live-action footage from a digital camcorder or VHS tape, add scrolling titles, music, and special audio effects, and then save your work as streaming media. Getting used to this technology now can only increase your effectiveness as a cutting-edge Web designer.

After Effects

Another fantastic program from Adobe is After Effects 4.1. After you have created a video in Premiere, you can import the file into After Effects to add high-end, film, and digital video quality effects to your work. As you can see in Figure 12.52, the interface looks very much like Premiere's, which makes it extremely easy to move from one program to the other. You can also use After Effects as a standalone application. It allows you to import files directly into it, generate effects, and save the files as QuickTime or AVIs.

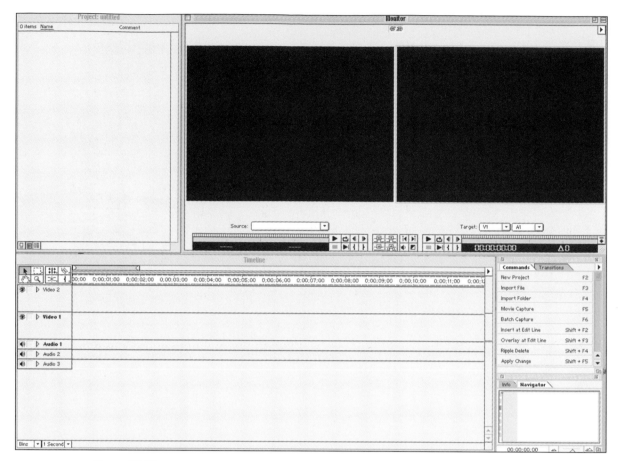

Figure 12.51

The Adobe Premiere 5.1 interface.

If you are interested in expanding into video production for the Web, you will definitely want both of these programs. Why? The best way I can answer that is to relate how I use the two. I use After Effects to create any special effects that are needed for my projects, such as flaming text or fireballs, complicated wipes and dissolves, and much more. I then import these elements into Premiere to build the final cut of my video, using Premiere's set of high-end tools to do all the cleanup work.

Video Plug-Ins

Both Premiere and After Effects accept third-party plug-ins. Many of these plug-ins are made for both programs and I definitely include them in both. Most of them are fairly expensive—ranging from $250 to almost $600—but you'll find that they are well worth it as you delve further and further into video production.

Some of the companies that produce plug-ins for these programs include:

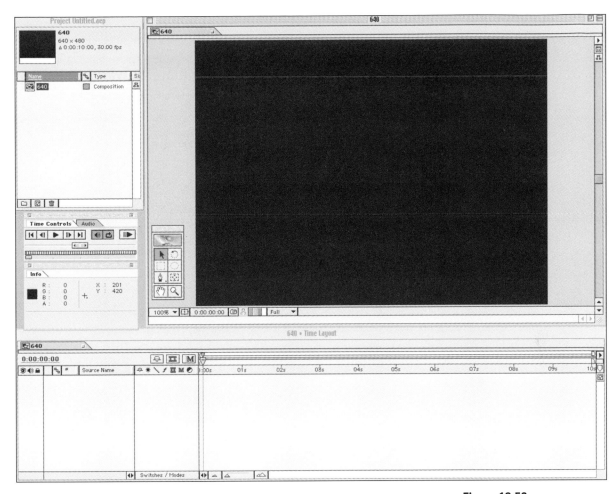

Figure 12.52
The After Effects workspace.

Boris FX

One of the most prolific developers, Boris produces plug-ins that create resolution-independent 2D and 3D titling, almost 200 original video effects, and more. Among these are AE (see Figure 12.53) and Continuum (see Figure 12.54). You can see the entire line of the company's products at **www.borisfx.com**.

Figure 12.53
The Boris AE package as seen on their Web site.

Figure 12.54
The Boris Continuum package as seen on their Web site.

Cycore Computers

These are creators of a plug-in set called Cult Effects. The set includes numerous filters that give you control over the saturation, luminosity, and other color channels, as well as a slew of displacement tools and special effects. You can see Cult Effects at **www.culteffects.com** or **www.cycore.com**.

The Foundry

The Foundry (**www.thefoundry.com**) creates a set of filters for After Effects that includes starbursts, light rays, warped reflections, etching (to make video look as if it were drawn by hand), and many more.

Many other companies create effects plug-ins for both Premiere and After Effects. It's well worth the effort to access your Web search engine and type in a query for Adobe After Effects plug-ins.

GoLive Actions

The following Actions plug-ins are not created by Adobe, but they are definitely backed by the company. Oliver Zahorka runs Out Media Design GMBH at this URL: **www.out.to**. He creates superb action sets that are placed into the Actions folder in GoLive and give you some of the coolest effects known to the Web right now. Figure 12.55 shows Oliver's home page, and the color section features some of the effects he features on his site.

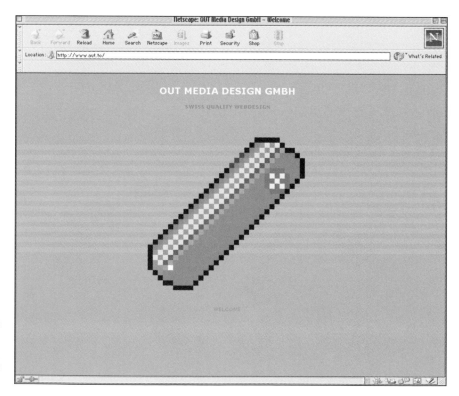

Figure 12.55
The Out Media Design GMBH home page, where you can obtain reasonably priced Actions plug-ins for GoLive.

The actions Oliver has created work with GoLive's DHTML creation system. They are part of the list (seen in Figure 12.56) that is available when creating rollover or DHTML effects. Among the plug-ins in this series are:

Note: Demos of some of Oliver's Actions plug-ins are included on the companion CD-ROM.

- Browser Test—Lets you set parameters to look for specific browsers and platforms.

- CSS Link—Looks for specific browsers and then links to the correct style sheet for that browser, making sure your work is viewed as you intended it.

- Delay Action—Lets you control when a specific effect or event happens.

- Execute JavaScript—Tells the browser when specific scripts should be triggered.

- MouseTrail—Lets you assign an image or text that follows the cursor around the screen. (This is my favorite, and I have to force myself not to use it too much.)

- Shake Window—Another cool effect that should be used sparingly. This one triggers the browser window to shake as if in an earthquake.

Figure 12.56

The current list of OUTactions created by Oliver Zahorka.

Again, you access these actions via the Actions window. You can set up a folder in your GoLive director that is OUTactions specific, letting you quickly find and specify the effect you want to use (see Figure 12.57).

This is just a short list of all the actions he has created. Some of them are free, others are very low cost. You can view the entire list and see screen shots of the controls at **www.out.to/actions/**. You'll be working with some of these actions, and seeing others in action (no pun intended) in Chapter 15.

Bringing It All Together

So what was the purpose of this chapter? It's important to know what tools are at your disposal when creating original and highly effective Web sites. Design is one thing, but content is everything. That has been proven over the long haul. A great design will attract people, but it seldom keeps them coming back. Intriguing and ever-changing content, though, will have people returning and talking constantly about your site(s). They'll talk about it in news and chat groups. Your hits will increase. Your fee for creating sites will go up. You'll become rich and famous. Well, okay, *rich* is a relative term. Let's say that you could easily earn a very good living designing Web sites, because your abilities stand not only the test of time, but also stay on the cutting edge of technology.

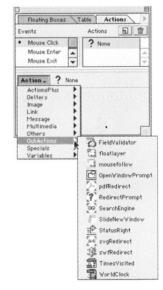

Figure 12.57

A special OUTactions folder created in the Actions window allows for quick access to the OUTactions plug-ins.

Moving On

And speaking of the cutting edge, you just explored only the Adobe line of products and read how they can enhance your sites; however, other products on the market can expand your content creation abilities. Chapter 13 looks at these other programs, most of them cross-platform, just like Adobe's. Following that, it will be time to bring everything together and look at how an entire site can be created using the techniques you've discovered throughout this book, incorporating the programs in this and the next chapter.

Chapter 13
Other Applications

As is the case with virtually every application, to get the most out of your Web site development, you will want to turn to other programs to help you build the best site possible. In this chapter, I'll identify and discuss some of the best programs for this purpose.

The Creativity Compendium

Building a Web site takes a strong knowledge of varied applications. You need to have a graphic artist's eye, a typographer's sense of flow, and, of course, the ability to get each link to work the way it's supposed to. The last chapter discussed Adobe products. However, many more applications are available to help you create award-winning Web sites.

You can consider the programs covered in this chapter as adjuncts to your creative tools. In many cases, it comes down to your way of working and your comfort in the way a program is laid out before you make your final selections. Use this section to discover some old, as well as fresh-on-the-market software that you can use as part of your site creation toolbox.

Creativity means many things when it comes to Web design. However, one area of creativity that is often overlooked is the way you can use a particular program to achieve your goal. Many programs on the market have, according to the developers, a certain purpose in life. Many of us look at it and say, "Well, that's great, but I don't have the need for a program that creates clothing patterns." But, if you take the time to look beyond the marketing strategy, many of these niche programs can have multiple uses well beyond their intended market.

That's what I'll be exploring in this chapter. Although I'll mention the tried-and-true products, such as Flash, Fireworks, and Freehand, you can incorporate many other utilities into your work that may not, at first glance, be geared toward Web design. (Call this a throwback to my old days when computers weren't around and I had to figure out how to make my vision happen for a commercial or television program I produced. I have never been one to look at anything and say it fits only into one small slot in a massive shelf unit.) By pushing programs to their limits, and finding new and creative ways to incorporate their power, you'll not only get more out of the program, you'll also achieve more satisfaction when your project is finished.

In various sections of this chapter, especially in the case of programs that aren't readily apparent as Web design tools, I'll give some walk-throughs. Many of these programs are included on the companion CD-ROM as demos or trial versions; others can be found on each company's Web site.

Many of these tools are low in cost. Almost all (especially the later programs) are available for less than $500, so they are well within the financial reach of many individual designers and small design firms. With that in mind, let's look at some of the programs available to assist you in your quest for Internet glory.

Macromedia

Yes, this is a highly competitive company to Adobe, but its tools are as familiar to some as a well-worn shoe. And if you already have some of these programs in your arsenal, you're well on your way to creative panacea. I'll start with the big kid on the design block, Macromedia, and then introduce you to programs that you might know of, but might not have considered, because they didn't immediately appear to have a place in your design kit.

Flash 5

This is the program that started it all in the area of fast-loading, high-quality vector-based animations (see Figure 13.1). However, as you probably already know, vector graphics are only the start of the Shockwave tool kit. Flash 5, released in September 2000, incorporates many changes that help your workflow if you use various Macromedia products.

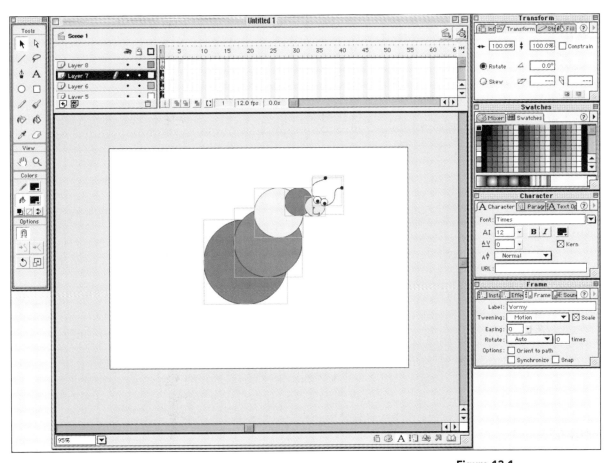

Figure 13.1

The Flash workspace. This latest version of the popular program has added many new features to help in your workflow.

Designers are really pushing the envelope when it comes to Flash productions. Not only can you use the program to create exciting home-page animations and virtually instantaneous-loading rollover effects, you can use Flash to produce Web-based games (**www.shockwave.com**), e-comic books (**www.stanlee.net**, one example is shown in Figure 13.2), and entire sites, such as the page shown in Figure 13.3 (**www.rbtwhiz.com**). Of course, you can also incorporate photographic images into your Shockwave animations (check out **www.williamleegolden.com** for a good example of photography usage), as in Figure 13.4, and mix and match

Figure 13.2
Stan Lee, creator of some of the most beloved comic characters, such as Spiderman, The Incredible Hulk, and The X-Men, is now creating e-comics created in Flash.

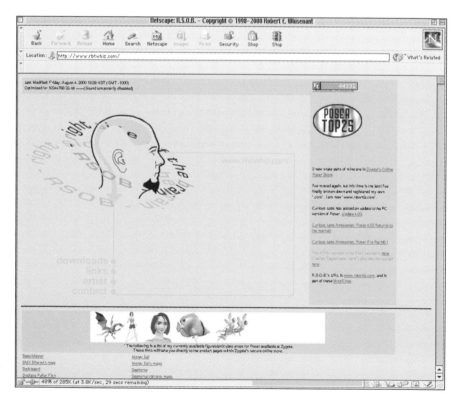

Figure 13.3
Robert Whisenant's site is a great example of creative use of Shockwave technology.

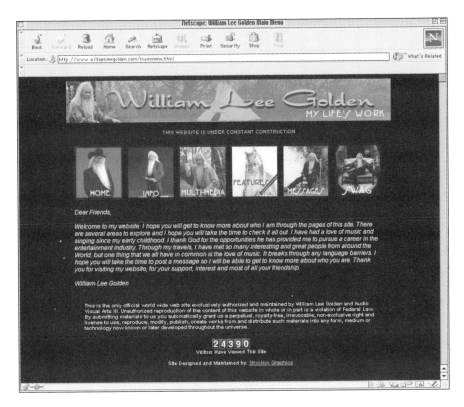

Figure 13.4

The Oak Ridge Boys' William Lee Golden used Shockwave to create a photographic montage on his site.

vector, text, and photographs into your files. These links are literally a miniscule chip off the tip of the e-iceberg. But they are a start to see how Flash is being employed in Web design.

Anyone who has explored Shockwave creation in the past few years has used Flash. It is, literally, the only product on the market (which gives it a decided advantage). Additionally, when you consider that the Flash player is available as a free download from Macromedia's site and that it is included in virtually every Web browser on the market, you're guaranteed the widest possible audience for your work.

Flash employs advanced vector tools (see Figure 13.5) to help you create your graphics and a TimeLine (see Figure 13.6) that will be familiar to anyone who uses other Macromedia products.

Fireworks 3

This program gives you the tools to create fully interactive elements, pages, and entire sites (see Figure 13.7). I consider Fireworks to be a hybrid with many of the tools and capabilities of Flash, but with some extras that help it stand on its own. You can import Flash files into Fireworks, modify them, and then save the final product as a Shockwave file.

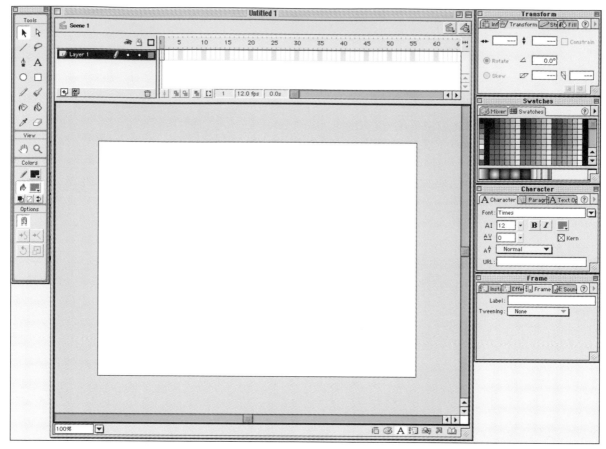

Figure 13.5

The Flash toolbox, which includes advanced vector graphic creation and modification tools, is located along the left side of the screen.

Figure 13.6

The Flash TimeLine is one that is very familiar to Macromedia product users.

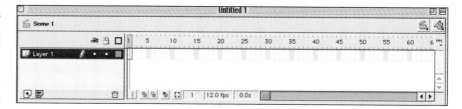

Other features in Fireworks are its ability to embed hotspots directly in your files, and its multiple Slice tools, the most intriguing being the Freeform Slice tool (FST), to create standard, as well as freeform slices (see Figure 13.8). Think of the designs you can come up with by using the FST to cut interesting shapes out of your image. One idea is to create interactive puzzles that visitors can put together (see Figure 13.9); another is to create non-uniform shapes that, through the course of an animation, build into the final image. By using odd shapes, you put your audience into the position of wanting to watch the entire thing to find out what's going to happen next. Additionally, when you use the Shockwave tool in GoLive, these hotspots and slices are automatically included in the page, leaving you very little to do but put the site on the Web and let people marvel at your work.

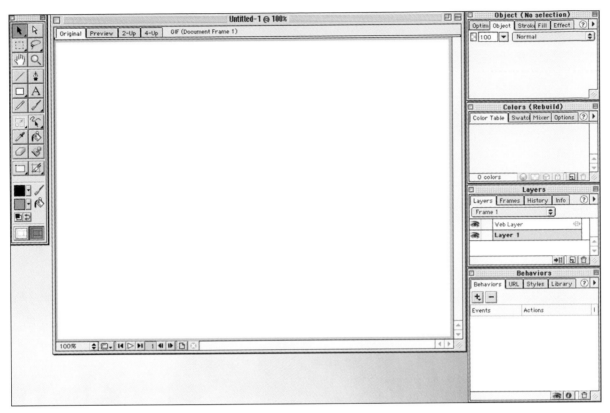

Figure 13.7
The Fireworks workspace.

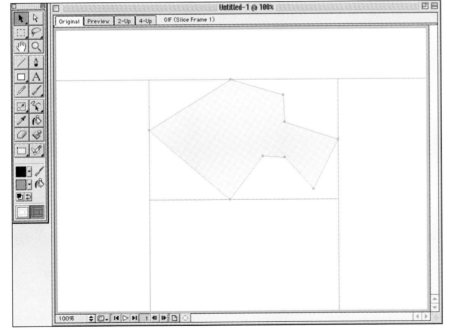

Figure 13.8
Fireworks offers free-form Slice Tools that allow you to create odd-shaped slices. This can be extremely beneficial to your designs.

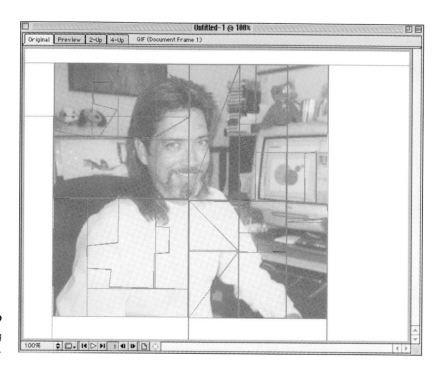

Figure 13.9
An interactive puzzle built using
Fireworks' Freeform Slice tool.

You can literally create all of your Shockwave files in Fireworks without ever opening Flash, so you should probably decide on whether you want both in your arsenal. However, I've found that the combination between the two, no matter how much I use one over the other, is beneficial. At the least, I have the options at my disposal.

Freehand 9

Freehand has long been the choice for professional page layouts. Its biggest competitor is Adobe Illustrator (see Chapter 12). Version 9 (shown in Figure 13.10) of this perennial program offers many much-anticipated additions that build upon the program's popularity. It also gives the ability to create Shockwave files.

This addition of Shockwave file-creation capability is an important and exciting element within Freehand. Not only can you build graphic elements for importation to Flash or Fireworks (not to mention the next program I'll discuss), you can now create entire Shockwave pages for your Web site. If you're versed in Freehand, you'll love this capability because you won't necessarily have to do much more than upgrade. Additionally, if you're new to Shockwave preparation, working within a familiar program gives you the chance to begin working with the format without having to learn another one if you're on a tight schedule. It's always better to test the waters before diving in.

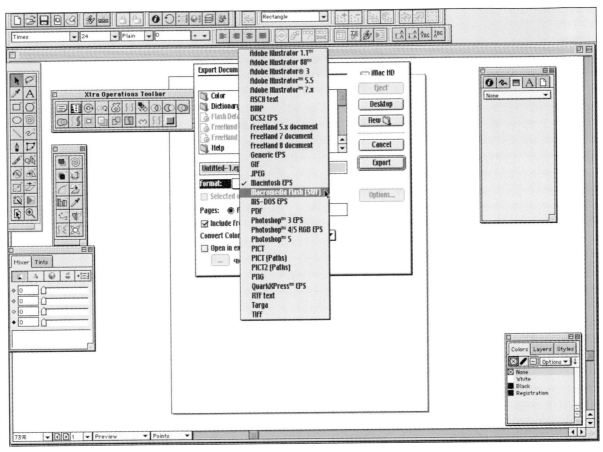

Figure 13.10
Macromedia Freehand includes the capability to export designs as Shockwave files for inclusion in Flash, Fireworks, Director, or directly to the Web.

Director 8 Shockwave Studio

And now we turn to the most powerful program in the Macromedia lexicon, Director (see Figure 13.11). This is a high-end developmental tool that has long been a workhorse for the development of interactive CD-ROMs, DVDs, and even in feature films. Of the latter, the computer effects in the *Star Trek* movies were created with Director. So, here's an application that can transition smoothly from low-bandwidth to cinematic displays without batting an e-eyelash. Director, however, isn't for everyone. It has a steep learning curve, thanks to its powerful scripting language, Lingo. In fact, of the two manuals that come with the program (the user manual and the Lingo dictionary), the Lingo dictionary is thicker than the program's. Additionally, the price is steep at almost $1,000, but if you can afford it and have the time to learn the intricacies of it, Director 8 Shockwave Studio is a must-have tool.

Although Lingo gives you the ability to create specialized scripts, it isn't totally necessary for you to learn it to make Director do its magic. Intuitive timeline controls (Director's timeline is called the Score) that mirror the controls found

Figure 13.11

Director 8 Shockwave Studio is the Lamborghini in Macromedia's product line, and is worth the time to learn it and the investment if you want to create interactive projects for the Web, CD-ROMs, and even movies and television shows.

in Flash and Fireworks let you manage all the elements in your *movie* (which is what animations in the program are called). Some much-needed revisions to the *Stage* (the main workspace) have Director afficionados happy as can be. What used to be a fixed area is now resizable (see Figure 13.12), allowing users to zoom in and out, scroll across the Stage, and make small adjustments more easily. While this isn't the place to go into great detail on the program, suffice it to say that this latest incarnation of Director makes it one to look into.

As the name states, Director 8 is being repositioned for Web creation with the focus on saving files in the Shockwave format; therefore, it's full name is Director 8 Shockwave Studio. Also, the way in which the family of programs interacts is really a dream. Create various animations in Flash, make modifications to your files in Fireworks, then import them into Director to build your long-form presentation; then save the final product in the Shockwave format for Web distribution. Or, use Director to build powerful movies and export them as SWF files.

Figure 13.12
Many of the changes in Director 8 Shockwave Studio make changing elements on the Stage a much easier task than ever before.

Macromedia "Xtras" Extensions

As I mentioned in the preceding section, Director uses an intense scripting language called Lingo. Numerous books on the market can help you learn Lingo and, if you already have some background in programming languages, you'll find Lingo to be an intuitive language. Basically, by using Lingo, you can create and assign specialized actions to take place at any given time along the movie's TimeLine, or create original interactive elements in your SWF files. If, however, you're not blessed with the ability to learn coding (me being one of them), dozens of Lingoists and companies can provide high-quality scripts for you to use. These plug-ins, known in Director-ese as *Xtras*, will become invaluable to you as you create Shockwave files.

Note: You can find a comprehensive list of Xtras at **www.macromedia.com/ software/xtras/director/.**

Media Lab

This Colorado-based company has, in its four years of existence, created Xtras that are virtually invaluable to anyone using Director for Shockwave file creation. The following sections discuss some of their plug-ins.

PhotoCaster

This product allows you to import layered Photoshop files directly into Director. As you can see in Figure 13.13, when you import a layered file, each layer can be made to appear as a separate *Cast Member* (the name for various elements ready to be incorporated on the Director Stage), giving you unprecedented control over your animations.

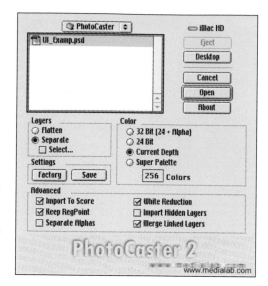

Figure 13.13
The PhotoCaster interface. Here you can choose to import a Photoshop file as separate cast members or as a flat image, as well as having control over numerous setups.

Effector Sets for AlphaMania

This Xtra allows you to create on-the-fly effects previously achievable only through Lingo scripting. Two sets of these plug-ins, versions I and II, give you the ability to rotate, swirl, colorize, blur, ripple, add drop shadows, and much more (see Figure 13.14). You can combine effects to create great animations that would have previously taken you hours to achieve.

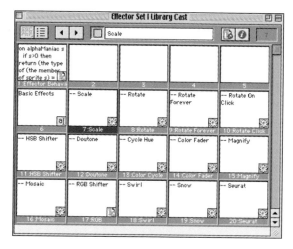

Figure 13.14
By combining Effector Set effects to your Director Cast Members, you can achieve advanced animations that you could accomplish previously only by writing Lingo scripts. Here, you see the Cast Member screen that shows some of the effects built into this great Xtra.

AlphaMania 2

This is another in a series of must-have Xtras if you plan on creating Shockwave files with Director for your GoLive sites. This is an indispensable set of Xtras if you plan on creating clean animations using non-vector–based images in your designs (see Figure 13.15).

You can find out more about these Xtras and others at **www.medialab.com**.

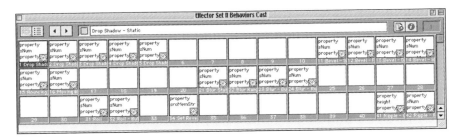

Figure 13.15
Some of the Cast Member properties associated with Effector Set II and AlphaMania.

Video Production Tools

Digital video editing is as hot today as 3D graphics creation. Additionally, its relevance to the future of the Internet and many production houses around the world is becoming more apparent. In the United States, High Definition Television (HDTV) is just around the corner. Other countries, such as Japan, have had HDTV (also known as HiDef) for years. Also on the horizon is an increase in bandwidth that will allow everyone high-speed access to the Internet. Those of you who are beginning to take interest in video production via the computer are on the cusp of a massive changeover; you could very well reap the benefits when the transition happens.

Apple

If you are a Mac user, two programs are available for video production. One is Web-based, with its browser plug-in coming standard on most systems. The other is a professional *non-linear editing* (NLE) package that is quickly becoming one of the favorites of computer-based video applications.

QuickTime

Still considered one of the best (read that cleanest) ways to provide streaming video to the Web, QuickTime (see Figure 13.16) is almost synonymous with streaming video. While other programs use proprietary *Compression/Decompression* (CODECS) to deliver video and audio, QuickTime lets you choose the CODEC that you want to use, from Sorenson (considered the best of the lot) to Cinepak, to H.263. It's also extremely inexpensive, under $50.00, for the full-featured QuickTime Pro version.

Final Cut Pro v1.2.x

This program is becoming extremely popular with desktop editors, even with a higher price tag than its close competitor, Adobe Premiere (covered in Chapter 12). Final Cut Pro (see Figure 13.17) is a high-end professional editing system that sports an intuitive drag-and-drop interface shown in Figure 13.18.

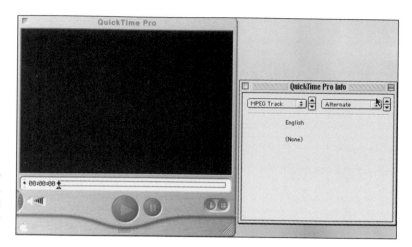

Figure 13.16
Apple QuickTime is a clean, low-cost, and highly regarded method of delivering streamable video on the Internet.

Figure 13.17
The Final Cut Pro splash screen.

Note: In and out points are the starting and ending points for a video clip or for an effect. The In time is where a particular video or effect will start, and the out point is where that particular video or effect will end.

Final Cut Pro incorporates a modular interface composed of tabs that give you access to audio and video, filters, and motion effects (see Figure 13.19). As you switch among the various elements, editing controls specific to that area appear. The main workspace is set up much like a standard editing bay with a preview "monitor" (called the *Viewer*) on the left that lets you set in and out points down to a specific frame of video, and the mix "monitor" (called the *Canvas*) on the right (see Figure 13.20). You have full titling capabilities, and the means to make text scroll (move in a vertical fashion) or crawl (move in a horizontal fashion) across the screen. You can use any typeface in your system or one that is stored in programs, such as Extensis Suitcase 9.

Real

The other extremely popular method for displaying and distributing streamable movies is with the RealPlayer. Real also markets RealProducer Plus, so you can edit your files directly in that format. Real videos are becoming so common on the Web that they are literally second only to QuickTime in the public's mind. Additionally, for many, Real video is the only way to provide streaming product over the Web.

Figure 13.18

Final Cut Pro allows you to drag and drop video from the preview screen to the Canvas. A menu of how you want the video placed appears when you do this.

Figure 13.19

Tabs accessible in the Viewer window let you work with specific controls that are specific to that particular header.

Figure 13.20
The "dual monitor" workspace.
On the left is the Viewer window.
On the right is the Canvas, where
you see your edited work.

Note: Audio and video take up
massive quantities of hard disk
space. If you are saving large
files to your hard drive, you
might want to consider purchasing a Zip 250 (also known as a
250MB Zip) or the 1 or 2 Gig
Jaz drives from Iomega (**www.
iomega.com**). Alternatively, you
can invest in a large capacity
hard drive that is used specifically for storing media files.

Note: If you are serious about
providing streaming video and
audio to your visitors, you will
want to consider saving your
files in both QuickTime and
Real formats. That way you are
guaranteed that almost all
your visitors will have immediate access to your work
without having to load a new
plug-in, restarting the browser,
and coming back to your site
to view your files.

The latest versions of RealProducer Plus and RealPlayer have fixed many problems associated with the display quality. Formerly, halos appeared around
sharp lines, giving an almost ethereal look to people, hair, and buildings.
They have done this by rewriting the CODEC, which is called RealVideo 8. It
has also helped with some performance issues and lower data rates.

You can find out more about Real's line of products on their Web site at
www.real.com.

Other Products

As I stated in previous chapters (and even in the Introduction), one of the most
fun aspects of graphic design is your ability to look beyond a program's main
reason for being to find new ways to make your vision come to life within
GoLive. In this portion of the chapter, I'll introduce some ideas that might
ignite some dormant creative sparks. Many of these programs are standalones
that have niche audiences, and in some cases, you might not have considered
using them in some of the ways I'm about to outline. That's cool, and that is
what this is all about—giving ideas that might be used in your upcoming
projects. Demos of many of the programs mentioned in this section are provided on the companion CD-ROM so you can follow along with the various
projects. Others not included (more than likely due to space limitations) can
be downloaded from the companies' sites.

I am also breaking this section into genres so these products are easier to find.
These include 3D (which is becoming a hot topic for Web presentations these
days), other animation tools, and seamless backgrounds. So, let's dive right in.

3D Applications

In many cases, presenting 3D content on the Web can be viewed as being as difficult as quickly providing streaming video. In many cases, providing full-motion 3D content means that you have to convert your file into QuickTime or AVI and then stream it in the exact same manner. However, developers are coming up with new and exciting ways to give novice, intermediate, and advanced users the ability to quickly present their visions.

As 3D moves into its next phase of existence, that of being included in more and more creative toolkits, it's fun to check out sites that employ the latest technology. By this time, nearly everyone has heard of Ananova (**www.ananova.com**), the cyber-newscaster that reads the headlines to you. She was the first computer-generated (CG) character used in this manner. The technology still has problems—some slow and slightly sloppy lip synching for example—but this is more of a problem of the phoneme engines that are used today and not really a bandwidth problem. Bottom line: Ananova is the harbinger of things to come on the Web.

Let's look at some programs (there are so many out there now) that can aid you in creating some 3D hosts of your own. We'll start with what I consider to be the best buy you could make.

Poser 4

If it isn't already, this program should be in your toolbox. Poser 4 is a character-based application that provides you with humanoid, animal, and fantasy models that can be easily posed and animated. The former MetaCreations program is now being distributed by Curious Labs (**www.curiouslabs.com**), created by company-dubbed evangelist Steve Cooper, program creator Larry Weinberg, and the team of programmers who have been with the Poser project since version 1. New ties with New York-based MetaStream give Poser users the ability to create low-bandwidth, high-quality interactive elements for the Web directly within Poser 4.

Poser 4 is the perfect program for non-3D artists to include 3D characters on their site. The Poser models are highly manipulatable, so you can easily create an original mascot for your own or your client's site. Because Poser is also one of my favorite tools, many Poser models are used in the projects throughout this book. All are high-quality models that—given the short length of time we have as designers to put a site together—save me from going nuts trying to build a whole new model in a 3D program.

Let's explore this program just a little bit further with a short exercise:

1. Start Poser 4 or the Poser 4 demo program that you can download from the Curious Labs Web site. To the right of the screen is a vertical bar that, when clicked on, reveals the numerous models at your disposal.

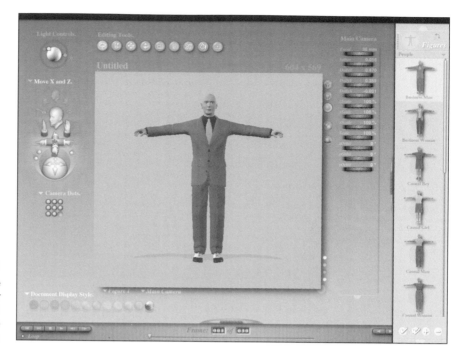

Figure 13.21

The Business Man will become the male version of Vanna White for your Web page. Use the Casual Man model if you are using the demo version of Poser.

The dots at the top of this model selection screen (see Figure 13.21) enable you to choose between Figures, Props, and more. For this project, choose Figures (the top button), and select either the Business Man (not available in the demo version) or Casual Man character by double-clicking on him. The model will load onto the workspace.

2. You need to add some hair. Move your cursor over the dots until Hair is highlighted. Click once, and in the controls to the right of this area scroll down until you find a male hair style that you like. Figure 13.22 shows the style that I chose. Double-clicking on the style automatically adds it to the model.

3. You control positioning of the various body parts by clicking on a part of the body and changing different parameters using the dial controls to the right of the workspace. You can also change the look of the body parts by modifying their sizes. If you don't want to fiddle with modifying each element, down to the position of each finger joint, preset poses are available that you can use; they are stored in the retractable tray where the characters are accessed under the Poses section. There are a number of preset poses ranging from Action to Sports to Standing sets. In this character's case, I positioned the character's arms and body so it looks like he is showcasing an item.

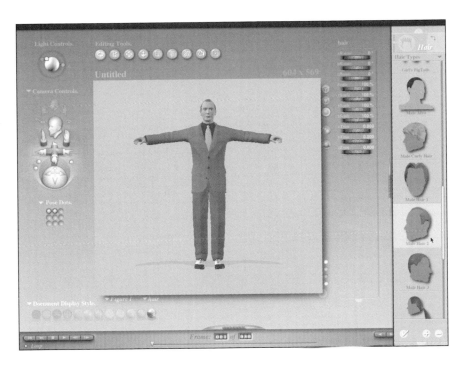

Figure 13.22

Adding hair to your model is as easy as double-clicking on the style you like.

4. To make sure that the figure looked as natural as possible in its final pose, I made a few more changes to the Bend and Twist parameters of the forearms. This change helped make the sleeves of his jacket look more natural. Figure 13.23 shows the final pose.

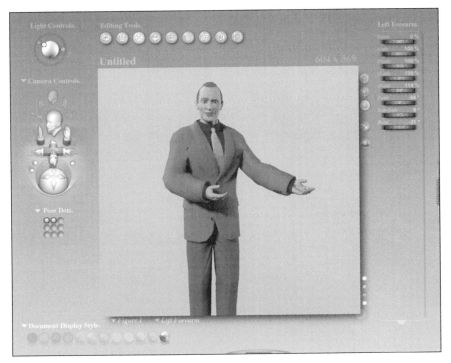

Figure 13.23

Our male Vanna (who I will now call Van White) is in his final pose following the setup procedures outlined.

Note: When you are working with 3D character models, it's important to take your time when positioning them. Even minor changes in the rotation or the bend of a body part can mean the difference between a realistic pose and one that looks contrived and unnatural.

Note: You cannot save your model when using the demo version of Poser 4.

Note: Unless otherwise noted, all the following programs are available in both Mac and Windows versions.

5. Now it's just a matter of rendering the image and saving it as a JPEG file. To do this, go to Render|Render Options. These controls are hidden at the top of the screen; simply move your cursor to the top and the pull-down controls will appear. Set the image parameters to 320×240 and make sure that Anti-alias is activated. After the file is rendered and saved, you can import it into Photoshop and create a layered image to place into GoLive using the Smart Photoshop tool.

Another Poser plus is the ability to change elements you don't need to be invisible. The GoLive and Prosper page you created earlier in the book used a Poser model's hand with the rest of the body made invisible. You can also render a model in sketch mode, making it look as if it were hand drawn, or use toon shading to make it appear more like a cartoon character.

Other 3D applications are available that you can use to create some fantastic highly original characters and creatures. If you have an interest in 3D modeling, and want to either extend your abilities or want to try your hand at it, you might want to check out these programs. I'm listing them in order by what I consider ease of modeling, although it's really your abilities and tastes that will determine which program works best.

Hash Animation:Master 2000 (A:M)

Animation:Master is a unique program that has an extremely avid user base. Modeling in A:M is, in my opinion, much more intuitive for the person who wants to jump in and give 3D character modeling a try. Using Patch Modeling, which is basically creating the exterior (or skin) out of patches made up of three, four, or five consecutive points (see Figure 13.24), you can create extremely high-quality models without the subsequent large file sizes that other modeling applications create.

Hash Animation:Master 2000 has been available for approximately ten years. It has pioneered many modeling and rendering techniques now found in the high-end (read: expensive) programs. Because it's under $300, you can't beat this as a powerful modeling application that is worth more than two to three times the going price. You can learn more about (and purchase) A:M program at the **www.hash.com** Web site.

Organica

Organica has been around for approximately five years now and, unfortunately, has not been updated since its creation. Nevertheless, it's still an interesting modeler. Like A:M, Organica has a unique style; it is a MetaBall modeler, which gives the feel of creating models with clay without all the mess and subsequent cleanup. Figure 13.25 shows a character in the middle of being created using the basic shapes that are the program's building blocks. You can find out more about Organica at **www.coolfun.com/INFO/PRODUCTS/Organica/organica.html** (and, yes, the capitalization needs to be typed exactly as it's shown here).

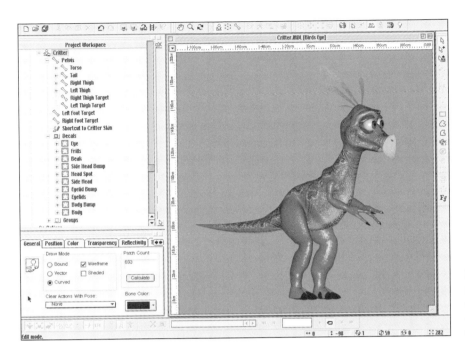

Figure 13.24

Hash Animation:Master 2000 uses Patch Modeling to create characters, organic critters, and scenic elements.

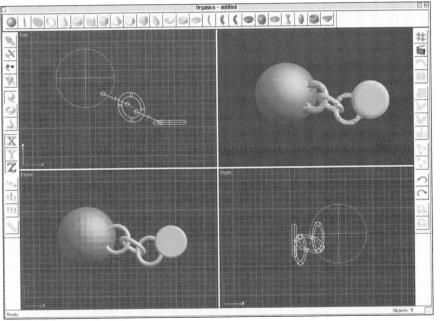

Figure 13.25

Organica is a unique program in that it is strictly a MetaBall modeler. While other programs now incorporate this technology, Oganica is the only one on the market that features only that technology.

The company also just released a fascinating new program named Illusion, which at the time of this writing was available for Windows only. This is a particle-effects software package that lets you easily create animated effects such as fireworks, clouds, gaseous materials, fountains, and more. You can save the animations you create in various formats for easy importation into GoLive. This program is extremely low-cost, yet is extremely high-end. According to the company info, Illusion was used to create effects for *Star Trek Voyager*, *Roughnecks: Starship Trooper Chronicles*, and other television productions.

Pixels:3D

This is a Macintosh-only 3D modeler that, incidentally, was my introduction to 3D creation. (So, I have a soft spot in my heart for this program.) While some work needs to be done to fix some bugs in the boning structure of the program, it is a powerful application that, literally, is the only one out there that only focuses on the Mac community. I created my first characters in this program, and I'm still considering making one, a creature I named Squash because of his immense size, the mascot for my company (see Figure 13.26).

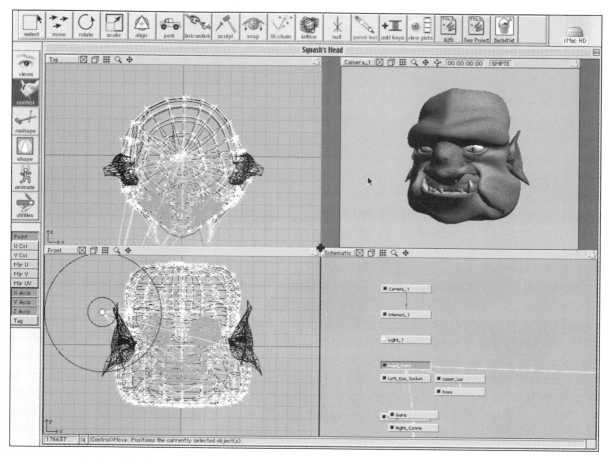

Figure 13.26

This is Squash, seen rendered in the upper-right window, and his mesh viewed from the front, top, and right side in Pixels:3D.

Pixels is also the first of the programs I'm discussing that has extensibility features. It uses a scripting language called *T/cl* (referred to as *Tickle*) that lets you create plug-ins and extensions for the program. In fact, many people have done so, and a wide variety of extensions are available for free or for a small price. Also, a new rendering extension called Tempest is probably one of the best and fastest renderers on the market. Check out Pixels and some of the extremely impressive work that has been created at **www.pixels.net**. Pixels:3D can only be purchased over the Internet from their site.

Amapi 3D

Template Graphics Software's (TGS) Amapi 3D (see Figure 13.27) is a hidden jewel of a modeler. Extremely popular in the UK, it has yet to gain much of a foothold in this country, due to various reasons. But, TGS is now beginning to make a marketing push for Amapi 3D which, to say the least, incorporates a *graphic user interface* (*GUI*, or *"gooey"* for those of us who love wordplay) that is completely different than any other modeling program on the market.

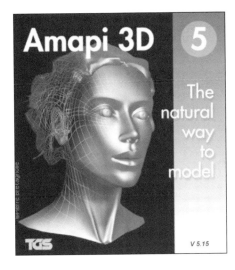

Figure 13.27
The least known program in the States, Amapi 3D by TGS is a modeler that deserves more recognition in the 3D world.

Amapi 3D's workspace is set up to represent a potter's wheel, and its main tool set design emulates craftspersons' tools (see Figure 13.28). Although you have the option to switch to a more standard tool set interface, once you get used to the default tools (and, trust me, it will take some time), Amapi 3D becomes a powerful and totally enjoyable experience. Also, unlike other modelers (which, on the average, incorporate a four-screen view of your model), Amapi uses one main screen (seen in Figure 13.29) that you can rotate incrementally in all directions. Again, this stays with its idea of emulating an artist's physical workspace.

To learn more about TGS and Amapi 3D, visit their site at **www.tgs.com**.

Cinema 4D

Maxon's Cinema 4D is another program with an extremely strong following. It comes in four versions, ranging from a beginner's version to a very high-end version with all the bells and whistles. The designers who use this program are avid about it and, judging from the work I've done in it, it's an extremely impressive package. The biggest problem is its steep learning curve. So, expect to spend some time getting past the basics with this one. You can find out more about the Cinema 4D family of products at **www.maxoncomputer.com**.

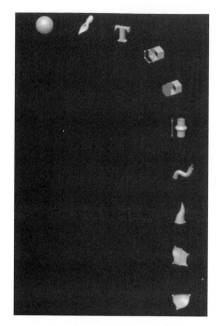

Figure 13.28

Amapi 3D incorporates a tool set unlike any in the industry. It takes some time to get used to, but when you do, the program becomes extremely fun to work in.

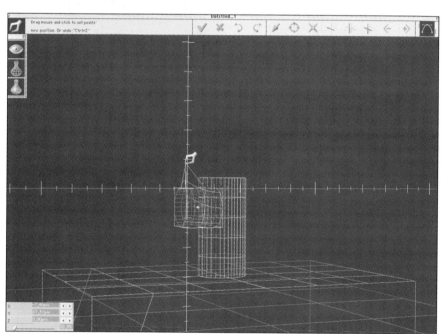

Figure 13.29

The main workspace of Amapi 3D is set up to emulate a traditional artist's table.

LightWave [6]

LightWave [6] is a top-notch program that is as professional as it gets, while retaining some semblance of affordability. Newtek's LightWave [6] (seen in Figure 13.30) has been used in a number of highly successful films, the latest being *Stuart Little*. Because of its scripting language, you can create plug-ins and extensions to increase the program's capabilities. This is exactly what was done to create the realistic fur and clothing movements for the main character, Stuart . Again, because of its power and depth, expect to spend time learning how to use this program. You can find out more about it at **www.newtek.com**.

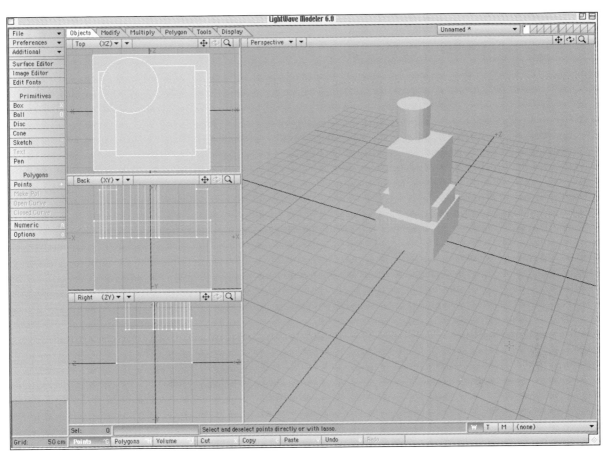

Figure 13.30

A look at LightWave [6]'s modeler. When you purchase this program, you basically get two-for-one, Modeler and LightWave, which is actually the layout program where you render your final image.

Other high-end 3D modeling programs you can choose from are:

- Form Z
- 3D Studio Max (PC only)
- SoftImage
- Maya (which is currently PC only, but will be released for the Mac around the same time as OSX).
- Houdini

Other 3D programs are on the market, and it would be a good idea to do some research, download demos when available, and find the one that works best for you.

Seamless Texture Creation

Seamless textures should definitely not be ignored when you are setting up your site designs. Consider the fact that they can be used in tables as a whole, table cells, and as backgrounds for your site. You can use them as JPEG or GIF images that highlight elements on your page. You have to be careful to not make the textures so busy with lots of bright colors and shapes that it fights your design. You've all experienced sites that include background images that literally make your eyes hurt when you see them. If you were like me, you left before the text loaded.

Unfortunately, so many people are using basic tools to create background images that appear like all the rest out there, that a dearth of creative ideas exists. So, it's important to really look at the programs you already own and try to envision how they could be used to achieve your objectives.

The programs I'm listing in the following sections are designed specifically to create seamless textures, others you wouldn't necessarily consider at first glance. So let's start out by looking at a cool program that is designed to do just one thing: Create seamless textures.

TextureMagic

This is a Mac-only program that was created by a Mac enthusiast in Germany, and he really did a great job. TextureMagic (seen in Figure 13.31) is very inexpensive, yet gives Mac users a wonderful tool to build great textures.

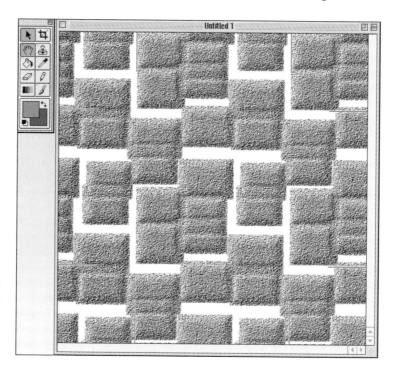

Figure 13.31

TextureMagic is an easy, yet powerful, program that gives Mac users the ability to focus on designing a texture without having to worry if the pattern's seams will match up correctly.

This program has only one purpose—to help you focus on the creation of original seamless designs without worrying about the intricacies of matching edges. To give you a better idea of how this works—and how easy it is to use—let's take a moment to create a texture:

1. Create a new file that is 256×256 pixels and 72dpi. This is a good size for background screens.

2. Double-click on the foreground color chip at the bottom of the toolbar and select CMYK Picker. Make the color C:72, M:0, Y:100, K:44, which is a nice shade of green.

3. First, you need to create a background. Select Effects|Lines and, in the information screen, select Precision: low, Color: colorful, Angle: 90, and Appearance: ink. At this stage, don't worry about the Presets. Figure 13.32 shows how the image will look.

Note: I haven't forgotten all the PC users out there. The texture that's created in this section is called WetTexture.jpg and is available in the Chapter 13 folder on the companion CD-ROM for your use, as are over a dozen other seamless files.

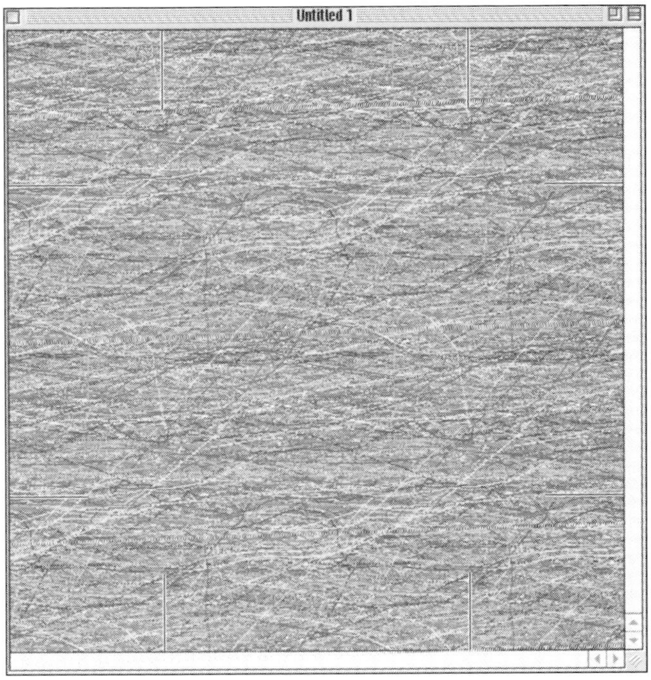

Figure 13.32
The base screen for the seamless texture you're creating in TextureMagic.

4. Choose Effects|Drops and set them up in the following manner:
   - Amount: halfway between few and many
   - Size: small
   - Variation: extreme
   - Lighting: dim
   - Covered Area: extremely blurred and no change
   - Emphasize reflection: should be deselected

   Figure 13.33 shows the screen and its setup.

5. Choose Filters|Add Bump twice to create some depth to the screen.

6. Select Filters|Add Aqua. In this screen, seen in Figure 13.34, select Simple Scanline Style and put the Strength between less and more. Make sure Preview is checked so you can see the effect that's being created.

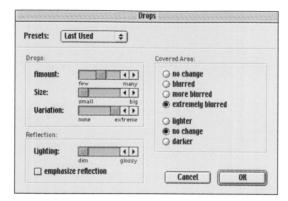

Figure 13.33
The Drops controls set up as outlined in the text.

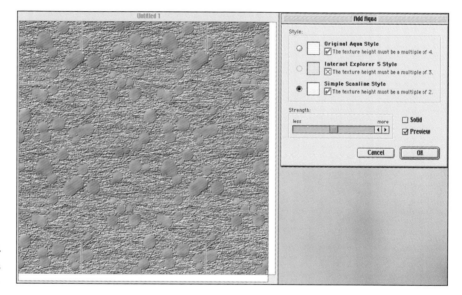

Figure 13.34
The Add Aqua command creates a scanline effect to your texture.

7. Select Filters|Blur|Gaussian Blur. Assign a value of 1 to this and click OK.

8. The final step is to select Filters|Saturation and set it to less. You now should have a texture that is extremely similar to Figure 13.35.

Save the image as a JPEG file. You can then import it into GoLive 5 as a seamless background. By experimenting with various settings and combining different image files inside the TextureMagic program, you can create endless textures for use on your Web sites.

You can order TextureMagic at this Web site: **www.artissoftware.com/ texturemagic/**. It's well worth the small investment.

ClicDesign

Here's a wonderful set of Photoshop and Illustrator plug-ins for background texture creation, although their main function is to create clothing materials. Designed for people in the fashion industry, or for people who like to create

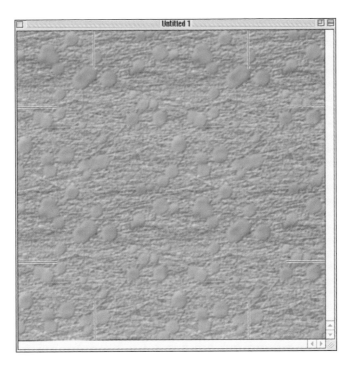

Figure 13.35

The finished texture created in TextureMagic.

clothing for Poser 4 or characters built in other 3D applications, ClicDesign (see Figure 13.36) has the capability to generate truly original textures for your Web site. Because of their main reason for being, it's easy to overlook the fact that the programs can be used for the purpose of texturing a Web site. Call it a hidden value-added feature, if you'd like.

The plug-ins include:

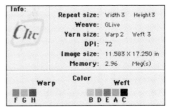

Figure 13.36

The ClicDesign series of plug-ins, although originally designed for the fashion world, can be used to create interesting fabric patterns for your sites.

- *PlaidMaker Plus*—Allows you to create plaid and striped fabrics. It can also simulate virtually any type of weave.

- *Colorvision*—Gives you the ability to change the color of scanned-in fabrics. It retains the texture and shading by working within Photoshop's Channels.

- *QuickRepeat*—Lets you create a design and then gives you the ability to create seamless patterns.

- *ArtLibrary*—Works within Adobe Illustrator to let you organize design sketches. Then you can create clipart and pattern libraries for importation to Photoshop or directly to GoLive 5.

Here's how PlaidMaker works:

1. To access PlaidMaker, open Photoshop 5.5, select File|Import|PlaidMaker Plus. This opens the controls that allow you to assign colors, patterns, and more for your pattern.

Note: For more detailed explanations of Warp and Weft, visit the Age Technology site at **www.agetechnologies.com.**

2. Warp and Weft are the two elements that determine the color setup for the pattern (seen in Figure 13.37). These are rather long, involved number/letter combinations, with the letters corresponding to the appropriate color chips along the right of the screen. The more combinations you assign, the more complicated the pattern. Use the code you see in the figure to assign your pattern. Feel free to change the colors to whatever you want by clicking on a color chip and assigning a new one.

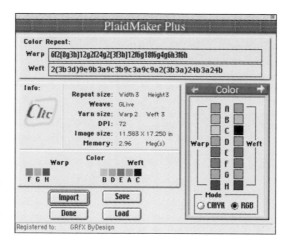

Figure 13.37

The screen that appears when you first open the PlaidMaker Plus Photoshop plug-in.

3. You can switch to other controls by clicking on the panel seen in Figure 13.38.

4. Switch to Weave and create a pattern by clicking on the pixels in the Pattern Box (see Figure 13.39). You can save the new pattern by clicking the Save button and giving it a name.

Figure 13.38

(Left) You access four areas by clicking on this bar. These controls give you access to the tools you'll use to create your pattern.

Figure 13.39

(Right) Creating a new weave is as easy as assigning a different pixel pattern in the Pattern Box.

5. Click the Load button in the bottom left of the PlaidMaker Plus screen to create your pattern. As you can see in Figure 13.40, I have created a tartan plaid that is taller than it is wide, so I could use it as a navigation bar background if I wanted.

ClicDesign's programs are available for Mac and PC.

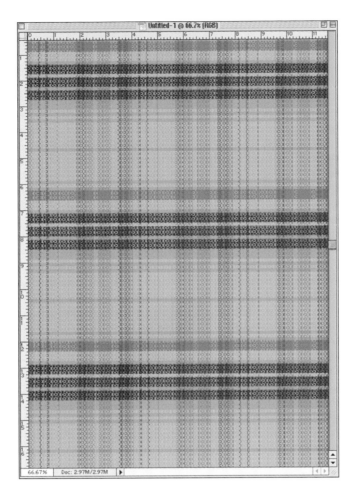

Figure 13.40
The pattern created in PlaidMaker Plus, which can be used as a background for a navigation bar.

EFFECT-ive Choices

As you can see, numerous programs and plug-ins are available that you can employ in various ways to help you create more exciting Web sites. With some creativity, and by looking at your programs in new and fresh ways, you can give your own or your clients' sites a completely original look.

Even more programs are out there that are both affordable and extremely professional. These include cell (which is short for cellular) animation programs that help you create fully-animated cartoons one frame at a time; even more Xtras for Director, and plenty of user-created textures and files that you can either download for free or for a minimal cost. Use your favorite search engine to locate these programs, or visit the various sites and go to their User Forum areas for links and more information.

Moving On

Now that I've gotten that out of the way, it's time to look at one more aspect of GoLive—its inclusion of WebObject technology for building sites. This technology is covered in Chapter 14. Then (in Chapter 15) we'll get into the really good stuff—building an entire site from scratch, while using many of the techniques and tips I've talked about up until now.

Chapter 14

What Are Those WebObjects Tools?

WebObjects are highly sophisticated tools that require an extra expenditure and, like WebDAV, a specialized server. This chapter gives an overview of WebObjects and how they can benefit your design strategy.

Note: If you haven't installed the WebObjects plug-in into GoLive 5, these tools will not appear in your Objects palette.

Design within a Design

Adobe has made a commitment to another design specification that, on the surface, duplicates many of the other tool sets, but is really a hidden gem—if you want to shell out quite a bit more money to use it. That's the WebObjects set of tools (Figure 14.1). WebObjects, in the most down-and-dirty sense, allows programmers to have a set of tools that are Java-based and employ integrated XML support. Modifications to these elements are then generated through the Inspector window.

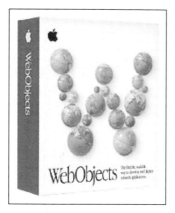

Figure 14.1
The WebObjects software has had its price dropped dramatically in an effort to make it available to more than just the multimillion-dollar companies.

Although all the WebObjects design and formatting work is done within GoLive, unless you have WebObjects Enterprise and WebObjects Server, your time and effort will be wasted. Your files or site that incorporate this format cannot be integrated or viewed without these. Recently, Apple announced an extreme price drop for this tool set—from a high of (gasp!) $50,000 to $699—and, by the time you read this, version 5 for Java will be out. Also, WebObjects is multiplatform. It's available for Mac OS 8.x and above, the soon-to-be-released OS X, Windows NT and 2000, Solaris, and HP-UX systems. What this means is that you can now have access to another set of tools that gives you unique design opportunities beyond all that are already included in GoLive 5.

It would be unfair here to go into great detail about working with WebObjects because they really are highly specialized tools. However, to ignore them completely also wouldn't be right. I realize that a $700 add-on to GoLive may not fit your budget, but if you are well off or are part of a design group with a budget for this kind of tool, this brief chapter will give you some added information about why WebObjects might be a good addition to your tool set.

WebObjects Tools

The WebObjects tools are located in the Objects window. This tool set is the sixth tab from the left, seen in Figure 14.2—the one that looks like an aqua colored W. The tool set consists of 18 objects, many of which, on the surface, look duplicative of the Basic tools. They really aren't duplicating the Basic tools, which you will soon find out. First, however, let's look at what each of these tools are.

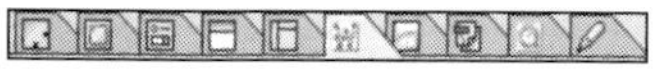

Figure 14.2
The WebObjects tab in the Objects window has a bluish W symbol on it.

The following list describes the WebObjects, from left to right, starting at the top row (refer to Figure 14.3):

- *WOImage*—Places a non-interactive image placeholder on the page.
- *WOActiveImage*—Depending on how this tool is used on the page, it can be used as an inactive, active, or active mapped image.
- *WOImageButton*—This tool, again linking to a graphic element, generates a forms request when a viewer clicks on the image.
- *WOEmbeddedObject*—Provides support for Netscape plug-ins.
- *WOApplet*—Generates HTML to specify a Java applet.

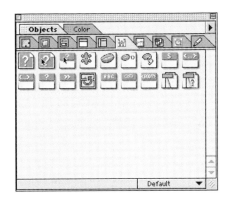

Figure 14.3
The WebObjects placeholders.

- *WOParam*—Works with a previous applet's parameter definitions.

- *WOJavaScript*—Lets you embed a script written in Java into a dynamic page.

- *WOStateStorage*—Causes repetitive or persistent information on a page to be stored in the page, rather than on the server.

- *WOGenericElement*—HTML is constantly evolving; this gives you the ability to accommodate empty HTML tags so new, unrecognized code (by current WebObjects technology) can be displayed. Doesn't work with a range of text.

- *WOGenericContainer*—Inserts a box container for elements that span a range of text.

- *WOConditional*—Specifies whether a part of an HTML page will be generated.

- *WORepetition*—Inserts a container that repeats its contents a specified number of times.

- *Table with WORepetition*—Same as WORepetition, except it places the container inside a Table element.

- *WOString*—Represents itself as a dynamically-generated string in an HTML document.

- *WOHyperlink*—Generates a hypertext link.

- *WOBody*—Used to specify a background image to display on the page.

- *WOSwitchComponent*—Lets you specify at runtime what nested image to display.

- *Reusable Component*—Inserts an unknown dynamic element that can be linked to any reusable component (see note).

Note: For a complete listing of reusable components, refer to the WebObjects user manual.

Incorporating WebObjects Elements

Just to give you a better feel for what you will deal with when working with WebObjects, let's look at the controls for one of these objects. Remember, unless you have the WebObjects program, you cannot incorporate these elements into your Web site. You would have to generate the entire code by hand.

The WOImageButton

First, take a look at the WOImageButton. When you place this button onto your workspace, the Inspector window changes to give you exacting control over your images and creating the subsequent forms:

1. To set up your image, go to the Inspector window. Notice the four tabs shown in Figure 14.4. In the basic tab, you can determine how the pop-up menu, when used, will treat the Source file. You also have parameter controls for the sizing and placement of the placeholder.

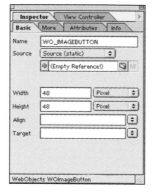

Figure 14.4

The Basic tab and the Source selections available for the image.

2. The More tab, shown in Figure 14.5, gives you controls at your disposal for creating server-side image maps.

3. Attributes (Figure 14.6) is a dual-purpose area. Here you can review the attributes assigned to that particular WOImageButton, as well as add new values (Figure 14.7), or delete ones you don't want.

4. The Info tab screen (Figure 14.8) provides you with a quick reference as to what the selected placeholder does and gives tips on when to use that particular element.

Figure 14.5

The options in the More section of the Inspector window let you create image maps. In this case, because no content is assigned, the Use Map option is grayed out.

Figure 14.6

(Left) The Attributes window.

Figure 14.7

(Right) Adding a new attribute to the WOImageButton.

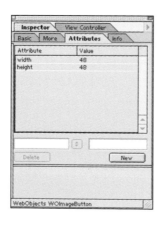

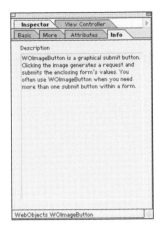

Figure 14.8
(Left) The Info tab screen.

Figure 14.9
(Right) The added selections in the Objects window.

5. Now look at the Objects window. Notice the pop-up screen (Figure 14.9) at the bottom right. You assign what type of image button the selected WOImageButton placeholder will be. It can be a singular element, such as a Frame, Form, or Head item, or it can have properties of all of them.

In the Workspace

Another area within GoLive where you can obtain information on your WebObjects-generated designs is the workspace:

1. With a WebObjects placeholder on the workspace, change the Source to Source (Dynamic), the Width to 240 pixels, and the Height to 100 pixels in the Basic area of the Inspector window. Under More, select Use Map. Now, in the workspace, select the WebObjects tab (fifth from left). As you can see in Figure 14.10, the parameters you assigned are displayed.

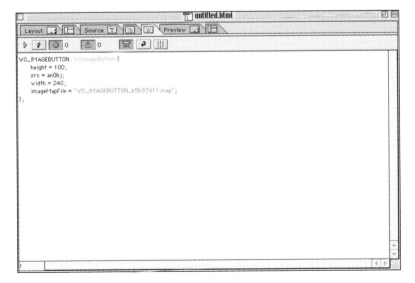

Figure 14.10
You can view attributes assigned to your WebObjects on the workspace itself.

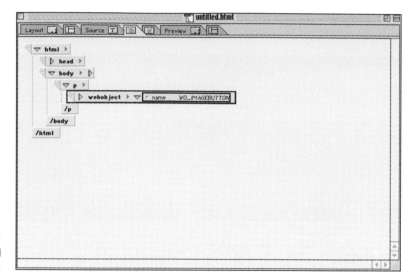

Figure 14.11
The WebObject element viewed in HTML Outline Editor mode.

2. In Source, you can see the WebObject as it is incorporated into the HTML script. And in HTML Outline Editor mode (Figure 14.11), you get a graphical view of the code and the WebObject placement within it.

A Final Word on WebObjects

As you build your pages using WebObjects and save them, you will notice different suffixes for your files. The standard WO suffixes are: .html, .wod (WebObjects declaration), and .wos (WebObjects script):

- *.html*—The Web page file defining how the page looks.

- *.wod*—The file that defines all the dynamic elements on the page, as well as the variables and actions.

- *.wos*—The file that defines the elements' behaviors.

WebObjects, until now, have for the most part been beyond the reach of most people because of its high price. However, with the massive reduction in cost, WebObjects could become more prevalent on the Web. However, if you do not plan on purchasing WebObjects Enterprise and Server, you don't need to put the WebObjects plug-in into GoLive 5 (unless you want to just play around with the components).

Moving On

So, now that you know what those myriad controls mean and you have a good idea of how to use them, it's time to look at how these controls can be incorporated into your Web site designs.

Chapter 15 follows along with the initial setup of my company Web site. The chapter will employ many of the tips and techniques outlined throughout the book, as well as give you insight into the thought processes that I used when I created the designs.

Part IV

Putting It All Together

Chapter 15

Constructing a Site

In this chapter, you'll be working with me as I redesign my company site. Numerous exercises will bring everything in the book to life.

Pre-Production Ramblings

As you begin your foray into advanced Web design, it's always nice to see how others have put together their sites. If you're like me, as I surf the Web, I constantly look at other people's work with a critical eye, dissecting how they accomplished a certain effect and how it all comes together into a cohesive whole. I don't do this with animosity because, no matter what the site looks like, someone has taken a great deal of time and put a lot of themselves into building it. If you consider this, no matter how much you might dislike a design or how poorly you think a site is put together, you can always find something worth looking at. It might be how the person designed their logo or how they laid out their links. It might even be the colors they used. Nevertheless, you can always derive something positive to take from every site you visit.

I personally have a pet peeve when it comes to personal and home business site creation, and that is with the belief that every link known to mankind has to be on the home page of a Web site. I personally hate to scroll for what seems like an eternity while trying to locate that one particular link that is tucked away between 50 other links on the left or right side of a page. I might be looking for news on the latest software upgrade from Company X, and that link always seems to be scrunched between a link to find out more about the life cycle of the Dodo bird and the average median rainfall in the Serengeti during the lunar eclipse of the first leap year of the millennium.

I'm a devout proponent of clean design that nurtures content over gaudy effects. Now don't get me wrong: Some marvelous "gee-whiz" productions are out there, and they have their time and place. However, a time and place exists for sites that don't oversell themselves by throwing everything at you when you first arrive and then forget to put any type of content in their e-space.

So, this chapter is not only going to follow upgrading the design of my company's site, it should also generate discussion about the reasons for what is done. You're not always going to agree with my choices—and I certainly wouldn't want you to. Sometimes, where I go with my site design might make you go, "Hmmm, I never thought of that." Design work of any flavor is 25 percent knowledge and 75 percent an extension of the person doing the work. It is this ratio that makes the creative process so fascinating for both the designer and his or her audience.

As you have discovered throughout this book, GoLive 5 has so much power that you could spend days and weeks working full-time with the program and still continue to discover new and exciting techniques.

Content Vs. Clutter

With that out of the way, I not only feel much better (thank you very much), but it's time to start looking into some pre-production strategies before putting together your site. First, you need to determine the main message you want to convey. What is this Web site's purpose? In this way, you have a good idea of the basic content and features you want to add.

The Personal Site

When you are designing a personal Web site, your main goal is to give friends and relatives a way to keep up to date on you and on your family's lives. You should have a minimum of the following:

- *A home page*—This page greets visitors as if they were your family (90 percent of them probably will be).

- *A "photo album"*—Make this page (or collection of linked pages) easily updatable.

- *An email link*—Add this link so family members can quickly send you messages.

- *A "diary" page*—Update this page as often as is necessary to let others know about the great events and happenings in your life.

A personal Web site shouldn't be too large and should be easy to navigate, because many family members won't have the first clue as to how the Web works. Build it for the lowest common denominator—that one person in your family that has never before touched a computer.

The Hobbyist Site

The Web is a wonderful place for the entrepreneurial spirit. With a little planning and basic marketing strategies, you can quickly create a site for people of similar interests. Suppose that your hobby is gas-powered remote-control (or RC) cars. It's a fairly simple procedure to build a site that devotes itself to your interest. In this case, your basic Web site would consist of the following:

- *A home page*—This page explains the purpose of the site's existence and outlines your interest.

- *A page of car types*—This element lists the type of gas-powered remote control cars you own.

- *A page with links*—This item will link to other RC enthusiasts' sites and to manufacturers.

- *A guest book*—On this page, people can leave your messages, add comments, and share ideas.

The hardest part of designing a Web site such as this one is in letting people know that the site is live. One of the best ways is to get in touch with a manufacturer via email (usually, someone in the marketing department) and let them know that you're building this site, that you'd like to link to their site and find out more about how they could put a link to your site in return (as in Figure 15.1), and that you actually use and will focus on their product. It's free, it's fast, and—by setting up a reciprocal link—you benefit from a built-in audience who already knows that company site is there.

Figure 15.1
An example of partnership links displayed prominently on a Web page.

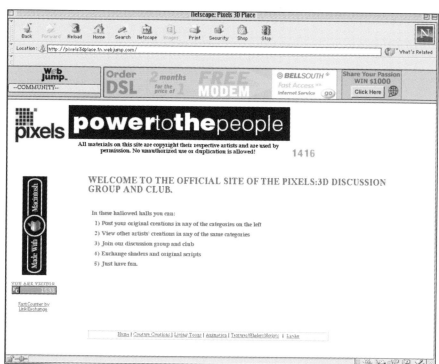

Figure 15.2
The home page for an e-group site created by the author in 1999.

Figure 15.2 shows a site I created about a year ago that was designed around a Mac-based 3D modeling program called Pixels:3D (**www.pixels.net**). The site was built using four frames: three static frames (the content never

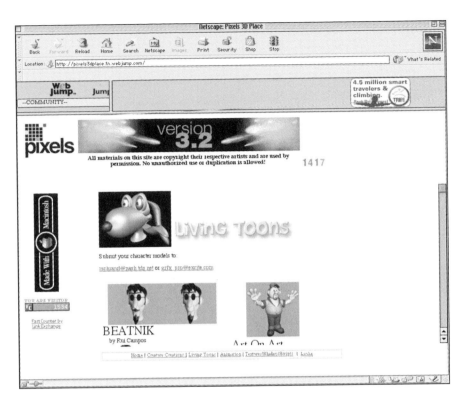

Figure 15.3
Content for each page of the site is revealed in the large, center portion of the page.

changes)—one at the top with the logo and legal information, the left side with the counter, and the bottom frame with the navigation links—and the center frame, where a selected page is revealed (see Figure 15.3).

The Sideline Business Site

Keeping with the entrepreneurial spirit, many of you have special knowledge to share or have a particular talent that you would like to offer for some extra income. The Web, as you know, is filled with this type of site. Unfortunately, many times, these sites lean so much toward what could be termed a personal site that it doesn't tell a visitor "Hey! I would love to do this for you, too!" If you have a talent (painting, sketching, caricatures, 3D modeling) and want to make some extra money at it, don't be shy when building your site. Your basic sideline business site would consist of the following elements:

- *A home page*—Its content should clearly state you offer your services for a nominal fee. It should clearly display links to each separate talent you have.

- *Gallery pages*—These pages should show thumbnails of your work. Each thumbnail should link to a page that shows the large version of the image (no larger than 500 pixels wide so that, no matter what service you use, you won't force people into scrolling around to view the entire image). You should keep these to one page per gallery.

- *A bio page*—This only focuses on why you're the perfect person to be hired to create work for the visitor.

You should include an email link on each page, so that visitors don't have to backtrack to find out how to get hold of you.

The Business Site

A business site is the same as a sideline business site, only even more focused on what you are offering. As you can see in Figure 15.4, my company's home page that has been on the Web for well over a year states a few of the services we offer. A good company site consists of the following:

- *An easily navigable home page*—This gives a quick, creative explanation of who and what you are.

- *Gallery pages*—These show the best of the best of your work.

- *A CGI form*—Visitors fill this out to obtain quotes.

- *A page of links*—This gives links to companies or individuals you have worked with, an email link to same, and possible quotes spouting glowing praise of your work.

- *A bio/background page on you and your employees*—If you have anyone else working for you, add these bios. It should also include any awards you have received.

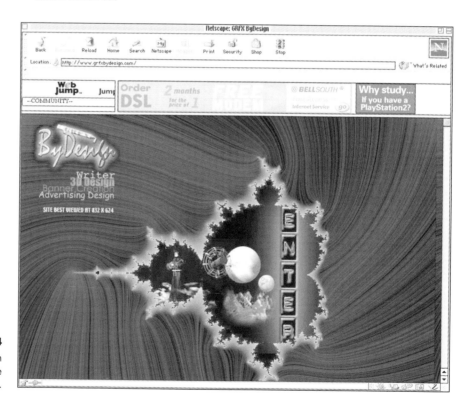

Figure 15.4
The author's home page splash screen that has been online since early 1999.

When it comes to any type of business site, whether to generate part-time work or for a full-time company, the worst thing you could do is put in too much information. Leave the visitor wanting more. Make them contact you to find out if you can meet their needs. And remember, nobody has the time nor wants to read long blocks of text when visiting a site. When it comes to bios, no one really cares where you went to grade school. What you need to focus on is the work you have created. That always speaks for itself. You have to be your own harshest critic, limiting your content to what you feel is the *crème de la crème* of your work...and you.

In other words, with a personal Web site, you do have a certain amount of leeway, and the "right and wrong" of Web-site design contains more gray areas than do company or corporate design rules.

The main thing to remember when you're building your site: Would you, as a visitor, really read or look at all you are adding to the content? More than likely you'll say no. And that's the perfect starting place to begin creating that world-class Web site you've always dreamed about.

Graphically Speaking

The more graphics you put on your site, the longer it will take for your page to download—no matter how well you prepared them for the Web. So it's important that the images you use convey the message you want to put out. You can look at this in two different ways—the hit-them-between-the-eyes imagery and the subliminal imagery.

Hit-Them-Between-the-Eyes

These are the type of images that show off your creative prowess so matter of factly that it's impossible to miss your talent. Figure 15.5 shows a good example. This is Squash, a character I was developing for an author friend of mine. Every time people see this big lummox, he becomes the center of conversation with people wondering how long it took me to make him, how he reminds them of some esoteric sculpture they once saw, etc. He has become so popular in many ways that I'm seriously considering making him my company's mascot.

Squash is the perfect example of a hit-them-between-the-eyes type of image. He makes people want to see more and, because of this, they will more than likely explore the site more thoroughly. You're bound to have one or more of this type of image stored on your hard drive, and you shouldn't give much thought about using them.

Subliminal Imagery

Very much the opposite of the hit-them-between-the-eyes type of image, subliminal imagery is the type that doesn't stand out. Taken as part of the whole, it gives the visitor a feeling of consistency and quality (or, in a worst-case scenario, the feeling that something is wrong or missing, thus conveying a lack of quality). In

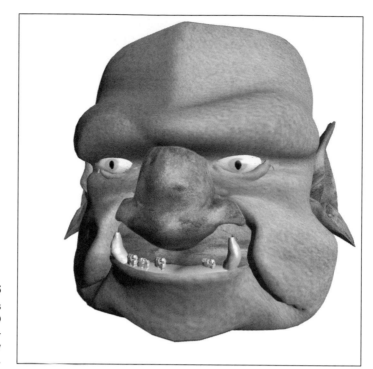

Figure 15.5

A hit-them-between-the-eyes type of image—in this case, a 3D character I created that I'm seriously considering making my company's mascot.

Figure 15.6

The Rubbirducks.com splash screen is a perfect example of creating powerful yet subliminal messages to your visitors.

the case of Figure 15.6, this splash screen is both fun and funny. Although its cartoonish nature hits you immediately, it subliminally projects a strong sense of quality and whimsy that is carried throughout the site due to the professional artwork. (You can see the color version of this site in this book's GoLive 5 Studio.)

Subliminal messages are also transmitted through the continuity of your site. What this means is sticking to your theme, making sure your pages reflect your vision of quality. That doesn't mean every page has to look the same, but a tying thread needs to be there throughout in order to make the site visitor comfortable. It could be as simple as taking each duck in Figure 15.6, separating them from the main image, and using a different one on each page of the site. It could be using the shower glass texture as the background for a navigation bar. One way or the other, by finding your theme and carrying it through on each and every page of your site, you will take a healthy step toward sending the message that you are someone to reckon with.

Site Roadmap

Before building a site, you should create an outline, so you know how each page will relate to the next. The outline process is simple—it can merely be a series of boxes to represent each page with lines connecting each one to indicate the links, like in Figure 15.7. Take a moment now to break down the site

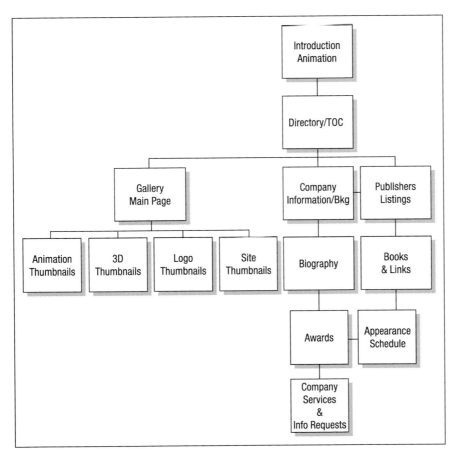

Figure 15.7
The base diagram for the site about to be created.

layout and what GoLive features will be used. Also, not everything is shown in this initial diagram, so it's important to know what pages are missing and why. Here's the layout:

- *Introduction Animation*—This page will be created with Adobe LiveMotion and will be a standalone Shockwave animation. The next section of this chapter will go into detail on what is used to build it. It will utilize the Smart LiveMotion placeholder. At the end of the animation, a rollover button will appear to link to the Directory/TOC page.

- *Directory/TOC*—(TOC stands for Table Of Contents.) This is the main home page, with links to all subsequent areas of the site. It will be the page that will be updated the most, so you should link it to a CSS in order to make sure that the revisions (when they occur) maintain the same look and feel.

- *Gallery Main Page*—This is the entryway to the various designs and models you have created. Thematic advanced rollovers will be created that will take the visitor to that specific area. This page will utilize tables. Artwork will be created in various programs, including Amapi 3D, Adobe Illustrator 9, and Adobe Photoshop 6. As you can see in the diagram, the topics for the sub-pages are Animation, 3D, Logo, and Site (meaning Web sites the company has designed).

  - *Animation Thumbnails*—This page will focus on some of the animations you have created. It will, again, utilize frames to display the thumbnails and short descriptions of the elements. It will also have links to pages containing each separate full-sized work, as well as links that allow visitors to download the files if they would prefer doing that instead.

  - *3D Thumbnails*—This page will focus on some of the 3D work you have created over the past few years. It will utilize frames to display the thumbnails and short descriptions of each image. Links will be created to take the visitor to a full-sized image.

  - *Logo Thumbnails*—This page will contain some of the logos you have created for various companies. It will utilize frames to display the thumbnails and short descriptions of each image. Links will be created to take the visitor to a full-sized image.

  - *Site Thumbnails*—This page will focus on sites you have created for yourself, as well as for clients. It will utilize frames to display thumbnails of the home pages and a short description of the sites. Links will be created to take the visitor to the sites themselves.

- *Company Information/Background*—This page will give a short description of your company, featuring some of the highlights since it was created. The page will contain no more than three paragraphs of text. Artwork will be created that employs 3D programs, such as Pixels:3D and LightWave [6], animations created with LiveMotion, and other art built in Illustrator 9 and Photoshop 6.

- *Biography*—This is a short personal biography. It doesn't need to be anything great, but it's almost obligatory these days. Do not—I repeat, do not—tell visitors where you went to elementary school, your collective Kindergarten through College GPA, nor reveal your sock size.

- *Awards*—A listing of some of the awards and honors you have been fortunate enough to receive. Try to keep it from being an ego study and, for the most part, quickly move through this section.

- *Company Services and Info Requests*—This is where you will list services your company provides. It will contain an area where visitors can request more information. It will also include a link so they can download a general rate card in PDF format.

- *Publishers' Listings*—This page will list the various publishers you have done work for, with logos acting as links to that particular publisher's site. This will not only include book publishers, but magazines and online publications in which you have been fortunate enough to be included.

  - *Books & Links*—This page will list the books you have either enjoyed or (if you are like me) written with cover illustrations and a short description of the contents. You should also provide links to various online retailers and, when possible, sample pages in PDF format.

  - *Appearance Schedule*—This will be an often-updated page that will feature a schedule of appearances. It will cover a three-month period and utilize frames and CSS functions.

Notice that the sub-pages for the Thumbnails pages were not included in the diagram; this varies, depending on how many samples you decide to use. Each of these pages will be set up as _blank links so that a new window is opened when the link is activated. Also not mentioned is the utilization of Actions for various image files. As you move through this chapter, you will see numerous mentions of and projects that include Actions that not only come with GoLive 5, but that are part of Oliver Zahorka's wonderful OUTactions package (described in Chapter 14). The site will use other programs as well, and 3D models provided by numerous companies and artists that often cost extra. If you like them and have the programs to use them with, I would highly recommend your purchasing from these various sources.

Philosophical Prattle

Although you aren't necessarily going to want to build this site as you work your way through this chapter, you can utilize the techniques discussed to create your own updated site. This is why you won't find many of the files I use. However, you can download demos of the various Adobe programs that I work with from the Adobe site (**www.adobe.com**).

I also like to create clean, unobtrusive sites that are visually appealing without the graphics taking center stage. Nothing is worse than a Web site design that is so heavily laden with images that the message is lost; and I know you've all seen advertisements or Web sites that have that problem. A site can be visually impressive the first time around because of its fresh look, but the main questions that should come to mind are: Does the content live up to the graphic representation, and does it deliver the content? Ninety-nine percent of the time you could probably answer "no" to both of those questions.

Also, these days, techno sites are hot. More and more people are creating graphics that represent futuristic control panels that almost make it seem as if my computer just gained a half a ton of weight. I enjoy that kind of imagery, and some great techno-art is being shown over the Web. But, if images don't have a tie-in to anything on the site, all the eye-candy in the world won't make it feel as if it were a perfect fit—sort of like that great looking pair of jeans that are a size too small that you keep trying to fit into.

Anyway, that's my philosophy on layout and design. Let's get started. Project 15.1 shows you how to build a Web site.

PROJECT 15.1 Home Is Where the Animation Is

Unlike movies and television shows, it's best to work from the beginning of your site and design pages as they fit into the overall flow. In movies and television, producers shoot all the scenes in a given setting, no matter where in the script the scenes actually fall. So, one day they could shoot sequences that appear at the beginning of the movie, 20 minutes into the film, and the ending sequence. Once all the scenes are shot, the film is taken to the editing facility and put into the right order. It makes sense to shoot a film that way, as it saves a lot of setup and tear down time. But, for Web sites, to create the look and feel you want, it's often best to work as you would write—from start to finish.

Note: Unless otherwise indicated, the background for all the pages of this site is white.

The Logo

I created my company logo in 1997 in a much older version of Adobe Illustrator. Because all updates of the program are built to be downwardly compatible, it was no problem importing the original file (see Figure 15.8) into version 9.

Note: The logo has been saved in three separate Illustrator 9 files: Pencil.ai, PaintDrop.ai, and Text.ai. They are available in the Ch15 folder on this book's companion CD-ROM.

Modifying the Illustrator File

You don't have to do much with the three Illustrator files per se, but you'll need to modify the Text.ai file slightly before importing the elements into LiveMotion. To accomplish this, do the following.

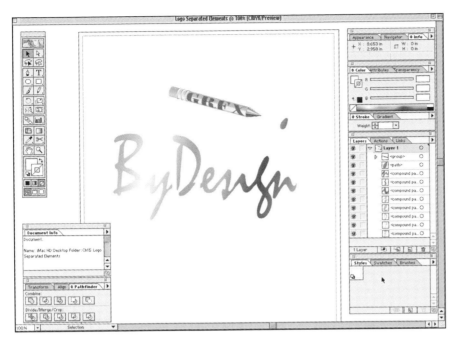

Figure 15.8
The three elements of the company logo.

1. For the logo, add a stroke to the script text to make it stand out more. Open the Text.ai file and click on ByDesign to select it. Choose Edit|Copy (Cmd/Ctrl+C) and then Edit|Past In Back (Cmd/Ctrl+B) to place the copy directly behind the original.

2. The background copy of the text is still selected. Click on the Stroke chip (the rightmost button in the second to last row) in the tools panel (shown in Figure 15.9) to bring it to the front and, if they aren't open already, open the Stroke and Color control windows (Window|Show Stroke and Window|Show Color). Select pure black for the stroke color and set the weight at 2 pt. This will create a 1 pt. black border around the text (see Figure 15.10).

3. Drag across the ByDesign text to select both sets and use Cmd/Ctrl+G to group the letters.

Preparing for the Logo Animation in LiveMotion

Now that all the logo elements are ready, you need to import them into Adobe LiveMotion in preparation for animating. These three Illustrator files consist of only a portion of the animation that will be built. The other files used in this section—if you want to use them—are on this book's companion CD-ROM in the LiveMotion_Elements folder. I'll be describing the positioning of elements and the addition of text to the screen, but you definitely need to have a basic working knowledge of LiveMotion before proceeding. The download comes with a user manual in PDF format, and I would urge you to go over it prior to moving forward.

Figure 15.9
The Illustrator tool set and the Stroke indicator chip activated, ready for a color and weight to be assigned. The Stroke indicator chip is the highlighted button at the bottom of the window.

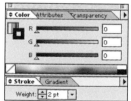

Figure 15.10
The stroke added to a duplicate copy of the ByDesign text.

The LiveMotion file dimensions are 640×480. The reason for this size (rather than something larger) is to accommodate people with smaller monitors (remember, 15-inch monitors are the average size) and for people who don't have video cards that accommodate higher resolutions. The length of the animation will be 15 seconds, the length of the music that you will add. To do so, take the following steps:

1. Place the TimeLine marker seen in Figure 15.11 at the 05s (five-second) mark. Where the marker is positioned along the TimeLine determines where any imported files will be placed.

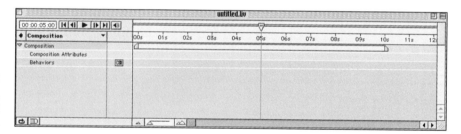

Figure 15.11
The TimeLine marker in position, showing where the imported logo files will begin.

2. In the following order, import the Illustrator files (File|Place or Cmd/Ctrl+I) that you created:

   • Text.ai

   • PaintDrop.ai

   • Pencil.ai

   This import process places the files in the correct layer order. After they are placed, position the pencil and drop, as you see in figure 15.12.

Now, add the other four files that will make up the animation: Fairy1.jpg, Fairy2.jpg, Fairy3.jpg, and Fairy4.jpg. These will be added to the beginning of the animation sequence. Also, a file named Caricature.jpg will appear at the tail end of this animation project.

3. Move the TimeLine marker to the 0s mark and, in the numbered order, place the fairy files. Move numbers 2 through 4 to the left edge of the

Figure 15.12
The logo elements have been moved into position.

workspace after they are placed. Once they are positioned, select all of them by Shift+clicking on each element in the TimeLine, and go to Object|Arrange|Send to Back so they are underneath the logo elements (see Figure 15.13).

4. Also at 0s, use the Text tool to type the following (each on separate layers):

   - Author

   - Graphic Design

   - 3D Design

   - Instructor

   Place these to the right side of the screen; they will appear as the fairy "flies" in.

5. At the eight-second mark (08s), use the Text tool to type in the catchphrase, "Helping Your Company Grow...ByDesign!" Put this on two lines, with "ByDesign" centered beneath the beginning of the phrase. Place this text so it is centered underneath the logo between the lower-case "y" and "g". Create another text layer by clicking on the workspace and typing in the copyright information. This should be centered under the catchphrase.

6. The final element to import before you animate the logo is the OpenAudio.aiff (Mac) or OpenAudio.wav (Win). Again, make sure that the TimeLine marker is at 0s (zero seconds) when you add it to your file.

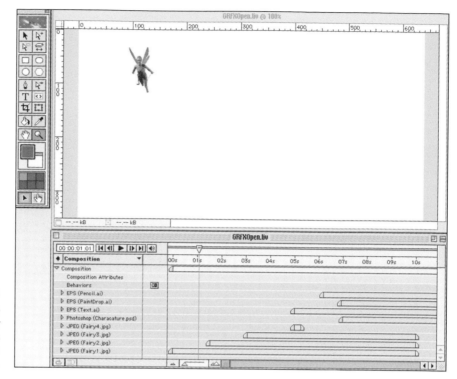

Figure 15.13
The Fairy files placed beneath the logo images in the TimeLine. For the fairy file to be seen in this image, I moved the animation TimeLine to 01s.

7. Take a look at Figure 15.14. This figure shows the TimeLine with all of the elements positioned where they need to go timewise. Now take a moment to look at the positions (detailed in the following list), starting from the bottom and working to the top:

- Fairy1.jpg is placed at the start of the animation. Using the Opacity settings, she starts off at 0% and fades up to 100% over a half-second timeframe.

- Fairy2.jpg comes in at 1.5 seconds, with a 0.5-second fade up while Fairy1.jpg fades out.

- Fairy3.jpg comes in 1.5 seconds later, with the fade-in lasting 0.5 second. The only difference is that Fairy 3 does not fade out. Rather, she flies off the left side of the screen just after the ByDesign text pops in.

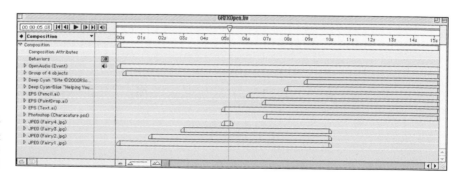

Figure 15.14
All the elements are placed at their starting positions, as can be seen in the TimeLine window.

- The four description lines (Author, Graphic Design, 3D Artist, and Instructor) appear at even intervals as the fairy appears to draw closer (see Figure 15.15). They all fade out at the same time just prior to the fourth fairy image appearing. Each text element has a drop shadow that was added using the technique outlined shortly.

- At 05s, Fairy4.jpg appears. No fade-in or fade-out occurs in order to give the appearance of her arm stretching out (see Figure 15.16) and magically making the Text.jpg image pop in.

Figure 15.15
The descriptive text appears as the fairy draws closer to the viewer.

Figure 15.16
The fairy is set up to look like her magic wand has made the ByDesign portion of the logo pop into existence.

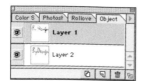

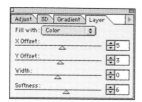

Figure 15.17

A new layer has been created that will be modified in the Layer window.

Figure 15.18

The Layer window with the parameters set to make the background Text.jpg layer appear as a drop shadow.

Figure 15.19

The fairy, having done her job, begins to fly off screen. Notice the drop shadow behind the ByDesign text.

- I added a second layer via the Object window to the Text.jpg image (see Figure 15.17) and, using the Layer controls (see Figure 15.18), I created the drop shadow you see in Figure 15.19.

- Immediately upon leaving the screen, the Pencil.jpg image flies in from the upper-left corner. Also, as you can see in Figure 15.20, it rotates as it moves toward its final destination.

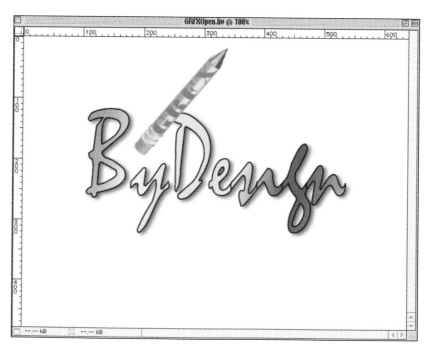

Figure 15.20

The Pencil at mid-rotation as it nears the end of its move onto the screen.

- The PaintDrop.jpg image has been squeezed down to 1 pixel×1 pixel so it is invisible onscreen. As soon as the pencil locks into place, the drop is expanded (see Figure 15.21), so it appears to have been dislodged from the tip of the pencil.

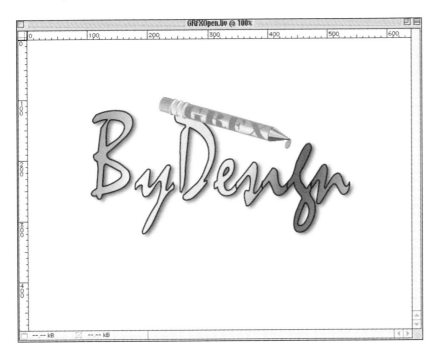

Figure 15.21
The paint drop is resized after the pencil comes to rest, so the drop looks like it's dripping from the tip of the pencil.

- To end the animation, at 13 seconds the catchphrase, legal information, and the Caricature.jpg image fade in to complete the scene (see Figure 15.22).

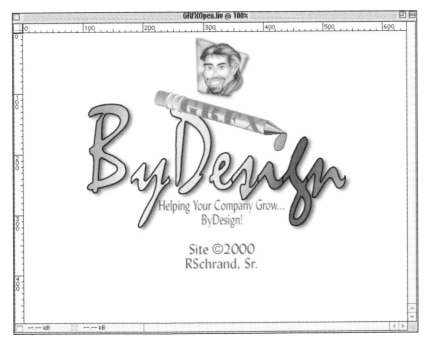

Figure 15.22
The final screen of the animation, ready to be imported into GoLive.

- Finally, music was added starting at the 0s marker.

Now that you have built your animation (whether working off the files provided on the companion CD-ROM or using your own), you need to save it as a standard LiveMotion file. Don't worry about converting it to Shockwave format because, as you've learned, GoLive will take care of that for you, thanks to the Smart LiveMotion placeholder. The finished GRFXOpen.liv file is available on this book's companion CD-ROM so you can study how it was put together; and the music bite I used is also there for the taking.

Create a Rollover Button in Illustrator 9

You probably noticed that I did not create a rollover link to take visitors into the site proper. I purposefully left this out, because I wanted to create the button elements in Illustrator 9. Certain effects I wanted to incorporate in the buttons are effects specific to Illustrator.

The button design itself can fall under the Subliminal heading described earlier in the chapter. I modeled it after the head of the fairy's wand (see Figure 15.23). Although the wand is extremely small—definitely not a focal point of the animation—and is seen for only a short period of time, designing the button to mirror that element gives the page a sense of continuity, even though the colors are different. This is the subliminal effect I hope to achieve.

Figure 15.23
This wand head from Poser 4 was used as the general design for the home page entry link.

Because you're already in the program, you will also create a starburst that will follow the movement of your mouse on the next page you create. You'll do this in GoLive using one of Oliver Zahorka's OUTactions plug-ins. Later on in the chapter, you'll use some of Illustrator 9's new features, but for this portion, you'll create fairly straightforward Illustrator images:

1. With Illustrator open, choose the Rounded Rectangle tool (seen in Figure 15.24). Hold down Shift as you drag the tool across the workspace to constrain the proportions. Don't worry about the size; just make sure it's a uniform square. After this is completed, switch to Outline mode (Cmd/Ctrl+Y) so you can see the center point of your rectangle.

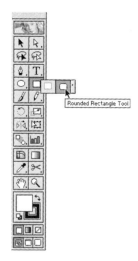

Figure 15.24
To access the Rounded Rectangle tool, click and hold the mouse button down over the Rectangle tool to expand the selections.

2. Turn Rulers on (Cmd/Ctrl+R). Create some guides based on the width, height, and center point of the rectangle by moving the cursor onto either the horizontal or vertical ruler, holding the mouse button down, and dragging a guideline onto the edge of the rectangle. Repeat the process until you have a guide placement as in Figure 15.25. Fill the rectangle with a yellow-gold to black gradient and use the Gradient tool to make the gradient go from upper left to lower right. Copy (Cmd/Ctrl+C) the rectangle and select Paste In Front. Reduce this copy 95%. Then, as the final thing to do, use the Gradient tool to change the direction of the gradient so that it's the reverse of the gradient in the original rectangle.

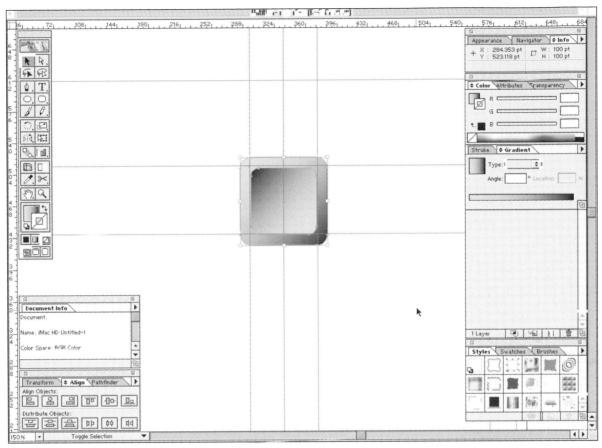

Figure 15.25

Placing guidelines onto the workspace helps you create other elements more accurately.

3. Using the guides, create a triangle above the larger rounded rectangle. Repeat the process in Step 2 to create a duplicate and reduce its size by 90 percent. Fill this copy with a light blue and the large triangle with a darker blue. Make sure the elements have no stroke. Shift + click to select both, and then use the Blend tool to create a gradient blend between the two.

4. Switch to Outline mode so this next part goes faster. Copy the blended triangle and select Paste In Front. Double-click on the Rotate tool and set the rotation to 90 degrees (see Figure 15.26). Repeat this process two more times, copying the copy, to place the triangles around the rectangle. Group (Cmd/Ctrl+G) everything except the small, center rectangle.

5. Select Copy and Paste In Front for this group. Ungroup the elements (Cmd/Ctrl+Shift+G). Repeat Steps 1 and 2 to change the blend for these triangles to a yellow-gold and yellow. Select the blue triangle group and rotate 45 degrees. Your button will now look like Figure 15.27.

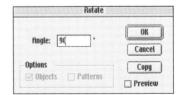

Figure 15.26

Access the Rotate control panel by double-clicking on the Rotate tool.

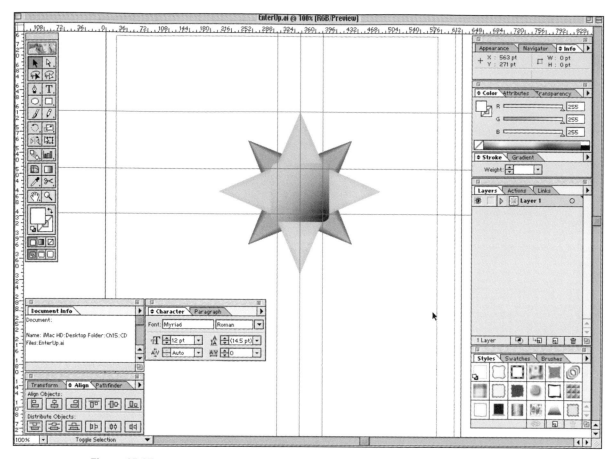

Figure 15.27

The completed Up
button design.

6. Copy the small, inner rectangle and select Paste In Front. Change the gradient so it is opposite to what it is now (black to yellow-gold, upper left to lower right). This gives the effect that the rectangle has been pushed in.

7. Using the Text tool, type the word "enter". Turn the text into outlines (Cmd/Ctrl+O) and group the letters. Resize them so they fit inside the smaller rectangle. Select Copy and Paste Behind, and change the color to White. Reposition the white text 1 pixel down and to the right. Copy the top layer of text again, select Paste Behind, and change the color to Black. Move this text group 1 pixel up and right. Select all three layers of text and group them. Make one more copy and select Paste in Front.

8. Use Punk and Bloat (Effect|Distort & Transform|Punk & Bloat). Change the parameter to +7. Your text will now look like Figure 15.28.

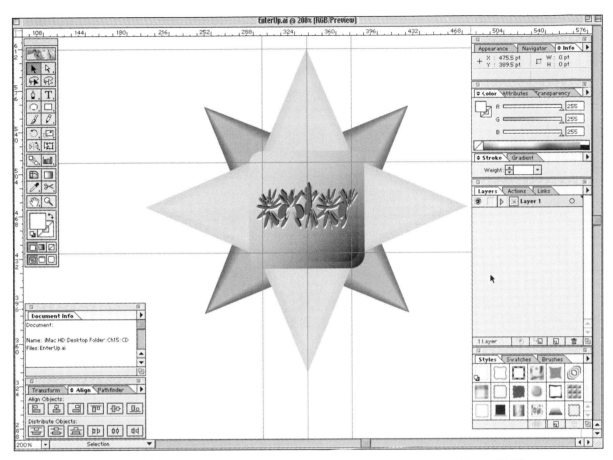

Figure 15.28

The "enter" text now looks like some sort of rune because of the Bloat effect.

9. Now create a box that is 1.5 by 1.5 inches by selecting the Rectangle tool and double-clicking on the workspace. This brings up the parameter controls. Select the button elements and resize them to fit within the box. Delete the box, and you're ready to save the file as HomeButtons.ai.

10. Delete one layer of text and one of the inner rectangles and save the file. Make sure you have the bloated text and the first inner rectangle chosen and save as EnterUp.jpg using the File|Export command. Choose the other text and inner rectangle and save it as EnterDown.jpg (see Figure 15.29).

11. To create the starburst, make a box that is .75 × .75 inches square. Use the Pen tool to create a line, change the Stroke to a yellow-gold, and make the Fill transparent. Duplicate this line and rotate 90 degrees. Select both lines, copy and select Paste In Front, and rotate the lines 45 degrees. Repeat this step one more time, rotating the lines 22.5 degrees.

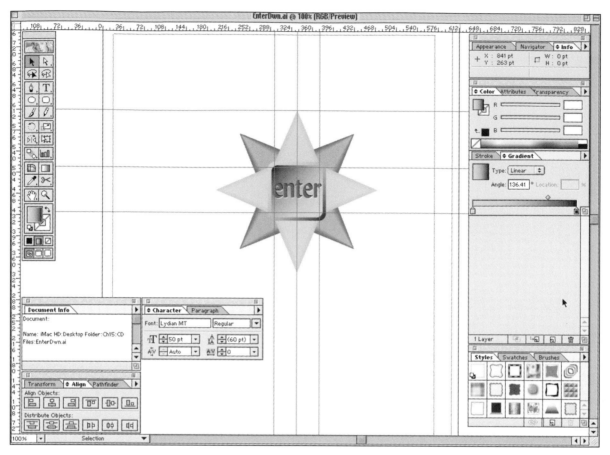

Figure 15.29

The completed Down button.

Scale two of the line sets down 95% and 90%, respectively, so that your starburst looks like Figure 15.30. Save this file as Burst.ai. You will shortly import this image as a Smart Illustrator image and save it as a transparent GIF.

Build the Splash Screen

Now, it's time to put the splash screen page together. So let's open GoLive 5 and get to work. Create a new site (in my case I called it CompanySite and placed it in a folder called ByDesign site). Inside of the master CompanySite folder, I created three other folders (PshopElements, LMElements, and IL9Elements) to store master files that I will want to use later. Once the site is open, create a media and a pages folder and you're ready to go:

1. Click once on the area at the top of your new page where it says Welcome to Adobe GoLive 5. It will turn into a text field. Highlight the text in this field and change the name to "Welcome to GRFX ByDesign". This is what will be seen in the browser headers when a visitor comes to your site.

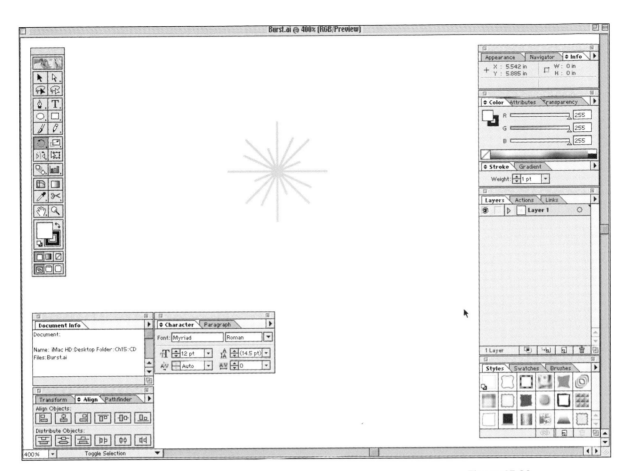

Figure 15.30

A starburst created in Illustrator 9 that will, when set up in GoLive, follow the movement of the visitor's cursor.

2. Place a Layout Grid onto the workspace; inside it, place a Smart LiveMotion placeholder (see Figure 15.31). In the Inspector window, click the folder icon to the right of the Source input field (see Figure 15.32) and navigate to the area where the GRFXOpen.liv file is located.

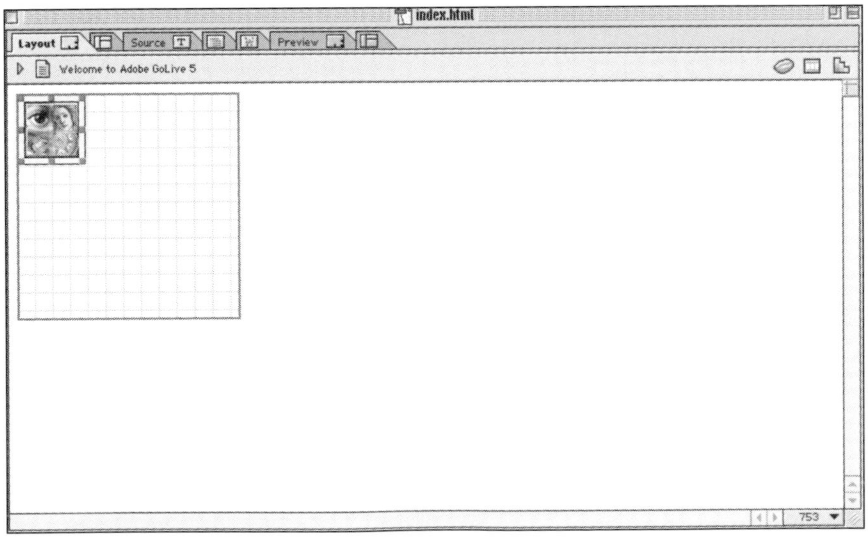

Figure 15.31

A Layout Grid and Smart LiveMotion placeholder positioned on the workspace.

Figure 15.32

Use the Source area in the Basic section of the Inspector window to link to an external file—in this case, the .liv animation you created.

Figure 15.33

Place the converted Shockwave file into the media folder you created.

Note: You should have already dragged both JPEG images into the media folder from wherever you have them stored. Refer to the User Manual if you do not know how to do this.

3. After LiveMotion is opened and the file has been translated to Shockwave format, you'll be asked where the new file should be saved. As you see in Figure 15.33, navigate to your media folder inside the site folder and click on Save. Once the file has been stored in the media folder, select the Layout Grid by clicking on the edge of the Shockwave image and center the grid using the center button in the main toolbar (see Figure 15.34).

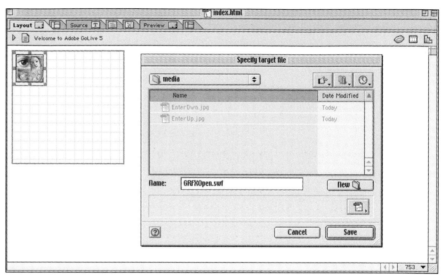

4. With the Layout Grid still selected, go to the Inspector window and change the grid's height to 604. This will give you enough room to place the Rollover placeholder underneath the animation. Move the placeholder so it butts up against the bottom of the LiveMotion placeholder and then link EnterUp.jpg to Main position, and EnterDown.jpg to the Over position. Once this is completed, click the Align Center button in the toolbar to center the placeholder in the grid (see Figure 15.35).

5. Finally, create a new page. Change the header to "GRFX ByDesign", but leave the rest of it blank for right now. Save the page as toc.html and store it in the pages folder you created. Now, you can finish linking the Enter rollover button to the page in the same manner that you link to images. Select the Rollover placeholder, and in the Inspector window, point and shoot to the toc.html page. Save your index.html page and get ready to move on to Project 15.2.

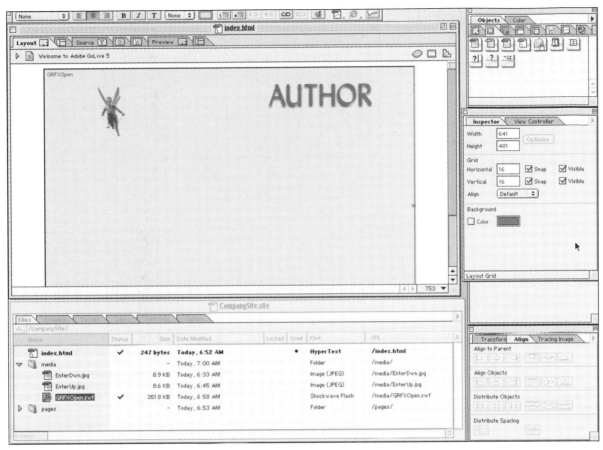

Figure 15.34
The converted LiveMotion file
and the Layout Grid centered
on the screen.

PROJECT 15.2 The Table of Contents Page

It's time to have some fun and create some interesting and seldom seen effects that you might not have known were possible. This is the gateway to the rest of the site, so it's the perfect time to add a little spice (without going overboard, that is). By your adding these effects, the visitor might be impressed enough to look at the rest of the site to find other interesting tricks you might have added. In this section, you will work with Illustrator 9 a bit more in-depth. You will also add tables to your page and create a style sheet. You'll also create remote rollovers. All the image files are available to you in the Chapter 15 folder on the CD-ROM.

Let me take a moment to discuss my design idea. You don't want to create anything heavy (I'm not crazy about an image that appears to weigh more than all my computer systems combined). It should be clean, easily read, and not force visitors to scroll down long lists of items before finding what they want. It's easy to get caught up in the look du jour which, at the time of this writing, is a Sci Fi and Fox Channel metallic plates look. It's definitely a cool look, and fits in with how the company should be displayed. The logo and caricature pretty well give the feel for what the site should be...fun and carefree.

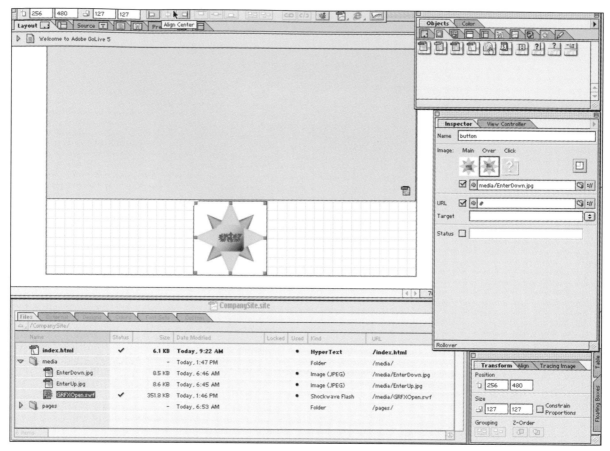

Figure 15.35

The rollover button, with the EnterUp.jpg and EnterDown.jpg images assigned, has been centered in the Layout Grid.

The Illustrator Files

First, you'll create the navigation bar that will be placed on the left side of the toc.html page. You'll use Illustrator 9 for this because it is so much faster to create clean vector art. After it's complete, you will import it into Photoshop for final tweaking:

1. Create a rectangle that is 50 pixels wide by 350 high. If Illustrator isn't set to display measurement information in pixels, go to Edit|Preferences|Units & Undo and set the General Units to Pixels in the pop-up menu (see Figure 15.36).

2. Using the Pen tool, create a hook like you see in Figure 15.37 at the top of the bar you just made. Deselect the Pen tool when you're happy with the hook and, using the Shift key, click on the bar so both are selected. If it's not open already, open the Pathfinder window and select the first Combine option to turn the two elements into a single element (see Figure 15.38).

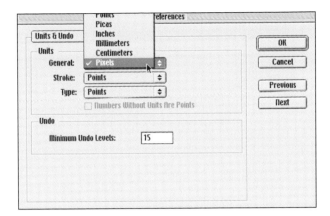

Figure 15.36
Change the way the measurement units are calculated by going to the Units & Undo area of Preferences.

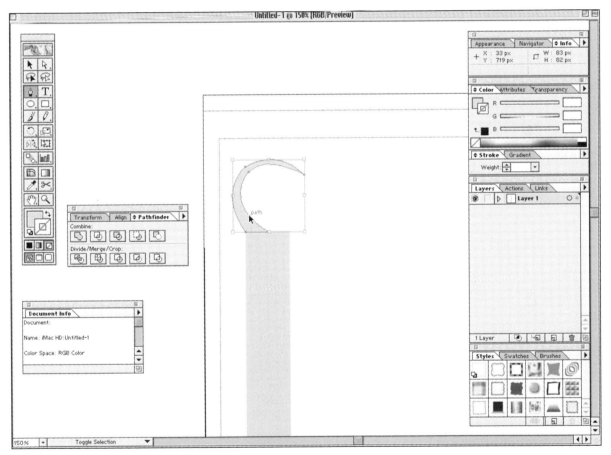

Figure 15.37
Using the Pen tool, create an arcing path that resembles a hook.

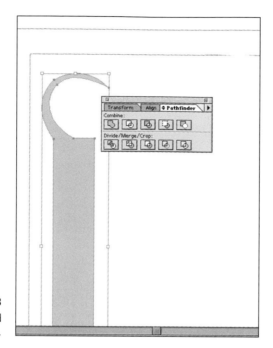

Figure 15.38
The hook and bar are combined using the Pathfinder controls.

3. Choose File|Place and navigate to the DesignInits.ai file from the CD-ROM. This is a grouped file, so click anywhere on it to select all the elements. Resize the window as you see in Figure 15.39 and drag the logo onto the page containing the artwork you just created. Place your cursor over the bottom-right control handle of the grouped logo (see Figure 15.40) and, while holding down the Shift key to constrain the proportions, resize it to fit inside the hooked area (see Figure 15.41).

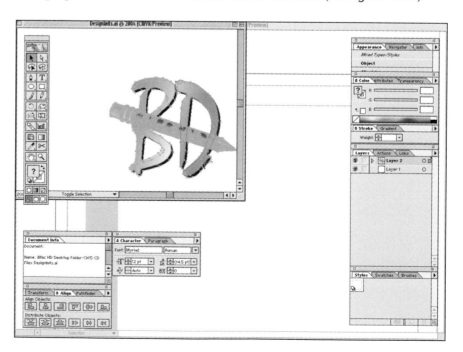

Figure 15.39
As with all Adobe products, you can drag and drop elements from one open window to another or from one program to another.

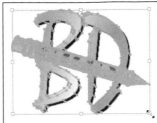

Figure 15.40
Place the cursor over the control handle to resize the selected object.

Figure 15.41
The resized logo placed inside the hook you created.

4. With this page still open, create another hook and bar that will be used on the right side of your Web page. Figure 15.42 shows the new hook that I created. Then, place a rectangle directly under that and grouped them as you did for the last graphic. Also, create a Rounded Rectangle at the bottom of the bar where you will write directions for finding the hidden rollovers in the left bar. Figure 15.43 shows what this one should look like.

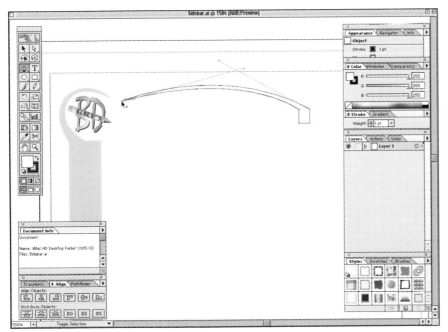

Figure 15.42
A new hook is created as part of a graphic that will be placed on the right side of the Web page.

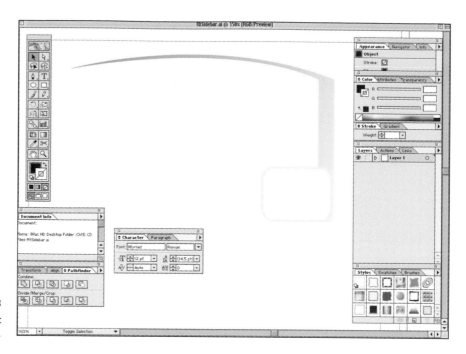

Figure 15.43

The completed Right Sidebar image.

Use the colors from the B in the logo, which automatically set the gradient from red-orange to yellow. Save this file as RtSidebar.ai. After that, write some welcoming text to the image (see Figure 15.44). Save this file as RtSidebarWlcm.ai.

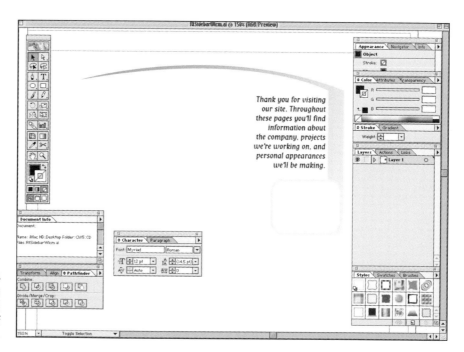

Figure 15.44

The welcome message added to the Right Sidebar. This will appear only on the Table of Contents page of the Web site.

Finishing the Sidebars in Photoshop

Now that you've created the artwork for the Table of Contents, you'll build a punch-in effect for the buttons inside Photoshop. You'll purposely use Photoshop so that you can quickly slice up the image. To do so, follow these steps:

1. Open the Sidebar.ai file in Photoshop. Because you will create buttons inside the bar that will become DHTML rollovers, you will measure out a half-inch block of the bar using Guides (refer to the "Adobe Photoshop User Manual" if you don't know how to set up Guides in your document). Save this file as Sidebar.psd, because you'll come back to it shortly.

2. Using the Crop tool, crop the image inside the guidelines, so you have a 0.5-inch by 1.153-inch block.

3. Duplicate this in the Layers window. This copy will become the Over state for the rollover. With the Rectangular Marquee tool, select an area inside the bar. Choose Select|Inverse to invert the selected area, and press Delete. Use the Command|Control+D keyboard combination to remove the selection. You now have an area in which an effect can be made using the Layer|Layer Style options.

4. For this rollover effect, I chose the Bevel and Emboss function and, referring to Figure 15.45, set the parameters so it will look like the bar punches inward when the mouse rolls over it.

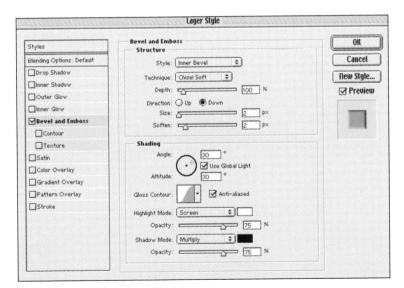

Figure 15.45

Set the Bevel and Emboss parameters like this to create a "punched-in" effect on the bar.

5. Add the text for the buttons using the Eyedropper tool to select a deep green from the bevel. The four buttons are:

- Home
- Company
- Publishers
- Gallery

Save each of these as separate files.

Note: You will find these files, marked SidebarButtonCompany.jpg, SidebarButtonGallery.jpg, SidebarButtonHome.jpg, SidebarButtonNorm.jpg, and SidebarButtonPublish.jpg, in the Chapter 15 folder.

6. For the RtSidebarWlcm.ai file, slice the image into five sections using ImageReady, making sure you slice the image as close to the edge of the text and screen as possible, as seen in Figure 15.46. Save everything except the large white area so that you won't have to use a floating window for other elements that will be placed on this page. In the lower screen area, add text telling visitors how to use the left Sidebar.

7. Slice the RtSidebar.ai image in the same way (see Figure 15.46), saving only the area that replaces the text area, so you can replace that section on subsequent pages.

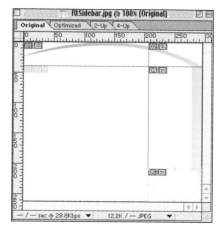

Figure 15.46
The RtSidebar.ai image ready for each slice to be saved. The large white portion will not be saved, because all that is needed is the bar.

Note: The OUTaction that will be demonstrated in this section is available for purchase at **www.out.to/**. If you don't already own it, you will not be able to complete that section of this chapter.

Build the Table of Contents Page

The last section gave you a good idea of how to build the main elements of the TOC page, but that's only a portion of the elements and effects that will be housed on that page. This next section of the chapter will deal with building the page itself, adding the effects, and adding text and a link so that visitors who might not have the Flash player for their browser (which is as close to an impossibility as you can get any more) can download it. The only people who will not be able to take advantage of the Flash technology are those who use a WebTV Basic to access the Web; these users, until the software is upgraded to provide Flash player plug-ins, cannot download the player, because the unit does not have the ability to store it.

Figure 15.47
The completed Table of
Contents page.

Figure 15.47 shows the layout of the finished TOC page. Let's break down a few of the elements that are there. Then, I'll go into detail on how the page was built:

- The navigation bar is on the left (see Figure 15.48). Notice the little upward-left pointing arrows, which indicate that those areas are Rollover buttons.

- The Burst.ai image you created earlier in the chapter is in the upper-right corner (see Figure 15.49). An OUTaction is attached to it, which will make the burst follow after the visitors cursor as it moves across the screen.

- A large white screen with another Rollover indicator (see Figure 15.50) is at the right. This area is linked to the rollovers in the nav bar and information appears there when the left rollover buttons are accessed.

Figure 15.48
(Left) The arrows to the left of the bar indicate Rollover buttons that are in place.

Figure 15.49
(Center) The Burst you created earlier in the chapter is finally coming into play.

Figure 15.50
(Right) This is a remote rollover area. Information will appear when the left-most rollover buttons are accessed.

Those are the most interesting elements on this page. All other pages will be built following this basic layout. You will make changes to specific sections, which I'll discuss when appropriate. So, let's get started in creating the toc.html page by taking the following steps:

1. If your site isn't already open, open it now. Then double-click on the toc.html page in the site window to open it. Remember, this is the page you created at the end of Project 15.1, and it should be a blank page. First, put a Layout Grid on the page, so you can more accurately position the elements. Change the dimensions of the grid to 640x464 pixels in the Inspector window.

2. Place an Image placeholder at the far left of the grid. The top of the placeholder needs to be at the bottom of the second grid line, as seen in Figure 15.51.

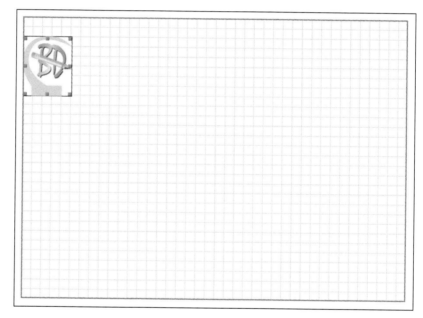

Figure 15.51

The placement of the first Image placeholder is important to the overall design flow. Here, the image has already been assigned to the placeholder.

3. Place a Rollover placeholder directly underneath the first one. The Main image will be the SidebarButtonNorm.jpg image available from the CD-ROM. Place three more Rollover placeholders under that, linking the Main image to the SidebarButtonNorm.jpg image. In order from top to bottom, the Over Image should be:

   • Company

   • Gallery

   • Publishers

   • Home

Underneath the last rollover button, place one more and link it to Sidebar2.jpg. Make this image both the Main and Over image. (I promise, you'll shortly find the reason to do this.) And to complete the nav bar, position an Image placeholder under the one you just placed, and link it to Sidebar3.jpg.

4. Using Figure 15.52 as a guide, place an Image placeholder and link it to Arc1.jpg. This is the first piece of the second hooked image that you created. Then place three more Image placeholders on the grid, using the Cmd/Ctrl+appropriate arrow keys to butt them up against the adjacent placeholder. Link them (in a clockwise order) to:

    *   Arc2.jpg

    *   TextBar.jpg

    *   ViewScreen.jpg

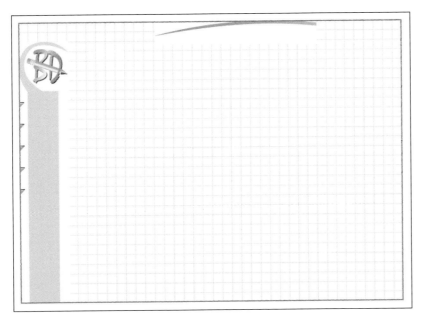

Figure 15.52
The first piece of the right-hand image needs to be placed at the top of the Layout Grid. You might also need to nudge the placeholders together so the elements are seamless.

The workspace will now look like Figure 15.53.

5. Now, add the image area that will become the information screen for the remote rollover. You need to place a Rollover placeholder just below and to the left of the elements you just placed. I have created five JPEG images—one that will be the blank screen when the cursor is away from the rollover buttons in the nav bar, and four text screens, one for each of the rollovers. These screens are the same width as the vertical images in the image placeholders above it, so if you place the rollover placeholder even with the left side of the upper placeholders, as in Figure 15.54, your grid won't resize.

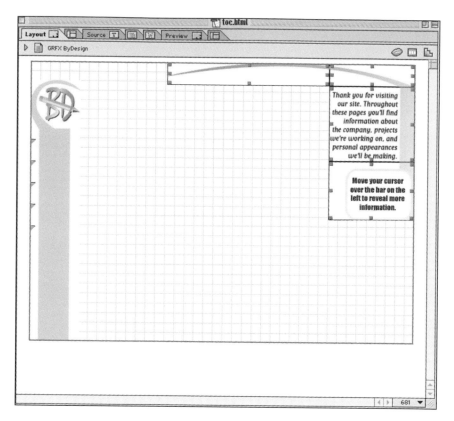

Figure 15.53
The right Sidebar in its final position.

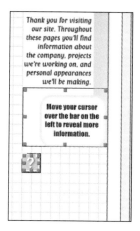

Figure 15.54
Because the new images that will be placed into the Rollover placeholder are the same width, align the Rollovers by their left edges.

6. Link the Main Image to RevealNorm.jpg. Again, this is just a white image that will make it look as if nothing is there. Give this placeholder a name (in my case, I called it Reveal).

7. Select the top rollover button in the nav bar (the one that links to the Company page). In the Inspector window, name this button Company. In the Actions window, choose Mouse Enter and click the New Actions button (the one that looks like a blank page immediately above the Actions screen). Select the Action|Image|Set Image URL (Figure 15.55). From the Image: pop-up, choose Reveal (see Figure 15.56). Link this to RevealCompany.jpg.

8. The white screen should come back once the visitor's mouse has left the rollover area. Select Mouse Exit in the Actions window and repeat the preceding Steps 6 and 7, this time linking to RevealNorm.jpg. Select Show In Browser to open your Web browser and see how your link works. It should do the same as you see in Figure 15.57.

It's now just a matter of setting up the rest of the rollovers to reveal their descriptive text. The rest of the related images are:

• Gallery and RevealGallery.jpg

• Publishers and RevealBooks.jpg

• Home and RevealHome.jpg

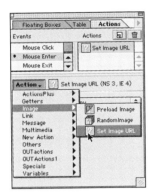

Figure 15.55
(Left) You need to assign a placeholder to work with the Company button.

Figure 15.56
(Right) Navigate to the Set Image URL and link to the company information image.

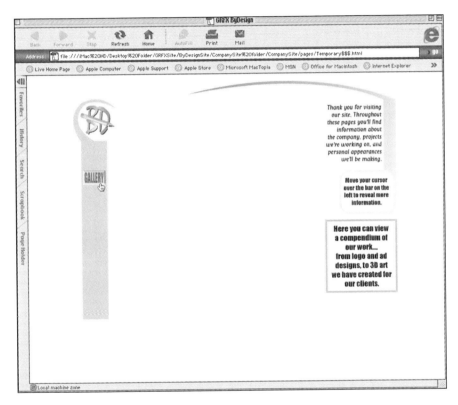

Figure 15.57
The completed remote rollover or DHTML rollover. The text screen appears at another location on the screen when a cursor is placed over the main rollover button.

You will notice one more remote rollover that you created beneath the Home button. This is one of those "surprise" rollovers to maybe bring a little chuckle to the visitor. Either that or—because of the subject matter I have placed in the remote rollover box—it could destroy tens-of-millions of computers world-wide, due to the ugliness of the subject matter. This rollover reveals a charicature done of me and is named Caricature.jpg. Using the same technique as before, create the remote rollover so my ugly mug (or somebody else's ugly mug) is revealed in the remote window.

Follow the Leader

And now, we come to one of the most amazing effects on the Web. Many people are using it, but it appears to be one of those effects that no one grows tired of seeing. You are going to use one of Oliver Zahorka's amazing OUTactions plug-ins called Mouse Follow. And it does just what it says: You can make an image follow the movements of the visitor's cursor as it moves across the screen. Again, this is not one of the free plug-ins that are included on the book's CD-ROM. You can purchase it for a very nominal feel at Oliver's site and, I would highly recommend it.

This part of Project 15.2 uses the Burst.ai file you created at the beginning of the chapter. You will use the Smart Illustrator tool to turn it into a GIF image with a transparent background and then set the parameters for the Mouse Follow action:

1. First, place a Floating Box placeholder onto the workspace and move it to the upper-right corner. Put a Smart Illustrator placeholder inside it, as you see in Figure 15.58.

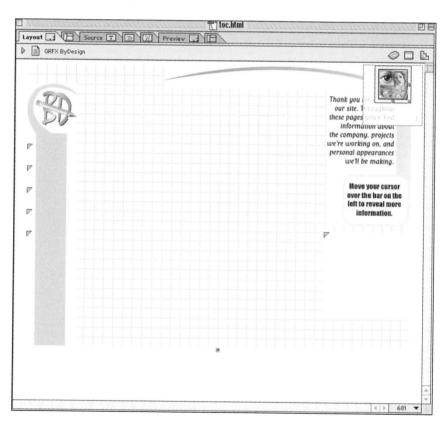

Figure 15.58

A Floating Box and Smart Illustrator tool at their starting point for the Mouse Follow action you're going to create.

2. In the Source field of the Smart Illustrator Inspector window, click the file folder icon and navigate to the Burst.ai file. Select GIF in the Conversion Settings control that comes up. Use the settings you see in Figure 15.59 to create a clean transparent file and click OK. Make sure that the new Burst.gif file is placed inside your site's media folder.

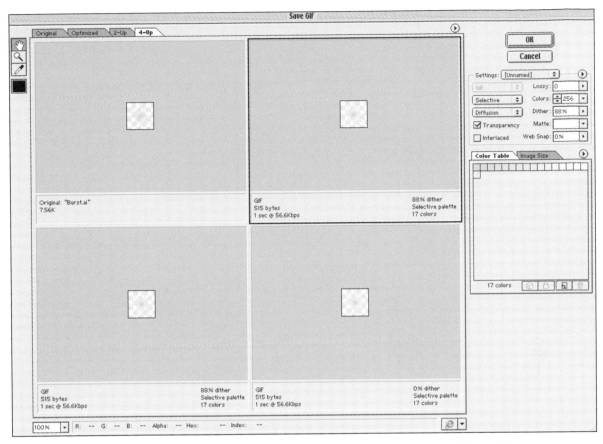

Figure 15.59
Use these GIF settings to create the transparent Burst file.

3. You can now either leave the Floating Box at its original size, or resize it to the Burst.gif image size, which is 44×44 pixels. You can resize the box manually by using the various points around the box, or by changing the width and height parameters in the Floating Box Inspector window. And, speaking of the Inspector window, give the Floating Box a name, such as BurstFollow.

4. This effect is created using a Head Action Smart tool, which is the second of the Smart tools with a question mark icon. This effect needs to be a head action, because it needs to load with the page, reacting immediately to the movement of the mouse. By creating the Head Action, it becomes one of the first elements to load (including the Meta tags and Title tags that are automatically placed when you create a new page). To place the Head Action Smart tool into the Head Action area, use the Toggle Head Section pointer next to the page icon just below the Layout tab of the workspace. When you do this, the Head elements area is revealed, as in Figure 15.60. Drag the Head Action Smart tool into this area.

Note: If you have limited RAM in your system, close down Illustrator, Photoshop, or LiveMotion (depending on the Smart Tool you've used), so you don't run into a memory problem. When a Smart Tool accesses the program, it opens it but does not close it down afterward.

Note: Giving a Floating Box (or layer) a name is a very important step, because you need to assign a named element to the effect. If you have a number of unnamed layers on your workspace, you may have a problem in finding the correct layer to which the effect should be applied.

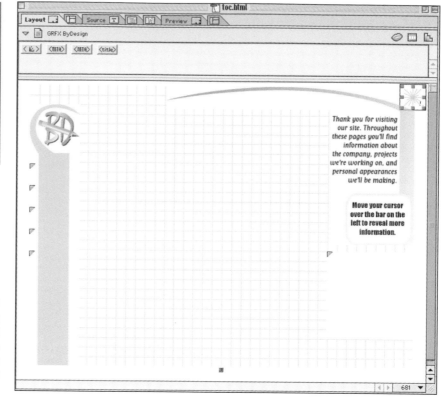

Figure 15.60

The Head elements are revealed by clicking on the Toggle Head Section switch next to the page icon at the top of the screen. You can now add new Head elements to your page.

5. The Inspector window has changed to the Action Inspector, where you see an Action pop-up menu, which is the same as the one you use when creating a smart rollover. Also, if you take a moment to open the Head section of your workspace, notice how the Head Action icon in the Head section has changed to reflect the MouseTrail action. Choose Action|OUTactions| MouseTrail|MouseTrailSlide (see Figure 15.61). The Inspector window might need to be expanded to show all the controls that now appear.

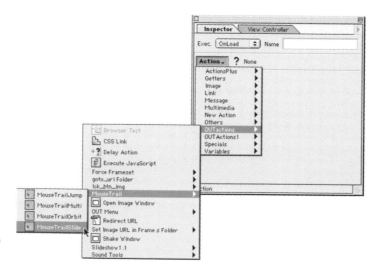

Figure 15.61

The path to the specific Mouse Trail command you want to use.

6. As you can see in Figure 15.62, you can set numerous parameters to oversee the control of the Mouse Trail effect. You don't have to change most of them when creating a basic mouse follow. In the Layer popup, select BurstFollow (or whatever you named the layer).

7. Now, select Show Coordinates In Status. You're doing this because you want the Burst.gif image to move through only a certain portion of the screen. If you left it free flowing to all the edges of the screen, when a person clicked on a button, the Floating Box layer could block out the link. By selecting this feature, you can find out the left-, right-, upper-most, and lowermost points where you want the burst to be confined. In the case of this page, you are containing the burst to the inner edges of both bars. You will need to activate your browser to see the coordinates, which appear in the lower-left area of the screen (see Figure 15.63).

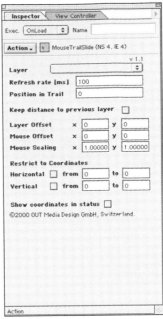

Figure 15.62
The Mouse Trail Action Inspector window with its numerous parameter controls.

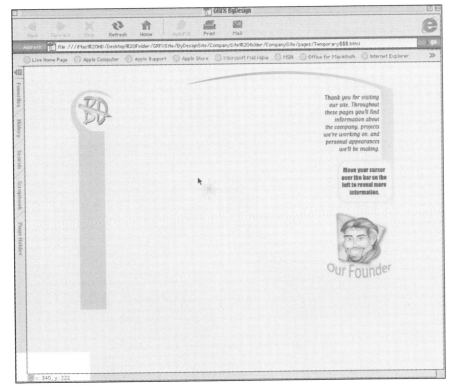

Figure 15.63
The mouse coordinates (x being left to right and y being top to bottom) shown in the lower left-hand corner of the browser window.

8. To save time and energy, type these coordinates into the Horizontal and Vertical fields of the Inspector window:

- Horizontal: 162, 669

- Vertical: 16, 435

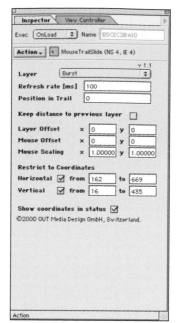

Figure 15.64

The Horizontal and Vertical coordinates are assigned so the movement of the burst image is constrained to a particular portion of the browser window.

This constrains the image between the two sets of vertical bars and also keeps it under the upper horizontal hook. Figure 15.64 shows the coordinates added to the Inspector window. Now, unless you want the mouse coordinates revealed to all your visitors (which can be a cool thing to do), you can deselect Show Coordinates In Status.

9. Now all that is left to do to finish out this page is add a dimmed logo image to the workspace and an informational text box. I also placed another Layout Grid just beneath the other one and put a Text placeholder in it. This bottom text box has a link to the site where visitors can get the Flash plug-in if they don't have one installed already. The finished layout will look like Figure 15.65.

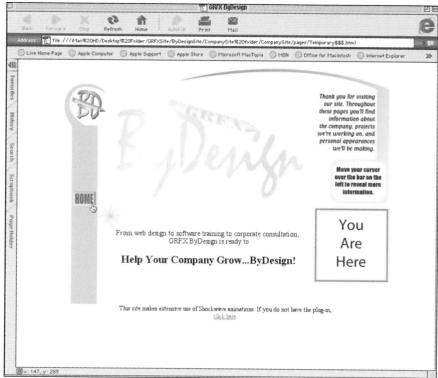

Figure 15.65

The completed toc.html layout as viewed in Internet Explorer. Notice how the burst graphic moves against the left nav bar without violating it.

PROJECT 15.3   The Gallery Page

To me, this was one of the most fun pages to do, because it allowed me to break out from the standard format of the site to display some of the work I have created for various projects. (These include 3D art built for my company and for other books, some of the ads and layouts I have done for clients, and links to other Web sites my company has built.) Many of the features of this Gallery.html page are duplicative of what you just did, but I have used them in different ways to utilize the little screen on the right side of the window. It also incorporates the _blank feature, so that the links open a new browser window when accessed. So, I will move through this section a bit faster, highlighting the ways I created the images used in the advanced rollovers, and pointing out a design feature that will be duplicated on subsequent pages.

The Gallery page has three sections, as you can see in Figure 15.66. These are: 3D Creations, Ad Design, and Other. The first two are self-explanatory; they will focus on the work my company and I have created in those various disciplines. The Other section features logos and links to Web sites I want to show off. The main things to remember when putting a page like this together is to show only the work that you think really stands out, as well as to show a good variation of your work. Don't show vast amounts of, say, CD tray card artwork you have built; instead, show one or two of the hottest designs in that category. Business people who visit your site won't want to wade through dozens of images that are, ultimately, repetitive. Figure 15.67 shows five categories under the 3D Creations header. That's the largest number of examples I plan to show, because each of the characters and scenes that are featured in that section are very different in stylistic approach. Some are cartoonish, some more photorealistic, and some tell a story (as is the case with the Snydlie link).

As previously mentioned, because this page contains elements that are very repetitive to the steps you went through in Project 15.2, you'll only work with the 3D Creations section. You can view the finished Gallery page at **www.grfxbydesign.com** to see the finished product.

Duplicating a Page

So you don't have to re-create the basic layout of the page, open the index.html page, remove any unnecessary elements from the page, and use the Save As… command. Rename the file Gallery.html and save it in the pages folder.

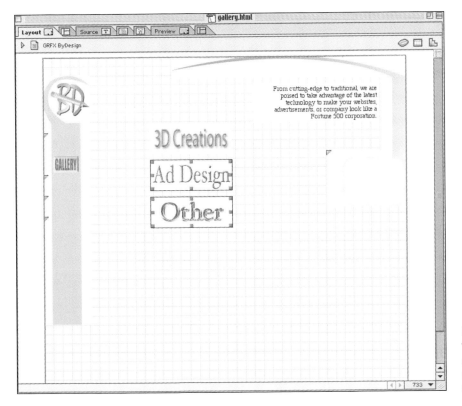

Figure 15.66
The Gallery page has three subsections that lead to very different categories of work my company has created.

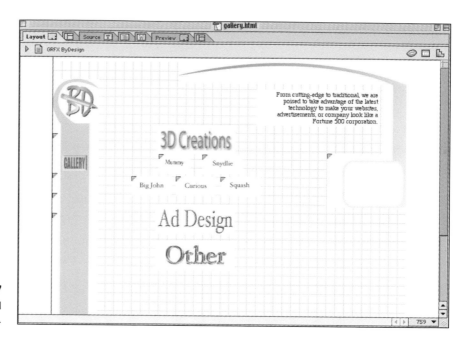

Figure 15.67

Five sub-categories is the most I want to put on this page.

Advanced Rollovers—Another Take

Because of the style of this page and the links I have created, the advanced rollover technique is, again, very much called for. That yellow-bordered screen on the right of the workspace was actually included specifically for this section of the site. As visitors move their cursor over the element names, a portion of that image will appear in that little window (see Figure 15.68).

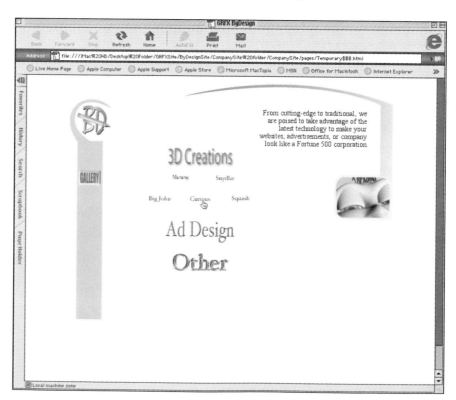

Figure 15.68

A look at the advanced rollover technique used in the Gallery page, as seen in the Web browser.

You have already walked through the creation of advanced rollovers, so the only thing I will discuss in this portion is how to incorporate the remote artwork into that section of the page:

1. Open the ViewScreenNoText.jpg image in Photoshop or in your photo manipulation program. Using the Magic Wand tool, set the tolerance to 10 and click once inside the screen area to select the interior pixels as in Figure 15.69.

2. Next, open one of the featured images. For the model you see in Figure 15.70, I selected a specific portion of the The_Gambler.jpg image and used Cmd/Ctrl+C to copy it to the clipboard.

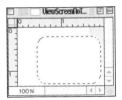

Figure 15.69

The interior pixels of the screen have been selected using the Magic Wand tool.

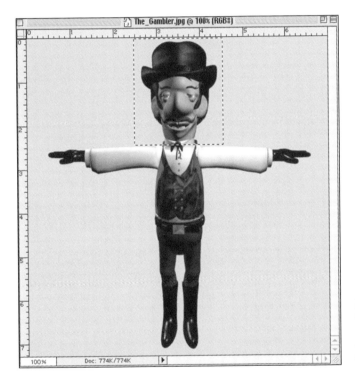

Figure 15.70

The section of the character image I want to be seen in the view screen window of the ViewScreenNoText.jpg file.

3. In Photoshop, first make sure that ViewScreenNoText.jpg is the selected image. Choose Edit|Paste Into (Cmd/Ctrl+Shift+V) to paste the image into the selected area of the ViewScreenNoText.jpg image (see Figure 15.71). The size of this pasted image is pretty close to the size you want it in the screen, but you want it a little smaller than it is now to show just a tad more of the character. To do this, choose Edit|Transform|Scale and resize the pasted image slightly so more of the character shows in the view screen.

4. Repeat this process for all the other images (which, by the way, are in the 3D_Images folder on the CD-ROM), saving each of the modified ViewScreenNoText.jpg files with appropriate, easily identifiable names.

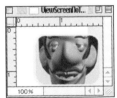

Figure 15.71

The character image has been pasted into the screen, ready to be resized. If you are happy with the way the file fits in the view screen area, then you can save your file for the site at this point.

5. Return to your Gallery.html page in GoLive. Because the ViewScreenNoText.jpg image on the page is now becoming an advanced rollover screen, delete the Image placeholder and replace it with a Rollover placeholder. Assign the above-noted image to the Main state. Then, if need be, reposition the new placeholder so it lines up correctly with the image above it.

6. Put an Image placeholder at the center portion of the screen and link it to the 3DHeader.jpg image. Place another Rollover placeholder below this. Link both Main and Over to 3D_Snydlie.jpg. The same image should be used for this rollover, because you want people to focus on the effect in the view screen. (You should have their attention grabbed by a single effect, rather than seeing multiple changes at the same time. That would effectively split their attention in a non-productive way.)

7. Using the method outlined in Steps 5 and 6, create the remote rollover effect, changing the ViewScreenNoText.jpg to the ViewScreenSnydlie.jpg image. Repeat this process for the other four images and their title rollovers.

The Full-Sized Images

With the advanced rollovers set, you need to create the pages each title rollover will link to. The easiest thing to do here is to create one new page and then replace and modify elements, saving each change using the File|Save As command. Take these steps:

1. With the new page open, place a Layout Grid onto the workspace. Place an Image placeholder into that, and because Snydlie has been the focus of the previous portion of this project, link to the SnydliePromoShot.jpg image. This will be the first of three images in this gallery section.

2. Now that the image is assigned, center the Layout Grid to the workspace. Extend the bottom of the grid so you can place a Layout Text placeholder and another Image placeholder underneath the picture. Write some introductory and explanatory text for the image, and then link the Image placeholder to the Button_Another.jpg image, which will become the hotlink to the next image. Position this button image against the right edge of the grid. Figure 15.72 shows the layout for this page. Save this as Snydlie1.html.

3. Delete the image from this page, place another Image placeholder in the upper-left corner of the grid, and link it to another of the Snydlie series of images. (The reason you put a fresh Image placeholder onto the grid is that, if you link to a new image from the existing placeholder, the new

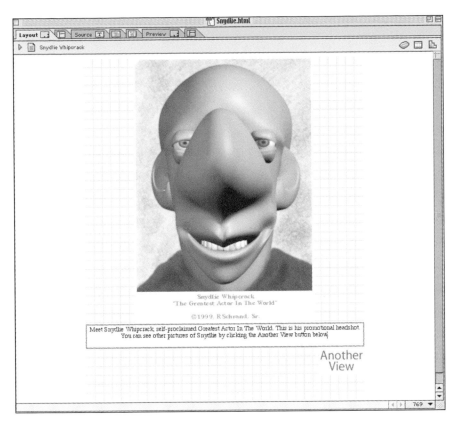

Figure 15.72
The first Snydlie page in
a series of three.

image will be resized to fit the dimensions already established. This can
often cause big problems if you go from an image that is larger to one
that is smaller; the second image will be expanded and will more than
likely look horrible.) Change the text to reflect the new image, add an
Image placeholder at the bottom left edge of the grid, and link it to the
Button_Back.jpg image (see Figure 15.73). Save the page as
Snydlie2.html. Now you can link the Back button to Snydlie1.html.

4. Repeat this process to create the third Snydlie page. This time, remove
    the Button_Another.jpg image because no more pages will be linked to
    this one. After saving it as Snydlie2.html, link the Back button to
    Snydlie1.html.

5. Close this window and, if it isn't already, open the Gallery.html file. Se-
    lect the 3D_Snydlie name image button and turn it into a link (see Figure
    15.74). Link this to the Snydlie.html page (the first of the series) and, in
    the Target field, either expand the pop-up menu and choose _blank, or
    simply type it into the text field. This will make the link—when acti-
    vated—open a new window in the visitor's browser (see Figure 15.75),
    while leaving the original window open behind it. Repeat this process for
    each of the other 3D image files that are part of the 3D Creations section
    of the Gallery.html page.

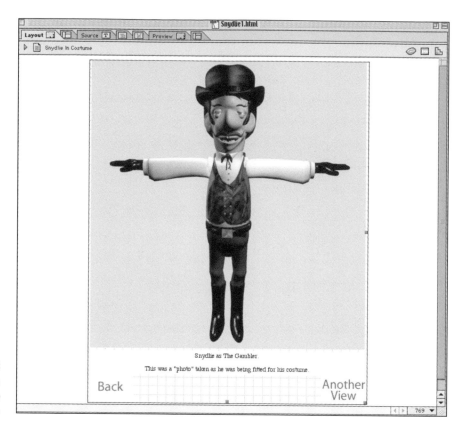

Figure 15.73
The second Snydlie page with a new button added that links to the first Snydlie page you created.

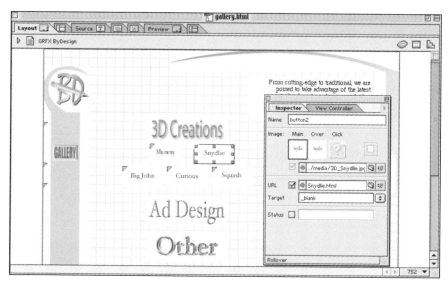

Figure 15.74
The Snydlie button has been turned into a link and is ready to be assigned a page to open.

Just for Fun

The Gallery page acts as an indicator of the type of work my company does. But it is also set up to be fun—almost like being a three-year-old during a trip through a children's museum when the Barney or Teletubbie exhibit is in full swing. Or, maybe during a high-stakes Pokemon trading card competition. Or, maybe I'm completely overstating the fun and adventure to be had while exploring this section of the site. But I digress.

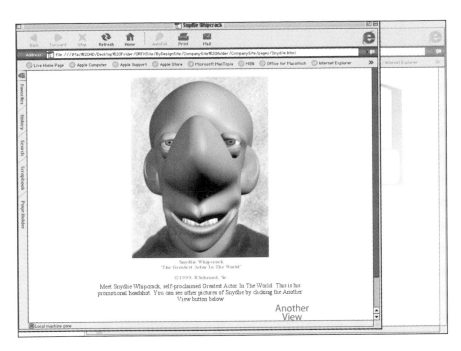

Figure 15.75
A look at the browser windows.
The one in front was opened
because of the _blank command
assigned to the Snydlie link
button on the main Gallery page.

One More Image Modification

One more modification needs to be made to this page. You want visitors to be able to easily see they are on the Gallery page. Many people are like me and rarely look at the top of the browser window to see what the page name is. (In fact, when I do look at the top, I often see that the site designers have forgotten to give the page a name and all I see up there is "untitled".) So, Gallery needs to be seen as part of the image content of the page. You can do this in two ways, the first being the easiest, but the second being less confusing to the visitor:

1. Select the Gallery rollover button and replace the Main image with the same one used as the Over image. This will effectively display the Gallery image, whether a cursor is over it or not. But, what it also does is continue to be recognized as a rollover button (see Figure 15.76). This can be slightly confusing to the visitor, as it appears that they can click on that button to go somewhere else in the site. It gives a subliminal message that they are not at the Gallery page, even though Gallery is constantly showing.

2. The best thing to do is delete the Gallery rollover and replace it with a plain Image placeholder. Link to the image that was used in the rollover's Over state. This way, as the visitor moves over the nav bar and when the cursor is on top of the Gallery image, the browser doesn't see it as a button (see Figure 15.77).

You'll notice that I also changed the image above the ViewScreenNoText.jpg image to one that does not contain text. I deleted that Image placeholder and put a new one in its place, because I changed the image to a skinnier one so I

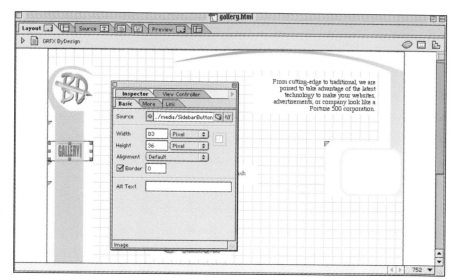

Figure 15.76
By keeping the Gallery area of the nav bar as a rollover button, a subliminal message is created saying that the page you're on is not actually the Gallery page.

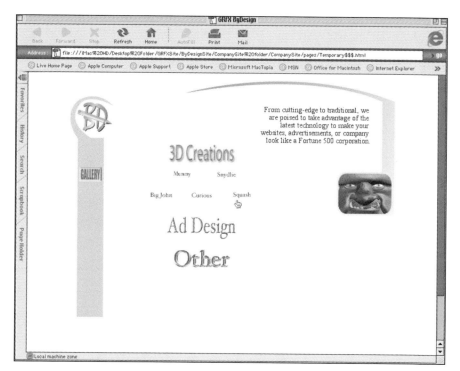

Figure 15.77
By switching the Rollover placeholder to a standard Image placeholder, no confusion arises as to what part of the site the visitor is at.

could have room to put a Text placeholder on the page. This way I can modify the text to an appropriate introduction for the specific content of the page.

A Final Thought before Moving Along

At this point, with the Gallery.html page designed in the way you want all the main section pages laid out, it is a good idea to use Save As to create pre-designed page layouts for the other sections. Delete the text inside the text box in the upper-right section and repeat Step 2 of the last project section to change the nav bar to reflect the section subject. From this point on, then, you can focus solely on adding content to your section master pages.

PROJECT 15.4 Adding a Table into the Design

I'm going to skip over to another page of the site design that is actually a sub-page, but that has some extra interest to it because of its overall purpose. This is the Company Services & Request page that is part of the Company section of the site. I want to move to this page now because of the various elements that will be added to it and to explain how it is designed to fit into the overall structure of the site.

Often, with pages like this, continuity is thrown out the window. It's almost as if the designer is saying that either the page is kind of a throwaway (so why put a lot of effort into it), or that the page is so complicated that you have no time to make it relate to the rest of the site. If a site's background is a solid color (white and black being most prevalent across the Web), or a texture image that looks like paper or stucco, it might be used as the background to the page. But all other design elements for the other pages are thrown out.

In the case of my Company Services & Request page, I wanted to definitely make sure that people knew that it was part of the overall design and not just a last minute addition. That's why the artwork for the page remains the same as all the rest of the pages of the site, only modified slightly so that it doesn't look as if something is missing. The most obvious instance of this is the removal of the ViewScreenNoText.jpg on the right side. No reason exists to have it there, so why not get it out of the way, where it doesn't take up valuable screen real estate? But, to make the exclusion of this element less glaring, I replaced it with the same image as the one above it. Again, this is a subliminal aspect to the design—one that says there's some thought to detail. Take a look at Figure 15.78 to see how the overall feel of the page changes when the viewer area is simply deleted and not replaced, and with the replacement image added. It gives a feeling of completeness.

Also, notice that the Company indicator is visible in the nav bar, just as it will be in all sub-pages for this section of the site. Again, this is a small element, but in the overall design, it is the small details that ultimately determine when a site truly stands out. It plays on those intangibles that make something great, rather than merely adequate. Think of a movie that stands out in your mind. What makes it so good? What makes it so much different than movies with similar storylines that it comes to mind before the others? It's the intangibles, those subliminal elements that are hard to qualify; yet without them, you feel that something is amiss. This is what you need to keep aware of as you build your sites, because its this focus on detail that will have people coming to you to build their sites.

With that said, it is now time to move on and look at the design and layout for this page.

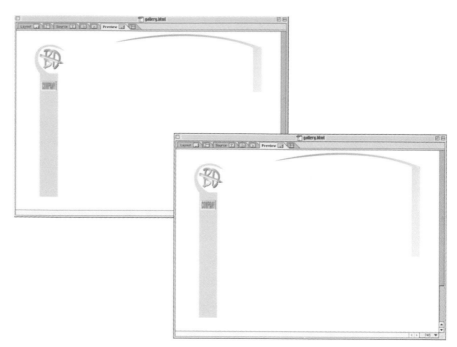

Figure 15.78
The difference between simply deleting an unneeded element and using a replacement figure that gives a less jarring transition between pages.

More Input...

A hit movie was made about 16 years ago called *Short Circuit* in which a robot kept demanding "more input" so that he could learn and become a living entity. Well, with the rapid expansion of the Internet and the changing climate of doing business on the Web, more input is definitely of more importance than ever before. Without feedback from the masses, it is virtually impossible to figure out how to set yourself apart from the ever-increasing crowd of competitors opening up e-companies. Thus, the need for a feedback page where you can gather the needed information.

Many Web surfers have little to no time to answer long, involved questionnaires. In fact, I would say many are like me and, at the first hint of a page that contains more than five questions, run like scalded apes without answering the first query. So, it is extremely important to think your questions through prior to building your page. The best technique is to think back on meetings you have had and recalling what the most-asked questions were (other than, "What's it gonna cost me?"). List them in order of frequency and then use the top four or five. Never put your prices out for display. Let potential clients request a rate card from you. This way, you build up a database of interested companies.

Using this as a guideline, open the questionnaire.html page (or the page you created to house this request form).

1. Put an Image and Table placeholder onto the grid. Link the Image placeholder to FillUsInHead.jpg.

Note: GoLive 5 comes with modules that aren't loaded immediately. You can find these modules in the root folder of your GoLive program, under Modules (disabled). Place these disabled modules in their appropriate folders within the Modules folder. For ease of placement, the disabled modules are situated in duplicates of the folders in which they are supposed to go, so all you need to do is transfer to the active folder with the same name.

2. Create a caption area for the table and drag a Smart LiveMotion place-holder in it. Then, add some text beneath the placeholder that fits with the animation you're about to add. In this case, it's an animation of a charging rhinoceros I created in Poser 4 using the Rhino model available on the Zygote Web site at **www.zygote.com**.

3. You also need to modify the table in the following manner:

   - Merge the middle and right cells of each row by selecting them and using the Control key, then holding down the mouse button (see Figure 15.79).

   - Add one more row of cells, so you have four instead of the default three.

   - Make the Width of the left cell 118 pixels and the Height 100 pixels.

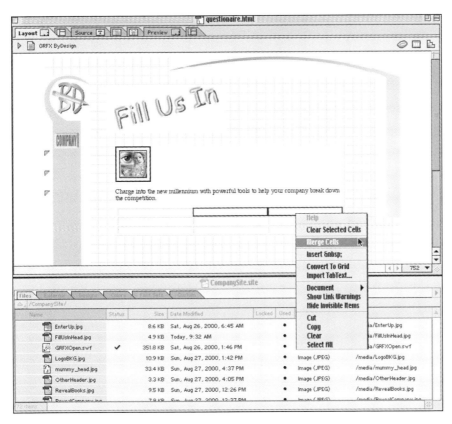

Figure 15.79
Merge the middle and right cells in each row of the Table placeholder.

4. Link the RhinoCharge.liv file to the Smart LiveMotion placeholder, saving the resultant .swf file to the media folder of your site. Now you have a Shockwave animation that shows a rhino charging and banging off the interior edge of the table placeholder.

5. Now it's time to start building the questionnaire. As you have no doubt gathered, you won't have many questions. All you do at this stage is get a general feel for what type of company it is, its size, and an idea of what type of work the potential client might want. Of course, you need a way to contact them, as well. So, in the left column of cells, type in the questions you want to have answered. Figure 15.80 shows the ones I have decided on using.

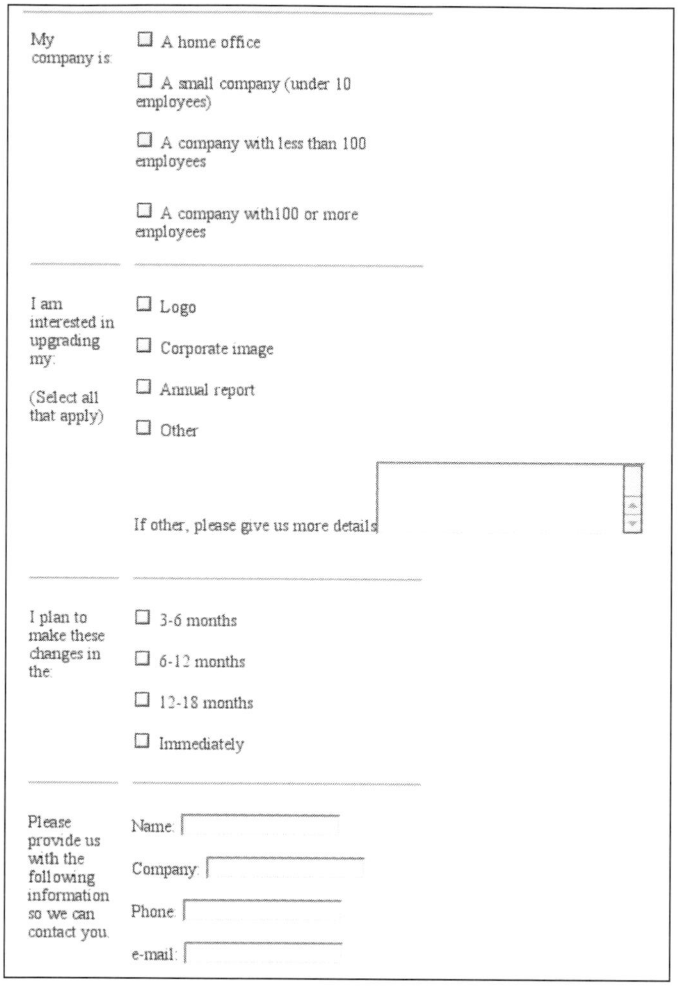

Figure 15.80

A short, non-intimidating series of questions. I purposely did not go into great detail about the potential client, so that he or she is more willing to answer the posed questions.

6. In the right column cells you will add response elements. These include checkboxes and descriptive text. You will also need a text field for question #2. Place a checkbox into the right cell; immediately next to that, type in the first possible response. Repeat this process for each response and question until the form is completed (see Figure 15.81).

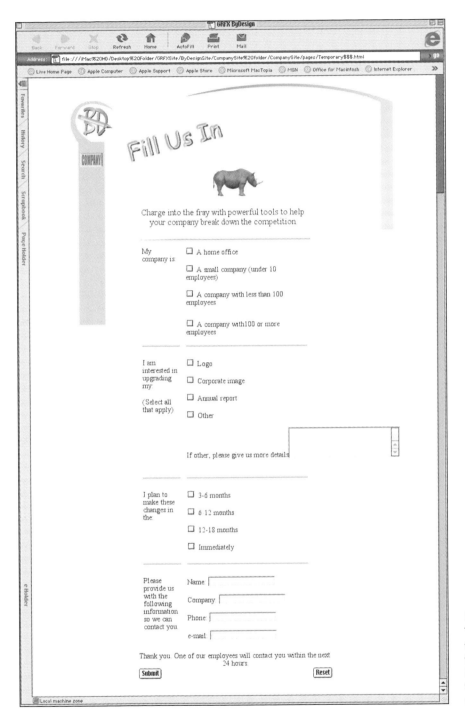

Figure 15.81

The completed questionnaire with the obligatory thank you text and Submit and Reset buttons added. I have combined two images so you can see the entire layout.

7. To complete the form, extend the Layout Grid and center a Text placeholder underneath the Table. Type a short thank-you note. Then place a Submit and Reset button below this. Finally, create a link to take the visitor back to the main Company.html page.

Note: Make sure that the company that houses your site files can handle scripts of this type. Check their online Frequently Asked Questions (FAQs) page or call them before setting up a feedback page.

Note: You can also access the Import Tab-Text feature by clicking on the right-pointing arrowhead button at the top right of the Table Inspector window.

Figure 15.82

Use the Import Tab-Text Browse button to import a properly saved spreadsheet file.

You need to link this page to a CGI/Perl script that will be stored in a separate folder. This allows the Submit button to actually do what it's supposed to do: Submit the information in a manner that is readable through your email program. Usually, if a provider allows form handler scripts, a folder will already be set up in your site's holding area. If not, just create a CGI folder in your site file where you can store the script file.

If you don't know how to set up a script or to create one, numerous sites on the Web can walk you through the creation of one or provide free scripts for download. One of the most comprehensive of these is at **www.cgi-resources.com**.

Other Table Tips

Not everyone is going to want to put a request form on their site. Many of you are probably working for companies that have an intranet set up, and you'll need to create pages that include company-specific spreadsheets filled with the latest sales figures. You really don't want to create a table inside GoLive and then fill in all those numbers, especially when you're supplied with a file that has already been completed. GoLive 5 allows you to import spreadsheet information while retaining the formatting of the file. If you're the one assigned to make this happen, here is a tip for importing spreadsheet data that can save you hours of time:

1. Open the spreadsheet file and resave it, making sure you save it as a tab-delimited text file.

2. Open GoLive and put a Table placeholder on the page that will house the spreadsheet information. In the Table Inspector window, click on the Browse button at the bottom of the window next to Import Tab-Text (see Figure 15.82) and navigate to your saved file. Your spreadsheet information will be inserted and formatted exactly as it was in the program that created it.

Another thing you can do is access a series of saved table styles, as well as save a table style you created. This way you can access a style you like very easily:

1. Open the Table window (Window|Table) if it isn't already. Two tabbed areas are here: Select and Style. Under the Select tab (see Figure 15.83), you can easily select cells and reformat them, as well as sort them based on criteria you set.

2. Under the Style palette, you can change the color of the text and background based on a pop-up menu seen in Figure 15.84.

3. When it comes to saving a table you have created, you use the Style area and type a new name into the text field at the bottom of the window (see Figure 15.85). Click Capture, and the style you created becomes part of the pop-up menu, as seen in Figure 15.86. This is particularly helpful if you have added specific text parameters, colors to cells, etc. You can easily reassign that style to any table you create.

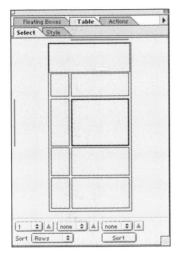

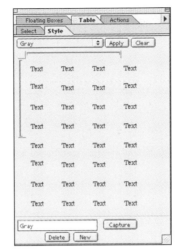

Figure 15.83
(Left) The Table Select window can make navigating between the various cells a breeze.

Figure 15.84
(Right) The Table Style palette. The brackets around portions of the layout image let you know which part of the table you have selected.

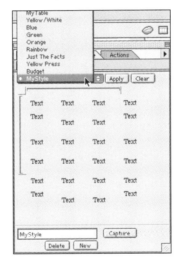

Figure 15.85
(Left) The text field where you assign a name to your Table style.

Figure 15.86
(Right) The new Table style you created is now accessible from the pop-up palette.

PROJECT 15.5 We Now Return to Our Regularly Scheduled Web Site

Because the only other page that contains any type of differences to the site than we have already discussed is the Company page itself, let's look at what was done to put that together.

Again, this section of the site is geared specifically to let potential clients know your qualifications, your company philosophy, and a little bit about your focus.

Case Study #1: Your Web site's content lists everything you've ever done since three days before you were born. You talk about your doctorates in computer science and paleontology. You discuss (in great detail, I might add) your expertise in Web and advertising design, logo development, product design, audio mixing, video creation, animation, and genetic research—all of which you have been doing for the past 20 years. The problem is, each of these study areas is given equal time on your site and encompasses way too many Web pages to navigate through. This gives potential clients nothing to grab onto when it comes to their particular need, which, in this case, is logo design. Also, the busy client doesn't have enough time to look at everything you have displayed. Although your work was interesting and seemed to fit with their corporate image, this potential client continues his search. He wants a logo specialist. Your first love and your strongest area might be logo design, but that wasn't transmitted to that visitor. So you lost the job (without even knowing it) to someone who specifically focused on logo creation.

Case Study #2: You have a business, like mine, that is still new. You have a degree in underwater basket weaving, and a small portfolio that shows the type of graphic work you have done for yourself, your friends, and your uncle's ice cream parlor. This includes Web design, logo creation, animation, advertising layouts, product design, and more. But you really enjoy creating logos and you feel that is your strongest talent. So you put more emphasis on that on your site even though you don't ignore your other talents. The same potential client who visited that other site visits yours. He sees you focus on logo design and likes some of the work you have done (remember, nobody likes everything). Your site is only five pages and has only four logo examples, but they are the best of the best that you have done. The logo hunter decides to give you a try.

No, they were not based on reality, although they very well could be. And yes, those were manipulative case studies. But if you really consider the underlying message, you'll see that it's often best to downplay yourself and focus on one or two areas that you believe are your premiere talents. You will notice when you visit my site that some things will be changed around, namely in the Gallery section you worked on with me earlier in the chapter. Subliminally, the way that I lined up the work I'm featuring gives the impression that my strongest talent is in 3D character design. I really enjoy doing that, but what I want my company to be known for is its product packaging and layout work. So, notice how that section has been reworked and how the focus has shifted.

I am also going to downplay my 28 years in the broadcasting industry, although I will mention the awards I received during that time. Although it seems that my focus should be on video production—while utilizing the various production tools, such as the 3D modeling programs, Web, and layout tools—I pretty much had my fill of that life. However, if a client needs that type of work done at some point, I'm more than positioned to handle whatever comes my way.

The Company Intro Page

So, you can have a quality page that touts your expertise without going overboard. Let's begin the page creation by opening the Company.html document:

1. If it isn't there, make sure the ViewScreenNoText.jpg is at the bottom of the right bar. It will be important to have it there as you build the subsequent pages of this section.

2. Now put a Text placeholder directly underneath the upper hook and drag it out so it's the same width as the hook image. This will become the Company section navigator area. Type in the following: "Corporate Philosophy | Biography | More Information". Set the text alignment to the right so your page looks like Figure 15.87.

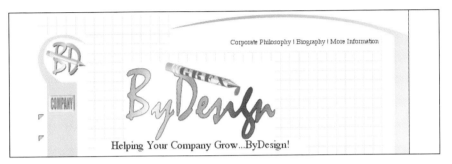

Figure 15.87
The link list set up in the upper-right corner of the page.

3. Add another Image placeholder and link to the GRFXLogo.jpg image.

4. Immediately underneath the logo, drag a Table placeholder and modify it in this manner:

   • Set the Width to 364 pixels

   • Add a caption area and make sure the text is set to Centered

   • Set Rows to 2

   • Set Columns to 1

   • Set the Height of the first row to 30 pixels

   • Set Border to 0

   In the caption area, type in the company catchphrase ("Helping Your Company Grow...ByDesign!") and set the text size to 5. Skip the first row and, in the second, type a quick blurb about the company.

5. The final thing to do on this page is select both the logo Image placeholder and the Table placeholder. In the Align window, select the center option in the Align Objects section. Your page will now look like Figure 15.88.

Next, set up the Biography page in the following manner:

1. Replace the ViewScreenNoText.jpg placeholder with a Rollover placeholder. For the Main screen, link to ViewScreenShake.jpg. For Over, link to ViewScreenCharacter.jpg. The basic page will look like Figure 15.89.

2. Select the rollover image and open the Actions window. Select Mouse Click and, if you have it, assign the Shake Window OUTactions action. Figure 15.90 shows the commands at your disposal. You can assign the number of times the effect will repeat, how many pixels the screen will

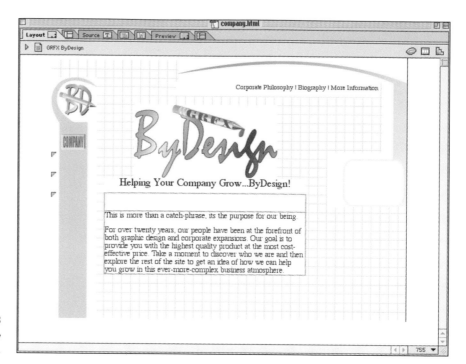

Figure 15.88
The completed company
introduction page.

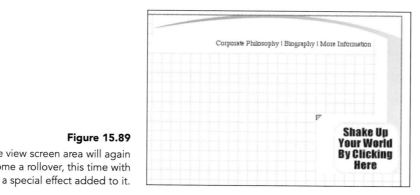

Figure 15.89
The view screen area will again
become a rollover, this time with
a special effect added to it.

Figure 15.90
The Shake Window Actions window and the controls available to
manipulate the effect. The movement of the screen has been
limited to 5 pixels in each direction.

move, and more. For this effect, set the Distance to 5, while leaving all
the rest of the settings as they are. This is a fun little effect that will
make the entire browser window shake. You want to give the visitor a
little chuckle before delving too deeply into the biography on this page.

3. Add a Table placeholder onto the workspace. Merge the middle and
right rows and columns of cells, leaving three rows on the left and one
large area on the right. Make sure you have the Caption option
checked. In the bottom left cell, place an Image placeholder and link it
to rschrand.jpg.

4. The final step for this page, and all subsequent pages in this group, is
to change Biography to a different color and make it bold. This helps
remind people what page they have accessed. Do this to the appropriate text for each page, so that a reference point is available for the

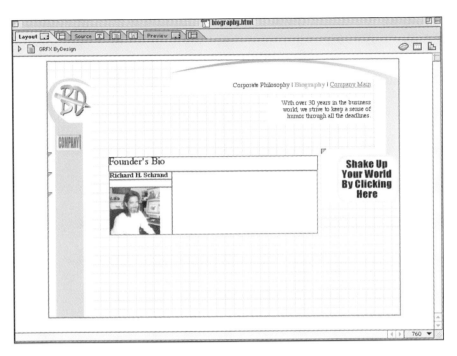

Figure 15.91
The bio page laid out and ready for the biographical information to be added.

visitor. Also, select Company in the left nav bar and turn it into a link using the Inspector Link area. Set the path of the link to the main Company.html page. The rest of the setup should look like figure 15.91.

The Corporate Philosophy page is pretty much set up the same way, so I think it's best to move on to the last area of the site.

PROJECT 15.6 The Publishers Page

The Publishers page is an important part of my site. It gives validation to the work I have been doing for the past few years. I also have to consider that most of the visitors who will initially view my site come from books like this and readers like you. This is far from being an ego page (although a savvy debater could easily say anyone who puts builds a Web page and talks about themselves is egotistical). Yes, it's pretty cool being a published author. Yes, very few of us out there are doing this kind of work. But, ultimately it shows potential clients that there is substance to the rest of the information given on the site. When they click on the link to a particular publisher or to a particular online store, such as Amazon.com or Barnesandnoble.com, and see the books for sale, it adds credibility to your words. So, I'd be remiss not to have a section of the site devoted to this area of my work.

Two portions will be housed on the same page, the first being book descriptions with links to the publisher and to the previously mentioned online bookstores. The second portion of the page will be a quick description of my appearance schedules, with links to any sites that would be applicable to that appearance.

Note: This effect only seems to work with Netscape Communicator and not with Internet Explorer.

Creating an Automatic Slide Show

The view screen area can be considered a catchall effects area. You have worked with remote rollovers, so that images appear inside the screen when a rollover button is activated, which is a pretty impressive effect; I don't know many people who are tired of that one. You used a Head item to set up the effect of the browser window shaking when the mouse button was clicked. Now it's time to use another Action feature that can be utilized in many different instances on any given number of pages:

Figure 15.92
Renaming the Rollover placeholder for easier referencing when applying the upcoming event.

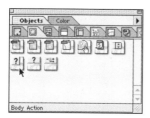

Figure 15.93
The cursor arrow is pointing to the Body Action element in the Smart Object window for easier referencing.

1. Place images 01.jpg, 02.jpg, and 03.jpg into your media folder. When using the Action you're about to create, the images must be numbered in sequential order.

2. Replace the ViewScreenNoText.jpg image with a Rollover placeholder. Make sure to name this one Stage (see Figure 15.92), which fits with the image you're about to add and makes it easier to locate when it's time to assign the action you're about to implement. Link the Main Image to 01.jpg, which is the view screen with an image of a stage inside it.

3. In the Smart tools area of the Objects window, drag a Body Action (see Figure 15.93) tool onto the workspace. A question mark icon that looks much like the Head Item tool you worked with earlier in the chapter will appear (see Figure 15.94), but will be invisible when the page is viewed on the Internet.

Figure 15.94
Here is what your workspace will look like after you place the Body Action element there.

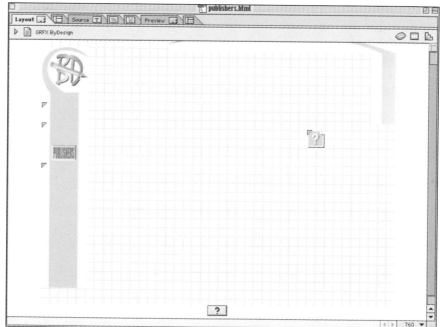

4. Click once on the Body Action element to activate it and bring up the Action pop-up menu in the Body Action Inspector window. Included with GoLive is a series of actions called ActionsPlus, which should be located on the GoLive installation CD. ActionsPlus includes a number of cool actions, including three SlideShow actions seen in Figure 15.95. If you have not installed this action set yet, I would advise doing it now. The ActionsPlus folder needs to be placed in the Actions folder located in Modules|JScripts. Make sure you place the ActionsPlus folder itself in there and not just the modules. Now you are going to create an automatic slide show using the SlideShowAuto action.

5. Select SlideShowAuto and set the Base Image to Stage (see Figure 15.96). Change # of images to 3. Even though you have 01.jpg assigned as the Main Image of the rollover button, you still need to include it in the number of images SlideShowAuto will cycle through. Then change Interval to 2 seconds. If you want the slideshow to loop, uncheck Stop At End Of Slideshow (which I have done). Figure 15.97 shows the Action window with the parameters set.

> **Note**: Once you have installed the ActionsPlus modules, you need to restart GoLive so the actions will be available to you. Make sure to save your publishers.html page prior to quitting the program.

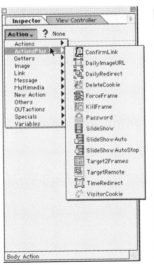
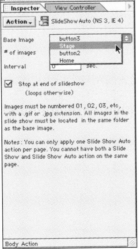

Figure 15.95
(Left) The full list of ActionsPlus actions included on the GoLive installation CD.

Figure 15.96
(Center) Select Stage from the list of available elements in the Base Image pop-up. The other choices you see listed are the other rollover buttons on the page.

Figure 15.97
(Right) The parameters for the SlideShowAuto effect.

6. Now select Show in Browser to see the slide show effect. The curtain will open and close in the view screen window, revealing the message seen in Figure 15.98.

Setting Up the Table

Again, this page will utilize the Table element. However, the setup for the table will be a bit different, and after it has been designed, you'll save it for use in other Web site designs you might work on:

1. Place the Table element onto the Grid in the position you see in Figure 15.99.

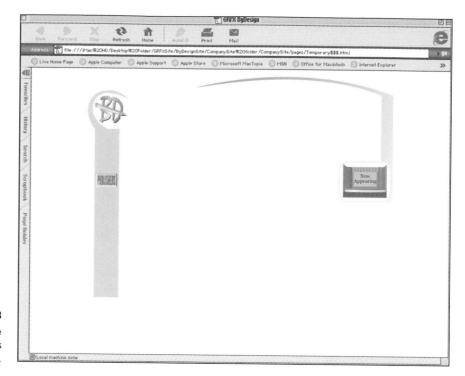

Figure 15.98
A look at the third frame of the slide show you just created as seen in Internet Explorer.

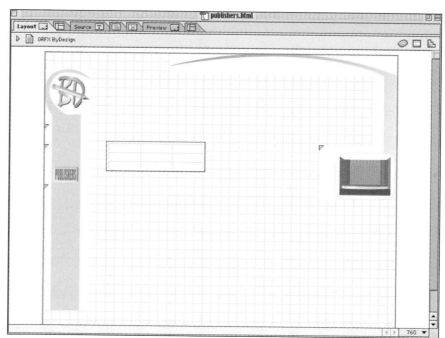

Figure 15.99
The position for the Table element for the Publishers page of the site.

2. Set the Table parameters as follows:

   - Rows: 24

   - Columns: 3

   - Width: 353 Pixels

   - Border: 0

   - Cell Space: 4

3. Begin modifying the cell layout as you see in Figure 15.100. For easier cell selection, use the Table window. Make sure the last row of cells remains at the default setting of 3 columns. As you can see, I am alternating between merging the middle and right cells and the left and middle cells. Each of the right cells of the modified rows needs to have the Horizontal Alignment changed to Right. The easiest way to do this is to select the cells in the Table window and set the Horizontal Alignment in the Cell Inspector window (see Figure 15.101).

Figure 15.100
The Table window showing the cell layout. I have selected the cells that were modified, so you can see the cell pattern that was created and which cells should be merged.

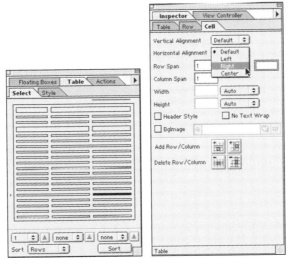

Figure 15.101
Modify the right cells of the modified rows using a combination of the Table Select window and the Cell Inspector window.

4. Switch to Style in the Table window. In the text field at the bottom of the window, type a name for this table style. (In my case, I called it AlternatingMergedCell. Click Capture.) The Style is now represented on the page (see Figure 15.102), and it becomes a part of the choices in the pop-up menu (see Figure 15.103).

5. Drag an Image placeholder into the upper-left cell. Make sure to place the Coriolis.jpg image into the media folder, and then link that image to the placeholder. In the field to the right of this, I have typed in some general information about the company and which books I have written for them (including, of course, this one).

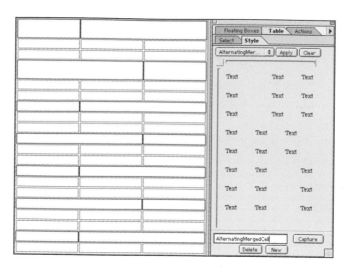

Figure 15.102
(Left) The new table style you created is now shown in the Style window.

Figure 15.103
(Right) The style you created is also available in the pop-up menu. It can be assigned to any table you place on the workspace.

6. In the cells beneath the text cell, place an Image placeholder. I linked these to the covers for, left and right respectively, this book (GL5Cover.jpg) and my other book published by the company (Canoma.jpg). Figure 15.104 shows the Preview screen and how this layout now looks.

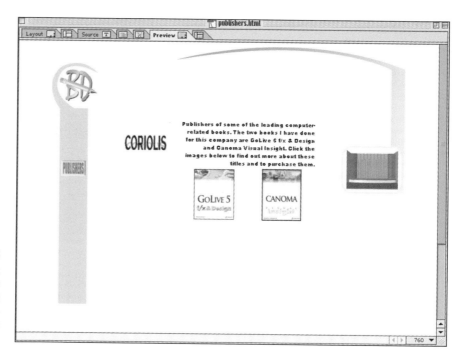

Figure 15.104
Using the Table layout you just created, you have a creative way of displaying your images and text that would be very difficult to accomplish without doing extensive HTML coding.

Create a Site Template Based on Your Design

GoLive 5 comes with three site templates that can be used when building your sites. However, you can also create a site template based upon your original designs. This gives you virtually immediate access to the design you created and you can use it to build new sites for yourself or other people. You can do so by taking the following steps:

1. After you have your design completed, duplicate the site folder. This is the folder that contains your master site file and the subfolders for the site. If you're on a Mac, move this folder into the Site Templates folder inside the master GoLive folder. If you're working in Windows, save the folder in that location. You can name this folder anything you want, although I would leave a space between the site name and the word "folder" (see Figure 15.105).

Note: When creating a site template you cannot have any files that have "template" in them. If template files are associated with your site, remove them prior to doing this step.

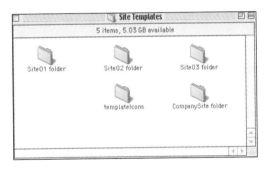

Figure 15.105
A look at the duplicated site folder placed inside the Site Templates folder in GoLive. This is a screen shot from a Macintosh computer.

2. Open this duplicated site in the same manner you would open any site. While holding down the Shift key, either select the Site Settings button on the top toolbar (see Figure 15.106) or go to Site|Settings. I prefer the former. The .site Settings screen comes up, as seen in Figure 15.107.

Figure 15.106
The .site Settings button in GoLive's toolbar.

3. Type a description of this site in the text field—make it as long as you want. You can also assign images to act as previews for both the layout and the structure of the page. Figure 15.108 shows the images I have chosen. Of course these images can be screen captures of a page, an element of a page, or something totally unrelated. After you finish, click on OK.

4. Select File|New Site|Copy From Template (see Figure 15.109). The selection screen comes up, allowing you to pick from all the template files in the Site Template folder (see Figure 15.110).

5. Give your site a new name and click OK. That's all there is to it.

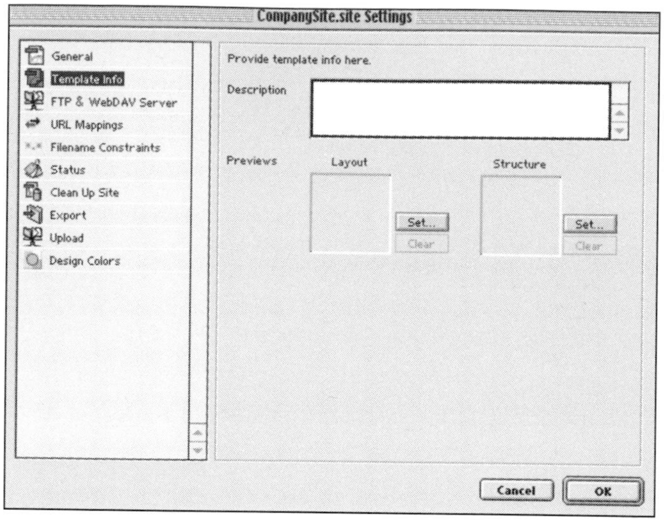

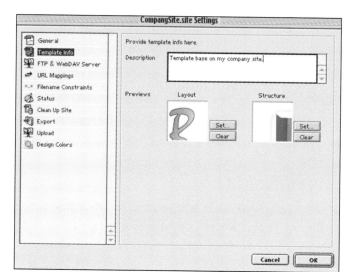

Figure 15.107
The .site Settings window that opens when you access the Site Settings command while holding down the Shift key on your keyboard.

Figure 15.108
You can type notes regarding the site template and assign images to help you recognize the design.

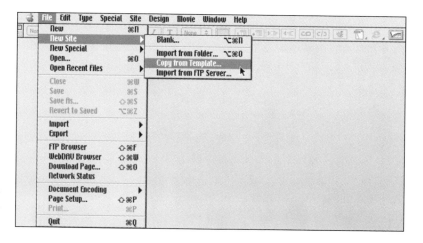

Figure 15.109
Create a new site using the Copy From Template option.

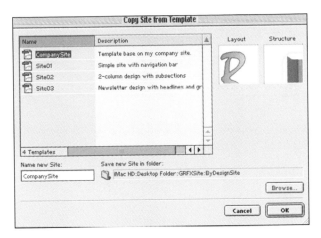

Figure 15.110
The Copy Site from Template
selection screen. All available
valid templates will be accessible.

Site-ings

The rest of the site pretty much uses the techniques, tips, and ideas outlined. You can view the completed site at **www.grfxbydesign.com** to see how it all flows. Also, take a few moments to see what modifications I might have made based on the subliminal layout I have discussed. I uploaded the site using the GoLive internal FTP client. The first time you do this, a screen will come up where you input your FTP connection parameters, click OK, and then the uploading happens automatically. You can then update the site by having GoLive search for newer files and replacing only them.

Change Is Inevitable

Yes, change is inevitable, but it seems even more so in the ever-shifting realm of Web design. New technology arrives every day it seems, making that wondrous effect you finally learned how to do seem like last year's clothing style. Still, a strong design that doesn't rely too heavily on the latest gee-whiz-golly effects is guaranteed to have a longer shelf life than sites that rely 100 percent on the latest technology.

The other inevitable change is the constant updating that must occur with your site. People will quickly become bored if the content of your pages doesn't change. Like moths to a light, if visitors realize that nothing new is happening, it's as if that light that attracted them has been turned off. Whey they can see and do different things every so often, it will generate return visits and increase your value as a Web developer. These changes could be as simple as replacing an image or two or offering some new content. They could be as difficult as a total overhaul of the site. A good rule of thumb when it comes to modifying your site(s): Change content approximately every month to month-and-a-half; change the entire site (design and layout) about once a year.

A Final Word

I want to thank you again for buying this book. I hope you find it useful as you delve deeper into the intricacies of site design using GoLive 5. I also hope you found the ideas and designs as fun to work with as it was fun for me to put together. Let me know the URLs of sites you have designed using the program. I'll create links to them from my site. In this manner, you can begin to build a library of design work that everyone can benefit from.

Until GoLive 6, have fun making all your site designs world class!

Appendix

Throughout this book, I have mentioned various Web sites where you can get more information about programs and plug-ins to enhance your GoLive 5 experience. Because it's difficult to go page by page to find a specific URL for a Web site that interests you, I have compiled in this Appendix a list of Web sites for you to check out. Many of these sites are listed within the pages of this book; others are Web sites that have come to my attention during the course of writing this book but, for one reason or another, didn't make it into the chapters.

This appendix is broken down into categories. All sites are listed in alphabetical order, based on either the company or the name of the program or plug-ins/add-ons.

Programs

Adobe

Because the deadline for this book did not allow for me to include demos of the various Adobe programs, here are direct links to the demo downloads:

- GoLive 5—**www.adobe.com/products/golive/main.html**
- GoLive 5 Actions Xchange—**www.adobe.com/products/golive/actions/main.html**
- GoLive Headquarters—**www.golivehq.com/**
- GoLive e-mail List—**golive-on@blueworld.com**
- GoLIve e-mail Digest—**golive-digest@blueworld.com**
- Illustrator 9—**www.adobe.com/products/illustrator/main.html**
- LiveMotion—**www.adobe.com/products/livemotion/main.html**
- Photoshop—**www.adobe.com/products/photoshop/main.html**

Apple

Here, you'll find Macintosh-specific video editing software, including QuickTime Pro and Final Cut Pro:

- **www.apple.com/**

Artis Software

Here, you'll find numerous programs for the Macintosh, including TextureMagic, which was discussed in Chapter 13:

- **www.artissoftware.com/**

ClicDesign

This company makes a series of software titles that are fashion-industry plug-ins for Photoshop and Illustrator:

- **www.agetechnologies.com/**

3D Programs

Curious Labs
Curious Labs is the creator and distributor of Poser 4 for Mac and Windows.
You can download a demo of the Poser program from this site:

- **www.curiouslabs.com/**

Hash, Inc.
Hash, Inc. is the developer and distributor of the popular Hash Animation:Master.

- **www.hash.com/**

Impulse
Impulse makes Organica, a modeling program and the new Illusion, a special
effects program.

- **www.coolfun.com/**

Maxon
Developer of the popular Cinema 4D XL and Cinema 4D GO applications.

- **www.maxoncomputer.com/**

NewTek
Creators of LightWave, the high-end 3D design and animation software.

- **www.newtek.com/**

Pixels Animation Studio
Makers of Pixels:3D for the Macintosh.

- **www.pixels.net/**

TGS Software
Here, you'll find the creators and marketers of Ampai 3D 5.1, another great
3D application with a unique interface:

- **www.tgs.com/**

Third-Party Plug-Ins

Catalog Builder
This is a fantastic add-on for GoLive that, unfortunately, I learned about after
the book was nearly completed. It was developed by Douglas Fairchild. To
learn about this essential extension, go to his Catalog Builder Web page:

- **www.catalogbuilder.com/**

OutActions

Oliver Zahorka was kind enough to supply some of these fantastic Actions for the companion CD-ROM. There are many more that he sells via his Web site, which I'm certain that you will want to get.

* **www.out.to/**

Contributors Sites

The following list features the Web sites of artists who contributed to the GoLive 5 Studio, the color section of this book:

* Miles Cruickshank—**www.flyingsolo.co.uk/**

* Douglas Fairchild—**www.douglasfairchild.com/**and **www.douglasfairchild.com/daddywasanoilman.html**

* Mike Grove—**www.graphicsbygrove.com/**

* Richard McLean—**www.designeffect.com/**

* Mike Swope—**www.blueplanetgas.com**

* Oliver Zahorka—**www.out.to/**

Index

If you like this book, you'll love these...

LOOKING GOOD ON THE WEB

Daniel Gray
ISBN: 1-57610-508-3
224 pages • $29.99 U.S. • $43.99 CANADA

Speaking from the user's perspective, this book provides a comprehensive, non-technical introduction to Web design. You'll learn how to design and create friendly, easily navigable, award-winning Web sites that please clients and visitors alike.

ILLUSTRATOR® 9 F/X AND DESIGN

Sherry London
ISBN: 1-57610-750-7
560 pages with CD-ROM • $49.99 U.S. • $74.99 CANADA

Features new information and projects on styles and effects, how to integrate with Adobe® Web products such as LiveMotion™ and GoLive™, as well as other enhanced features. With real-world projects, readers learn firsthand how to create intricate illustrations and compositing techniques. Readers also learn how to work seamlessly between Illustrator® and Photoshop®.

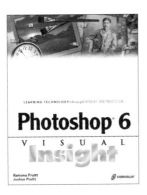

PHOTOSHOP® 6 VISUAL INSIGHT

Ramona Pruitt and Joshua Pruitt
ISBN: 1-57610-747-7
344 pages • $24.99 U.S. • $37.99 CANADA

Learn Photoshop's basic features, including layering, masks, and paths, as well as intermediate functions, such as Web graphics, filters, and actions. This book teaches the most useful Photoshop techniques and allows readers to use these in real-world projects, such as repairing images, eliminating red eye, creating type effects, developing Web elements, and more.

ADOBE LIVEMOTION™ F/X AND DESIGN

Daniel Gray
ISBN: 1-57610-676-4
352 pages with CD-ROM • $49.99 U.S. • $74.99 CANADA

Presents step-by-step projects for creating dynamic effects with Adobe's latest Web program. A 32-page color studio illustrated the program's advanced capabilities, including animation. Working in conjunction with other popular graphics and Web software, such as GoLive™, PageMill®, Freehand®, and Illustrator® is covered.

The Coriolis Group, LLC   Telephone: 480.483.0192 • Toll-free: 800.410.0192 • www.coriolis.com
Coriolis books are also available at bookstores and computer stores nationwide.

What's on the CD-ROM

A number of companies have supplied demos of their programs, exclusive discounts on products, and files. Unfortunately, as this book was being written, Adobe was updating many of their programs, including Photoshop, Illustrator, LiveMotion, and Premiere. Therefore, the latest Adobe demo software (including GoLive 5) is not included on the CD-ROM. You can download the latest demos of Adobe software at **www.adobe.com**.

Included on the CD-ROM are:

- All of the image and animation files used in each of the chapters.
- ArtisSoftware—TextureMagic (M) lets you generate high-quality original seamless textures to use as backgrounds on your Web sites.
- Bias—Peak LE (M), a top-notch audio editing program.
- CharacterMotion—LifeForms (M/W), Gives you the ability to create humanoid animations.
- Sonic Foundry Programs (W) - Demos of many of this company's audio and audio/video programs. This includes demos of Acid Pro, SoundForge XP, and Vegas Video.

and much more, including:

- Free audio loops from SoundForge.
- Over a dozen royalty-free original seamless textures.

System Requirements:

Macintosh

- PowerPC-based Macintosh computer
- Apple System Software version 8.6 and 9
- 48MB of RAM*
- 70MB of hard-disk space.

Windows

- Pentium 200 MHz (or faster) or compatible processor
- Microsoft Windows98, Windows NT 4 (or later) with Service Pack 3, or Windows 2000 OS
- 48MB of RAM for Windows 98*; 64MB RAM for Windows NT 4*
- 50MB of hard disk space.

* RAM requirements based on all modules being active.